JEAN BLACKBURN

Jean Blackburn

Education, Feminism and Social Justice

Craig Campbell and Debra Hayes

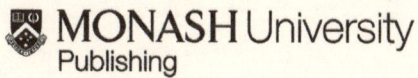

Jean Blackburn: Education, Feminism and Social Justice
© Copyright 2019 Craig Campbell and Debra Hayes
All rights reserved. Apart from any uses permitted by Australia's Copyright Act 1968, no part of this book may be reproduced by any process without prior written permission from the copyright owners. Inquiries should be directed to the publisher.

Monash University Publishing
Matheson Library Annexe
40 Exhibition Walk
Monash University
Clayton, Victoria 3800, Australia
www.publishing.monash.edu

Monash University Publishing brings to the world publications which advance the best traditions of humane and enlightened thought.

Monash University Publishing titles pass through a rigorous process of independent peer review.

ISBN: 9781925835274 (paperback)
ISBN: 9781925835281 (pdf)
ISBN: 9781925835298 (epub)

www.publishing.monash.edu/books/jb-9781925835274.html

Series: Biography

Design: Les Thomas

Front cover image: Jean Blackburn, *The Age*, 14 July 1989. Reproduced with permission and courtesy of Fairfax Syndication.

Back cover image: Jean Blackburn, Chancellor of the University of Canberra 1990–1991. 1994 Portrait by Robert Hannaford, reproduced with his kind permission, and that of the University of Canberra Art Collection.

A catalogue record for this book is available from the National Library of Australia.

Printed in Australia by Griffin Press an Accredited ISO AS/NZS 14001:2004 Environmental Management System printer.

The paper this book is printed on is certified against the Forest Stewardship Council ® Standards. Griffin Press holds FSC chain of custody certification SGS-COC-005088. FSC promotes environmentally responsible, socially beneficial and economically viable management of the world's forests.

TABLE OF CONTENTS

Abbreviations vi
Acknowledgements ix
Preface xii
Introduction xv

Chapter 1   An unsatisfactory childhood, 1919–1932 1
Chapter 2   School and the independent girl, 1933–1937 23
Chapter 3   University, communism and war, 1938–1941 39
Chapter 4   Wartime public servant, and marriage, 1942–1950 61
Chapter 5   Suburban life and beyond, 1951–1966 96
Chapter 6   Career at last, 1967–1973 135
Chapter 7   Schools Commissioner: Whitlam government years, 1974–1975 181
Chapter 8   Schools Commissioner: Fraser government years, 1976–1980 217
Chapter 9   Curriculum theorist and educational activist, 1981–1989 266
Chapter 10 Feminist matriarch, 1990–2001 313

Conclusion: Thinking about the life 358
Notes 371
Select bibliography 409
Index 423
About the authors 433

ABBREVIATIONS

ACE	Australian College of Education
ACER	Australian Council for Educational Research
ALP	Australian Labor Party
ANU	Australian National University
ASIO	Australian Security Intelligence Organisation
ATF	Australian Teachers Federation
AWEC	Australian Women's Education Coalition
CAE	College of Advanced Education
CDC	Curriculum Development Centre
CERI	Centre for Educational Research and Innovation
CP	Communist Party
CPA	Communist Party of Australia
CSIR	Council for Scientific and Industrial Research
CSIRO	Commonwealth Scientific and Industrial Research Organisation
CWWW	Council for Women in War Work
DOGS	Defend Our Government Schools
DSP	Disadvantaged Schools Program
ERDC	Education Research and Development Committee
IWD	International Women's Day
JB	Jean Blackburn
JBPP	Jean Blackburn Personal Papers
KU	Kindergarten Union
LCL	Liberal and Country League

Abbreviations

NAA	National Archives of Australia
NHA	New Housewives' Association
OECD	Organisation for Economic Co-operation and Development
PGC	Presbyterian Girls College
SB	Susan Blackburn
SBCD	School Based Curriculum Development
SC	Schools Commission
TAFE	Technical and Further Education
TEASA	Tertiary Education Authority of South Australia
TTUV	Technical Teachers Union of Victoria
UAW	United Associations of Women
VCE	Victorian Certificate of Education
VSTA	Victorian Secondary Teachers Association
WCTU	Women's Christian Temperance Union
WILPF	Women's International League for Peace and Freedom

*To the memory of Jean Blackburn,
and in support of all teachers, politicians, parents, bureaucrats
and citizens who share her vision of the school as a place
where a more just society might be imagined.*

ACKNOWLEDGEMENTS

Thank you to:

Susan Blackburn, for seeding the idea and doing everything possible to make sure we had access to a full range of family contacts, photographs and other sources.

Keith Foulcher, who contributed an extensive commentary on our draft text which improved it no end. Jenny Palmer, for her commentary and editing suggestions. Each critically engaged with the argument as they were given opportunity. Dean Ashenden and Raewyn Connell, for being a source of encouragement, ideas and information.

Our interviewees, who responded to our requests with generosity. They are listed in the bibliography.

Stuart Crawford and his colleague archivists of the National Archives of Australia, who made our many weeks of research in Canberra both comfortable and productive. Archivists at the University of Adelaide, University of Melbourne, Public Records Offices in South Australia and Victoria, and librarians in the state libraries of Victoria, South Australia and New South Wales, for providing a courteous and efficient response to our requests.

Two online resources have provided essential resources for this work. Without *Trove*, hosted by the National Library of Australia, letters to newspapers written by Jean Muir/Blackburn would have been almost impossible to find. The *Australian Dictionary of Biography*, hosted by the Australian National University, has been referenced often during the writing.

Many others have provided contacts, information and encouragement that have made the work a pleasure to research and write. They include Don Aitkin, Margaret Allen, Hugh Blackburn, Effie Best, Jill Blackmore, Barbara Burr, Lyndsay Connors, Judy Ferguson, Carole Hooper, Carol Johnson, Jan Lingard, Bob Lingard, Susan Magarey, Janet Prior, Helen Proctor, Fay Redgrave, Susan Ryan, Roger Scott, Dick Selleck, Pat Thomson, Margaret Vickers, Fran Waugh, Nadia Wheatley, Kay Whitehead and Wayne Urban. Loine Sweeney deserves special mention as a generous informant on a difficult period in both Jean's life and her own as they planned the Centenary of Women's Suffrage in South Australia in the 1990s.

We have tested our writing on a number of people who responded with generosity. They include Hugh Blackburn, Susan Blackburn, Bob Lingard, Susan Magarey, Loine Sweeney and Kay Whitehead. Judy Gill encouraged Jean Blackburn in the 1990s to write autobiography. The short essays subsequently produced were crucial sources for the first two chapters of this book. Judy also helped by reading an early draft of the last chapter. Nevertheless, the authors take sole responsibility for the published text.

The conferences of the Australian and New Zealand History of Education Society (ANZHES), Australian Association for Research in Education (AARE) and the International Standing Conference of the History of Education (ISCHE) have provided valued forums for the discussion of our papers on Jean Blackburn.

Robert Hannaford generously allowed us to reproduce the image of his portrait of Jean Blackburn (see back cover). Alex Stalker-Booth of the University of Canberra kindly arranged the photographing of the portrait for use in the book. Margaret Haselgrove and Rosey Boehm also helped with images from the 1980s and 1990s.

Acknowledgements

We thank our respective partners: for Craig, Keith Foulcher, and Deb, Gaby Mason. We are fortunate that our research and writing occurs in loving and secure spaces.

PREFACE

In 2018, the national challenge of providing school education that provides fair and equal opportunity to all Australian children remains monumental. After nearly fifty years since the Whitlam government initiated massive educational reform, the struggle to achieve effective public policy design and implementation remains. In order to achieve fairness, financial sustainability and effectiveness, Australian schooling must reach without discrimination all children: children of the First Australians; children who have arrived here from all parts of the earth; those born here across the full range of social and economic circumstances, and those growing up in country towns, remote areas, capital cities or sprawling suburbs. The public financing dimensions of this task are massive and politically fraught, but no more so than the expectations and judgements of parents, teachers, employers, educationists, international performance assessing bodies and of course the students themselves.

When the Whitlam government first took on all this by establishing the Australian Schools Commission in 1974, the challenges it faced were not very different. But that government had the great good fortune of the availability of Jean Blackburn, whom they appointed as one of their inaugural Schools Commissioners. Blackburn's work, especially through her particular responsibilities for the Disadvantaged Schools Program and Special Projects, had immediate and enduring success in reducing educational inequality, and liberating creative, new and better approaches to deep-seated schooling problems. Blackburn, working alongside her Commission colleagues, produced a flourishing new, improved and successful education practice.

Preface

Jean's story is remarkable and an important part of Australian history. Born in 1919, she grew up through the Depression, the Second World War, post-war reconstruction and the arrival of millions of migrants fleeing war-ravaged Europe. Always focused on education she saw how our schools succeeded or failed in providing to all these young Australians what she rightly believed to be their fundamental right, that is quality education to develop their talents and equip them for a successful and constructive working life. Blackburn, an early female graduate in Economics from the University of Melbourne and later a teacher, had a long intellectual and personal preparation for her Commission work. She spent decades immersed in democratic socialist thinking, and researched education policy for reforming governments. She brought massive intelligence and passion to her work, enhanced by her hugely valuable approach of appreciating teamwork and learning from others.

It is a pleasure and an encouragement to read this biography and understand how Jean, a woman of her era, managed her responsibilities as a mother and a wife, and worked out how to come to terms with policy environments far from her own best preference, to achieve progressive reform. She attracted lifelong friendships and the great loyalty of colleagues. Her rigorous approach and clarity of thinking affected many who came within her orbit, of whom I was one.

I was a part of the advisory committee that worked with Jean along with Commission Chair Ken McKinnon and others on the pioneering breakthrough investigation into the educations of girls. The report of this investigation, *Girls Schools and Society*, was powerful. It detailed the ways in which schools contributed to the social, economic and cultural disadvantages suffered almost universally by Australian women. It highlighted the great loss to the nation of the talent, energy and potential commitment of so many girls who were failed by schooling that taught them to limit their hopes and ambitions. The report had consequences. A national plan for the education of girls grew from it, and girls' school experiences and outcomes improved dramatically and quickly.

When, a few years later, I became Minister for Education and Youth Affairs and Minister assisting the Prime Minister on the Status of Women in the Hawke government, Jean's work was never far from my mind. It was always a source of insight and motivation to pursue reform. I consider myself fortunate to have retained contact with Jean over the years, and to have benefited from her incisive thinking, her marvellous capacity to detect and reject the merely fashionable or superficial in policy ideas, and her unswerving direction towards education as the central means of reducing inequality and discrimination, and liberating talent and ambition. As well, she was excellent company.

Jean died in 2001. Now we have this comprehensive, informed and authoritative biography. I know many will read it to be reminded of Jean and her powerhouse thinking. I hope anyone who grasps the importance of education to everything we hope for our country and our fellow citizens will also read it. Australian education still needs Jean Blackburn. We don't have Jean herself but thanks to Craig Campbell and Debra Hayes, the co-authors of this biography, we do have reliable and extensive records of the work she did, the people she influenced, the big impacts she had on Australian schools, and thus of the generations of students whose schooling has benefited from her profound advice.

Susan Ryan AO

INTRODUCTION

One morning in early December 1972, Jean Blackburn had a tutorial scheduled with some of her students at Bedford Park Teachers' College in the southern suburbs of Adelaide. It was a typical December day, the promise of another blistering Adelaide summer tempered for the moment by the breezes that stirred the shady gums and swept the low hills of the Bedford Park campus. The teaching year was winding down ahead of the Christmas and New Year break. Yet this was no ordinary Australian December. Days before, on December 2, a new national government led by the Labor Party's Gough Whitlam had decisively won a federal election.

There had been no Labor government since 1949. There had been no government-elect since the 1940s with such an ambitious raft of policy promises, from foreign affairs through to labour relations, national economic development and then to urban renewal, education and social welfare. Whitlam was not for wasting time. He formed a temporary government with two ministers only. This government ended conscription for the armed services and recognised the Peoples Republic of China. Australia also ended its participation in the Vietnam War.

One of Whitlam' short-lived portfolios was Minister for Education and Science. Shortly after election, Whitlam contacted economist and university Vice-Chancellor, Peter Karmel, asking him to chair a committee that would plan the implementation of Labor's election policy for schools. Karmel agreed, but there was a condition. There was a person without whose help he was reluctant to assume the challenge. Whitlam accepted Karmel's nomination for Deputy Chair of the planned Interim Committee of the Schools Commission.

Jean Blackburn's tutorial was well underway when there was the kind of interruption that students and teachers resent. 'There's a phone call for you, Mrs Blackburn.' Jean left for the office. 'Ennor here', announced the voice at the end of the line. The voice told her that the Prime Minister wanted her in Canberra for several months. He had a job in mind for her. 'And I was almost opening my mouth to say, "Yes, and I'm the Queen of Sheba"', but what she recalled saying was that she was in the middle of a class and would ring him back. She telephoned her husband, Dick, with the story. 'Who is this Ennor? And is it a joke?' Dick told her that Hugh Ennor was the head of the federal Department of Education; it was not a joke, and she should decide whether she wanted to take the job. She thought 'Yes, I do' and Jean Blackburn's career in national education had begun.[1]

Several people have attempted brief summaries of Jean Blackburn's impact on educational thought and policy in Australia. In his book on the rise of economic rationalism in Australian public policy, Michael Pusey wrote that Peter Karmel 'was greatly helped by a brilliant sociologically oriented researcher, Jean Blackburn, who subsequently became one of the leading [Schools] Commissioners. Jean Blackburn is one of Australia's truly remarkable women of modern times'.[2] This is certainly true, but there was more to Jean Blackburn than her educational work. Hers was a twentieth century life that was shaped by great historical events. From the late 1930s through to the 1990s she was also a maker of history – sometimes only in minor roles, but from the late 1960s, in major as well. Jean Blackburn's story contributes to Australian histories of communism, feminism and social democracy as well as the transformation of public policy in education.

Introduction

This biography of Jean Blackburn has a dual purpose. We have written our understanding of her personal story as she struggled with family, education, career, marriage and motherhood through to old age. We also write of her contribution to the making of public policy, especially in education. In looking to this dual purpose, we try to breach old separations, the domestic from public life and the biography of a person from their intellectual history. There are consequences for the narrative balance in this approach, but we have been careful not to introduce an imaginary gap between Blackburn's public and private life. Susan Magarey and Kerrie Round pursued this issue in their biography of Roma Mitchell. They quoted an informant, Deirdre Jordan, who also plays a part in this biography: 'Her private face was no different from her public face – she was the same whether walking on the beach ... or presiding at public functions.'[3]

There were few facets of Jean Blackburn's life before 1972 that did not help shape the crucial fifteen years that followed. The legacy of those fifteen years in turn shaped her later years. Appointments in the 1990s, when she was in her seventies, included foundation Chancellor of the University of Canberra (1990), Chair of the Victorian State Board of Education (1991) and Chair of the Steering Committee planning South Australia's celebration of the centenary of female suffrage (1992).

As Jean Blackburn's biographers, we seek to illuminate several themes that run through her life story as it traversed social change across the twentieth century. The barriers to women building professional careers was one of them.[4] Through the late 1940s and into the 1960s especially, Jean struggled to fulfil the expectations raised by her education and employment during the Second World War. Despite the problems, including discrimination against her employment due to Communist Party membership, she remained resilient. Jean Blackburn emerged in the 1970s as an energetic and singular leader in Australia's educational transformation.

A related theme in this biography is Jean Blackburn as a feminist. The consequences of Jean's family life as a child and young woman drew her towards feminism but reading the feminist classics from the 1940s expanded her understanding of the experience. She co-wrote two significant texts in the history of Australian women and feminism.[5] As a feminist formed before the 'second wave' from the late 1960s, she lived long enough to experience the rise of women's liberation, the growth of women's studies, and the succeeding post-modernist influences on feminism from the late 1970s. The story of Jean's engagement with feminism is a story of what feminism could mean for women of successive generations.

Jean was a socialist for most of her life. She joined the Australian Communist Party in 1938 and left it in 1956. Her commitment to social transformation played out in several areas. This theme raises questions for her biographers. How did her socialist and social justice commitments develop over time, and how did they contribute to the programs for which she was responsible in the Schools Commission? How did she connect her feminist and socialist commitments, including the occasionally competing demands of gender and class in her social justice thinking? Jean had engaged in the struggle for Aboriginal rights in the early 1960s, so racial equality was also an active social justice issue for her. At the heart of the Schools Commission's Disadvantaged Schools Program, of which she was the major architect, were issues of social class and equal educational opportunity. Jean thought deeply about class, gender, ethnicity and race. Their impacts were each conceived in relation to the other as she developed programs for state action in education.

We add at least three more themes to this list, and they are of a different order. One relates to the idea of 'networks' of relationships. Family, school and university connections provided longstanding friendships. They often existed as political associations as well. They provided Jean with contacts that helped make her emergence into public life possible. Such connections were especially effective as Cold War passions declined, and reforming Labor governments were elected from the late 1960s in both South Australia and the nation, and a little later in Victoria. This theme provides one of several potential explanations for the emergence of Jean Blackburn as a remarkable policy maker and public intellectual.

Another theme concerns her approach to education as a potentially transformative experience for individuals and society. She had a view that a challenging education was not for a select few, but for all. She believed in its power to make good and sensible citizens, and to improve society generally. Its significance was much more than as an instrument for individual advancement and economic development. Her thinking about curriculum, and more broadly, the roles of schools and universities, was that they should critically engage, and improve the experience of being human.

And by no means finally is the overarching theme of Jean Blackburn as a remarkable woman, who struggled to overcome multiple constraints on her emergence as policy maker and public intellectual. Such constraints included her family of origin, her schooling, her communism, her suburban isolation, her marriage, the consequences of motherhood, her existence within bureaucracies – and always the threat of personal depression, and the failures of her body to support her intentions. There is a paradox in this of course. Without the obstacles perhaps there would have been less in terms of the fearlessness, fortitude and even controlled wrath, as she sought to change the world. They probably aided her capacity not only to 'read' existing social and political circumstances, but also to seize opportunities and recognise latent capacities for change.

We are aware of the longstanding arguments about the defects of biography as historical writing. It is true that biography can overestimate the contribution of individuals to the histories of their times. It is also true that biographies may contribute to a necessary argument for the significance of human agency in history. Biography can not only make individual agency visible but also show that its impact is contingent on historical circumstances. As an operative in the Department of War Organisation of Industry from 1942 to 1945 Jean Muir, later Jean Blackburn, doubtless made little difference to the organisation of the home front in winning the war. However, another argument will be made about her agency in the operation of the Schools Commission in the 1970s.

In an essay on educational agency, Barbara Finkelstein wrote that biography can act as a lens through which the origin of new ideas may be explored. It allows a study of social choices and possibilities as individuals and groups develop, as they construct meanings, form communities, build institutions and lead their lives. Biography 'provides an aperture through which to view relationships between educational processes and social change'. Biographies are essential for the exploration of the intersection between human agency and social change.[6] As Jean's biographers, we believe that this is well illustrated through her life story.

Barbara Caine has written that in recent times the role of biography in the history of feminism, for example, has become less about the lives of exceptional individuals, less the story of heroic victories on the way to women's emancipation. The focus has shifted to broad collectivities and social movements.[7] It is in this spirit that we explore Jean's life. She was one of many who made significant contributions to Australian feminism, socialism and education over the course of the twentieth century. At times she led. Her influence was obvious, but it waxed and waned as the contexts, her relationships with other individuals, institutions, agencies and groups, changed. We have written our story as much from a social history perspective as any other. We believe Jean Blackburn's story illuminates many issues in the history of Australian women in the twentieth century.

It is important to comment on our, the biographers' relationship to the biographical task. Debra Hayes has worked in university schools of education for many years. Her research often occurs where there are high levels of poverty and social inequity. Her work has aimed to describe the impact of these factors on young people's educational participation and achievement. Much of her earlier research explored the changing character of gender policies and their impacts on schooling and young people. She did not know Jean Blackburn personally. The coincidence of her research interests and feminist commitments allowed for a potentially insightful and sympathetic analysis of Blackburn's policy work in the years surrounding the Schools Commission.

Craig Campbell's research has focused on the social history of Australian schooling; the impacts of changes in educational policy on specific populations, whether they be children, youth or families, from the nineteenth through to the present century. At the same time, he has a history in teacher unionism. He also brings direct experience of Jean Blackburn to the work. They travelled together on an educationally oriented study tour of China in early 1976. They met again when Jean was preparing the Schools Commission study of 15 to 16 year olds, and in her period of curriculum activism in the 1980s.

It is unusual for biographies to be co-authored. The writing process required high levels of cooperation in the search for a relatively unified authorial voice, consistency of approach and interpretation. We believe the benefits have outweighed the disadvantages as together we have thought through the meaning of the events, circumstances, persons or texts as they were relevant in the telling of this life. We also agreed that despite our efforts, there could be no single set of interpretations that encapsulate the life of another. In saying this, we consider that the images, usually photographs, that are reproduced in this book have an important role to play. They suggest a wider range of possible narratives and interpretations possible for the telling of Jean's life than those that occur through our text alone.

This brings us to our sources. They are extensive. The interviews we conducted, and those otherwise available to us ranged in focus across the entire period of Jean Blackburn's life. There is a belief that Jean herself never produced autobiography. In one respect this is true, but in another it is not. She drafted autobiographical narratives for the years of her childhood through to early womanhood, but she also talked to a series of interviewers, including Peter Biskup, Tony Ryan and Wendy Lowenstein about her life.[8]

The most substantial of the written archives are the Jean Blackburn Personal Papers held by the National Archives of Australia. They reveal her work and preoccupations as Schools Commissioner. There are other relevant archives, also in the National Archives. Both Jean and her husband, Gerard (Dick) Blackburn and several of their friends were watched by the Australian Security Intelligence Organisation (ASIO) from the 1940s to the 1960s. Like any source, the ASIO files are not always trustworthy, but we are grateful for their existence, even if their targets were not. One substantial collection of Jean's personal correspondence survived because her daughter, Susan Blackburn, lived in Melbourne while Jean was in Adelaide. Letters Jean wrote to Susan from the 1960s through to the 1980s have informed the biography. Susan also wrote several pieces reflecting on her childhood and family history including for example, what Jean was cooking for her family in the 1950s – and on what it was like to have communists as parents. She also wrote a book on her grandfather, Jean's father-in-law, the labour legend, Maurice Blackburn.[9]

In 1979 Jean addressed a conference of the Australian College of Education. Her paper was titled "Quality is not what it was".[10] She began by reporting a telephone conversation with someone who wished her well as she prepared for a trip to Europe and the United States on behalf of the Schools Commission.

> "Goodbye Jean, keep fighting the good fight."
>
> "I would, if I knew what it was."
>
> "If we knew what it was, we'd win it, wouldn't we?"[11]

The exchange captures a little of the intangibles associated with Jean Blackburn's life and career. There is a recognition of her effort in the fight for good and just schooling in Australia. There is her hesitancy in believing she had the answers. There is also an indication of the solidarity which she inspired among great sections of the Australian educational community, for the winning of the fight.

Many of our interviewees talked about their interactions with Jean. Lyndsay Connors, a Schools Commissioner herself some years after Jean's appointment, spoke of the impact of their first meeting when she interviewed Jean for a newspaper story, probably in 1974:

> I found her quite forbidding. She had a kind of aura … forbidding, and yet also engaging and warm. She had this enormous dignity … but she was very forthcoming. She wasn't difficult to interview. And she had a robust sense of humour, often ironical, with a delightful throaty laugh.
>
> And, I guess from that first meeting on, whenever I think about Jean, you know when people say, 'a beautiful mind', I think of her … I mean, there are plenty of people who are clever. But I just thought from the start she had a beautiful mind. She was very serious and caring, and ethical. And I could tell that from the start. And very concerned about – she had that ability to, express her concern about making it a better world for everyone. I hadn't heard anyone talk much like that before, in a spontaneous way and without being pompous or self-conscious. It was a very genuine concern I think, and she was very prepared to ask hard questions. Especially of herself. But right from the start I thought: 'This is amazing to be in the presence of somebody like that'.[12]

Recollections such as these lead to thoughts about the consequences of the general approval and even admiration of biographers for their subject. We have of course no desire to write anything approaching the life of a saint. Jean Blackburn was no saint, but she has certainly inspired strong statements, for example, Jean 'was the most influential feminist educator in Australian history'.[13] The website of the Australian College of Educators describes Jean as 'the nation's philosopher queen of education; a ferocious intellect; a notable scholar; a courageous thinker; and a compassionate and inspiring advocate'.¹⁴ One of our interviewees made an argument that she was Australia's Simone de Beauvoir: in 'importance, absolutely not', but 'in significance, temperament, and character, in many ways, yes'.¹⁵

David Gonski was the foundation orator of the Jean Blackburn Memorial Lecture, initiated by the Australian College of Educators and held at the University of Melbourne on May 21, 2014. Gonski said that Australian schooling was unfairly funded: that the money was not going where it was needed. He argued that funding should follow national aspirations in education, and surely one of these was that no person should be held back from a good education because of the circumstances of their parents, nor the under-resourcing of their schools. He asked the national government to rethink its policies for Australian education, to rethink its response to the report of the committee he had chaired in 2011. In reiterating arguments made by Jean some forty years earlier, Gonski referred to the continuing relevance of her contribution to a still yet to be achieved ambition – a schooling system that provided a fair go for all children and youth in Australia.¹⁶ It is our hope, as her biographers, that Jean's story will inform and inspire others who choose to continue her work.

Chapter 1

AN UNSATISFACTORY CHILDHOOD, 1919–1932

To be born in 1919 – as a female – was incompatible with the future I was unconsciously designing for myself.[1]

I entered University High School in 1934, when I was 14 years old. I sometimes feel that my life began with this move.[2]

At University High School in Parkville, across Royal Parade from the University of Melbourne, Jean Edna Muir found more than a school; she found herself. Before then, Jean thought of her life as occurring in a waste land. When writing about her childhood at the end of her life, she represented it as quite unsatisfactory.

Jean Muir was born on a Monday, July 14, 1919. In later years as she sought to make sense of her life, she was happy to celebrate the coincidence that July 14 was also Bastille Day, and her birth-date, the 130th anniversary of that symbolic event in the overthrow of semi-feudal oppression. It augured well for the making of a radical life.

More relevant to Jean's actual life were the social circumstances of families in Melbourne in the early twentieth century. Many had been shaken by the impact of the Great War. Abroad and in Australia Bolshevism and fascism challenged democracies in the 1920s and 1930s. Australian populations sustained another shock in the Great Depression. There were demographic and social changes affecting families also. Family size was contracting, and gender roles were changing in the broader society and within families. Jean's parents came from very large families, but the 'demographic transition', the move towards fewer children in families was reflected in her own. Jean's mother would have three children only, as would Jean herself.

By the 1920s there were opportunities for more women to make lives other than the expected, but the opportunities usually remained contingent on the social class and ethno-cultural origins of their parents. Racism was entrenched. Many Aboriginal Australians did not have the right to marry freely, and many children were forcibly removed from their families. At the same time, some women had increased control over their fertility though its exercise was officially deplored. It brought more freedom, especially for better-educated middle-class women. They could pioneer professional careers, especially if they did not marry. This was new in early twentieth century Australia. Apart from school teaching such opportunities barely existed in the nineteenth century. Women lower on the social scale had fewer options. The rise of the legally enforced male breadwinner wage arguably made things worse for many women.[3] The basic male wage was supposed to support a dependent wife and three children, in the process contributing to the confining of most women to the role of 'housewife', full-time mothers and wives. In later years, Jean, as a 'dependent' married woman, would experience the expectations and discriminations involved in such an approach. Her own mother certainly did.

The rise of the suburb in Australian cities, including Melbourne, also affected the lives that women led in the new century. Houses on blocks of land that were large enough to be gardened were increasingly available. The increasing separation of the suburbs from the centres of employment contributed to the rise of the housewife. Such changes in the social and physical circumstances of Australian life helped frame Jean Muir's early life.[4]

Her parents, Clarice Edna Witt (Claire) and Leslie Allan Muir (Les) had married in June 1914 at the Mt Erica Methodist Church in High Street, Prahran.[5] They each attended the local Prahran Methodist Sunday school and public school. Claire had been friends with Les's sisters. Both of Jean's parents were raised in large working-class families of six and seven children each; both families mostly dependent on the wages that a sole semi-skilled breadwinning father could earn. Each family, though poor, was 'respectable'.[6] Claire Witt and Les Muir were both 24 years old when they married. The wedding was modest, the reception in an upstairs room in an arcade off Chapel Street, Prahran. If Les's speech was brief, 'On behalf of my wife and myself, I thank you', the departure for the honeymoon was more dramatic. The borrowed car failed to start until Les remembered that he had not switched on the engine. Everyone spilled onto the street to watch them leave for their few days of honeymoon at Lakes Entrance.[7]

Clarice (Claire) Witt was born in 1890. Following the death of her mother, also named Clarice, Claire assumed housekeeping duties for her father Edward and her younger siblings. At the age of twelve she was officially exempted from completing school.[8] Her new responsibilities were great considering that her father worked for the post office. He was often away on regular overnight rail trips interstate, sorting mail. Edward gave Claire a weekly housekeeping allowance. She shopped, cooked and cleaned not only for her father but her two brothers and a younger sister who was reluctant to share the burden. 'She [Claire] didn't complain though – just accepted it.'⁹ This resigned attitude towards domesticity and domestic labour endured through her life. Such a life and the resignation and confinement that went with it, never appealed to her daughter.

Figure 1.1 Jean Blackburn's parents on their wedding day in 1914. Les Muir and Claire Witt were both minimally school-educated. They were from working class families – but Les had ambition.
Photographer unknown, courtesy of Susan Blackburn.

Claire's housekeeping responsibilities meant a prolonged courtship for her and Les, but as Jean later reflected, her obvious household '"management skills" were doubtless attractive to my father given the upwardly mobile trajectory on which he had launched ... without discounting her good looks and generosities of spirit'.[10] Les's mother liked Claire but thought she looked sad. She was 'quiet'.[11]

Les Muir, also born in 1890, spent his early life in country Victoria. His father, Thomas, was a ganger on the railways at Wychitella and elsewhere. After he was disabled by a back injury, the railways allowed his wife, Caroline, to assume the role of station mistress. This gave the family an income while Thomas was laid up, either in bed or on crutches. Later the family lived near Ballarat and then Hawksburn. While in Ballarat, Les was involved in an incident that caused him enduring shame. It is possible that it affected relationships with his own children into the future. There would be small tolerance when it came to their apparent failings. He had not forgiven himself for his own. At age ten, he had been briefly entrusted with operating the level crossing, opening and closing the gates that allowed trains and road traffic to pass unimpeded by the other. He fell asleep, and the Adelaide-Express ploughed into the gates. He confided the story to his granddaughter in 1981, when he was 91.[12] The family eventually moved to Prahran where the railways put Thomas on light duties.

Les's mother, Caroline, was keen on church and the Rechabites, a mutual aid society with a strong temperance mission for working-class people originally founded in England. Like Claire, Les lost his mother early. She died when he was twenty-three: 'I can remember sitting on the form in the dining room when she came and told me she was going to die'. This occurred in Prahran soon after the turn of the century. There were six siblings, three older and three younger, four girls and two boys. The older sisters looked after the household, including the younger children. The family was poor. As had been the case for Claire Witt, there was no thought of schooling beyond the elementary.

Les worked before and after school, delivering papers. Les also had a Saturday job for a well-off doctor's family, scrubbing a veranda, gardening, attending fowls, raking gravel, cleaning shoes and the like. He had begun working for money when he was eight.[13] He grew mint which he sold to local greengrocers. From an early age, Les believed he knew all about the relationship between leisure, labour and 'earning a quid'. School had little to do with any of it. It came as a surprise some time later when his daughter announced that she wanted to go to high school. Les would be full of objections based on his own experience and feelings about work, life and women – and his belief that prolonged schooling was irrelevant to the making of a life.

Les Muir finished with school when he was thirteen. He had not liked it much – the best part was rifle shooting, part of cadet training. He secured an apprenticeship in the motor trade, to a carriage-making and mechanical engineering firm.[14] He had an instinct for tools and engines, and his skills developed quickly. All cars were imported into Australia at this time and spare parts were in short supply. Les and a fellow apprentice had access to a lathe and everything else necessary to make spare parts from scratch. He liked making things. He talked in later life about the car he and fellow apprentices surreptitiously built and drove.[15] The garage attracted people who lived in Toorak. They were more likely to own cars than people who lived elsewhere. He got to know the car owners.

After finishing his apprenticeship about 1909, Les went to work for Dalgety's, a merchant firm powerful in rural Victoria, and indeed, across Australia and New Zealand. Opportunities presented themselves within its motor vehicle division. The company had agencies for car manufacturers that included Rolls Royce, Buick and Mercedes. Les remained with the company until 1919, the year of his marriage.

During the Great War (1914–1918) Les Muir chose not to volunteer for the armed forces, but he was part of the effort to convert small lorries into ambulances for shipping overseas. By the end of the war other businesses were providing substantial competition for Dalgety's vehicle and garage division. His acquaintance with car owners, including 'squatters from Victoria and New South Wales', led Les to a significant contact, the managing director of the British Imperial Oil Company, Ernest Wagstaff.[16] The company was the Australian branch of what became Shell, the Dutch-Anglo oil conglomerate. Les asked for and was given a job as a carburettor expert. He thought that working for such a company was more promising than Dalgety's and events proved him right. British Imperial Oil began to expand its operations and soon Les became a manager, responsible for equipping the company with some 2,000 lorries to be used throughout Australia, New Zealand and the Pacific islands. This was around the time his daughter Jean was born. Later, with Shell, he would be responsible for Australia-wide transport operations and the pioneering of hot-mix road paving in New Zealand.[17]

In many respects the young Muir family had made significant steps from the working class into the middle class. In theory managers were middle-class, but in this case, what is still occasionally talked about as 'class consciousness' lagged well behind an improving economic and social positioning. For his family there would be no rush towards unnecessary consumption, in either goods or services.

Frugality was, of course a common characteristic of the new, the 'moral' middle class. But for Les Muir, the frugality involved was extreme, and closely related to both his and Claire's experience of childhood. Jean's father never intimated that there was money for anything beyond the basics. The Muirs apparently belonged to the 'not well-off' class. The children, and their mother were made to understand that 'any overstepping of bounds of frugal living could bring disaster'.[18] Parental attitudes towards schooling barely changed either. The teachings of the Rechabites also retained significance for the family.

The family was not poor, however. Some things previously denied became possible. Home ownership was an early aspiration, much more possible for rising middle-class families than those of the working class. Upon marriage, Les and Claire moved into a house that Les had had built 'to avoid getting into debt' at 27 Moama Road, Malvern East.[19] It was there that each of the children were born: Allan Edward (1916), Jean Edna (1919) and Leslie Thomas (1924). In 1914 Malvern East was a new suburb. The block was on a subdivided former market garden. Jean, the second child and only daughter, lived there until she was twelve. Then the family moved a couple of suburbs north to Hawthorn. This was a shift up in the world. Les had taken advantage of low land prices during the Depression. He designed the new house, with its view over the Yarra River, to include a workshop under the main roof. To Jean and her elder brother Allan, it seemed a 'rather grand house'. Its achievement did not quite fit with Les's claim of near penury. 'When our father proudly announced that it was fully owned without debt, both my elder brother and I felt, when we compared notes late in our lives, that we had been "had"'.[20]

Figure 1.2 Jean, about 3 years old, with her elder brother Allan. Jean's father, Les Muir made his career in the motor industry. It is no surprise that there was a child-size motor car for the children to play in. It was probably made by their father, c1922.
Photographer unknown, courtesy of Susan Blackburn.

Figure 1.3 Jean, about 6 years old, with her two brothers, Les the baby and Allan. They are photographed in the front yard of the suburban block in Malvern East. The family was already on the way up, especially in terms of home ownership, c1925.
Photographer unknown, courtesy of Susan Blackburn.

It was not only home ownership that marked this family as different from many working- and even middle-class families in the 1920s and 1930s. Les had owned cars from before he was married. After marriage, there would be two cars, one for Claire as well. Car ownership in Australia before the 1950s was hardly universal, and two cars in one family signified social rank. The family was 'well-off'. There were also once yearly family holidays in Marysville and Lakes Entrance. Les enjoyed overseas travel in 1938, in England, France and Switzerland. The knowledge that her father had money stashed away somewhere, inaccessible to his family, caused family tension then and into the future.

Jean did not remember her childhood with affection. In retrospect, she thought of herself as a rather dreamy child, even a 'cuckoo in the nest'.[21] She laid out several objections to her childhood as she wrote her odd pages of autobiography late in life. They usually circled around her father, Les, specifically the connection between her father's earning power and his assumption that this entitled him to near absolute authority over his wife and children. One of the works that Jean enthusiastically read before beginning university was Marx and Engels' *Communist Manifesto*. There were contemptuous comments there about the bourgeois family, and a primitive critique of the subjection of women and children in the family. ('The bourgeoisie has torn away from the family its sentimental veil, and has reduced the family relation to a mere money relation.') Jean became convinced of the economic foundation of patriarchal oppression. The near unassailable authority of her father, perhaps tyranny, was based on his economic power: 'he was the supreme example of small scale unaccountable power. Its basis was the fact that as sole income earner, he believed he had the right to call every tune'.[22]

At some point early on, Jean decided 'never to be financially dependent on anyone, or to cede the power that went with that dependence'.[23] Jean insisted that she understood the humiliations involved in dependence from an early age. This did not mean she was always independent into the future, especially for stretches of time in the 1940s and 1950s. Nevertheless, the dependency issue was in part responsible for a growing distance between herself and her parents over the years. Before Claire Muir's youngest son, Les Thomas, left home, Claire confided in him about a pattern of problems with her husband. They were set soon after marriage. One of Les's demands was that Claire should see her own family no longer.[24] She resisted this, but in the main, Claire complied. Jean understood why her mother mainly accepted her ordained role, but Jean's incipient feminist outlook resulted in a growing alienation between mother and daughter.[25] Claire herself eventually felt that she had 'lost' not only her daughter, but Jean's older brother Allan as well.[26]

Both Jean and her brothers lived in fear of their father. Jean insisted that Les was 'no monster' despite the strappings that she and her brothers endured. Jean thought he was 'performing his expected male role in the family as he understood it' though the beatings were for reasons she 'seldom understood but which might broadly be classed as defiance'.[27] Risk of harm often follows a challenge to the presumption of men that they should control women – and the young. An earlier judgement that her father was a 'violent man' was tempered by later conversations with contemporaries about how their families also operated in the period.[28] Current understandings suggest that there are many reasons why the children of abusive parents sometimes excuse the damaging behaviours, but most are linked to historical constructs of gendered roles in families. This approach became Jean's approach, though it did not stop her feeling aggrieved about her father's behaviour and its consequences into old age.[29]

Jean developed survival skills as she lived with the continual threat of a displeased father.

> The really big incident was when the back of my primary school tunic was chewed up in the cogs of the trolley my father bought for my younger brother. By that time I had become a practised liar, to escape the razor strop punishment of which our father was the *aficionado*. I came to admire the fecundity of my inventive powers about how this happened. I forget the outcome but it was a long playing saga.[30]

Many years later, in 1968, when Jean's own daughter was forming a relationship with a young man from Sri Lanka, Jean passed on tactical advice:

> I think you should protect yourself by saying nothing to Nana and Grandpa. Because their knowledge and experience has been limited … they tend to reduce everything to the most petty terms, and do succeed, despite one's conscious rejection of their views in tarnishing whatever one holds dear. This is why I have never been able to talk to them, and was reduced to constant deceit when I lived with them. Such deceit I now regard as legitimate protection in the young in such a situation.[31]

The beatings may have slowed in the 1930s when Allan, Jean's older brother, called a halt to it. He pointed out that given his size and strength he could 'floor' his father if he ever laid hands on him again.[32]

Jean's father's attitudes towards saving, consumption and money in general were unbending. There would be no scented soap, bought toilet paper, fizzy drinks or too-heavy a use of butter, though eventually there would be a pianola for family sing-alongs. Cardboard inserts prolonged the life of shoe soles with holes in them.[33] On one occasion Jean was sent on an errand to a local shop. On the way home, she lost the change, an ha'penny. Les, 'a skinflint' according to his granddaughter Susan, sent Jean to re-trace the route and find the coin. As she wandered the streets of East Malvern in the failing light, she probably anticipated a beating when she arrived home.[34] For Jean, the story of the lost ha'penny encapsulated an unsympathetic, authoritarian and parsimonious upbringing, but it was also a story of a childhood set during the Great Depression, though Les was securely employed through the 1920s and 1930s. Few families would have been tolerant of children losing money of course. But a ha'penny?

The second objection Jean had to her childhood was the want of good talk and reading. This is a constant theme in her autobiographical writing. Though her mother, Claire, had little education: 'She remembered, and taught me before I went to school, the poetry she had learned in her truncated educational experience'. Jean remembered the poems, able to perform 'A little best girl' and 'She's nobody's mother' until late in life.[35] It was thin gruel, for neither parent had an interest in books. There were no books in the house other than 'how to' manuals, recipe books and 'the telephone directory and the Bible'.[36] Jean developed an interest in books and eventually school, despite her family. Her desperate struggle for an education beyond the elementary was a personal experience that conditioned Jean's thinking as she made her contributions to Australian educational reform some forty years later. She described her childhood and home:

> a strange household in that my parents talked hardly at all to each other, they hardly talked to us, there was never – there were no books in the house and in fact I don't think either of them ever read a book throughout their whole adult lives; not even newspapers, because that was a waste of money … and

so in lots of ways it could be called a very culturally deprived childhood.[37]

There were visits to relatives on Sundays which did involve lots of talk, but in Jean's recollection, no-one ever *said* anything. Daily talk was of the practical here and now. There was little discussion of the family's past, a point of contrast with Jean's future husband's family.[38] Many decades later, these memories of a culturally impoverished family life were corroborated by Jean's younger brother, Les Thomas. Overt affection between family members was in short supply.[39] Some of the relatives were hazardous. Jean was sent to holiday in the country with one set where she was forced to watch pigs being killed, a scarifying experience that helped turn her into an occasional vegetarian.[40] Books she read were cast-offs from friends at school. At some point one friend gave Jean a small collection that included novels by Mary Grant Bruce and some of the *Anne of Green Gables* series.[41]

The school to which Jean was sent in 1925 was the Lloyd Street Higher Elementary in Malvern East, the only school most of its students would ever enter. Jean was brutal in her appraisal. There was no library, and the teachers were 'what I regarded as sadists'. 'I vividly recall being strapped in Grade 2 because I didn't maintain the required distance between hand and eye in writing.'[42] In the process of that strapping, the teacher made sure she broke each of the bangles Jean was wearing, gifts from her parents on their return from travel in New Zealand.

That her handwriting never approached the desired standard may have been part of the problem. For teachers, perhaps it was the common frustration with the 'underperforming' but clever student.[43]

Jean was often in trouble. The school was 'not a very intellectually stimulating place', the experience was a 'hard, controlled, limited grind'. She was sent out of class for various misdemeanours. Thankfully the headmaster, Mr Chambers, to whom she was sent was 'benign', less intimidating than he first appeared.⁴⁴ Jean's schooling belied the promise of the New Education reforms that were supposed to have improved the learning experience for children in the new century; but she did learn to read, and that was the beginning of 'liberation'.⁴⁵ She practically learned the set readers by heart. Of all their content, she loved the poetry most, some of it moving her 'almost to a state of transcendence'.⁴⁶ She fancied herself 'as a famous reciter and things of that kind'.⁴⁷ She spoke poetry to the air on solitary walks, inventing forgotten lines towards the end of a poem. She found other material to read, even if the school did not support a library. Some of the parents of her school friends subscribed to publications such as *The Schoolgirls' Own*, which Jean was able to borrow. She was also startled to discover that in friends' homes, there was interesting talk. At home conversation seemed to be query driven, along the lines of 'Who left the bathroom light on?'⁴⁸

Jean conceded that she ended up doing 'quite well' at Lloyd Street Higher Elementary despite her parents' lack of interest. She won a reputation as a writer of compositions that were passed around among teaching staff. Yet she found the authoritarianism at home reflected in the school, the teacher as unassailable boss. The drawing of a banana was typical. Propped up on the teacher's desk was a banana to be represented in pastels. Moving on from the line of the base curve could only occur after the teacher had approved the effort. Rubbing out was anathema. Step by locked step the class moved towards a completed image of a banana.⁴⁹ Why things were done this way was a mystery to Jean, though the learning of drawing in this manner was standard practice in Australian schools at the time.

Jean was somewhat grateful for the arithmetic she learned, the increasingly arcane intricacies of rods, poles, perches and troy weights. With fellow students, she was able to calculate the time required to fill a bathtub while it drained at a slower rate. 'We did all that reading, writing and calculating in an atmosphere where humiliation, the witnessing of it and the fear of it were powerful motivators. There nevertheless was a genuine concern that everyone [should] learn the basics.' She also learnt that other barely hidden curriculum: never to speak uninvited, to attend to 'infinitely detailed instructions about how, and in what sequence, to perform every task', and to 'subject our wills to the teacher/leader' – apparently never quite to the extent that Jean needed to in order to avoid trouble. She continued to be considered a disruptive influence; she 'talked too much'. She continued to be removed from class, told to report to Mr Chambers, the bemused school head. She felt that teachers disliked her.[50] Jean disliked and occasionally 'hated' her elementary school.

As a girl, Jean also learned to darn, sew and knit, and to 'bathe baby-substitute dolls while boys did ... sloyd'. (Sloyd was a craft-based school subject that was expected to improve hand and eye coordination, and the gap between mental and manual labour.) As Jean told graduates at the University of Melbourne in 1988, with sarcasm: 'If there was a message in this, I didn't get it'.[51] The 'it' in the message was social engineering towards the acceptable female subject.

Thinking about her schooling later, Jean decided that Les, her father, was responsible for this mean education. The school as a higher elementary was designed to occupy children for the years of compulsory attendance though there was a possibility of entry to a high school, the sub-intermediate class, but this was uncommon. Students in the higher elementary classes apparently on such a track rarely lasted the distance. Jean could recall 'only one who, like me, stayed till the bitter end'.[52] She only met one other student from Lloyd Street at Victoria's sole university when she was an undergraduate. These limits to schooling suited her father who 'was attracted by this low cost terminal education of his daughter destined for housekeeping'.[53] Education would, if anything, be unhelpful in 'catching' a future husband who would support her for the rest of her life.[54] Her father also believed that parents had no obligation to financially support children 'beyond the point where they could leave school and earn their own living'. On passing his Intermediate, Jean's older brother Allan was quickly apprenticed. Les Thomas, five years younger than Jean, had an easier time of it, attending Scotch College, very close to home, and then University High.

At elementary school Jean became aware of the circumstances of families affected by the Great War. There were children in her class who had lost fathers, and others 'whose fathers lived a half-life, immobile in a rugged armchair, detached from families and visitors in an inner world of unforgettable horrors'. She could be moved to tears by lines from *For the Fallen*: 'They shall grow not old, as we that are left grow old', and the playing of the Last Post, bugled at school assemblies. But there was also a distance from the 'medalled men who spoke on such solemn occasions as Anzac and Armistice Day about Empire and duty'.[55] She felt a little 'unworthy', uncomfortable that few in her near family on either side, had joined up for 'the war to end all wars'.[56] At least Ted, her mother's younger brother returned from war 'to tell the tale'. Discomfort with the evidence of the recent war contributed to the beginnings of Jean's pacifist sentiments.[57]

Jean was at Lloyd Street from 1925 to 1932, eight long years. It could have been shorter had she been moved to high school from the sixth grade, but that possibility had entered the heads of no-one. Nevertheless, a determined intervention in Jean's future came from an unexpected quarter. Claire, Jean's mother, was not as uninterested in her daughter's education as she appeared. She did occasionally talk to Jean, as Jean 'sat on the doorstep endlessly creaming fat and sugar for cakes and cookies' on a Saturday morning. Claire encouraged Jean to 'get as well educated as possible'. Devoted to running her father's and then her husband's households from the age of twelve, Claire's formal education was limited, but she could make soap from fat and caustic soda – and after marriage 'she saved sixpences from the household allowance' Les paid her, 'and banked them in case her children might have special needs'.[58] While at high school and even some time beyond, Jean would have recourse to this fund. When, at the end of Jean's time at elementary school, the possibility of a transfer to a high school arose, Jean's mother would be sympathetic.

Claire had a widowed aunt, Jean's great aunt Con, who lived in Essendon. Claire took Jean with her on visits, and these stimulated Jean although conversation was often restricted to how families might be fed at little cost. It was the Depression. Even though Jean, tending towards vegetarianism, was revolted by Con's exposition of how to feed a family for two days with a sheep's head, other talk was often interesting. Con found humour in the varying predicaments of humankind. Both Con's daughters were being educated for professions: one in pharmacy. Con was 'a bright light among a multitude of boring relations', and Jean believed that Con and her daughters were in her mother's mind when the question of Jean and University High School arose. Predictably Les said 'No!' but Claire was overheard, shouting: 'Of course she must go'.[59] Though given little credit in Jean's writing towards the end of her life, at least one or two teachers at Lloyd Street Elementary must have helped with preparing her for the tests associated with the application for enrolment at the high school. The protests made by her father, about wasting education on girls, the expense of the uniform, and University High being on the other side of the city, and so on, were neutralised. Jean was startled; she barely remembered another instance where Claire stood up to Les and faced him down.

Jean had to fight for her sense of self in a usually unsympathetic family. The children did not develop strong bonds with each other, though Jean and Les Thomas became closer later in life.[60] Jean's father dominated the family; his attitude towards females was conservative, bordering on misogyny. Despite the want of respect in her own family, Jean eventually came to realise that historically there were new possibilities for women. She would join

> the generation of Australian women who would see, and play an active part in expanding the opportunities for married women to participate in full employment. The size of families fell as contraception became more reliable and as changed patterns of employment opened up more jobs where physical strength was not a major qualification.[61]

Regard for children and their place in families was changing, along with the reduction of children's participation in labour, paid or unpaid. Compulsory education added to the pressures that reduced the size of families. If Jean's family was slow in imagining a different, perhaps more humane way to manage children, Jean seemed to have had enough spirit to work around restrictive demands. She would make a life different from that ordained by her father and modelled by her mother.

Education was at the heart of her fight to make a different life for herself. The first round was to win an enrolment at University High. Jean passed the selection exam: 'And it really changed my life. And that partly explains my, the great passion about schooling which I have had forever'.[62] Patriarchal opposition was in retreat, but only for the time being. It would regularly reassert itself during Jean's high school and university career.

It was difficult for her father to conceive of any possible benefit from investing in a girl's education. It was rational to apprentice his sons along similar paths that he had pioneered. Like his father, Jean's elder brother, Allan worked for Shell most of his life. According to Jean's analysis of the situation:

> The world in which I grew up needed no 'discourse' to bolster sex stereotyped futures. In our home the father brought home the bacon and the mother cooked it. The realities of our own home situation were confirmed in the homes of our schoolmates. By the act of marriage women were excluded from such occupations as teaching and Government public service jobs above tea lady and cleaners. That's how we learned how the world was. We prepared for it in school.[63]

Jean Blackburn's childhood and youth played out in the years following the Great War. A few years of greater national prosperity were soon undermined as agricultural prices fell from the mid-1920s. The streets of Melbourne, like other Australian cities, were partly peopled by men who had survived the war in damaged condition.

An Unsatisfactory Childhood, 1919–1932

The year of Jean's birth saw the formal end to the war at the Treaty of Versailles, but the peace only lasted twenty years. The onset of the Depression made the Bolshevik revolution and communism look good to many, as Germany, Italy, Japan and Spain underwent crises that led to at best highly authoritarian, and at worst, fascist regimes. The capitalist democracies often looked feeble in comparison. The League of Nations, the great international hope after the Great War, failed to win the support of the United States. The Soviet Union only joined when it began to fear the eastern ambitions of leaders of the Third Reich. These international politics were not merely context for the coming years as Jean Muir completed high school and university. They were to be a significant part of her life.

Jean crafted the stories of her childhood into a settled autobiographical narrative. They were useful in explaining the life that came. In this form they helped her to explain the emergence of her feminism as well as other social and political engagements. She was to live a life in radical opposition to that of her mother. Claire Witt's life was a warning against financial dependence on a man, either as husband or father. It was a warning against too elementary an education and marriage to a man who had little regard for women – though Jean had only a nascent sense of this as a child and youth.

Jean's narrative of herself when young tended to downplay the significant interventions that Jean's mother made as Jean was schooled. Nevertheless, the absence of books and engaging talk at home, made books and intelligent conversation essential for the life Jean was to make for herself. As she resisted her father, preparing to take control of her own life, Jean endured bruises, the wrath of her father. An early indication of the emerging person was the ditching of her family's church, Methodist for the Presbyterian, at age twelve.

Atheism would come not much later, when she was about fourteen.[64] And for all the faults with which she charged 'the school', it emerged in Jean's regard as an essential institution for escaping her family and class cultures, which she experienced as debilitating. The narrative of an unsatisfactory childhood was more than a construct of old age; its truths contributed motivation for the life to come. Jean's childhood also provides a possible explanation for some of the troubles that she endured throughout her life: a recurring lack of confidence and an unsteady sense of self-worth.

Chapter 2

SCHOOL AND THE INDEPENDENT GIRL, 1933–1937

> When I came back from Lyonnesse
> With magic in my eyes,
> All marked with mute surmise
> My radiance rare and fathomless,
> When I came back from Lyonnesse
> With magic in my eyes![1]

Catherine Forster, one of Jean Muir's teachers at University High School, wrote these lines in Jean's autograph book. Jean was startled. It took her a while to understand, and she did not completely grasp their meaning until she witnessed the effect that some poetry had on some of her own students many years later. The 'I' who came back from Lyonnesse was Forster's description of Jean, demonstrably in love with the poetry she had read – the student with 'magic in her eyes'.[2]

Neither her family nor her limited schooling to this point prepared Jean for the challenges of University High. She and fellow students coming in to the sub-Intermediate year were asked to read four novels, two by Walter Scott and two by Charles Dickens. They were to be tested on the novels' plots and characters, with no teacher guidance to help. Jean worried. Her prior education and reading had not prepared her for challenges like this and she was embarrassed by her ignorance.[3] She also suffered a sense of insecurity in this new community of girls. Generally, her fellow students were from more established middle-class families. Some were from Jewish families who had settled in Melbourne after fleeing Nazi Germany. Nevertheless, before long, Jean decided that she had found a home. This school community provided Jean Muir with an 'exhilarating' experience.

University High was academically selective. Even though Jean had little good to say about her previous school, Lloyd Street, she was grateful for the teachers there who had told Jean's parents that University High could be a good place for her. Jean was thinking along similar lines. Next door to her family's Hawthorn home was a neighbour whose grandson attended University High, the best of all schools as far as he was concerned. Jean had a bit of a crush on him, and although she later recalled that she knew little about the possibilities in secondary education, she imagined following in his footsteps.[4] There was not much other information available to her apart from her father's belief that such schooling was an ill-afforded luxury. She had not known that she could have entered University High three years earlier. It became a refrain in her autobiographical reflections: how little she knew and how difficult it was to learn of opportunities that may have been available. Teachers from Lloyd Street arranged for Jean to sit the entrance test for University High in 1932 when she was thirteen.

University High had an unusual establishment for a public secondary school in Melbourne. It was founded in 1910 as a practising school for secondary teachers in training, decamping from its original site in Lygon Street, Carlton, to its present Parkville campus in 1929. Victorian governments had been slow to provide public high schools, and private and church school interests successfully opposed state high schools for many years.[5] In this respect, Victoria lagged New South Wales with its superior public schools and high schools founded in the 1880s. Nevertheless, Frank Tate, the Victorian Director of Education from 1902, wangled the beginnings of a system of public high schools a few years prior to the Great War, though most were in country towns.

Schools such as Melbourne High and University High were academically selective, their status protected by the small numbers of students accepted for enrolment. Such schools were meritocratic, not democratic institutions. They looked as much to the church colleges as other government schools in developing their cultural identities. Their founding staffs adapted the approaches that had begun to transform the church-founded colleges in the late nineteenth century, with their prefects, school magazines, student clubs and games.[6] For Jean, the experiences and privileges associated with a school such as University High did their transformative work. Before long she was reading, thinking, writing and talking about things that were alien to her family. She rapidly conceived the ambition to go on to higher education. On the other side of Royal Parade was the University of Melbourne. Students were very aware of the university, often visiting the campus for school assemblies in Melba Hall. Becoming a university student was an aspiration that Jean soon shared with her classmates.

So, in 1933, the height of the Depression, Jean Muir was on the tram to the city from her home in Hawthorn. She was uniformed in a green gingham dress, beige gloves, white straw hat with school badge on the band, green jumper and blazer. For winter, there was a navy box-pleated tunic, white blouse, tan tie, navy felt hat and woollen gloves. Jean's father was far from impressed that her blazer alone cost £5.[7] On the way to school she was shocked by 'real world' lessons as she passed the soup kitchens feeding the unemployed.

Despite her early discomfort, Jean took to the academic curriculum with enthusiasm. The school 'felt like coming home'. It was 'exhilarating in ways I hadn't previously encountered'.[8] Alongside the encouragement to reading and serious study, she developed a taste for argumentation'.[9] In later life Jean thought that the school was an English grammar school 'transported to an alien clime', taking for granted that its students were clever, that they wanted to learn. Its teaching methods were close to those of the university, 'verbally based'.[10]

Some of the school's teachers had a profound influence on her. This was a period in which many remarkable women, almost always unmarried, brought great energy, scholarship and a sense of the possibility of independent womanhood to their female students at schools like University High. Alice Hoy wrote about several of them. They were among the first generations of women who had been accepted into degree studies in Australian universities. Dorothea Marshall was one, 'an exceptionally vivid and stimulating teacher' who left a lasting impression with her 'lessons in history, and in all branches of English literature, composition, and even grammar'.[11]

Ada Knowles was Jean's form mistress for the Leaving year. She was completing her own degree at the time. Modern European history and economics were her teaching subjects, and through her teaching, she helped attach Jean to the wider world. Years later when Jean taught at Presbyterian Girls College in Adelaide she taught roughly the same subjects. She thought that she stimulated a 'similar response from students'.[12]

A little earlier while teaching at Geelong High, Knowles had begun an annual instalment plan, giving £25 to the University Women's College, 'In token of her continued gratitude to those who made her education and place in the world's work possible'. Born in 1892, she was 43 when she taught Leaving subjects to Jean. In 1936, she was appointed to the inspectorate, a member of the Board of Secondary Inspectors. She knew the role that a university education could play in the transformation of a woman's life, and she had a greater influence on Jean's development than any other teacher at the school.[13] Alice Hoy acknowledged her 'vigorous stimulating teaching and her interest in individuals', her 'friendliness, her professional competence and her practical advice'.[14] Such women provided lessons in female achievement, independence and influence, and whether articulated or not, lessons in lived feminism.

Jean readily admitted that not all her teachers were admirable. The worst she thought were some of the long-serving males. One of her physics teachers insisted that a metal object and a piece of paper dropped from the leaning tower of Pisa would arrive on the ground at the same moment. It took until the next lesson the following day before he confessed that a vacuum would be required to make it possible. Jean was relieved, remarking loudly, 'Now you're talking!' The teacher reported her to the headmaster for impertinence.

The subjects Jean loved were English, history and economics, the last being for the most part economic history. Economics 'confirmed for me that the class struggle was the central feature of history'. Jean studied the rise of labour movements and the genesis of socialism. Before leaving school, she had read Engels' *The Condition of the Working Class in England* (1845).[15] She took to heart the dire results of enclosures and the conditions in the factories of the Industrial Revolution.

Initially the study of English literature was a challenge for her. Never having read novels more demanding than *Anne of Green Gables* and 'trashy romantic novels', the set texts demanded concentration 'quite beyond my experience … As I progressed, the pleasure gained rated higher than the pain.'[16] The subject nurtured Jean's passion for poetry: 'The four years at UHS gave it an historical frame and a wider and deeper base'. Tennyson was an early favourite, though much of the poetry studied was devoted to military and imperial themes. Catherine Forster, head of the girls' section, was the English teacher who rivalled Ada Knowles for Jean's respect and affection.[17] Only much later did Jean realise that in her curriculum there was 'damn all about Australia, its history or poetry'. In thinking about the subjects she studied, Jean came to regret not keeping on with mathematics into her senior high years. Its absence became an issue as she pursued her economics major at university.[18]

Belonging to University High filled Jean with pride. She became both a house captain and a prefect. The houses were named after former students who died in the Great War; hers was Saltau. She participated enthusiastically in bellowing songs 'about cricket and every other possible sport', and the school song borrowed from England, 'The best school of all'. In Jean's later view, the sexism, solidarity and patriotism of it all, were 'typical of the times'.[19]

Figure 2.1 Jean, third from the left, in a senior year at University High School. Friends not identified. Jean loved her school, and several of its women teachers. She was a prefect and debater, but also a budding feminist, pacifist and socialist at high school. c1936.
Photographer unknown, courtesy of Susan Blackburn.

Jean recognised in later years that academically selective public schools had a huge advantage over other public schools in developing an affinity between students, teachers and learning – the development of schools as communities where students enjoyed a strong sense of belonging. In 1936 the sixth form girls went to Ferntree Gully for a class camp. There was a Clark Gable film to enjoy, but also a day visit from Inspector Ada Knowles.[20]

In contrast to her difficult years at Lloyd Street Higher Elementary, Jean was 'rather popular' at University High. Her younger brother, Les, a junior at the school, 'bathed in the reflected glory of that popular, tall house captain and senior prefect'.[21] The strongest of Jean's friendships at school was with Rivkah Brilliant, but she had other close friends as well, including Yetta Bardas. She and her friends visited each other's homes on weekends, occasions that gave Jean an insight into the possibility of a family life 'beyond the somewhat emotionally cold model of my own experience'. With school friends were also walks in the Dandenong Ranges, the beginnings of a lifelong pleasurable recreation.[22] Years later, Jean's friend Rivkah wrote about the experience of being a student at University High:

> we had been well and truly inducted into the belief that knowledge was to be highly valued, there'd been some crack women teachers who were erudite without being remote and who somehow or other gave us a feeling that we were all involved in a democratic enterprise that was in no way impersonal.[23]

The friendship with Rivkah was not plain sailing. Recounting Jean's version of the relationship, her daughter Susan wrote: 'The girl was from a very intellectual family and seemed to Mother's starry eyes to embody this world. The friendship was thus very narrow: the girl grew irritated by it and then threw mother off, although the two became friendly again at Uni'.[24] In thinking back on her fellow students, at least those who made it to the Leaving year, Jean thought that almost all of them were the children of teachers, civil servants or high-income parents 'with a commitment to education'. Many of the girls from families whose fathers were grocers or builders failed to last the distance. Some of the friendships Jean made at school were continued into later life; they were 'friends who shared significant interests'.[25]

During these teenage years Jean had little in the way of a social life. Money was limited, and homework was ever pressing, as were household chores: ironing, cleaning the bathroom, scrubbing floors, while her brothers were in her father's workshop being introduced to the magic of the lathe. Claire, Jean's mother inducted her into cooking, but there was still not much talk other than how to save money, and what might be had for tea.[26] None of it was of much interest to Jean. Her younger brother recalled an incident from those years that showed where her interests really lay. Jean was told to take young Les to the pictures. It was a long walk, and Jean 'in typical form' gave him a lecture on the current state of the world. She rebuked him for his relatively dispassionate response to the litany of injustices: 'How dare you ... those poor people!'[27]

Sex was not talked about at home and Jean thought she was probably more ignorant about it than other girls of the same age. She did develop attractions to boys, but fear of judgement and pregnancy cast a 'terrible pall over it all'. There was some kissing and holding hands. Men's jokes about 'buns in the oven' enraged her.[28]

As was the case when she was a child, the tension and conflict with her father continued through her teens. Once yearly there was a family trip to relatives in Ballarat. At half way would come the break, a thermos of tea and food on the side of the road, and the children getting into trouble. It was Jean's turn to have offended and she was put out of the car and over a fence, and left, as Les drove on. Her brother, Les Thomas, was distressed: it was 'dreadful to me'. Eventually Jean was collected, presumably having learnt a lesson yet again. Les Thomas thought Jean got more than her fair share of trouble, perhaps because she was 'gamer than we were ... she could put words together. And she would speak back to him'.[29] In later years Jean modified some of her anger over her father's behaviour. She accepted some fault, but she was afraid of him through her teenage years. 'Positions [of] which he disapproved were interpreted by my father as a rejection of his authority. The statement over a family dinner that I was an atheist made all hell descend'.[30]

Remaining at University High after the Intermediate year was a struggle. Les tried to have Jean leave at the end of 1934; however, there were teachers who defended her. 'I didn't know this till a good time later, but my form mistress rang my father and said that would be absurd and I must go on. So he said, well, he wanted it understood that I was to be a primary teacher.'[31] Towards the end of the next year when Jean was sitting for the Leaving certificate, Les tried again. Jean was to qualify as a primary teacher in case she did not marry. This meant that she was not to return to school for the final Leaving Honours year. Primary school teachers did not need Leaving Honours, nor were they bound for the University of Melbourne as part of their training. This time there was Ada Knowles to contend with. She had the good fortune to know, despite Jean's excellent Leaving results, that she would not be accepted into primary teaching. Her Leaving certificate lacked a subject, drawing. She would have to return for the Honours year, studying the necessary Leaving drawing at the same time. The case was strong, though Les was likely unimpressed by Knowles telling him that Jean was 'university material'. Jean wrote later: 'It was typical of the workings of our family that my father had not discussed my future with me, regarding all decisions he reached in isolation (especially if expenditure was involved) as his prerogative as the income provider'.[32] Ada Knowles was a good ally for Jean, but despite temporary defeats, Les Muir held to the long-term objective. Jean would go into the workforce sooner than later, and she would receive a restricted education. However, the experience of University High had made Jean less malleable, and she had an ally at home, though she hardly registered it sometimes. Although there were annoying and upsetting victories for Les yet to come, he faced defeat in the long term. Jean had her mother on her side.

There was no escaping a world in trouble in the 1930s. Among Jean's fellow students were boys and girls whose families had fled Nazi terror. Girls from refugee Jewish families influenced her as they helped politicise 'the school, and expanded our concern for fellow human beings'.[33] She, along with some of her fellow students, were surprised to discover anti-Semitism in their own families.[34] A school friend, a boy who had arrived in Melbourne as a refugee lent her a copy of a banned book by the British communist, Palme Dutt, that made the case against fascism. The book circulated among the school's senior students.[35] The lender also partnered Jean in a school debate. She drew closer to admiring the communists, but her developing pacifism held her back.[36] She did begin to think that the communists were the most vocal and effective opponents of fascism. A school debate addressed this very issue: 'That the salvation of the world lies rather in Socialism than in Fascist dictatorship'. Jean and her team lost this 1935 debate, arguing 'Yes', but the topic was not unusual. Another debate in which Jean argued was the question of equal pay for men and women.[37] This education, along with her observation of the social effects of Depression meant that Jean Muir would leave University High a socialist.[38]

In later years, Jean speculated about her experience of school. She realised her good fortune in getting a full secondary education at one of the few selective public high schools in Victoria. She was disturbed that for most students, school education only became interesting once they had left.[39] The elementary years were overwhelmed by rote learning and the basics. Talk, argument and ideas arrived too late for most young people. In later years she ruminated 'about the intellectual and social pros and cons of selecting students for special treatment, and at what age and on what measurable grounds that may be admissible within a democratic society'.[40] She realised that she had barely heard of the university before this school. Being there allowed her to imagine joining her friends and going on.[41] Because University High was an 'approved' school, its syllabuses were designed and examined within the school itself, though not for the Honours year. This enabled a curriculum about which its teachers were possibly more enthusiastic. Jean's enrolment and experience at University High survived the introduction of fees in 1933 and attempts to rein in the school's relative autonomy from closer Education Department control.[42]

Schools such as University High pushed their students towards good results in examinations. Jean worked hard, and her results were creditable. She passed all her subjects, including Latin and French, gaining her Intermediate in 1934. In the next year, the Leaving, she did well in English, European history, British history and economics. Jean's Leaving Honours results a year later, were not as she wished. She gained first class honours in English and was placed second in the state, but in both histories, the honours were second class, and there was a mere pass in French.[43] She would not win the desired scholarship to the University of Melbourne. Her future seemed subject once more to her father's will.

Despite this failure to win a scholarship, Jean could have gone to the university at the end of high school by accepting a bond from the Education Department. She could have qualified as a secondary teacher, and then have been obliged to work for the Department. In return her university fees and a living allowance would have been paid. This was another example of Jean being unaware of the possibilities open to her. When she arrived at the university a year later she was surprised to find peers from University High 'whose academic performance I easily surpassed'. They were not only having their fees paid but had living allowances in return for a three-year bond. She guessed that she was still 'an unworldly person, and remained so, or I would independently have sought out ways of getting a university education without a scholarship'.[44] Jean had not seen any way of resisting her father's intentions following her failure to win a scholarship. 'There was no fall-back position'. Jean went teaching at seventeen years of age. Her father won this round.[45]

1937 was Jean's year as an apprentice, a junior teacher. From here the expected path was entrance to Melbourne Teachers College in 1938. Jean decided otherwise. She would recover her future. Her Leaving Honours result could be repaired – she *would* win a scholarship. She enrolled in French and economics at night school, on top of her teaching load.

The year was difficult, but it was not without its benefit. Jean rose daily before 5am to work on her night school subjects for two hours. She walked to school, taught all morning, followed by lunchtime instruction. The headmaster explained the Herbartian steps of well organised teaching. Jean appreciated the instruction and she liked the head. She worked with other junior teachers, skilling herself for copy book writing, singing and nature study. Blackboard art and music had to be mastered at after-school classes elsewhere, with junior teachers from other schools.[46] The weekly pay was twenty-eight shillings and four pence. The teaching itself she quite enjoyed, getting on well with the children.

There were problems, however. Jean decided that the level of conversation in the Hawthorn primary school staffroom was dire, and she 'had to find some way out'.[47] The problems apparently were not one way. Jean committed an unpardonable sin by 'taking' another staff member's tea cup. Unless conversation was one to one, fellow teachers were not to be addressed by their Christian names, a convention Jean had little time for. 'It was a rather sad place in its way, but enormously intolerant and narrow-minded, and I decided I wouldn't spend my life in such surroundings'.[48] She was working with teachers like those whom she thought she had escaped when she left Lloyd Street years before. Jean thought that a want of married teachers was a problem. Attitudes towards unmarried women in the first half of the twentieth century were often dismissive, often unkind. Jean appears, at least in relation to the elementary school-teacher women, to have shared a prejudice. Later, she became increasingly occupied with the disadvantages and discriminations suffered by married women, rather than the circumstances of the unmarried. She was hardly alone in all this. The fictional portrait painted by Christina Stead in *For Love Alone* of such elementary school teachers in the 1930s is close to scarifying.[49]

Matters were not helped when the budding seventeen-year-old socialist attended, with an older fellow teacher, probably Con Warneke, a film about the civil war in Spain. In sympathy with the republican cause, Jean bought a large badge, 'Food for Spain'. When she wore it next day the headmaster instructed her to remove it. Unless she did so, her signature in the time book would not be accepted, and her wage for the week would be lost. She gave way. 'I was humiliated', and it confirmed her views 'of how power operated'.[50]

Con Warneke encouraged Jean's reading of Marx. Con was someone whom Jean could trust, a refuge when there was trouble. It was probably she who warned Jean against bursting into the staffroom, 'excited by the *Communist Manifesto* and [urging] everyone to read it'. The friendship persisted for many years.[51]

Jean's night school instruction occurred two evenings each week. It was a good experience. Her mother helped by driving Jean from the 'site of my singing and drawing humiliations' after school to the tram stop. 'She brought food to me in the after-school classes which were part of primary training, she didn't charge me board on the condition that I saved the greater part of my slender "pay"'. Jean interpreted the assistance to mean that her mother supported her ambition towards the university. Claire advised Jean to play up to her father, to charm him, but Jean would have none of it. Claire sighed: Jean was 'too like him' to wheedle favours.[52]

Her French teacher thought Jean should be able to improve her grade but she detected little gift for languages, and there could be no enrolment in an Arts degree without a language. The economics teacher at the night school thought Jean was terrific, much more proficient than his day students at an expensive private school. He distributed her essays to his day students, using them to inspire. Jean studied labour movements in Britain, the United States and Australia. She made another friend, a boy who had been expelled from Melbourne Boys High. He was her fellow economics student. As they walked and talked together, he reinforced Jean's socialism and helped convert her 'hatred of violence' into pacifism.[53]

Along with the early morning rising, Jean spent the greater part of every weekend at the public library, especially the excellent Hawthorn public library, only a half hour's walk from home. With all the study and teaching, this was the year that she decided in retrospect, that she 'learned how to work'.[54]

At the end of the year, Jean's results were good. She improved her French to second class honours, gaining first class in economics. In economics, she came second in the state. 'Triumphantly, I reapplied for a senior scholarship.' A form letter told her she was ineligible as a part-time student. 'As may be imagined, I was deeply cast down at this confirmation of the outsider that I was.'[55] Neither she nor her parents 'knew the system'. It was, to use a phrase popular in the 1980s, one of the hidden injuries of class. Such problems were a theme in Jean's early life experience. Some students, and some families were continually disadvantaged because they simply lacked knowledge, not only about gate keeping rules, but about what opportunities might exist on the other side of the gate.

Jean Muir had long experience of not knowing, of being outside the networks that knew how to access educational opportunity. She was almost brought down by her prolonged enrolment at a higher elementary school. She had only discovered through fortuitous encounters with a neighbour's grandson, that a school such as University High existed. In 1937 while teaching, she worked early mornings, nights and on weekends for a year, for a goal that was never attainable. She could not access a scholarship. It was not until her university years that she discovered that by being bonded as a prospective secondary teacher she would not only have had her university fees paid but could also have received a living allowance. 1937 was a valuable year for Jean, but in a mainly negative sense. It improved her understanding of what was wrong with the world, but at the expense of her main goal, getting to the university.

Chapter 3

UNIVERSITY, COMMUNISM AND WAR, 1938–1941

So, when I got to university and into my honours economics, which was, as you can imagine, a very conservative school. I mean, this was coming out of the Depression and Copeland, the professor had been a great advisor to governments and so on and so forth ... So I got into the honours economics and, of course, I immediately joined the Labour Club and I soon became assistant secretary and then secretary of the Labour Club and then its first student president. I also in 1938, which was the year I entered university and which was the year of Munich, joined the Communist Party.[1]

Jean Muir's effort to achieve university enrolment remained uncertain of success. She was determined nevertheless. She knew that her 'kind of people', people 'who enjoyed the contest of ideas' went there. The other contest that impeded her enrolment, that with her father, was perennially tiresome. Les Muir resented 'any further calls on "his" earnings'.[2] No doubt against his wishes, Jean decided that she would not spend her working life as a primary school teacher, despite fine assessments by the school head and an Education Department inspector. She resigned from the Department at the end of 1937, having the small satisfaction of refusing to sign the letter, 'Your Obedient Servant'.[3]

The deciding moment had come. Could she enter the University of Melbourne despite the want of a scholarship and the opposition of her father? Jean went to his desk, surreptitiously inspecting his tax files. She decided he could well afford the £40 per year fee. Her mother supported her. Jean and Claire reasoned that if his income made Jean ineligible for a free place, then he earned enough to pay the fees. Jean could earn some money for additional expenses. The 'postponed struggle with my father was reactivated'.[4]

Surprisingly, yet another of Jean's educational misadventures helped with the decision-making. Jean had applied for a scholarship to Ormond College, a Presbyterian affiliate of the University, not realising it was an all-male college. She was offered tutorials in the college, but this was not what she was after and she turned the offer down. However, when Claire intervened once more with Les, the Ormond offer was an argument for his assistance. While Jean wept, or so she wrote, Claire contested the claim that he could not support her. 'We never talked about what we were up to, but it was my mother who enabled me to move out of primary school teaching, into the University of Melbourne – as I passionately desired.'[5] Jean marvelled at the campaign executed by Claire. She was almost as surprised by it as was her father. In truth, the 'tyrant' appeared to have a weak spot. When roused, and that occurred so rarely that it came as a shock, Claire was difficult to resist. Jean overheard her mother shouting: 'Of course she must go!' Why, she argued, they would be *wasting* the scholarship to Ormond (in fact, there was no scholarship, and Jean had already rejected the offer of tutorials). 'Waste' was never a virtue in Les Muir's view.[6]

In the end, Claire prevailed and Jean entered the University of Melbourne in 1938. Her mother used her savings to kit Jean out for the new life. Les had not given up the struggle though, as he imagined the conditions that might lead to the withdrawal of his forced cooperation. He would not have long to wait. Would he wish to harbour not only an atheist but a virtual Bolshevik in the bosom of his family?

In 1938 the University of Melbourne was in its eighty-sixth year. It had survived an embezzlement scandal and had consolidated its several roles in Victorian society. It trained and educated young men and some women in the professions such as law, medicine – and secondary teaching. It had assumed the topmost position in the system of public and private schools, controlling the most prestigious of the credentials to be gained across the education system. It played its role in adding distinction to the governing class. One of its law graduates, Robert Menzies was Attorney General in the Commonwealth government, and only a year away from becoming Prime Minister. The University performed a significant civic role, dignifying the city of Melbourne. It educated men and women in classical, modern and professional subjects and granted degrees, producing significant intellectuals and others who had and would continue to have a profound influence on Australian culture, business, politics and society.

Enrolment at the university was achieved mainly as a result of public examination success. Scholarships were far too few for youths from poorer families to achieve easy entry. The university fostered a cultural milieu with which the educated middle and upper middle classes were comfortable, shaped as much by the residential colleges, usually church-affiliated, as by the lecture halls of the university itself.⁷ The site was contained, having 'the air of an English village centred round its pond'.⁸ The university also harboured a left-liberal and radical minority. By Jean's time the lake into which communist students had been tossed from time to time by their fellow students had been filled. The new Union building hosted student sociality, and student clubs and sports were encouraged. Several clubs fostered political engagement: the Student Christian Movement, Labour Club and University Peace Group all leaned left. Academic staff sometimes involved themselves in the clubs.

In the mid-1930s there were 2,500 full-time students, and a further 1,000 who were part-time.⁹ It was a student body both small and large enough to form a society in which strong attachments to the institution, to its teachers and fellow students were possible. As Jean's friend and future sister-in-law, Louisa Blackburn said:

> There was the Graduates' Union – you could get a meal there. There was the Union House, which was wonderful. We had this wonderful vice chancellor called Medwell, who came in 1937 and he got the Union built. It was in spanking new condition, and everything was lovely. There were a lot of night meetings going on and a lot of activities, the theatre and so forth: it was really terrific.¹⁰

At the same time, the university did not lack critics. The political activity of many students, along with 'the excesses associated with student japes' could inspire condemnation in press and parliament, and this was certainly so, before, during and after Jean's undergraduate years, from 1938 to 1940.¹¹ Jean had entered an institution which had the capacity to engage and shape her even more profoundly than her high school.

In her first year Jean studied Economics I, Economic History, and English Language and Literature. Her school record justified enrolment in the honours stream and her university results were consequently expressed in class of honours. In second year came French as well as Economics II and the History of Economic Theory. In her third and final undergraduate year in 1940 she studied Economics III and Political Institutions. She did well for the most part, gaining three firsts in economics subjects, equal first place in Economics I, but a mix of seconds, and the predictable pass in French, giving her a second-class degree overall.[12] Her continuing interest was in economic history, developing also an interest in public policy. Throughout her undergraduate years, politics conditioned her studies and extra-curriculum. She joined the Labour Club and Communist Party within weeks of her enrolment. 'As a committed Marxist', the economics she was taught early in her course, the 'micro-economics' and 'macro theories', raised problems, 'until I encountered Keynes, recently published very late in my degree, with whose theories I developed a connection'.[13] Jean's want of sufficient mathematics also had an impact, but negative. 'So I would never have made a marvellous economist when it got to the stage of – with the three dimensional diagrams and calculus and things – I was really quite out of it.'[14] In Jean's time undergraduate classes were large. The teaching staff were few in number. The 1939 enrolment in economics was 731.

The Faculty of Commerce was established in 1925, though economics under various labels had been taught from the first decade of the university. A separate Department of Economics was established in 1944, after Jean's time, but before then an honours stream in economics existed within the Faculty of Arts. Students were directed by Douglas Copland and then Wilfred Prest as the professors. Many of its most successful students were offered Rockefeller-funded study overseas. Some were to become leading Commonwealth bureaucrats during the coming war. If Jean was not wholly in tune with the kind of economics taught, she was happy enough with Copland's intention to train professional economists capable of contributing to government. Copland himself was determined to influence government policy.[15] Both Copland and the research professor in economics, L. F. Giblin, left the university at the outbreak of war for senior positions in the Commonwealth public service.

As Jean continued into Economics III her fellow students were increasingly men. In one statistics course with many students, she thought there were only two women: herself as a student, and Jean Polglaze, the lecturer. Significantly though, she insisted that she never 'felt put down as a woman by the economists', and she developed friendships among fellow students.[16] One was with Bruce Williams, a future vice-chancellor of the University of Sydney and significant figure in the development of national employment policy many years later. Jean's honours thesis was 'a small scale empirical study' on the economics of public housing. There was no supervision, and with a topic the significance of which she did not fully grasp, her result was 'indifferent'. She had been advised against her desired topic, 'women's wages'.[17]

Ian Turner is one of many who have written about the strength of the left in his generation of university students in Melbourne. They were born:

> into a world where those who had survived the shambles of the First World War had resurrected the ability to hope. But

hope died many deaths – in 1929, with the Wall Street crash; in 1933, with Hitler; in 1935, in Abyssinia; in 1937, at Shanghai; in 1938, at Munich; in 1939 in Spain. These were the social and political impressions of our childhood and early adulthood, and they shaped our lives. An end to poverty amid plenty. Down with capitalism. The united front against war and fascism. *No pasaran!*"[18]

Jean Muir, though a couple of years older than Turner, was part of this committed minority within her generation of university students. Among the many controversies that excited student passions in the 1930s, none was more significant than the Spanish Civil War. The communist-led Labour Club was firmly on the side of the republicans, as were most socialists and left liberals in Europe and elsewhere. On the other side were the supporters of General Franco, backed by a deeply conservative Roman Catholic Church. The fact that Stalin and Hitler intervened in the civil war on opposite sides made the struggle in Spain not only an apparent rehearsal for the coming resumption of the Great War, but a broader struggle between communism and fascism.

The fallout from the great debate at the University of Melbourne in 1937 over the Spanish Civil War was still being felt in the year that Jean enrolled. Several people have written about the debate and its effects. Manning Clark's narrative was quoted in large part by B. A. Santamaria in his autobiography.[19] Santamaria for the Catholic right had led the argument for the Church and Franco, 'When the bullets of the atheists struck the statue of Christ outside the cathedral in Madrid ... those bullets were piercing the heart of Christ my King'. Nettie Palmer and Jack Legge led for the left, an argument that 'ignorance, superstition, poverty and domination were to be no more.' The audience, of between 800 and a thousand divided into 'two howling mobs'.[20]

Jean Muir had already come in on the side of the republicans during her time as a junior teacher at Hawthorn primary, nor did she have much time for capitalism. That her father was likely on the other side of the argument possibly consolidated her growing convictions. Her reading of economic history, and observation of the Depression (not over as late as 1938), joined her to the generation written about by Turner. For them socialism was the only organised and just alternative to the failings of capitalism. Jean decided not to announce her memberships of the Labour Club and the Australian Communist Party at home, but soon enough she was selling the communist newspaper, *The Guardian*, outside Flinders Street Railway Station in the city. It was there that Ada Knowles bought a copy. Ada affectionately greeted Jean but cryptically remarked that this 'was not quite what she meant'.[21]

If Jean was to commit to the Communist Party, she needed to rethink her pacifism. She decided that successful opposition to fascism would likely demand action beyond pacifism.[22]

Before the year was out Jean was an assistant secretary of the Labour Club. Its president was Dick Blackburn, and by 1939, she was the secretary. The Club had a history stretching back to 1924. In 1935 the then Vice-Chancellor of the University, Raymond Priestly, was writing about the management of its activities, and the hostility it inspired. Would discipline be required for those who opposed the Club and the Anti-War Society? What could be done about the attacks on the Club in 1935 by allegedly drunk students 'using tear gas bombs'? Did some of the hostility come from the Melbourne University Regiment, whose licensed canteen might be a source of the problem, though the University had no control over the regiment? The Vice-Chancellor decided not to speak at the invitation of Club secretary, Jack Legge, on proposed repressive measures by the federal government against the Communist Party. Yes, the Labour Club could show the film *Ten Days that Shook the World*, but only to a university audience. One university Council member, J. G. Latham, a senior conservative politician and later a high court judge, argued that the film should not be shown. *The Argus* newspaper would likely make a big issue of it.[23] The problem of managing left and right within the university intensified as war approached.

1938 was a busy year for the Labour Club and its members. Helen Palmer co-edited the *Melbourne University Magazine* with its argument for the compatibility of 'culture' (non-aristocratically based) and socialism.[24] Dick Blackburn invited students who believed that socialism was the only way of 'using the tremendous social benefits of medicine, engineering, agriculture and science within the limits of the present social system' to join the Club. In almost every issue of the student newspaper *Farrago* there were activities advertised: establishing a 'Left Book Club Discussion Circle' and an anti-Japan meeting jointly sponsored by the Student Christian Movement and the University Peace Group. There was a protest against problems with the cafeteria. An appeal for the relief of Chinese students was organised. The Labour Club hosted a talk by Brian Fitzpatrick on the defence of civil liberties even though the international situation was alarming. It invited students to a Labour Club camp, organised other meetings, one on collective farming in the Soviet Union, and another for Dick's father, Maurice Blackburn. He told students that extreme pacifism was useless and impossible unless a country became socialist and surrendered its privileges.[25] In a letter to *Farrago*, Dick

Blackburn wrote that imperialism had to be eliminated if war was to be eliminated. Women's equality, anti-Semitism, Aboriginal rights as well as international affairs were further subjects for Labour Club meetings. In July, Ralph Gibson, co-founder of the Club, and now a full-time Communist Party organiser, spoke at a Club meeting, arguing that communism was the only true patriotism.[26]

As secretary of the Club, Jean worked on a cause close to her heart: government scholarships for students 'from lower income homes'. After a setback, she was reported as saying: 'This must be the beginning and not the end of our campaign. The Labour Club believes that the position should be more vigorously put before the people of this State … The Labour Club has already suggested that a student demonstration be arranged'. Melbourne was becoming a 'rich man's university'.[27] She issued a club secretaries' joint call for assistance to Spanish refugees. She organised a combined University Peace Group and Labour Club camp at Healesville. On 11 July 1939, Jean was reported as claiming 'that the combined democratic, Polish, and Soviet forces could withstand those of the Fascist powers'.[28] Statements like these, born of the 'popular front' strategy of the Comintern, would prove an embarrassment when the Soviet Union came to an arrangement with Nazi Germany a few weeks later.

On 23 August 1939, the German-Soviet Non-Aggression Pact was declared. Some Communist Party members resigned, but most adapted. The Party shifted its popular front, anti-fascist argument, to one which opposed the 'imperialist' war. A fortnight after the pact was signed, the European war began in early September with the invasion of Poland. The Labour Club held together though not without ruction. Not all Labour Club members were communists, and Jean took some credit for the club continuing to contain, if not embrace, Trotskyists, Fabian socialists, 'right wing Labor supporters' as well as its usually dominant Communist Party members.[29] 'Our annual policy retreat into a boarding house in the Dandenongs ... left us divided about the war until the German invasion of the USSR'.[30]

In retrospect Jean wondered at her and her comrades' 'gullibility'. 'We said to ourselves that this was the consequence of the failure of the West to support collective security with the USSR, and that it was really an imperialist war'. Though she insisted that she had had reservations about the Soviet Union from early on (the 1930s trials of old Bolsheviks disturbed her), 'nevertheless ... the Soviet Union we regarded as the people's country and so on ... So, I was opposed to the war.' Such an argument had minimal support among the population at large let alone within the university, 'and of course I was madly teased and so on around the university'.[31] 'For me, and I would guess that this was a position widely shared among communists in the university and beyond it, the German attack on the USSR [in June 1941] was a relief that initially took no account of the bloody price it exacted from our Soviet comrades.'[32]

Jean ran for election to the SRC a month after the beginning of war, but her policies were compromised. She expressed no support for the war effort, only support for the Red Cross, and 'freedom of thought and speech'. She was not elected.[33] As a prominent leader of the Labour Club and the communist students on campus in 1940, Jean had to argue the official line of the Communist Party, ultimately determined in the Soviet Union. The Communist Party's opposition to Australia's part in the war was often regarded with suspicion and contempt, not only on campus, but beyond. The Party supported both the deeply unpopular pact between the Soviet Union and Germany, and the Soviet invasion of Finland. Under the circumstances, the

Menzies government felt well justified in banning the Communist Party under national security regulations in June 1940.

Rivkah Brilliant, Jean's old friend from University High, was involved in the same student organisations. Like Jean she joined the Labour Club and Communist Party: 'I believed what Stalin had said – we communists were of a special mould'. She also sold the communist newspaper, spoke at meetings and 'sneered at social democratic and bourgeois clap-trap'. Trotskyists, Nazi apologists and Catholic 'stooges of the bigoted Santamaria' were but some of the Labour Club's colourful assortment of enemies. Attitudes towards the Soviet Union were the source of endless discussion. The favourite venue for regularly held Labour Club conferences was a 'grotty, ramshackle, broken-down old wooden guest-house at Tecoma' in the forests of the Dandenong Ranges outside Melbourne. Plenty of socialising, and singing of the 'The Workers' Flag' and 'Harry was a Bolshie' marked the occasions.[34]

In 1940 Jean became the Club's president. This was the year for keeping a low profile, but *Farrago* continued to report the self-education camps, the organisation of meetings on and off campus, social events and proselytising among potential new members. The Club remained at the heart of the more or less organised left at the university.[35] Early in the year prominent Labor politicians were invited to give talks. Among them were John Dedman and John Curtin. There were study circles on imperialism and Russia, social research into the slums of Carlton, and a class offered on public speaking. Towards the end of 1940 Jean appeared as speaker for a meeting of the newly formed Australia-Soviet Union Friendship League. She shared the platform with communist trade union leader Jim Healy of the Waterside Workers and an organiser of the Left Book Club.[36]

Figure 3.1 Jean Muir (second from the left, standing) with members of the University of Melbourne Labour Club, c1940. Others identifiable are Louisa Blackburn (standing next to Jean), Don Porter and Peter Hamilton are standing on the right. Rosemary Porter is sitting alone in the middle row. Alan McBriar is one of the remaining men. A difficult time for the Club, with Communist Party members in control. The Non-Aggression Pact between the Soviet Union and Germany had been signed, and Jean was President of the Club.
Photographer unknown, courtesy of Susan Blackburn.

Inside the Labour Club, and under Jean's presidency, there was often turmoil. One of its vice-presidents was pressured towards resignation given his opposition to Ralph Gibson being welcomed as a speaker at a Club meeting. The student newspaper, *Farrago*, reported a plot for a mass resignation by the executive in the hope that the 'moderates' could be got rid of, and the 'extreme Left' installed more securely.[37] In May, residential college students – a 'national anthem singing horde' – disrupted a Club study meeting. The invited speaker, Jack Blake, was in the throes of blaming Britain for the Non-Aggression Pact and justifying the Soviet Union's invasion of Finland as a forward and necessary self-defence.[38]

Many in Melbourne believed that the campus was a hotbed of disloyalty. The Vice-Chancellor, John Medley, announced the decision of the University Council that the university was not to be used for subversive activities. Clubs should seek permission from the Vice-Chancellor before bringing in outside speakers or distributing written material, a ruling that had to have been directed at the Labour Club. Prior to this, Medley had been a vocal defender of freedom of expression and debate, so this directive was new, but not draconian in its implementation. After a letter by 31 staff to newspapers resisting censorship of the communist and trade union press, a prominent university Council member demanded staff take a loyalty oath. Medley insisted that all staff were loyal.[39] A Conservative Club was formed on campus to counter the Labour Club.

In 1941, Jean had completed her degree, but she was still on campus working as a research assistant, and still involved in political activity. She talked at one meeting about different kinds of socialism.

> Jean Muir ... advocated revolutionary methods. She stressed the fact that the basic difference between the two schools of thought lay in their interpretation of the state. Evolutionary socialists assume that in a democracy power is vested with the majority. Revolutionary socialists believe this to be an illusion; the state is owned and controlled by the same minority, who own and control the means of production. Their desire to maintain their wealth and privileges caused them to oppose with all the means in their power any move to reconstitute society in the interests of the bulk of the people. Consequently, no worthwhile change in society could be achieved without first of all dismembering their machinery of oppression.[40]

One of Jean's last university-based interventions was to support hunger strikes by two trade unionists, Ratcliffe and Thomas. Jean believed that their defence of trade union rights showed that 'the spirit of Eureka is not yet dead'.[41]

Jean found many of her friends, some lasting a lifetime, in the circles that intersected with the Labour Club and her study of economics. Slightly older students whom she admired included Helen Palmer. Rivkah Matthews described Helen as 'ever thoughtful, ever well balanced, one of those entirely committed people who never fall into fanaticism and whose rationality never leads to neutrality'. Helen was the daughter of Nettie and Vance Palmer, the prominent Australian writers. Dick Blackburn was the son of Maurice Blackburn, a Labor, then independent, member of the federal parliament, anti-conscription leader and civil rights lawyer. Helen Palmer and Dick Blackburn were prominent members of the student left. Dick was described by Rivkah Matthews, with his 'tight blond curls and a Grecian profile', as 'something of a guru', given his father's role in the labour movement.[42] According to his sister, Louisa Blackburn, Dick and Jean became romantically involved, with possibly more interest by Jean in Dick than the other way round.[43] Others associated with the left who became, and often remained, Jean's friends included Eric Russell, Alan and Maud McBriar, Marjorie Pizer, Sam Cohen and Rod Bretherington. The friendship with Rivkah Brilliant (Matthews) resumed from their high school days.

In the last year or two of Jean's time on campus a person who was to be significant in her later life was making his mark there as she left. Jean knew of this brilliant young economics student, and he certainly knew who she was given her prominence on campus.[44] This was Peter Karmel who more than anyone apart from Jean herself would be responsible for initiating her later career.

All this activity made for a busy life. Most nights were taken up with meetings, making it more a political than a 'social' life although there were boyfriends at various times during Jean's years at University High and the University. Les and Claire took a hand, encouraging boys, especially the son of Les's boss at Shell though Jean herself disliked him. Another boy at the university liked Jean a lot but was put off by Jean's communism. Les and Claire were keen for her to marry. In May 1940 one of Jean's cousins married. Jean attended Betty Witt's kitchen tea, and then was one of her four bridesmaids, each of whom were dressed in white.[45]

Jean revealed as little as she could to her parents about her politics, but men in her father's office began to make comments about his notorious, communist daughter. Les insisted she give up the Labour Club. She refused. He said he would not pay her university fees, but when notices arrived from the university that Jean would be excluded from lectures, 'He coughed up'.[46] The question of how much longer Jean could last at home was answered, probably in her final undergraduate year. Louisa Blackburn found her in the university cafeteria. There had been an argument with her father that morning.

> Oh, it was something about breakfast, and she hadn't done whatever she should have done, or at the right time, or in the right way, or done the eggs properly, or something, and her father got furious with her and she answered back, and so forth, and he said she couldn't stay in the house any longer. There were probably other reasons but that brought it to a head. She was in the cafeteria – I saw her in the cafeteria – it was an odd time of morning, and she was in a state. When he threw her out she'd picked up a handful of underwear and she was sitting on

the tram in tears and suddenly realised that she had bras and panties and things all over her [*laughs*] – you can see it all, can't you? She didn't know where to go, and I said she could come and stay with us.[47]

She stayed a week or so at the home of Maurice and Doris Blackburn. She may then have gone to Con Warneke. From that point on, Jean never returned to her parents' house to live. In 1941 she found more permanent quarters, living at the institution close to Ada Knowles' heart, the University Women's College.[48]

It was Dick Blackburn who really caught Jean's attention as a potential boyfriend and possible lover. His sister painted the picture: 'He went round – this little curly headed bloke – with a cafeteria tray, banging on it and recruiting people to the meetings'.[49] Jean told her daughter about him in later years. 'Apparently he was very grim and stern', taking his communist commitment very seriously. As the occasion demanded, he would deliver Jean lectures on her duties as a Party member. Dick had entered the university at 16 years of age, and left before Jean finished, but he came back to Melbourne from time to time and continued to engage in Labour Club affairs. His first job as an agricultural scientist was in rural Victoria. He wrote to Jean: 'his letters to her made her furious because they were full of analyses of the political situation, but contained no tender messages.' Despite Dick's comradely seriousness, and occasional imitation of rather uncouth, supposedly 'proletarian' manners, Jean was attracted.[50] He asked Jean to keep a look out for his sister, Louisa, who began university in 1939.

In 1945, a Communist Party newspaper interviewed Dick on his reasons for joining the Party. He said that he had grown up surrounded by labour politics and had been handing out 'how to vote' cards at booths since he was seven. 'The idea of socialism was never new to me, but as I grew up and heard first hand of the inner workings of the Labor Party, I doubted whether it would ever bring socialism about.' He had no contact with the Communist Party until he was a student of agricultural science at the university. He joined the Party in 1936.[51]

Jean's first meetings with Dick's family went reasonably well. Maurice, Dick's father, had but a few years longer to live. He had been immersed in Labor politics in Victoria and nationally since at least 1908. He founded his still prominent law firm in 1922. He was expelled from the Labor Party in 1941 when he refused to conform to its ban on membership of the Australia-Soviet Friendship League. A little later, in 1943, he lost his federal parliamentary seat to an 'official' Labor candidate.[52] However, Maurice Blackburn was not a communist. The communist party leader, Lance Sharkey, denounced him on more than one occasion.[53] Dick thought his father should have been more radical, and in an early conversation between Maurice and Jean, Maurice confided that he and Dick were not that good at communicating. In his last election campaign, Communist Party opposition helped defeat him. Jean also met Dick's mother, the parent Dick was closer too. Doris Blackburn was also a longstanding activist. In 1913, she had been Vida Goldstein's election campaign secretary. In the late 1920s Doris was president of the Women's International League for Peace and Freedom (WILPF). Her pacifism lessened as she saw the growing threat of fascism. She was a 'forceful woman with a flair for organisation who responded purposefully to the wrongs, injustices and wasted lives she saw around her'.[54] Jean may have respected her political engagement, but took to her less easily than she did to Maurice.[55]

At the end of 1940, Jean had completed her degree. With her results there was no going on to a research degree and the best option available was to stay on, employed as a research assistant for staff in economics. She lived in the Women's College where she tutored and made another friend, the future philosopher, Gwen Taylor. Low wages as a research assistant, as well as war events, helped convince Jean to decide that for 1942 she should seek work outside the small world of the university.

Political activity remained difficult following the banning of the Communist Party in June 1940. There was the marking of time until the great events of 1941. In June of that year, Germany invaded the Soviet Union, and in December came the Japanese attack on Pearl Harbour, and weeks later, Darwin. The Communist Party now supported the allied war effort. The allies now included the Soviet Union, the British Empire, including its dominions such as Australia, and the United States of America. By the end of 1942 the ban on the Communist Party had been lifted by a new Labor government in Canberra, and the comrades were again advocating a popular front strategy, supporting the allied effort in the war.

This period also saw a strengthening of Jean Muir's feminism. She had not only been influenced by her fellow students and the women teachers at University High but had viscerally felt the oppression of unreasonable patriarchy in her own family. At university there were friends – and their mothers, women like Nettie Palmer and Doris Blackburn – who were feminists. Such influences helped Jean's emancipation from her immediate family, that element of the suburban middle class she would have condemned for its mean-mindedness. Women such as Ada Knowles, Nettie Palmer and Doris Blackburn had voices quite separate from the Communist Party's approach to the 'woman question'. Nevertheless, the Party numbered many strong women among its members including Katherine Susannah Pritchard and Jean Devanny. These women developed activist roles of significance, even though the male-dominated Party was conservative in relation to gender.[56] Another influence was the peace movement which was often led by women during the inter-war years.[57] Jean's commitment to feminism grew as her experience and reading reinforced each other, but there was a long way to go for her, and Australian feminism.

From the late 1930s and throughout the 1940s, Jean accepted the Party as her intellectual and political home. During her student days and early years as an unmarried woman, Jean's growing sense of freedom was not much contradicted by her communism. It was only later that she discovered that the Party's organisation and culture was strongly patriarchal. In 1940 Jean turned 21. She had escaped the tyranny of her father and felt increasingly free to make her own life. She was a university-educated woman who had turned away from the lives of her mother and other women in her family. She remained angry that her struggle to get a good and interesting education had been so difficult, and she knew that this was a condition experienced by a great many other women.

During her university and high school years Jean Muir became a participant in the debates and politics of a distinctive Melbourne left, given classic definition in Manning Clark's essay contrasting Melbourne with Sydney. Clark observed that Marxism as an influence was stronger in Melbourne. It had been rejected earlier by the philosopher John Anderson in Sydney, and his views influenced more than one generation of students, intellectuals and cultural warriors from New South Wales.⁵⁸ The memory and experience of participating in the diverse energy of the Melbourne left was an important element in Jean's history, for her sense of self. Not many years later when she went to live in Adelaide, it was the communal, though fractious energy of this environment, that she would miss.

The stories of Jean's youth and young womanhood are about social class as well as politics and gender. Her grandparents' generation were impoverished and working class, but in Jean's childhood and youth, the family was on the way up. Her father was a skilled tradesman and then manager of increasingly substantial enterprises. For a young socialist, Jean's family narrative originated in a desirable working-class background, but it was complicated thereafter. She was alienated from her emergent and unimaginative, yet upwardly mobile middle-class family. Its approach to education was a further mark against it. Jean's social class history helped frame a life that put the correction of social injustices caused by class at its centre.

It is easy to allow the political story to dominate the telling of Jean's life in the late 1930s and early 1940s. The last words should be given to her future sister-in-law Louisa Blackburn who talked about Jean as

> very popular at university. She was a personality and I never met anyone who didn't like Jean. She was just warm – the thing that came across to us was – she often got really down and wouldn't talk about things, but she was such a warm person. You know that smile of hers which was radiant – it was just beautiful, and you sort of felt you were gathered up.⁵⁹

Jean had 'found herself' at University High School and the University of Melbourne. She was not only critically engaged with her education and the crises of her times, but had emerged as a person willing to argue, to take a public role in the way these crises played themselves out. The first phase of the struggle with her father was over but there was a continuing residue of resentment on both sides, and on Jean's side, damage as well; nor would she ever become a version of her mother. At the same time many of Jean's peers valued her friendship and she was often admired. She had loved and was in love. There was still 'magic in her eyes'.

Chapter 4

WARTIME PUBLIC SERVANT, AND MARRIAGE, 1942–1950

She thought marriage bourgeois, but she went to the altar.
Il y avait une fois she thought marriage bourgeois,
je ne sais quoi made her principles falter.
She thought marriage bourgeois – but she went to the altar.[1]

Hair–brown
Eyes–blue
Features–regular
Height–about 5'5"
Build–medium, large hips
Wears gold Hammer & Sickle badge[2]

Jean Muir began work as a public servant from early 1942 at the height of the fear of Japanese invasion. She was employed by one of the Commonwealth government departments reorganising the Australian economy towards winning the war. This was her first experience of contributing to the making of government policy and it taught her that the state could be more than a conspiracy of the ruling class. Jean married in 1943 but for the duration of the war many of the discriminations against the employment of married women were suspended. It was in 1945 with the birth of her first child that she was separated from the world of paid work. At this point she was confronted with having to make a different kind of life, one where necessity rather than aspiration set the boundaries. For all its frustrations, Communist Party membership provided both life and meaning outside of the domesticity that came with being a wife and mother.

Early in 1942 Jean Muir, Helen Palmer and a couple of other friends went hiking the Bogong High Plains in northern Victoria. Back in the city, as they walked along Collins Street, Jean noticed a building that had been occupied by a Commonwealth government department, War Organisation of Industry. This was in the period when much of the federal government remained based in Melbourne. She decided to ask if there might be a job, even though she was sensitive about, even ashamed of, her second-class honours degree. Next day she was seen by Sydney Butlin, director of the economics division within the Department. He had come from a lectureship at the University of Sydney and was in the process of establishing a policy branch. He had no hesitation in offering Jean employment, so 'trailing clouds of debt', and pleased to leave her university life behind (some of which she described as 'neurotic'), she responded well to the question, 'When can you start?' She began work a week later.[3]

The Department of War Organisation of Industry had been established in June 1941 by the United Australia Party government led by Robert Menzies. It was supported by John Curtin, leader of the opposition Labor Party, as part of the move towards a 'total' war effort, the kind of government department that Menzies had observed on his wartime excursion to Britain. One of its aims was to divert labour from non-essential to essential industries. In the process, it would reorganise industry itself. Not much was achieved early on. One problem was overlapping responsibilities between the ministries responsible for the economy, but with the new Labor government, and an energetic minister, John Dedman, the interventions rapidly escalated. Dedman 'had revealed a distinct liking for making public ascents into the economic heights and ... soon showed more practical gifts and an administrative diligence, resolution and tenacity that made him one of the most reliable and trusted members of the [Curtin's] team'.[4] He was also the Minister in charge of the Council for Scientific and Industrial Research (CSIR), chair of the production executive in cabinet, and a member of the war cabinet.

Of the ministers for whom Jean Muir/Blackburn worked in the 1940s, 1970s and 1980s, she had the most time for Dedman. He was interested in economics and the government planning that might improve social and national life. Partly inspired by the work of John Maynard Keynes, Dedman had enrolled in economics at the University of Melbourne during Jean's undergraduate years there. He was a pragmatic Labor Party socialist, not so interested in the full nationalisation of industry, but in strategic interventions and socialisations, especially in banking. For a place in the ministry he had the support of Prime Minister Curtin. He had entered the federal parliament in 1940 as member of the Geelong electorate of Corio.

The task for the Department of War Organisation of Industry was huge, and potentially conflict ridden, not only with businesses, large and small, but the trade unions. Two persistent opponents were the banks and the newspaper proprietors. Mistakes were made: the imposition of clothing rationing led to panic buying and attempts to restrict the supply of liquor saw a black market develop. Better progress was made elsewhere. The new 'victory suit' conserved materials. Tails on shirts were shortened. Pink icing was banned from wedding cakes (white was okay). Women, it was thought accepted the restrictions and rationing more easily than men. Department stores became hostile as retail advertising was restricted, including in the lead-up to Christmas.[5] However, these were relatively small examples of the greater work of the Department. In early 1942 fibre and jute goods were restricted. Manufacturers were required to provide information on workers available for war work. Some occupations were 'reserved', and men were not allowed to join the armed forces if employed in such an occupation. In 1943 it was estimated that some 300,000 workers had been shifted from former occupations to war production. Paul Hasluck, as historian of the domestic front during the war, noted the 'dourness' of the regime, but he also wrote that 'None of the criticism was fundamental. It referred mainly to decisions which had caused sectional or personal inconvenience or affected sectional or personal interests.'[6]

Dedman's biographer thought that he was not a great politician. He was too determined and idealistic, leaving himself and his departmental officers open to avoidable criticism as the machinery of economic reorganisation became more intense.[7] In 1943 he was forced to create a public relations unit. 'The general public saw Dedman as the minister for "austerity", or even "morbidity".' He was lampooned by newspaper cartoonists.[8] Artie Fadden, then leader of the opposition in the federal parliament was a predictable critic, but Arthur Calwell and Jack Lang, Labor men, were often hostile as well. By 1944 as the emergency began to pass, critics accused Dedman and the government of not relaxing restrictions, manpower regulations and the rest, quickly enough. Dedman was perhaps less effective towards the end of the war, but there were significant achievements during his time as Minister such as Commonwealth means-tested assistance to students in universities. There was also the other work on post-war reconstruction which inspired a generation of Labor intellectuals and public servants, including Jean Blackburn. The Department of War Organisation of Industry concluded on 19 February 1945.[9] Dedman became Minister of Post-War Reconstruction, taking over from Ben Chifley when Chifley, not long before Curtin's death, assumed Curtin's responsibilities as Prime Minister. By then Jean had given birth to a son and had left public service employment.

So, at the centre of a maelstrom of domestic wartime activity was the Department of War Organisation of Industry. What was the job that Jean Muir, later Blackburn, performed from April 1943, and with whom was she working? The first job she was given was to calculate how much meat suitable for human consumption could be saved by banning dog racing. She enjoyed that: 'I did quite a number of things like that, which were in a way more investigative journalism than economics'.[10]

One of her main tasks was to write, assisting in the policy making and persuading process. Jean was surprised, and then pleased, that what she wrote was often well received. She wrote speeches for the Minister. If something was good Dedman would ask who had written it. Sometimes it was Jean, and he let her know it was good. She thought this was a lesson for all government ministers in how to deal with underlings. In an interview, Jean said that she also worked on cabinet papers, briefing her minister:

and you'd say, you know, this is the history of this issue and the options appear to be this, this and this, and this option is being recommended, it doesn't seem as good as this other option for this reason – that kind of thing. So it was a good sort of training in policy work and I enjoyed it greatly.[11]

There was an interruption to this work, at least on highly confidential papers, when it registered among her superiors that she was a communist. She would not be given access to those papers, but that 'didn't last very long actually, it gradually drifted back'. It is likely that neither her immediate boss, Trevor Swan, nor Dedman himself was much concerned about her.[12] At the same time there were aspects of the work she disliked: the survey work that was required for planning, the knocking on doors, seeking information on household income for example.[13]

Figure 4.1 Jean Muir, clerk in the Commonwealth public service, Department of War Organisation of Industry, c1943. She is happy at work, even writing speeches for the Minister on occasion, and she is on the cusp of marriage to Gerard (Dick) Blackburn.
Photographer unknown, courtesy of Susan Blackburn.

Jean was quite aware that in peacetime she would never have had such a job in the Commonwealth public service. Before the war, it was only men who could be appointed as clerks, and they made up the majority of public service employees.[14] Women had the lesser shorthand and typing jobs. Nor was Jean discriminated against in terms of salary. She received a full 'male wage' because it was a 'male' job. For a time, she was the only woman at her level in her unit. As she had in economics at the university, she remained quite comfortable with being the rare woman in a group of men.[15]

In September 1942 Jean attended the YWCA Blue Triangle Victory Fashion Parade held at the Town Hall in Melbourne. Clothing courtesy of the Myer department store apparently demonstrated that rationing could still lead to fashions that were both 'patriotic and smart'. During the event, the principles of rationing 'were outlined by Miss Jean Muir, who said that the coupon issue was meant only to supplement a wardrobe, and not to supply a new one – it would take about three years before a complete wardrobe could be supplied from coupons. People who criticised the allotment of coupons did so based on their own needs, and not on the supply available'.[16] In 1944 she was participating in the debate over the Labor government's referendum that proposed an increase of Commonwealth government powers not only over the economy but health, transport, employment and social welfare. She spoke at the Business and Professional Women's Rooms, McEwen House in Melbourne, her subject being 'The referendum through a woman's eyes'. We presume she advocated a 'Yes' vote though there was feminist criticism that women's rights and needs as a specific issue in the referendum had been ignored.[17]

Trevor Swan was employed by the Department of War Organisation of Industry in 1942, coming from an assistant lectureship in economics at the University of Sydney. He was Jean's immediate boss, and she got on well with him. While with the Department he developed procedures for the statistical analysis that might lead to the efficient deployment of 'manpower'. Later he drafted key passages of the government's white paper on full employment, published in 1945. He went on after the war to a key advisory role with the incoming Menzies government and assumed the foundation chair in economics in the School of Social Sciences at the newly established Australian National University.[18]

H. C. ('Nugget') Coombs was another person with whom Jean had dealings. Through the war and for decades after, he was an extraordinarily influential public servant. His position as Director of Rationing from April 1942 meant that he and his work were crucial to the work of Jean's department. When the government established the Department of Post-War Reconstruction under Chifley in December 1942, Coombs was its first Director-General. He continued as a significant figure in War Organisation of Industry work. With a colleague, Edmund Foxcraft, Jean, had some responsibility for liaison between the two ministries.[19]

Coombs was a leader of the generation of public servants who regarded nation building and strong interventions in the organisation of economic and social life as essential if the disasters of the years following the Great War were to be avoided. These public servants were Keynesian in approach, willing governments to operate the economic levers that might foster economic development, national security and social welfare.[20] Coombs' biographer, Tim Rowse, also makes the argument that Coombs was responsive to feminist agendas from the 1920s into the 1940s. He was ready to contemplate women in the workplace on conditions equal to those of men, unlike his political masters, Curtin and later Dedman. They saw the war as a temporary interruption to the gender order in employment that had been normalised in the early twentieth century.[21] Nevertheless, under Chifley's political leadership, and that of Coombs in the public service, there was a cultural change in the Australian public service and its approach to economic and national development that would survive the Menzies years, only to seriously falter with the rise of economic rationalism and neoliberalism in the 1980s. Jean's boss, Trevor Swan, and Jean herself, though a relatively minor public servant, identified with this new planning, interventionist approach in government.

War Organisation of Industry became a large department before its eventual absorption into Post-War Reconstruction in 1945. By 1944 it employed more than 300 staff. It had offices in all Australian states. People whom Jean had originally come across through Labour Club meetings and circles, such as Brian Fitzpatrick, worked there for a while. There were others like Tom Critchley whom she likely met for the first time in the Department. She made other contacts through participation in the affairs of her trade union.

Jean joined the Clerks Union. She had not been in a union before and was excited about the possibilities. Part of the experience was to witness the internecine struggles between various elements of the labour movement. Union meetings often degenerated into shouting matches with people storming out. Jean thought the conflict had its origins in lingering resentments from the bitterness of debates over the Spanish Civil War. Regardless of their cause, meetings were awful: 'that was the toughest thing I've ever been in'.[22]

Jean with fellow Communist Party comrades Marjorie Pizer and Muir Holburn, also working in the Department, established a branch of the Party within War Organisation of Industry. They also established a Federated Clerks' Union branch in the Department, spending time recruiting members. Mainly put together by Pizer and Holburn, their little branch publication, *The Woiker*, the "Woi" standing for "War organisation of industry" was a gossipy rag with serious intent from time to time.[23] Its first issue printed a message of support from Dedman. Its aim was to 'give Union members a feeling of solidarity and unity, not only with all clerks, but with all people whose work and aim it is to defeat fascism and win the war'.[24] The committee for the office's union branch met at lunchtime once weekly. It was headed by Jean as 'shop steward'. An early campaign was better rates of pay for typists.

By 1943 the communists had no problem with fighting the war or supporting a re-elected Labor government, though attempts at a more formal 'united front' with Labor were rebuffed.[25] *The Woiker* argued that a Labor government would continue the 'strictest control' over private enterprise. It reassured readers that 'the question at issue is NOT socialism, although the government's opponents will attempt to ride this horse harder and harder as the elections come nearer.'[26] *The Woiker* supported women as being as capable as men. Towards the end of 1943, with Jean re-elected unopposed as shop steward, *The Woiker* discussed international politics. There was a sceptical article on the Atlantic Charter, criticising 'that greedy clique of Slavs who pose in London as the Polish "Government"' and an advertisement for a pro-Soviet play at the New Theatre.[27] Another article protested that too few children from fourteen years of age continued to attend school: 'Over 50% of Australian breadwinners have to keep a home going for a year on what it costs fully to provide for one boy at a certain Melbourne private school for the same period'. A somewhat anti-racist poem insisted that the 'fuzzy-wuzzys' in New Guinea who helped fight the people's war should also enjoy the coming 'people's peace.'[28]

In late 1943, Jean was defeated in an election for the Assistant Secretary of the Federated Clerks' Union (Victorian branch): 1,687 votes for Dunbar, 1,173 for Blackburn.[29] She was part of the Communist Party's strategy to increase its influence in the unions but the clerks' union was not a promising field of activity even though there were a couple of prominent Communist Party members, including Ted Hill, involved in its leadership. The union did not support equal rights for women in employment. The strength of Catholic Action in the union at state and national levels was on the rise. After her run for assistant secretary the Party proposed Jean for union president. The leaflet in support described her as a 'virile young woman'. She did not win. By the late 1940s the Federated Clerks' was a right-wing union and when the Labor Party split in the 1950s it was one of the few unions which disaffiliated from the Labor Party altogether.

Jean Muir and Dick Blackburn remained interested in the University's Labour Club. They attended its conference at Tecoma in the Dandenong Ranges in 1942 with some fifty others who managed 'to leave their books' for long enough. Dick, 'recently returned from the Mallee' gave a review of international affairs. Jean led a session on 'Australia's part in the people's wars'.[30]

Back in the department Jean, Marjorie Pizer, Muir Holburn and a few others put together a review for which they wrote parodies of well-known songs. Not only fellow staff but the Minister enjoyed it; a 'great success'. One song began 'I can't give you anything but love baby', sending up their own department for banning the production of a litany of goods that would in normal times have been available to mothers and babies. It ended, 'A pram without frills will have to do your scottie baby'. Presumably it was performed with Scottish accent, Dedman being of Scottish origin.[31]

Then there was Jean's participation in the Council for Women in War Work (CWWW). This was her first major involvement in a women's organisation, and advanced her feminist understanding, though the more significant event would be the shock of being sidelined from employment by motherhood.[32] One object of the Council was to improve the percentage of the male wage that women could earn, though its overall aims were broader, in support of women and their conditions of work after the war as well. Jean was on the Council's Victorian executive with Mollie Bayne and Kathleen Fitzpatrick. The Council was 'non-party and undenominational' with subscriptions invited from individuals and affiliating societies. It gave 'advice about whether this job was 100 per cent, 80 per cent [of a male wage] or whatnot and lobb[ied] about it'.[33]

In 1943 Bayne edited for the 'Research Group' of the Left Book Club of Victoria, a group that did not include Jean, a booklet on women in the war. Fitzpatrick wrote the introduction: 'In war-time women are eagerly welcomed as workers of inferior status'. The injustices were especially salient for women of lower-middle and working-class families. Mothers were 'cruelly over-worked', the male wage was insensitive to the range of family needs in health, education and housing. A special problem for the efforts to improve women's lot was the disunity between unmarried and married women: 'The well-being of each woman should be the concern of all women'.[34] An essay later in the book expressed anxiety about what would happen after the war. 'If we fall back into the unplanned scheme of things in which only "profitable" businesses are undertaken and social services languish and slums flourish, women will fall back too.' Social planning controls should not be surrendered after the war.[35]

The Council was but one of the organisations working on behalf of women during the war. Jessie Street's United Associations of Women (UAW) was one of the more important. A shift occurred in the demands by feminist organisations, more towards equal rights, pay and conditions in employment, the elimination of all forms of sexual discrimination, as opposed to the earlier concentration on domestic issues, especially support for mothers and families.[36] There was a National Women's Conference organised by Street in November 1943, one aim of which was to put together a Women's Charter. H. V. Evatt for the federal government made travel permits available for interstate delegates. Two of the Communist Party members who attended, both intent on a 'new order' were Jean Blackburn from Melbourne and Elizabeth Johnston from Adelaide, both from the Federated Clerks' Union. Party member Katherine Susannah Pritchard from Perth was one of the main speakers at the conference.[37] It is possible that this was the first meeting of Jean Blackburn and Elizabeth Johnston. If so, it was the beginning of an association that would last fifty years. When the Charter agreed to by the conference was presented to government in early 1944, Evatt rather than Curtin received it, possibly signifying a lack of interest by the Prime Minister.

Amid the demands of her political commitments and working life, Jean was also treading a circuitous path that eventually led to marriage with Dick Blackburn. Each had relationships with others prior to the final decision to marry. Although the timing and details are unclear, Jean's daughter recalled a conversation with Jean where she talked about a relationship with a young man who joined the air-force and was killed in combat. Jean found herself pregnant by him, and an abortion followed. As biographers we were not surprised that we found it difficult to discover more than bare details about these events and their significance in Jean's life. She would certainly have needed to hide the fact of her pregnancy from her family and employers. The grief that Jean must have felt following her double loss was all too common in wartime Melbourne. Regarding the abortion, it is possible that abortions were a little less difficult to procure during the war, but the experience would still have been traumatic, the more so because of her lover's death.[38]

At one point, at a time Jean felt sure that she and Dick were together, Dick was taken with another comrade. This was a terrible blow. Hyrell Ross was a school teacher and an attractive woman 'with a tremendous personality' according to Louisa Hamilton, Dick's sister. Sometimes Jean could feel bitter that her attraction to Dick left her vulnerable. There was a Party conference in Sydney possibly in late 1941 or early 1942, which Dick and Hyrell both attended. Not long after, they turned up at Dick's parents' home announcing their engagement. It did not last long, but Jean was both devastated and jealous. Louisa had a theory about why Dick had felt the need to get engaged: a sense of duty because of the affair. It ended when Dick discovered Hyrell was also involved with another comrade, Judah Waten. Hyrell and Judah would marry in 1945. Jean and Dick, Hyrell and Judah would visit one another over the years to come, but there were tensions in the friendship.[39]

When Jean and Dick were together again. Dick was taken home to meet Jean's parents, Les and Claire. In honour of Jean and Dick's marriage on 2 April 1943, and perhaps following the surprise of it, Trevor Swan penned the verse that begins this chapter. She had thought marriage 'bourgeois', but 'she went to the altar'. Hume Dow and Margaret McArthur were the witnesses.[40] The scattering of family and friends during the war, as well as austerity, meant that the ceremony was modest, in a government registry office. Jean continued at work, enjoying the 'privilege' of paid, professional work despite marriage, for much of the remaining year of the war.

Figure 4.2 Jean's parents, Les and Claire Muir, c1947.
If Les was not keen for Jean to have more than an elementary education, Claire, despite a life devoted to domesticity, provided the support Jean needed to establish a life as an independent and well-educated woman.
They both looked forward to Jean marrying, though not to another communist.
Photographer unknown, courtesy of Susan Blackburn.

In 1944, a few days short of a year after Jean and Dick had married, Maurice Blackburn died. He was hospitalised for just two or three days before his death after a brain tumour began causing terrible headaches. To be in easy reach of the hospital, Doris stayed with Dick and Jean in their St Kilda Road flat. Maurice had had a difficult war, losing his Labor Party membership, opposing various regulations seeking to give federal governments new powers, losing his federal seat and holding out against conscription to the last. It was a big funeral. Senior clergy of the Presbyterian, Methodist and Anglican churches pronounced on Blackburn's goodness and principled nature. He was, according to Anglican Dean Langley, 'the fearless friend of the worker'. The federal Labor government put aside any grudges and seven ministers, including Prime Minister Curtin, attended the funeral. Other institutions sent representatives and wreaths. State politicians were there, as were union and state Labor Party leaders, and representatives of the Left Book Club and May Day Committee. Brian Fitzpatrick attended for the Council of Civil Liberties, Ralph Gibson for the Communist Party and Judge Foster for the Women's Employment Board.[41] Jean herself was unable to attend. Maurice Blackburn's other son, also Maurice, had a new-born child, and Jean volunteered to look after the baby so Maurice and his wife could go.

Jean became pregnant around April 1944. She resigned from her job in early 1945; Bill was born on January 16. Resignation from paid employment was the expected thing under such circumstances and Jean and Dick had no thought that it could have been otherwise.[42] Dick could still be away for stretches of time even though he had finished work at Walpeup Agricultural Research Station in north-west Victoria in 1943. He worked after that in the Department of Labour and National Service as an industrial hygiene officer. He had not been allowed to enlist; his job was on the reserved list.

Motherhood radically transformed Jean's life. Sometimes she felt like a single parent. She feared leaving the city for isolated country locations that were often where Dick's work was centred. As Jean saw it, even when he was living in the city:

> Dick was able to ignore paternity by floating into the maternity hospital for ten minutes on his way to his Party obligations as secretary of the St Kilda branch or as time [was] needed to prepare ... for a weekly Party broadcast on the achievements of collective farms in the USSR. It was the Low Point of my life, only exceeded by his acceptance, without talking to me about it, of a job in the CSIR [Council for Scientific and Industrial Research] in Adelaide.[43]

Between marriage and motherhood, it was the latter which was the more momentous.

> Now, stuck in a smelly, monstrously expensive upstairs flat, cut off from the world, the reality dawned. Bill spent every afternoon being pushed around in the pram; Nettie Palmer was the only person I knew near enough to visit on foot and I spent some most interesting times with her, listening to her experience in the Women's Movement. Moving further afield to Chapel Street and Halls' second-hand book store, I bought a worn copy of Rae Strachey's *The Cause*, a history of the Women's Movement in the UK. I was horrified by my ignorance of many aspects of women's lives, and properly indignant about the late passage of the Married Women's Property Act.[44]

Bill cried weeks on end, a victim of the mysterious colic.[45]

Figure 4.3 Dick and Jean Blackburn with their first-born child, Bill, c1945.
Still living in Melbourne, but soon to shift to Adelaide.
Photographer unknown, courtesy of Susan Blackburn.

The Pacific war ended on 15 August 1945, and the challenge of returning service men and women to civilian life taxed governments, businesses, and no doubt, very many families. The federal Labor government, with John Dedman now in charge of post-war reconstruction, continued to plan for the future, but Robert Menzies was back, leading a new Liberal Party. At the 1949 election his appeal for less planning, the end of rationing, and more recognition for Australia's 'forgotten middle class', the class that apparently had little to gain from the 'dead hand of socialism', was to initiate an alternative future for Australia. These events and the effects of the Cold War, including the founding of the Australian Security Intelligence Organisation (ASIO) in 1949, was to make the coming decade a difficult one for Jean and Dick Blackburn.

Dick won his job with the CSIR in Adelaide in February 1946. Despite the lack of consultation Jean had no option but to make the inter-city move with him. She had no income apart from Dick's. He began work as a research officer in the division of soils in March, Jean and Bill following in April. Dick was working once more as an agricultural scientist and was again often away on field trips. At one stage, he was home only every second weekend. Jean had no friends or family in Adelaide other than the odd comrade acquaintance. Despite the limited participation in Communist Party activity that she could manage as a young mother she began to develop a small circle of acquaintances.

There was a severe housing shortage in Adelaide after the war. The two roomed rented flat, in an old house with an enclosed veranda used as a kitchen and bathroom, was at least subject to fair rent controls. It was cheaper than the Melbourne flat. Dick's wages as a research scientist with five years pre-war experience 'were slightly less than mine in WOI where I had been paid the full male rate'. The Blackburns had no savings and no furniture to speak of. Packing cases and a lumpy double bed had been their furniture in Melbourne. They did the job again in Adelaide. 'The early years in Adelaide were the leanest of my life – and not just in a monetary sense. Dick, I found, was away employed as member of a soil mapping team, more often away than at home'. They had to adjust to one another after his absences. Jean talked about how Dick, having been away for weeks, was eager for physical intimacy, whereas she had been preoccupied with issues of the children (the second child, Susan was born in early 1947) and needed time to regain her emotional and physical responsiveness. Dick's absences meant multiple frustrations. At home Jean was cooking lots of minced meat 'disguised in various ways'.[46]

There was no car and no telephone. It is at this point in Jean's story that personal depression begins to be mentioned as a more regular part of her life.[47]

At some point early on, Jean met up with her old Melbourne friend, Bruce Williams, who was lecturing at the University of Adelaide. Giving in to her 'shameful desire for more money' and knowing that 'there was no way back into public policy areas', she took up his offer of casual employment, marking Economics I essays. Bruce thought she should enrol for a higher degree, qualifying her to teach in the expanding university sector. 'Dick brought me down to earth by asking where I would find the money to do this.' Her 'outlaw academic position' was confirmed, and she knew again the problem of being economically dependent on a man.[48]

Even though Jean was getting to know fellow Party comrades, there was the disheartening realisation that the intellectuals among them were few. In later life she said that in her early days in Adelaide all the intellectual company she had was Elizabeth Johnston and more marginally, her husband Elliott, and a couple of medical doctors.[49] A couple of old Melbourne university friends now in Adelaide were difficult to contact; they worked during the day, and no-one had transport for easy visiting. Bill was 15 months old when they arrived in Adelaide, and as had been the case in Melbourne, Jean spent much of the day with the pram, 'pushing him around to fill in time'. At least Bill 'was a physical comfort and delight, and quick on the mental uptake'. She was amused by his reasoning when at a slightly older age he announced that people who placed floral arrangements on graves were 'silly' since the dead could not appreciate the effort. When Bill was two, Jean tried him out in a local kindergarten, but he objected vociferously. There would be no respite from full-time motherhood.

For herself Jean thought back to her year at night school and teaching at Hawthorn primary. It might at least be possible to do some serious reading. This proved to be the case and her 'self education went ahead'. She was living only a few tram stops from North Terrace and the Public Library and this enabled her to read her way through George Elliott, Leo Tolstoy and Fyodor Dostoevsky. 'The big excitement was that one could borrow from the Reference as well as from the Lending library.' She concentrated on reading classic feminist works, the history of the women's movement, and later, in the 1950s, sociology. She was particularly keen on a book by Alva Myrdal and Viola Klein, Swedish feminists, who had written about women and their labour.[50]

On February 26, 1947, Jean and Dick's second child, Susan was born. By then Jean was becoming a little less isolated, but she still felt hard done by 'as I languished in two rooms with a two-year-old and a three-week-old baby in a city where I knew no-one'.[51] Nevertheless by now she was writing to the newspapers. In *The Advertiser* she defended the Soviet Union against the charge that its experiment was a 'monstrous and tragic failure'. She wrote that the Soviet Union was a socialist society, only part the way to communism.[52] Another of her letters contained a vigorous defence of Marx and Engels. Their materialist philosophy did *not* mean men were mere creatures of their environment, 'The very fact that they [Marx and Engels] organised working people to struggle in order to establish a society where the means of production were owned in common is in itself sufficient indication of their views' and 'Their philosophy is certainly materialist in that it excludes supernatural forces, but they attacked the mechanical materialism which asserts that man is what his environment makes him, without any suggestion that he may react in an active fashion to that environment'.[53] Later in 1947 she wrote a sarcastic dismissal of a Country Party leader's statement that blood would flow before the bank nationalisation debate was concluded. Jean thought that his fears required weighing up 'the relative merits of mattress and garden as the hiding place of his hoard'.

> Whenever the interests of a small section of the people are threatened by an act which will benefit the overwhelming majority, then that section knows reasoned argument can't win it the support of the majority. So it deliberately tries panic. The case of the bank nationalisation proposals sets a new high in this line of 'persuasion.' It is generally agreed that control of credit policy is important in determining the level of employment. Why should such a power be wielded by a few people responsible only to their share holders rather than by a public institution responsible to all electors? That is the issue in the banking controversy. If the opponents of nationalisation have something to say which affects that issue, let them say it, and allow any dispassionate observers to judge facts, not hallucinations.[54]

In May 1948 Jean took part in a public meeting in the Institute Building on North Terrace, arguing the case for federal power over rents and prices. Opposed were leaders of the League of Rights, Eric Butler and E. C. Finn.[55]

Moving to a city that she did not know and where initially she had no friends and family, was not the only problem Jean had with Adelaide. It was much smaller than Melbourne, and more obviously dominated by an 'establishment'. In 1947 Adelaide's population was just over 382, 000 while Melbourne's was 1,226,000. South Australia's politics were increasingly dominated by Tom Playford and the Liberal and Country League (LCL). Playford had been premier since 1938 and would remain so until 1965. The LCL government was socially conservative, though a great user of state instrumentalities to advance industrialisation during and after the war. The electoral system was firmly weighted against the growing number of working-class and other metropolitan electorates in favour of the rural hinterland.[56] Jean lived her first 27 years in Melbourne, and her last 55 years in Adelaide, but she retained a lifelong sense of Melbourne as her intellectual and spiritual home.

After the war, in 1946, the New Housewives Association was founded in Sydney, developing several suburban branches. How soon it took on the character of a 'front' organisation for the Communist Party may be speculated about, but its relationship to the Party was clear enough in Adelaide as it got under way in 1947–1948. As a comrade who had been in Adelaide well over a year by this time, Jean Blackburn learnt that she was to be president of the local branch, and Winifred Mitchell, another young mother and recent arrival in Adelaide, was to be the secretary.[57] Jean and Winifred retained these roles in the association for the duration of its brief three years of existence. They also became lifelong friends.

Jean wrote about the organisation and her history with it. After her time with the Council for Women in War Work, this was her second experience of running a women's organisation, though this one would be subordinated to the struggles of the working class as defined by the Communist Party. Nevertheless, it would help her think more clearly about the social consequences of women becoming wives and mothers, the subject of a booklet she would write in the early 1960s. The experience also led to the beginnings of a significant disenchantment with the Communist Party itself. Years later Jean concluded that a double masquerade had been asked of her in leading the New Housewives. She was expected to masquerade as a 'housewife' and as a 'proletarian'. She may temporarily have been the former, though it was not the principal way she thought of herself, but she certainly did not believe herself to be the latter.[58]

There was a much older and larger Housewives Association that had been formed in the Great War. It acted mainly as a consumers' advocacy group, its thinking marked according to Jean by 'narrow economism'. During the 1930s and 1940s it became politically conservative.[59] The Women's Christian Temperance Union (WCTU) was a power within it. There was room for a more radical, left alternative, although in South Australia at least, the WCTU was more accepting of working with communist women than other groups.[60] The proportion of Australian women not in the paid workforce, working at home as housewives, was large. It could reasonably be argued that they had an interest in wages determination (their husbands'), the costs and provision of food and housing, social welfare, and schooling for their children. Increased child endowment, equal pay for women and the establishment of neighbourhood markets to bring cheaper goods to housewives were among the New Housewives' goals.[61] If housewives could be organised they had the potential to be a force for the left.

Jean thought that in the 1940s there were very few left-oriented women's organisations in South Australia. The women's organising committee in the Labor Party was prohibited from associating with non-Labor organisations and Labor women were unable to appear on the same public platforms as communist women. In several states there were women's auxiliaries attached to unions, their role being to support union campaigns. However, in South Australia they had little presence except for the Miner's Federation. The auxiliaries had no role to play in union governance. The decision to call a strike for example was not women's auxiliary business, but during a strike the auxiliaries were expected to leap into action, suppressing all thought of the hardships being visited on them and other families.

In South Australia 'we attempted to organise working-class housewives', to 'draw them closer to the Party'.[62] Fortnightly lunch-time discussion meetings were held 'at our grotty headquarters in the Jewish Club Rooms upstairs on the corner of Hyde and Pirie Streets'. Jean's children and others were 'crawling around their feet', though childcare was supposed to be organised. Sandwiches were prepared for those attending. The women organising were mainly Party comrades, Dympsie Slater, Flo Edmonds, Audrey Robertson and Gloria Gartens, besides Winifred and Jean. Gloria was a typist in the Party office and may have been there to keep an eye on the emerging organisation.[63] Tess Caust, who was also involved, became one of Jean's long-lasting friends. 'We were all much of an age – in our late twenties'. Up to fifty women attended meetings. Jessie Street, Australia's most prominent feminist leader, drew the largest crowd when she was visiting Adelaide. The New Housewives had committed to the Women's Charter that Street and the UAW had organised a few years earlier. Other meetings might have guest speakers from the 'ban the bomb' campaign, trade union auxiliaries, the WCTU and the League of Women Voters.

A roneoed newsletter was produced and small suburban branches were organised. Each group did what its members wished; some made 'bread flowers' and macramé, though Jean and Winifred were 'a bit sniffy' about that activity.[64] Several of the branches bought and shared sewing machines and vacuum cleaners. Socialising house-work and childcare were high on the New Housewives' agenda. Jean acknowledged 'the hundreds of women with whom I talked on the doorstep, and who often would ask me in and confide in their loneliness about the most intimate details of their lives'. Jean learnt that women's difficulty in controlling their fertility could overwhelm relations with their husbands. 'They had no access to or knowledge of birth control, and frequently referred to the monthly means by which they attempted to "bring it off", and to husbands considerate enough as they saw it "not to bother them much"'.[65]

These experiences affected Jean's feminism. Up to this point her feminist thinking was framed by her reading around the suffragist movement and the women's struggle for control over their wages and conditions of work, their property and children as married women. 'I began to see that there were other oppressions, that they were not all material, that they affected all women, and that the control of one's body was pretty central to them.' She had been deeply affected, often upset, by the stories of the women she talked to.

The shortage of housing in Adelaide provided a political opportunity as well as a welfare issue that the New Housewives pursued. Many families were forced to live in caravans, so Jean and other members worked their way through the caravan parks in Adelaide's southern suburbs. It was difficult for Jean and the others as they managed their own lack of transport and young children whether at home, kindergarten or school. Many of the caravan dwellers were receptive to their interest, and a march was organised, targeting the headquarters of the state government's Housing Trust. There were plenty of regulations left over from Depression troubles for authorities to use against street demonstrators. Though the march and meeting with placards was small, it attracted some press attention. In dealing with Trust officials Jean and fellow organisers experienced the same dismissive treatment from 'minor bureaucrats' that the caravan park inmates had told them about.

Another demonstration was called one Mothers' Day (probably in 1948 or 1949). The New Housewives wore their aprons and sang 'On Mother's Day, Mothers Say – No More War'. They were getting better at avoiding police attention. 'We succeeded in walking around the city in casual formation and it was quite some time before the police dispersed us.'[66]

In June 1949 Jessie Street, on behalf of the Women's Charter Movement, secured a formal deputation to Prime Minister Ben Chifley. Tess Caust participated on behalf of the New Housewives in Adelaide. The Charter was a useful rallying point for feminists and women's organisations in the 1940s and early 1950s, though Street and the UAW suffered during the Cold War. Street and the UAW were accused of being too close to the Soviet Union and communist influence.

Events in 1949 initiated the end of the New Housewives Association. The ill-advised miners' strike, the miners' union branches often led by Communist Party officials, mobilised most organisations associated with the Party. The federal Labor government also mobilised but in opposition. Communist Party insistence that the New Housewives support the strike meant that many of its members, already sensitive to communist influence, left the Association. The fear of 'red bogies' seemed especially strong in South Australia. Jean wrote that 'The NHA was already a proscribed organisation by the ALP [Australian Labor Party], and as the general situation heated up, reassuring the membership beyond its politically committed core that they were not being used by the CP was becoming increasingly difficult'. Jean argued that the New Housewives' support for the miner's strike was:

in effect, the death knell of any possibility it may have had of becoming a mass organisation. We collected food and clothes for the miners' women's auxiliaries and sponsored their visiting speakers. On the one hand it was gallant solidarity; on the other a foolish act of self destruction. I see it in the second light …[67]

In Jean's ASIO file, it was noted that she spoke in July 1949 at Adelaide's 'speakers' corner' in Botanic Park at a meeting convened by the Miners' Campaign Committee.[68] The miners' strike failed when confronted not only by the army but by the unpopularity it endured, especially by women trying to keep their families going, cooking an evening meal as supplies of coal for electricity generation were exhausted. The failure of the miners was also a failure for the Communist Party. Its influence in the union movement and beyond would diminish through the 1950s. When the Labor government in Canberra was replaced by the Liberal-Country Party coalition in 1949, the Cold War in Australia intensified and banning the Party resumed its place as a priority of the federal government. The failure of the New Housewives was collateral damage, but it took one more act to terminate it altogether.

The Communist Party decided to end the organisation, replacing it with a Union of Australian Women (UAW).[69] Neither Jean Blackburn nor Winifred Mitchell had any role in the discussion that led to this decision. 'We were summoned and informed of the decision.' That was one blow, the other was that Jean was excluded from leadership in the replacement organisation. Winifred survived a further fifteen months, but then she was peremptorily dismissed from the UAW. According to Winifred's account as reported by Jean, 'the Party did not want any "bourgeois" women (for which Winifred reads "moderately well educated") in the leadership of "its" women's movement.' For Jean, the experience finally raised to prominence the issue of the Party's attitude towards women with children. Both she and Winifred had small children, and the sacrifice in time, money and energy to run the New Housewives was substantial. There was little thanks.[70] Leadership of the Union of Australian Women in South Australia went to the more proletarian wives of Communist Party 'functionaries'. 'Class, not sex' dominated the Party's approved version of the women's movement.[71] Many years later Jean wondered 'why we allowed the Party to dispose of our energies in directions which we took no part in designing'. She had not felt the same in Victoria, but then again, 'I guess I was very young and inexperienced and had always had my own "mass base" in the political activities I undertook, so attaining a degree of autonomy and respect'. In Victoria she had not had 'to beat the breast and pretend one was a proletarian really'.

Win Mitchell wrote later that in Adelaide in the late 1940s she was sustained by her friendship with Jean.

> Many years after the wounds of these years had healed we were able to compare our scars, astonished that we had been such unresisting victims, that we had been prepared to accept humiliating treatment, restricted lives and limitations on our thinking.[72]

According to Jean, 'The leadership of the CP in SA was aggressively working-class male, and high-handed to a degree which would not have been tolerated in the larger and more socially varied Victorian Party'. But then again, she thought, there was the top-down 'democratic centralism' that organised all the communist parties associated with the Soviet Union at the time. If the movement towards communism was to occur, disciplined orchestration was easily justified.[73]

There was a second women's group that Jean engaged with, again at the behest of the Party. This was International Women's Day (IWD) with its origins in Australia in the 1920s, but only becoming a presence in Adelaide in 1938.[74] Jean became secretary of the South Australian organising committee in 1948. Again, the challenge was managing reluctant children as she went to meetings. Bill and Susan Blackburn remembered these experiences with no affection.[75] IWD suffered from the tensions that surrounded other women's organisations in the early Cold War. In Adelaide there were 'small meetings, luncheons or concerts organised by socialist or communist women'.[76] Jean's emergence as secretary in 1948 brought her to the notice of ASIO as 'active' in left-wing circles in Adelaide. Its agents watched her progress through another mainly communist organisation, the Consumers' Protection League, along with the New Housewives.[77] Jean had discovered IWD while in Melbourne and had participated in its activities there. In Adelaide, as elsewhere, the idea was that IWD could bring together a broad coalition of women. They included members of the WCTU and League of Women Voters. It was WCTU members whom she quickly grew to respect and like. The committee met in Willard Hall in Adelaide, the hall belonging to the WCTU.

At the 1948 annual luncheon, Jean was an advertised speaker, along with Phyllis Duguid, Elizabeth Johnston and Maud McBriar. Jean was involved at a leadership level in the IWD for only a year or so. Duguid, wife of the Aboriginal rights campaigner, Charles Duguid, outlined the history of IWD, Johnston talked on raising living standards, McBriar on the struggle for peace, and Jean on 'widening democracy'.[78] With Maud McBriar, a friend from University of Melbourne days, recently back from England where she had received attention from MI5, Jean was about to shift her main political interest from women's organisations towards the peace movement, though she may not have thought of it in those terms.[79]

The eight years between 1942 and 1949, were significant years for Jean Muir then Blackburn. By the time she arrived at 30 years of age in 1949, she had had a wealth of experience in work, marriage, motherhood, and feminist, labour and communist politics. She had also been forced to make a new life in a new city. The move to Adelaide coincided with another crisis in her life. She was out of the labour market and the public service. From the centre of things during the war, she was now on the margins. Instead of advising a federal government minister, she and her husband had become a 'threat' to Australia, worthy of the attention of the new ASIO. Neighbours knew they were communists because Jean and Dick tried to sell them copies of the local communist newspaper. One neighbour was concerned enough to write to ASIO:

> Remember me telling you about Mrs [Doris] Blackburn's son [Dick] who lives near us. Well they are out and out Commos, both he and his wife go around houses on Sunday morning trying to sell the *Tribune*, and now the latest is he has gone to the Rocket Range. I thought that Security Officers were very particular about who went there.[80]

In the Department of War Organisation of Industry, Jean had felt a flush of confidence: 'I suddenly knew that I was okay, which I had never really thought about before. I suddenly realised I could do this thing and that what I did was well appreciated by the people around me and I was okay.'⁸¹ But this would be tested over the coming years. She loved her children and her husband, but she did not love her life. With what regularity she was brought low by depression is unknown, but it became an enduring feature of her life. Her daughter believed that her unhappy childhood experiences had left their mark.⁸² But whatever its causes, it was only one side of Jean's life. There were also great bursts of energy, and always the application of an intellect that could change the organisations and people she touched.

Her experiences during this period developed Jean's understanding of feminism and the women's movement. Marxist theory had early on developed a critique of bourgeois marriage, and formally at least, the Bolsheviks had declared the equality of the sexes, so the organisation of women, and women as comrades, was an acceptable objective for the Australian Communist Party. Nevertheless, female comrades were generally corralled into organisations that were either peripheral to the main game, class and industrial warfare, or they were to be constituted as 'support' groups. This certainly happened during the coal miners' strike of 1949. Jean began to feel battered by the approach, especially by the way she and Winifred Mitchell were excluded from the decision terminating the New Housewives Association. 'But our experience with working [together] as women was an experience which – however monitored and controlled – led us – and certainly led me towards a feminism which later flowered, and was [less] able to be so monitored and controlled.'⁸³ Jean's contacts in these years with feminist women and organisations as had occurred through the development and campaigning for the Women's Charter for example, gave her a foundation beyond the Communist Party for continuing to engage in the women's movement.

Figure 4.4 Jean in 1950, free of the New Housewives Association,
but with a renewed personal feminist commitment.
Jean was about to devote her energies to the peace movement.
Photographer unknown, courtesy of Susan Blackburn.

At the same time, Jean was reading feminist literature. This included the eighteenth century classics by Mary Wollstonecraft which she encountered before coming Adelaide.[84] There was also the influential exposition by Ray Strachey's *The Cause*, written in the 1920s. That work had its faults, as Barbara Caine has shown, but as an introduction to the history of the women's movement in Britain it opened a new world to Jean.[85] At a time when she had very little money, she bought Jeanne Young's biography of South Australia's pioneering feminist, Catherine Helen Spence, 'lured into this wild extravagance by tributes on the dustcover from two women I already admired – Alice Henry and Vida Goldstein'.[86] She was also reading whatever she could find of interest in the South Australian Public Library.

The New Housewives had provided crucial new understandings important in Jean's developing feminism. It was not only the women in the caravans, but working-class women who lived in suburbs near the Islington railway workshops who talked to Jean. Their loneliness, their fear of unwanted pregnancies, these spoke to Jean not only in ways that extended her understanding but touched on some of her own trials. Jean said that 'being a mother … made her a feminist'.[87] Such reading, contacts and experiences took her well beyond the argument by Communist Party leader, J. B. Miles, that the woman question was all about women being drawn into the proletarian struggle 'to smash the rule of the capitalist class and set up workers' rule'. For Miles, history itself had 'determined that the masses of women are inert and uninformed, even more than men'.[88] As Joyce Stevens opined, 'The politics of family life and housework had to wait more than forty years for a new wave of feminism and for the development of an expanded socialist theory' before the issues that were moving Jean and many others were addressed.[89]

This period of Jean Blackburn's life was full of frustration. With her husband Dick away often, the children and the politics were not enough. Jean felt that she had lost a great deal in gaining her own family. Though the job she had loved had gone at the end of the war, Jean did not lose her sense of how government had operated in the war and might also operate in a post-war reconstructed Australia. Government had been able to reorganise the economy and society, often to good effect. As part of a generation of wartime public servants, she and they continued to see the possibilities for government action in the remaking of citizens and society. She likely thought the experience proved that some form of state-led socialism was possible.

For the time being, Jean could only look on. Many of her former colleagues in wartime government, indeed many of her fellow economics students at the University of Melbourne, all men, were making careers for themselves in the public service and universities. She also wanted a career like that. Despite these difficult years, there was no diminution of either her humanity or emergence as a resolute and articulate thinker and speaker, as an engaged intellectual on the side of greater social equality.

Chapter 5

SUBURBAN LIFE AND BEYOND, 1951–1966

A party was held at the Blackburns' home in Glenunga on the Saturday night of the poll. When the news came through on the wireless that the vote was 'No' [to ban the Communist Party] there was great rejoicing. The celebrations went on for hours. I [ASIO spy] did not reach home until after 2 am.[1]

The circumscribed domestic round, the absence of productive satisfying work, and the social isolation engendered by the prevailing suburban cult of privacy all tend to make the housewife a frustrated, intellectually inbred person who, having little else upon which to lavish her attention, is in danger of fussing unmercifully over her children.[2]

Jean shifted house with her family in 1950 and established a new life in suburban Adelaide. Her sense of isolation was overcome as new friends were made and old friends from Melbourne turned up. The mid-1950s saw Jean going back to paid work, and a short time later, she made the momentous decision to leave the Communist Party. It was a decision that endangered her marriage because her husband Dick was a 'lifer', one who would never leave the Party. In the mid-1960s, now with a third child, Jean was reading education at the University of Adelaide. That study would lead her to teachers' college employment. Her socialist politics continued to be exercised through her commitment to the peace movement, her work in Aboriginal advancement, engagement with Helen Palmer's *Outlook* magazine, and the publication of her own *Australian Wives Today*. But before she left the Communist Party, and for a few years thereafter, she had first to survive a period of heightened Cold War activity.

The Blackburns' new house at 78 Allinga Avenue was in Glenunga, a new suburb close to the Adelaide Hills, south-east from the centre of the city by about seven kilometres. It eventually became a respectable suburb of the middle class, though in the 1950s it was socially mixed. In the late 1940s the price of land was still controlled, the Allinga Avenue block costing about £200. Jean's mother gave her £100 and a friend lent a similar amount. Les Muir did not help. He retired from work in 1950, continuing to be well-off. Shell's investments had not suffered during the war, and its superannuated managers shared in the wealth. Les believed that if any of his money went to Jean, it would simply end up with the Communist Party. He remained opposed to her.[3] The new house was modest but was not quite ordinary. A comrade architect from Hungary, Andrew Benko, designed it. Benko attracted ASIO attention for writing an article discussing 'revolutionary architectural design and structure' in an Adelaide newspaper.[4] From this house, each of Jean and Dick's children would go to government schools, Linden Park Primary, and then Unley High.

Dick and Jean developed the garden. Adelaide suburban houses of the 1950s were usually built on blocks of land large enough for fruit trees and vegetable plots out the back, with lawn, ornamental trees and shrubs at the front. A consequence of having a house like this was that there was supposed to be room for people to come and stay. One early visitor was J. B. Miles, recently displaced by Lance Sharkey as Communist Party national secretary and now assuming the role of the 'grand old man' of Australian communism. Miles visited 'outlying branches to rebuke members for their inadequacies'.[5] Other visitors included the family of Joe Goss who stayed for several months.

Joe Goss was a recent arrival from England. He and his wife Esther had been members of the Young Communist League in London, but Joe was a chronic asthmatic. He was told that unless he moved to a dry climate he would not live long. His doctor recommended Adelaide in Australia. Joe's brother, Jim, knew of Dick Blackburn in Adelaide as a possible contact.[6] In preparation for his family's migration Joe made the trip to Australia where he met Dick, but from there the plans were tragically interrupted. Esther was diagnosed with terminal lung cancer, and Joe returned to his two daughters and dying wife in London. When Joe and his girls eventually arrived on Anzac Day in 1952, they went straight from Outer Harbour to the Blackburns. The girls were in a bad way. Not only were they grieving the death of their mother, but also the loss of their friends, grandparents, other relatives, their neighbours and schools.

Judy Goss was twelve, and her sister eight when they arrived to a warm welcome at 78 Allinga Avenue. Jean took the girls under her wing, organising the girls into primary school. In Judy's words: 'Jean was very affectionate, very gentle, very kind – but I think it was very stressful for her to have us staying there as you can imagine: a young woman with two young children of her own'. Judy could not get over the fact that the Blackburns had a garden. There was nothing like that where they had lived in London.

Jean provided the girls with their first feelings of security in a long time. Judy was grateful that Jean helped her through the trial of Grade 7 domestic arts. Each girl simply had to have 'a basket with an elasticated cover'. Jean did some mothering – there appears to have been limited amounts of fathering. Joe Goss, Judy's father, 'was a very, very dogmatic committed communist. And he told me [Judy] as quite a young child, that the Party came before everything, before his family'. As a twelve-year-old, Judy organised her sister, Bill and Susan into plays which they performed for the adults. She looked at the family and noticed that Bill was very close to Jean. Jean was often worried about Bill for a reason that Judy could not have guessed. When he was four years old, Bill's heart was noted as 'abnormal', with a 'systolic murmur'. Bill's sister believed Jean's concern was more likely caused by his behaviour. He often swung between over-excitement and withdrawal.[7]

Figure 5.1 Judy and Joe Goss, recently migrated from London, with Bill Blackburn, c1952. The Goss family came to stay with Jean and Dick Blackburn before establishing a home for themselves.
Photographer unknown, courtesy of Susan Blackburn.

Like Jean at the same age, Judy Goss loved poetry. For her thirteenth birthday Jean gave her *A Book of Verse for Boys and Girls*, inscribed 'with love from Jean 1952'; it became a treasured possession. Towards the end of their time with the Blackburns, Judy noticed some tension between Jean and Dick. She wondered how much say Jean had had in them coming to live in Glenunga. In late 1952 the family moved to the other side of the city and close contact with Jean was lost, though they saw Dick from time to time at Party events. Years after Jean left the Party, Joe Goss also left the Communist Party, transferring to the Socialist Party of Australia, the party formed by comrades who remained attached to the Soviet Union.[8]

One of the obligations of being a communist was to help migrant communist families with accommodation, and the Blackburns were soon hosts to a German family who stayed some weeks. The boy shared Bill's bedroom. Judy Goss and her sister had shared Susan's. Later again, in the middle of Jean's leaving the Party in 1956, comrades Rosemary and Donald Porter were sharing the house. Rosemary was ill which, according to an ASIO report, threw an additional burden on Jean.[9]

But Jean's problems at this time were not confined to the pressures that came from other families in the house. She also chafed against the sexual division of labour expected by the Party. Her treatment at the end of the New Housewives Association and the more general political economy of motherhood were also involved. The burden of looking after children fell heavily on her. Susan wrote that her mother 'yearned for intellectual stimulation and adult company and told us in no uncertain terms when we were naughty that she did not want to be stuck at home with us'.[10] Perhaps the wonder of it is that resentment of the role did not interfere with Jean being a loving mother, and an empathetic host.

In 1951 the Menzies government decided to ban the Communist Party. The legislation passed in parliament but was rejected as unconstitutional by the High Court. The government then went to the people in a referendum to change the constitution. The Labor Party increasingly riven by Catholic right and socialist left finally decided to oppose the powers sought by the government. Communist Party comrades campaigned hard, especially in the unions and factories where the Party had influence. The referendum proposals were defeated with New South Wales, Victoria and South Australia all voting against.

There were many victory parties that night, including that hosted by Jean and Dick Blackburn. Anne Neill's report on Jean and Dick's party is quoted at the beginning of this chapter. Comrade Anne Neill lived a few streets away from Jean and Dick in Glenunga. Her real name was Freda Bennett and she had been a member of the conservative Liberal and Country League since 1936. She had been involved in the Women's Peace Council in South Australia after the war but became increasingly concerned about communist influence within it. She was recruited to ASIO in 1950. She made herself available as an unpaid typist to Elliott Johnston who was secretary of the South Australian Peace Council. Johnston was a communist and a lawyer on the rise in Adelaide. He recruited Neill to the Party in 1951. Neill was then in a good position from which to report the activities of South Australian comrades to ASIO over the next ten years. She kept an eye on Elliott and Elizabeth Johnston, Jean and Dick Blackburn, and many others. Though quite ill by 1960, she did not go gently. Just before Christmas in 1961 it was not only the citizens of Adelaide who were bemused by her headline articles in the *Sunday Mail* about subversion in their midst. So too were the many members of the Party whom Neill named.[11] Though out of the Party some five years in 1961, Jean did not escape Neill's public revelations.

The peace movement had fair support in the early 1950s beyond Communist Party circles. Cold War circumstances that included the threat of nuclear war and concern over the 'spread' of communism in eastern Europe, Korea and China often led to a sense of imminent apocalypse. In supporting, and sometimes taking a lead in organising peace organisations, the Communist Party had a dual purpose. One certainly was to avoid another war potentially more terrifying than that of a few years before but the other was to defend the Soviet Union from perceived threats. For many socialists, the USSR remained the promise of a better, more just world, the kind of world that capitalism would forever remain incapable of building. As the labour historian Ian Turner put it, the struggle for peace was the struggle for socialism.[12]

In 1948 comrade Graham Smith was the first secretary of a newly formed South Australian Peace Committee. Elliott Johnston attended the World Peace Congress in Warsaw at the end of 1950. There was a national Youth Carnival for Peace and Friendship in Sydney in 1952. In 1955 there was a great petition launched by South Australian unionists, church leaders and academics 'to outlaw atomic war'. Within two months it had gathered 16,000 signatures.[13] Jean put a lot of work into recruiting signatures for one of the 'Ban the Bomb' petitions. She also had the unpleasant job of collecting subscriptions that enabled the employment of a Communist Party organiser in the peace movement. She joined the executive of the South Australian Peace Committee, but after working on one of the petitions, she noticed something that disturbed her. In the peace movement, there was an increasing absence in speeches by comrades of outright condemnation of atomic weapons. Having raised the question in the Quaker's meeting hall where peace movement meetings were held, 'the penny dropped and I knew the answer, so I sort of beat a retreat from that'.[14] The answer, she realised, was that once the Soviet Union had developed its own nuclear weapons, the communist parties and worker's organisations belonging to Cominform were no longer to condemn them in quite the same way. From this point, Jean began to disengage from intensive peace movement activity, but not altogether by any means.[15] Her peace work shifted to the revivified WILPF. In 1956 an ASIO agent recorded her comments on a future strategy for the peace movement at a meeting of the South Australian Peace Conference.[16]

While still a communist, Jean had a letter in *The Advertiser* in August 1953. The new Chinese republic should be admitted to the United Nations, 'a quarter of the human race' could not be ignored. The Korean War was not an argument for keeping China out of the UN. China had 'already suffered from imperialisms' and now there were 'the fire-eating statements of MacArthur'. (General Douglas MacArthur advocated the bombing of China in the Korean War.) Australians' feelings about the new Chinese government were irrelevant, 'because it enjoys the support of the Chinese people'. The letter concluded: 'unless we accept this principle, the whole basis of UN falls to the ground and we all face a war of extinction'.[17]

The Party continued to sustain a social life for its members and Jean continued to participate even if she was becoming less enthusiastic about the organisation herself. The New Theatre, like those with the same name in other Australian cities, was meant to spread socialist ideas and culture. A drama of the Korean War, *Land of Morning Calm*, was put on in Stow Hall in 1952. It had first appeared in the Youth Carnival for Peace and Friendship. The Adelaide production was terrible according to a press review, lacking in stage direction, with amateur actors who knew so few of their lines that it was easier to follow the prompt to find out what was going on. Nevertheless 'Good work was done by Alan Miller, Jean Blackburn, and Yvonne Geary'.[18] Ann Neill was occasional wardrobe mistress in productions of the New Theatre.[19] She turned up everywhere, listening and reporting to ASIO.

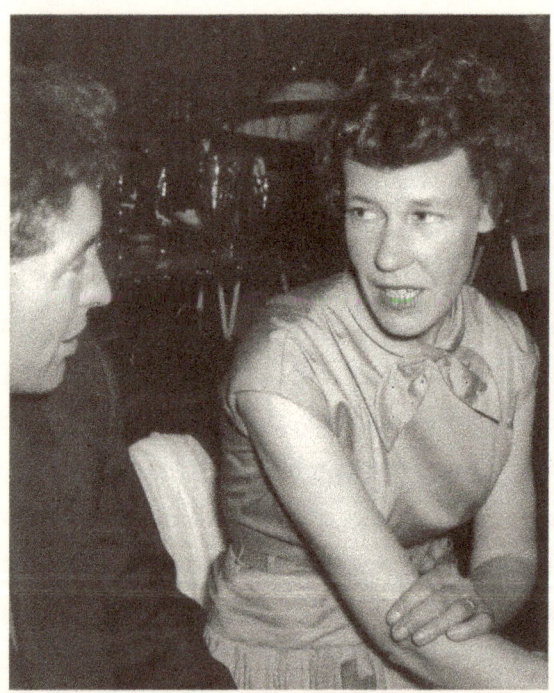

Figure 5.2 Dick and Jean at an event at Burnside Town Hall, not far from their new house in Glenunga. Jean has one year left as a member of the Communist Party of Australia, 1955.
Photographer unknown, courtesy of Susan Blackburn.

Jean grew tired of the demands being made of her by the Party. She was fair game, having her own house, no paid work and 'only' a couple of school-age children to look after. There were annoying moralistic judgements to put up with. Why would she want a luxury item like a refrigerator? If the Blackburns could afford that, they could increase their weekly Party dues. This parsimony, the virtue made of scrimping had plagued Jean's childhood and adolescence, and it was *still* with her. Prominent comrade Jim Moss apparently told her that she should not complain if Dick was away with his work so much. She should simply be grateful he had provided her with such a nice house. 'I suddenly thought to myself – poo. I'm going to get right out of this. I'm going to get a job. I got a job.' The job would not be the right job of course. A comrade teaching in a private school! Moss had also been the one to announce that the Union of Australian Women, the replacement for the New Housewives, would not require bourgeois women in its leadership positions. By this he meant Jean. Another comrade, Haury Pyle, at one point told Jean that she had a lot to live down. What did he mean? 'He said well, having an honours degree in bourgeois economics – what could be worse?'[20]

Jean thought that school teaching was the obvious job for her. There would be the hours and holidays that suited a mother with children. She also needed work close to home. Jean applied to the South Australian Education Department. It is not clear whether ASIO was involved, but her application was not accepted because she was unwilling to teach anything anywhere. Other married women applying for teaching were treated better. Jean believed that the South Australian government had made a commitment to the Returned Services League that it would employ no more communists.[21]

A little way up Portrush Road from Glenunga was the Presbyterian Girls' College (PGC). Would it be interested? In late 1953 or early 1954 Jean applied for an advertised position as an English and history teacher. She had little relevant experience and no teacher qualification. This was not a problem however because South Australia was still decades away from requiring professional qualifications for the employment of teachers. The baby boom was on its way of course and teacher shortages were already an issue – qualifications to teach were far from the immediate issue. As had occurred in the war it was again becoming possible for married women to be employed in some occupations, though in government jobs such as teaching, employment remained 'temporary' for many years. Neither tenure, promotion nor superannuation were possible under these circumstances.

One might have thought that PGC would have been wary of Jean, but its headmistress, Ruby Powell, employed her immediately. The school had something of a 'blue stocking' reputation and had fair autonomy despite the Presbyterian church. Whether Powell was aware of Jean's background is unknown, but Jean's honours degree was sufficient for employment. No doubt Jean interviewed well. She was to work part-time, teaching economic history, her great love, to two Leaving classes, and history to two junior classes. The latter would be a challenge. She found a 'how to teach history' book and agreed that planning a seventeenth century English meal might be a good thing to do with students. So at the age of 34, Jean was once more in a workplace where she was valued, where it was okay to read and talk about all sorts of books and ideas, and there were students who responded to what she had to offer. Some of her teaching colleagues,

Ellen Christensen in particular, headmistress of the school from 1957, were intellectuals worth engaging with.[22]

In later years Jean wrote that she had not been comfortable about teaching in a high-fee private school, even though it was within walking and cycling distance from home, but she believed that she had no real alternative.

> My indignation at being excluded from public employment, my longing for colleagues – and my recent decision that I wanted a washing machine, telephone, a car, none of which we could afford [...] Now, the education for which I had fought for love of it had monetary value ... Dick was not keen about my desire to rejoin the workforce, responding in words I later found common among husbands. These affirmed that it was okay for me to seek paid work, but only if I could continue to assume the household responsibilities I presently bore.[23]

Ellen Christensen's partner, Cecil Teesdale-Smith was Elizabeth Johnston's sister, and a woman with a communist history. Christensen did not resile from communist friends and acquaintances. In these women at PGC, Jean found friends who became part of her life for years to come. Cecil was a famed teacher of English. After she retired she passed books on to Jean with her commentaries written at the back.[24]

Going to work was a crucial move for Jean. 'I guess I felt, since observing the situation between my parents and between my father and the family, I'd long been convinced that the equality of women depended fundamentally on their ability to earn their own livings, and I still believe that.'[25] A sense of growing independence may have contributed to Jean's next major decision.

Jean left the Communist Party in 1956, the year that ruptured loyalties of communists across the world. Jean Blackburn was part of a mass exodus. Jean, like many, had had reservations for years, but nothing was perfect, and overall, the cause appeared greater than the doubts. However, in 1956 all that changed. First came Nikita Khrushchev's 'secret speech' that condemned the crimes of Josef Stalin, reported in the *New York Times* after its initial delivery in February. The Communist Party in Australia went into denial. Comrades were not even to talk about it. Then there was Hungary, in turmoil for much of 1956 as its governments attempted to decrease or manage the control of the Soviet Union over its affairs. Late in the year, October through November, there was a mass uprising. On November 4, Soviet troops moved on Budapest suppressing the revolt. By then, Jean had already left the Communist Party. Events in Hungary confirmed the decision.

Jean's reasons for leaving did not simply revolve around the de-Stalinisation speech, nor Hungary. For some years she had been doubtful about the show trials and disappearances of comrades in the Soviet Union. She was also disturbed by the treatment of Tito by the Soviet Union as Yugoslavia determined its independent socialist destiny. She had also been unhappy about attitudes towards women in the local Party and believed she had seen through the hypocrisy of the Party in its policy towards atomic weapons and peace. She was tired of being thought not proletarian enough, with suspicion aroused by her intellect and education. By 1956 Eric Russell, an old friend from University of Melbourne, had a job at the University of Adelaide. They talked while Dick spent three months away in Brunei for work. Jean had the time and space to think. 'I found strength to take this "traitorist" step through my close friendship with Eric

Russell, who lived nearby.'²⁶ Jean's daughter, Susan wrote that Jean left the Party 'when he [Dick] was in Brunei and when he returned he shouted at her telling her she was "a grain of sand" who would make no difference to the great forces of history which were bringing the revolution'. He insisted for a very long time that Khrushchev's speech was a forgery.²⁷ As a nine-year-old, Susan noticed that her parents were arguing more than usual. Jean later told Susan that she had considered leaving Dick at this time. When she suggested that perhaps they should divorce 'he wouldn't hear of it'.²⁸ Jean's decision made things difficult for Dick, but he soon assumed the presidency of the local branch of the Friends of the Soviet Union.²⁹

Susan told the story of Judah Waten visiting the Blackburns around this time. Waten was becoming prominent in Australian literature; his novel *Alien Son* was published in 1952.

> In the late fifties I recall occasional visits from the large, loud and dogmatic communist writer Judah Waten, who had been a friend of my parents when they lived in Melbourne. According to what my mother later told me, when Waten challenged my father [in front of Jean] as to how he could continue living with 'that renegade', my father said, 'If I had to choose between the Party and Jean, I'd choose Jean any day.' He must have been torn, because his lifelong loyalties to both the party and his wife and family were very firmly entrenched.³⁰

There is evidence to suggest that Jean felt some embarrassment, even shame, that she had gone along with the Party for so long. Dean Ashenden talked with her about it, some twenty years or more later:

> My sense of it was that it was an absolutely humiliating and scarifying experience ... Nonetheless she wasn't going to do what so many of the disillusioned Left did, and jump straight

into some other enclosed intellectual system … Her one intellectual and political certainty was that it is not possible to be certain. She was sceptical of any finding or conclusion, including particularly, and sometimes paralysingly, her own, but also temperamentally/psychologically, and by conviction, incapable of shrugging her shoulders and walking away.[31]

This suggests that leaving the Communist Party was a crucial factor in Jean's intellectual development. The social equality, social justice objectives remained powerful, but scepticism, the demand for an argument or course of action that was based on clear evidence became more powerful than perhaps it once had. Yet, in an interview years later with Wendy Lowenstein, Jean had not forgotten the benefits of being in the Party either. She had learnt how to organise and that you were not 'entirely a private agent because you had to behave in ways that made you acceptable to other people'. Lowenstein suggested that the experience had been 'enormously' educative, and Jean agreed.[32]

John McLaren has written about 'the revolt of the intellectuals' within the Communist Party following the events of 1956. For them it was intolerable that the Party leadership for some months refused to admit the existence of the Khrushchev speech, thereby disallowing debate on its contents. The Party also went into denial over events in Hungary. In Melbourne Ken Gott, Ian Turner and Stephen Murray Smith contacted Helen Palmer who in 1957 established the magazine *Outlook* for dissident comrades.[33] Jean was also in contact with Helen. Ian Turner wrote that *Outlook* provided a refuge for intellectuals who had left the Party, it was a place to 'lick wounds', to 'regain our intellectual and emotional health and vigour'.[34]

Helen Palmer had ended up in New South Wales after her years at the University of Melbourne. She wrote books, but also taught in public high schools. Like Jean she had trouble finding paid employment, or in her case, being re-employed by a state education department after attending a peace conference in Beijing in 1952. She was forced to wait eighteen months without appointment, finally being re-employed as a temporary teacher in 1955. Her trajectory after leaving the Party was different from that of Jean. She developed her criticism of the Soviet Union from an increasingly favourable view of communist China. She wanted to open discussion not only about the secret speech by Khrushchev, but a broad range of socialist ideas. She was expelled from the Party for her trouble, but with the support of an editorial board, began *Outlook* in 1957.[35] The Party 'banned' the magazine before it even appeared. In its first editorial, *Outlook* promised a forum for Australian socialist views and attention to 'major problems facing us today'. Topics might include the welfare state, the role of political parties, living conditions and 'the way to economic and cultural independence'. According to Helen, socialism was a proven alternative to existing social systems, but in the USSR and elsewhere 'the price to be paid ... in human values has been too high'.[36] *Outlook* was clearly 'revisionist'.

Support and discussion groups followed the publication in Sydney and Melbourne and then Adelaide, attracting men and women who had never been Party members as well as former comrades.[37] Jean's most substantial piece for *Outlook* was published in 1959. 'Shine, O Shine them Pots!' began an argument that anticipated her 1963 publication, *Australian Wives Today*. It exposed the reactionary policy of the Labor Party, still diffident about the rights of married women to paid work. She praised when warranted: the Communist Party had finally improved its policy on women.[38] Later, in 1961 she wrote about the difficulties that arose in South Australian government schools following the 1940 Act introducing religious instruction. Palmer had recently written a longer piece on free, compulsory, secular and 'protestant' public schools.[39]

In early 1962, Jean and about twenty-five other 'Adelaide socialists' met to form the Adelaide Left Club. Ian Turner had recently taken up an appointment in the University of Adelaide's history department. Turner's wife, Amirah, took over as *Outlook* representative when Jean stepped down in 1963. As head of department and professor, Hugh Stretton made more than one appointment of historians with communist associations. He was one of several University of Adelaide academics who were to become significant in Jean's life. It is likely that Turner's arrival provided the impetus for the formation of the club. He wrote often for *Outlook* where Jean did not, but Jean was the named Adelaide contact for *Outlook* and the club.[40] The range of topics discussed by the *Outlook* group in Adelaide was wide, including foreign policy and the question of state aid to non-government schools.[41] Jean had begun her engagement with education policy.

Jean also contributed a brief review of the 1960 Adelaide Festival of Arts. The 'Hiroshima panels' attracted a good crowd. Tickets to many events were too expensive for most people. The contradictions of the event were on display in a play by a 'West Indian Negro' about shack-dwellers 'in the straight-jacket of poverty'. In contrast to the play's subject, the Festival audience was full of 'gay, elegantly garbed' veteran theatre goers. Jean noted sympathetically another South Australian real-life drama being performed in the Supreme Court. Anti-establishment local newspaper proprietor Rupert Murdoch was facing charges of libel for allowing *The News* to criticise the conduct of the Stuart case, in which an Aboriginal man was on trial for murder.[42] In 1962 Don Dunstan spoke to the Adelaide Left Club on

Aboriginal affairs, a rare interest for South Australian politicians of the time.[43]

Almost certainly reducing her dependence on the Communist Party for social contacts, Jean developed relationships with a number of University of Adelaide academics. Most of them were men employed in economics and history. Several, including Eric Russell, who had arrived in 1952, had University of Melbourne student histories. Hugh Stretton, though five years younger than Jean, had been an undergraduate there also. With Jean, Russell was involved in the peace movement. He wrote on disarmament for *Outlook* in its first year, 1957.[44] His intellectual loves – economics, history, literature and philosophy – matched those of Jean. She admired his conversational strategies. He was prone to announcing the end of a discussion in which he had lost interest with the peremptory: 'Not of general interest'.

> They were kind of soul mates, really. My mother loved to have intellectual discussions, and she could not get that from my father. I think my father had worked out very early in the piece that my mother was always going to win a discussion and he wasn't going to enter into those any more ... most of those old communist party friends were not terribly good for a good intellectual discussion either, but Eric was, and they were very close.[45]

Geoffrey Harcourt, another with a University of Melbourne history, arrived in Adelaide with his wife, Joan in 1958. Harcourt later wrote about Eric as a 'complex many-sided man and there were reserves within reserves. Once these were penetrated, his companionship and support were unbelievably rich.'[46] Jean also became close to Eric's wife, Judith. Geoff and Joan Harcourt recalled their first meeting with Jean. While they were at dinner with the Russells, there was an urgent knocking at the front door. Jean was upset; she and Eric moved elsewhere into the house to talk. It did not take long, and she was gone.[47] It was to Eric that Jean had turned for counselling as she prepared to leave the Communist Party two years before.

In 1951 Peter Karmel arrived in Adelaide, appointed to the chair in economics as a 27-year-old. He and Jean had been aware of one another since their student days at the University of Melbourne. They were linked to some degree by mutual friends in economics working at the University of Adelaide. Peter and his wife Lena were also parents of students at Jean's school, PGC.[48] In 1966 he became the founding Vice-Chancellor of Flinders University in Adelaide.

Another of Hugh Stretton's appointments in history was Ken Inglis in 1956. He and his first wife, Judy, an anthropologist, also helped with Jean's transition out of intellectual isolation. Judy Inglis became Jean's guide as together they visited Aboriginal communities in South Australia. About the same time that Jean met Judy Inglis, she met Denise Bradley, married to a university academic. Judy and Denise were younger than Jean and she was happy that neither had personal recollections of her earlier communist self.[49] At last Jean's isolation from the intellectual life that had caused her such despair when she first arrived in Adelaide was coming to an end. 'I knew various academics ... I was asked to parties and I gradually got to know quite a lot of them'.[50] Former University of Melbourne acquaintances and friends in particular gave Jean a network of significance over the next several years.

A year or so after the events of 1956, Jean and Dick decided to have a third child. It may well have signified a reconciliation between them. Observing the little ones at PGC, Jean had found herself yearning for another baby, or in her words, she 'was getting clucky'.[51] Hugh was born on 3 March in 1958. There are two possibilities for the choice of name 'Hugh': Dick was related to the poet Hugh McCrae, and the other was Jean's respect for Hugh Stretton.[52] They may well have reinforced one another for the final decision. Jean finished teaching to be at home for Hugh's five pre-school years – but the experience this time was better than with Bill and Susan. Having friends, some of whom lived nearby made a difference. Joan Harcourt, caring for a baby of her own, found warmth and companionship with Jean. 'Jean was very kind because you'd call by and have coffee and talk, and with other young women who had small babies … That was a great support to me coming to a city I didn't know'. Unlike the men, Joan noted, the women did not have [paid] work to occupy them during the week.[53]

Figure 5.3 Susan, 11 years, Jean and Bill, 14 (in his Unley High school uniform) with the new baby, Hugh, 1958. Jean interrupted her teaching at Presbyterian Girls College to care for Hugh in the years before he began school.
Photographer Dick Blackburn, courtesy of Susan Blackburn.

Judy Inglis also had a child around the same time as Jean. Judy joined those encouraging Jean towards study for a higher degree, and she was soon talking to a prospective supervisor in the economics department. According to Jean, he insisted that she take a subject that involved survey work, knocking on 'thousands of doors'. This was the last thing that Jean wanted. 'I said, "I've been there, I've done that", and I'd made up my mind I would never knock on anyone's door uninvited again.'[54] She did not enrol in a research degree, but the feeling that she had missed out by not doing so remained an issue for her, never quite going away.

After she left the Communist Party, Jean was cold-shouldered by many of her former comrades, but with Dick still in the Party there remained substantial engagement with several communist families.[55] Some of her former comrades barely missed a beat as joint holidays, weekend visits and the like continued. The extended family of Tess and David Caust was particularly important. David was one of only a couple of medical doctors in the Party. With marriage to Tess came children, and the children of the Blackburns and Causts were friends. Tess Caust had sisters, Mary Miller, a unionist and communist, and a New Theatre activist since the 1940s, and Gwen Slade. Margie Ward, David's sister, was a teacher who had also left the Party. Each of these women, Tess, Mary, Gwen and Margie were in Jean's continuing post-Party circle of friends. John Sendy, an organiser and later Party president, named David and Tess, Marjorie Johnston (Elliott's younger sister) and Graham Smith as members of the Party's Edwardstown branch who were the main questioners in Adelaide of the Party's reaction to the events of 1956.[56] These former comrades were sympathetic to Jean even though she left the Party when most of them remained. Eventually Tess and David left, but for them it was to join the 'Maoist' break-away, the Communist Party of Australia (Marxist-Leninist). Jean and Tess found plenty to talk about apart from politics, though Jean could be irritated by dogmatic assertion from time to time. Susan Blackburn wrote of the camaraderie, though focusing on the pre-1956 period. The families mentioned were those that remained friends after 1956.

> The Party provided them with a surrogate family who were indeed much more congenial than most of their own relatives. In turn, their Party friends and communist sympathisers like the Causts, the Smiths, the Millers and the Johnstons had children whom we met with frequently and some of whom became our friends. Party meetings were occasionally held in our house, and there were Communist Party picnics at Belair National Park.[57]

Graham and Sally Smith's family had reason to value their friendship with Jean. After the war, Graham had performed his proletarian duty by working in a factory, but with a wife and young children to support, he needed a better paying job. In his case ASIO was effective. A number of job applications around 1950 looked promising, but then the message would come through: there was no job after all. In gathering despair, Graham tried the Commonwealth Bank for a clerical position. All was fine, he was employed, and then came the retraction. Graham wept in front of the bank's employment officer. He went around the corner to Elliott Johnston who talked to him about claiming a month's pay because of dismissal without notice. On the way to Elliott he had met Jean. She told him to write to Nugget Coombs, whom she had known during the war. Coombs was now Governor of the Commonwealth Bank in a time when it also performed the functions of the later Reserve Bank. Jean told Graham that she doubted the bank had specific policies that would deny him a job. She thought it was a 'local' decision. Graham did as advised, and a week later there were two letters for him, a local one telling him that there was a job after all, and the other from Coombs, 'I think by now you would have heard from the office of the Commonwealth Bank in South Australia. Yours faithfully, H. C. Coombs'.[58]

Dick Blackburn's workmate at the CSIRO, Ted Jackson, and his wife Mary became important friends of Jean. It was Ted Jackson who sat down with Jean in 1963 to work on *Australian Wives Today*. Another friend, Maud McBriar, back from England with negative MI5 and therefore ASIO assessments, worked at the University of Adelaide, unable to get a job elsewhere despite her science credentials. She was involved in peace organisations with Jean through the 1960s.[59]

Figure 5.4 At the beach with friends and old comrades, from left, Mary Miller, Jean Blackburn and Rosemary Porter, 1966. The families and friends of Tess and David Caust often shared beach holidays around Christmas.
Courtesy of Susan Blackburn.

In the week after Christmas in 1966 many of the friends were at Christies Beach together. Jean wrote to Susan: 'Tess is just 'round the corner here, with Marg Ward's girls staying, and Gwen popping up and down. They all send their love ... Today the Smiths and Porters are coming for the day. I feel weak'.[60]

At the same time as Jean was leaving the Communist Party, Bill developed an illness, the symptoms of which seemed to fit with rheumatic fever, another problem for his heart. He spent some two months as a ten-year-old in the Adelaide Children's Hospital and after discharge, though active, he fatigued easily and was 'habitually pale'. The consulting doctor saw no reason why he should not lead a normal life, except that his parents should guide him 'away from highly competitive sport'.[61] The concern for Bill continued through Jean's life. As a teenager he had few friends, and those whom he did have were so interested in technical things, including the building of radios, that in his sister's mind at least, 'they were impossible to talk to'.[62]

For the Blackburn children, having communist parents had its consequences. There was the fun of the New Theatre productions and the fundraising *Tribune* fetes, and socialising with other communist families, but there was also a wider Adelaide society to deal with. Susan wrote:

> Somehow word got around about local communists. This led to a few children at my primary school ... pointing at me and calling me a communist, and suggesting I needed to go and live in Russia. I was particularly hurt that the mother of my best friend of the time refused to let her play with me out of school hours. It seemed to be just another case of stigmatising those who are different in some way. At least I did not appear

different, like the daughter of Plymouth Brethren parents in my class at primary school: she had to wear long plaits and long skirts …[63]

Later again, in 1961, with Bill now sixteen, and Susan fourteen, there were the Anne Neill revelations in the *Sunday Mail*. 'This resulted in another outburst of name-calling and finger-pointing at school', this time high school. Susan remembered herself and Jean walking around the Glenunga neighbourhood, 'my mother pointed out to me the house where Anne Neill lived: "that spy" as she called her, but without much animosity'.[64]

Susan remembered being taken on peace marches through the streets of Adelaide. From 1958, her new young brother was pushed along in a stroller. These were agreed activities for Jean and Dick. Jean would have nothing to do with more obvious pro-Soviet Union activity after 1956 – unless Dick's work in the Australia-Soviet Friendship Society made it unavoidable. In 1960 the renowned Russian cellist, Mstislav Rostropovich was in town for concerts with the Australian Broadcasting Commission. Dick and Jean hosted a reception for him at 78 Allinga Avenue.[65]

In watching what went on with her children at school, Jean occasionally intervened. She knew she could not confront corporal punishment head-on at Linden Park Primary.

> I was pretty canny about that. I invited a departmental psychologist to come out and talk about the matter and then I said, what would you do if your child was being whacked and she said, I'd raise hell. But I got in very well with the mothers and with the teachers by and large and it was much better than it had been in my day but still terribly over controlled.

Jean was less effective at Unley High. Her queries about the absence of history in the curriculum of higher stream students were received with indifference. She thought the school authoritarian, a 'rather awful place'. She learnt 'how powerless parents were' which made her more supportive of parents' rights to engage with their children's schools 'down the track'.[66] Jean had begun thinking about what good schools might look like many years before, but with her own children now in the system, and her being a teacher, there was an incentive to think about the issues more systematically.

Because Susan's parents were engaged with the wider world, beyond the cultural boundaries of 1950s South Australia, Susan had access to unusual books and magazines. Her father collected his *Tribunes* for on-selling each week from the International Bookshop. He brought publications home, among them an art book from 'Shankar's Annual International Children's Art Exhibition', which resulted in a yearly publication of children's paintings. Jean and Dick 'gave me this bumper book every Christmas, and its children's paintings from all over the world ... were a revelation.'[67] There were subscriptions to *China Reconstructs* and the *UNESCO Courier*, their colourful photographs of life elsewhere than Adelaide appreciated. Dick brought home the *New Statesman, Listener, Vogue, Good Housekeeping* and some excellent children's magazines. He co-subscribed to them with CSIRO work mates. Jean made most of Susan's and her own clothes, so the women's magazines were welcome.[68] Enid Gilchrist's publications provided many patterns. At the same time, Susan was aware of problems. Her parent's view of the world was incongruent with what seemed to be happening around her. She found it difficult to envisage 'revolution in a quiet backwater like Adelaide. I could not make much sense of any of this'.[69]

In the early 1950s, Dick was the owner of a car. It took the family visiting or black-berrying in the Adelaide Hills, and there were annual trips to Melbourne to see Jean and Dick's families. Dick's mother had won election to the House of Representatives in 1946, but she was defeated in 1949 and again in 1951. Susan seemed to enjoy meeting her grandparents, but Doris Blackburn could irritate Jean as she went on about her commitments and her wonderful family (the Horderns). At that time Doris was much more accomplished in feminist, peace and labour politics than Jean and Susan suspected some rivalry on Jean's part in response.[70] With her own parents, Les and Claire, Jean remained guarded. More to her liking was the meetings with old friends like Con Warneke, and Jock and Jessie McLeod.

Right at the end of this period, Jean acquired a car of her own, a Volkswagen. It was not an easy ride, Jean having trouble mastering the clutch, but it added to her sense of independence. It was also at this time that Jean and Dick first travelled to Europe. Jean came back 'absolutely determined that we should live closer to the European lifestyle of enjoying good things … it didn't amount to a lot except in the culinary sphere, more wine-drinking … and the purchase of a few ceramics'. The making her own clothes phase passed, and Jean would go clothes shopping with Susan. They encouraged one another as they bought.[71] Guilt at spending money was no longer in the ascendant. Adelaide and its increasingly educated middle class were changing. Culturally, the biennial Adelaide Festival of Arts was transformative. Jean had been a reader from youth, but new interest in theatre and film, the arts in general enriched her life.

Despite the building of a different kind of life, especially after her period of entrapment at home Jean continued to battle with 'highs and lows ... more pronounced than most people's'. David Caust tried her on different medications. He thought at one point that she may have to be hospitalised.[72] She would manage without that, but despair and weeping recurred, and was 'worse around menstruation'[73]. It is possible that a realisation that her marriage was less than she had once hoped it might be may have played a part. That Dick had opposed her enrolment in a research degree was a source of occasional bitterness. Increasingly Jean and Dick's paths through life diverged. Old sources of tension continued. Jean's language was quicker than Dick's. She could argue him down and when she was very strong, he would retreat completely from the contest. Yet, at the same time there was loyalty, one to the other, and a companionship, often loving, that survived through the coming decades. There were things they could do together quite happily. They included attending theatre, gardening, collecting long-playing records of classical and other music, going to and talking about film – and travelling. When Jean was so depressed that she took to her bed, Dick efficiently ran the children and household. He was in some wonder, though not necessarily admiring, of Jean's 'rich emotional life'. Picking up the pieces was a role he had rehearsed with his mother as a youth. Doris Blackburn was also subject to debilitating collapse.[74]

Between 1959 and 1962 Jean took an interest in Aboriginal communities and their organisations in and around Adelaide. Judy Inglis took Jean on visits to the Point McLeay reserve, a former mission south of Adelaide. Judy rented a flat attached to her house to a former resident of another reserve they visited, Point Pearce, on the Yorke Peninsula. Judy became interested in the lives of 'part-Aboriginal families living in or near Adelaide', getting a grant from the University of Adelaide to conduct research. She began interviewing and surveying families living in Adelaide. She was aware of the problems that might arise from an anthropologist 'meddling' in Aboriginal community affairs but decided to join the Aboriginal Advancement League. Outside the League's business, she supported Charles Perkins' advocacy for 'a private member's bill to replace the present Aborigines Act with a new Act that would remove all legal restrictions on Aborigines while still enabling welfare services to be provided'.[75] Labor lawyer and politician Don Dunstan was actively involved. His visit to Point Pearce some years earlier had left him appalled.

Judy and Jean attended meetings of the League, run by the non-Aboriginal Presbyterian minister, Charles Duguid.[76] The two women were not great supporters of the well-meaning Duguid and the orientation of the League which they tended to see as prolonging Aboriginal dependence on white sponsors. Judy and Jean thought independent Aboriginal organisations, run by Aboriginal people, were the preferable alternative. All the same, they were aware that the League did much good and helped many Aboriginal individuals and families.[77] In early 1962, Judy moved to Canberra, but Jean, now on the executive of the Advancement League, remained active. At the annual meeting of the Federal Council for Aboriginal Advancement in 1962, Duguid and Jean represented the South Australian League. Jean's mother-in-law, Doris Blackburn, a co-founder of the national League and its conference, joined the national education subcommittee with Oodgeroo Noonuccal (then known as Kath Walker) among others.[78]

While Jean remembered her involvement with the League as rather peripheral, Duguid did not. He contacted ASIO complaining about communist influence in the organisation. ASIO noted that 'Jean Edna Blackburn is one of the main causes of this influence although she is believed not to be an actual member of the CP of A'. In April 1962, an ASIO agent wrote a hostile assessment of Jean's activity. Agents may have written what they thought their superiors wished to read, but whatever the case, Jean was accused of being 'the real troublemaker', her 'criticism is always destructive and is designed to embarrass the government'. 'She is adept at putting words into the mouths of the Aboriginals' when she visited a reserve and she was 'inclined to interpret their statements in a way to suit her own particular ends'. In the same report Duguid was also portrayed negatively, as a dogmatic 'fire eater'. The report noted that Jean had been named in the Anne Neill articles.[79] In both South Australia and nationally governments at this time had plenty to be embarrassed about in relation to Aboriginal policy. It was too convenient to construe any and every criticism as a communist plot.

Jean remembered being involved in rather mild politics in this area, helping prepare deputations and submissions for example.[80] Later she looked with favour on the emergence in 1964 of an alternative grouping to the League, the Progress Association, led by Malcolm Cooper. Jean got to know current and former inmates from Colebrook Home at Blackwood in the Adelaide Hills, for a while tutoring one young woman in university economics. She was aware of the terrible educational disadvantages under which Aboriginal people laboured. Almost no Aboriginal students completed secondary school. Jean met men and women whom she came across again several years later in the Schools Commission. They included Lowitja (Lois) O'Donohue.

Keri Rani has assessed the interview that Peter Read conducted with Jean about her engagement with Aboriginal affairs in Adelaide, suggesting that wisdom in hindsight affected Jean's judgements. The issues were more complex than Jean remembered. She talked about Duguid as encouraging 'Uncle Tom' behaviour among Aboriginal people, but this was not quite fair. It sidelined the fact that many Aboriginal people wanted and needed the assistance of Duguid and the League to manage the terrible disabilities that white assimilationist Australia imposed on them.[81]

Jean's friendship with Judy Inglis came to a sudden end in 1962. Judy and her family moved to Canberra at the beginning of the year, and then, six months later Judy was dead, killed in a car crash. Her death affected Jean deeply.[82] In 1963 Jean had wound down her Aboriginal engagement. She was back to work at PGC and studying for a Diploma of Education. Her attention had shifted towards women, and education.

It was most likely in 1962 that the Victorian Fabian Society asked Jean to write a booklet on the circumstances of married women in contemporary Australia. It was published as *Australian Wives Today*. Jean had read widely on the topic of women and marriage and believing she had relevant experience, agreed to do so.[83] Norman McKenzie's book on Australian women came out in 1962.[84] There were contentious reviews and letters in various publications concerning its worth. *Nation*, a magazine to which Judy Inglis and Jean had contributed, published one of the more hostile reviews. It may be that the Fabians were responding to this controversy when they commissioned Jean. The Fabians were closely associated with the Labor Party, so writing for them was possibly a significant act for Jean, especially when members of the Communist Party criticised the resulting publication. Ted Jackson was on the executive committee of the Victorian Fabians. He worked with Jean to achieve the publication. In *Outlook*, Jean had defended McKenzie's critique of existing women's organisations, and insisted that married women's right to work was a key issue for the women's movement.[85] Gisela Kaplan has noted the significance of the post-war suburban expansion on feminist thinking in the 1950s and early 1960s. Isolation, poor services, lack of mobility and dependence on husbands for money let alone access to secure employment were only several of the many problems.[86]

Australian Wives Today is a tour de force, continuing to read well today. The range of reference is wide. Contributing disciplines include sociology, demography, history and economics. Each were engaged to produce a convincing argument about the wastage that occurs when women who could *do* and *be* so much more were confined to housewifery. The writing is taut and direct, laced with arresting phrases. A wealth of policy suggestions is included, many of which were taken up over the next twenty to thirty years. Enabling older, married women to enrol with minimal economic hardship in universities as the Whitlam Labor government made possible in the early 1970s was but one of many suggestions. Child care reform, shopping hours extension, working hours flexibility, removal of barriers to employment and promotion, each of these and more were part of the case. Jean found the work of Viola Klein and Alva Myrdal especially useful.[87] Where Australian-specific research and data produced insufficient evidence for the argument, Jean was adept at the critical use of international studies of women in or out of labour markets. Though undetectable to readers who did not know Jean's family history, *Australian Wives Today* not only reads as a fine contemporary study of women and work, but an analysis of her mother

Claire's life, and that of her own, her husband Dick's beliefs on the duties of married women (and men), and those of other friends and acquaintances.

We do not reproduce the argument here, except to draw attention to some of the booklet's insights. Jean noted that the confinement of women to the home was historically recent; it was not a *natural* condition of womanhood. There was no convincing evidence that the children of women in paid work were any more likely to be delinquents than those whose mothers were confined to the home. There was the problem of the husband who is 'brought up to expect a housewife to wear a perpetual apron and to be virtuously preoccupied with domestic duties … inclined to protest against any modifications to his cherished domestic legend'.[88] In an era of the professionalisation of work, continued investment in voluntary activity by women with time on their hands would go nowhere. 'Cakes baked and clothing made in homes for local fetes suffer from the economic disabilities of small scale industry'. The frustrations of the women doing the baking were only alleviated by the social activity involved as they were likely 'in desperate need of activity or companionship'.[89] Dependent wives lose the ability to 'stand on an equal footing' with their breadwinning husbands. Women's intellects are dulled by staying at home too long. It was unfair to divide men and women, the one with paid work and careers, the other as producers of the finer, cultural parts of family life: 'Is there not something unjust in a system which condemns one half of the human species to an ulcer-racked life in an office or factory while the other debates languidly the artistic merits of egg-shell blue as against primrose for the south-west wall of the rumpus room?'[90]

Jean was also concerned that children could be deprived by home confinement. They deserved more than what mothers could provide.

In an echo of her former admiration of the Soviet Union, she asked 'Where are our Pioneer Palaces?', institutions that could improve the quality of childhood.[91] Under-employed married women constituted a reserve labour force, its existence concealed by misleading official employment statistics. Jean gave the last words in the argument to Myrdal and Klein. Many causes of marital unhappiness could be alleviated if paid work was not monopolised by men. Relationships could be more truly companionable if based on more equal access to contacts and stimulation both inside and outside the joint home.[92]

Because Jean Blackburn's future career was to be in education, it is worth looking at some of her thinking about education in *Australian Wives Today*. We have already mentioned her advocacy of improved access to higher education for mature-aged, married women. She was highly critical of the gender divide in teaching and management roles in schools as well as within the promotion hierarchies, and the increased predominance of men through the levels hierarchy in education, from primary to secondary to tertiary. She made a strong argument that would recur in the future, that 'only a small proportion of girls capable of it receive tertiary education'. Being born a girl 'was a hazard girls must surmount in order to be educated'. Educational opportunity was not just about social class and geographical location, 'sex' had to be considered as well.[93]

After writing the draft, Jean asked Ted Jackson to edit it.[94] Presumably his work was useful enough for Jean to decide that he should be named as co-author. The work's significance is encapsulated in a comment by Peggy Mares, a friend of Jean from later in the 1960s:

> It shows how all that time in the 1960s she was raising the same issues through to the end of her life really. Change in that

area was incredibly slow. And she was raising the issue, really of child care ... equal pay and things like that ... And it's that preoccupation with the *system*, and in a sense, that's what made her different from most feminists.[95]

A strange review of the booklet appeared in Helen Palmer's *Outlook*. A weakness of Jean's argument resulted from its attachment to 'the moral standards of the nineteenth century'.[96] This was nonsense really; the reviewer, an old friend of Jean's, apparently confused Jean's concern to ground the argument historically, with a belief that Jean's assumptions about women were of the late nineteenth century. Jean would have been disappointed, but the reception elsewhere was positive, though Dick was not quite convinced. The booklet was taken up in several teachers' colleges as well as being read by the Fabians.

The focuses of the women's movement evolved in the late 1960s, so Jean's booklet represents a statement from a particular moment in history, although the issues that she raised failed to disappear for a very long time. *Australian Wives Today* showed that Jean could still write extended, evidenced, appealingly argued and useful policy-oriented documents, despite not having done much in that line since the 1940s.

In 1963 Jean decided to credential herself for teaching. For a graduate working in secondary education, the one-year Diploma of Education at the University of Adelaide was the obvious means. But a difficulty arose at PGC, Jean's former school. A teacher left unexpectedly, and Jean was needed to take classes. She returned to the school, studying and attending lectures part-time. She was looking after three children (Hugh had yet to begin school). Dick's field work continued to demand long absences from home. All this and teaching was too much, and she came down with pneumonia.[97] Once recovered she pressed on. There was a new challenge at school. Jean was to teach ancient history, a subject that soon fascinated her.

Jean completed her Diploma of Education at the end of 1964. In the next year, Dick and Jean travelled to Europe for three months. On the return to Adelaide there was no place for her at PGC until the beginning of the following year. The heat in the Cold War had lessened and Jean found a term's work in an Education Department girls' technical school. Despite her socialist ideals, presumably prioritising the education of working-class children, she did not like it much. The girls were not as pleasant to teach as the middle-class PGC girls and the staffrooms compared unfavourably. In the write up of an interview, probably with Judy Gill, Jean was reported as saying 'she could not abide the totally anti-intellectual environment of the technical school in which most of the students and a good proportion of the teachers viewed education as a job to be done with minimal effort and even less enthusiasm.'[98] Such observations were likely true enough, but one might also ask how accomplished Jean was as a school teacher. There is not much evidence since doors into classrooms are usually closed. However, there is certainly evidence of girls appreciating her work at PGC. Claire Woods, whom Jean taught in 1963 and 1964, said that Jean was:

> a fantastic teacher of year 12 History at PGC ... [she] taught her [Claire] the power of reason. She said Jean had them all reading *Utopia*, going through it in detail, exploring the ideas and explaining the logic ... she remembered Jean lending her own books ... she made the point, later picked up by others, that Jean never talked down to anyone, treating students as if they were as intelligent as she was.[99]

One of her new Adelaide friends, Denise Bradley, observed some of her lessons. In her words, 'She was an okay teacher but not that great.'[100] Jean thought a great deal about the circumstances of teaching. Good work by teachers is not only dependent on individuals' personalities, previous education and skills, but the circumstances of their schools and school communities. Over these, teachers usually have little control. Later, Jean set about improving them as a policy maker, not only by recommending additional resources but by encouraging teachers to work together, and with their local communities. Jean knew the limits of what could be achieved by teachers working in isolation.

Jean's work for the Diploma of Education went well. It was a long time since she had studied at a university, but as a mature-age student (she was 43 in 1963), she was determined to shine. She gained top distinctions in each of the four main subjects and took out the New Education Fellowship prize. Her reading in education was both prodigious and critical, setting her up for employment in teachers' colleges, and late in the 1960s, working on the first of two Karmel enquiries into education.

According to her daughter, Jean's decision to leave the Communist Party did not result in many changes at home. 'The twelve volumes of the collected works of Lenin, printed in Moscow and bound in bright orange boards, were quietly moved from the bookshelves in the living room to the obscurity of the top shelf in the linen press.'[101] In 1961 there were the Anne Neill revelations in the *Sunday Mail* to be endured. Neill revealed that after joining the Party, Elliott Johnston had said he would take her to meet Jean. Neill ended up a member of the Glenunga branch of the Party where she was indeed 'introduced to Mrs Jean Blackburn, wife of Gerard (Dick)'.[102] In all Jean was mentioned three times in the articles. Perhaps she was lucky that the articles did not appear while she was teaching at PGC. What might the parents of Jean's students have thought? As it was, Jean survived Anne Neill and the *Sunday Mail* relatively unscathed.

In the 1950s through to the mid-1960s Jean had left rentals for her own house with a garden and had found work that she enjoyed, though how reconciled she was to teaching as a long-term occupation is uncertain. She found friends and colleagues with whom she could talk ideas. She had escaped the intellectual rigidities of the Communist Party. Now, as an independent intellectual she could assess the arguments and make her own judgements as never before. She retained older friendships that mattered to her and made new ones who would be important for her future. She survived the worst of Australia's Cold War. She had three children whom she loved. She had written and published a remarkable essay on women and work and had triumphed in her education studies. Jean's daughter Susan recorded the continuities, the presence of the Jean who dated back to the 1920s and 1930s:

> she would sometimes stare dreamily out the kitchen window and spout poems while doing the washing up – mainly Keats and Wordsworth and the romantics. (Bill and I, doing the drying-up, used to squirm with embarrassment.) She kept up with the latest in literature and we often traded books and recommendations together. She also devoured history works and some biography (I recall a lot of discussion about Simone de Beauvoir), plus books about politics and educational philosophy.[103]

Jean was also continuing to manage challenges in her life related to the changing character of her marriage, alarming mood swings, and other bouts of ill health stemming from fatigue. Her deep depressions and then elevated 'highs' were known to friends, but they were mitigated to some degree with their support. Her network of friends, especially those in the universities, would play a key role in assisting Jean in the imminent next stage of her career, the period when she made her most significant contribution to educational policy in Australia.

Chapter 6

CAREER AT LAST, 1967–1973

[My] career, if you can call it that, was accidental and it didn't really take off until I was 50 years old.[1]

I am not for the revolution because I fear its consequences more than I hate a capitalism, which I see some hope of improving.[2]

Jean's career gathered pace once Hugh commenced school in 1963 and she began a teacher preparation program at the University of Adelaide. Her results were outstanding and brought her to the attention of senior staff at Western Teachers College. In the 1960s there was a rapid increase in students at all levels of education, mainly as a result of the post-war baby boom. Demand for teachers, and therefore lecturing staff to provide teacher training, outstripped supply. A former peer at the University of Adelaide, Rae Blessing, was on the education staff at Western. Upon Jean's return from European travel in 1965, Rae recommended Jean to Rod Esselbach, head of Studies in Education.[3] It was to be the first in a series of recommendations that fast-tracked Jean's career. Esselbach in turn put forward Jean's name to Eric Pfitzner, principal of the college, but it was Kevin Gilding, a senior lecturer and progressive educator, who convinced Pfitzner to take her on. George Williams, vice-principal of the college, was worried about her communist background but Jean began teaching at Western in 1967.

Figure 6.1 Jean Blackburn, the teachers college lecturer.
She joined Western Teachers College in 1967 and transferred to the newly opened Bedford Park College in 1969, late 1960s.
Courtesy of Susan Blackburn.

Jean's appointment to Western lasted two years, immersing her in an environment where many of her colleagues and students were, like her, the first in their families to participate in tertiary education. She was there two years. Although groaning under the weight of a rapid increase in student numbers, the staff of the college shared a belief in the emancipatory power of education. It was a culture that reflected a classic teachers' college tradition where the prime job was not research but teaching how to teach.[4] While not academically oriented, Western was responsive to growing social unrest, including opposition to the Vietnam War and the social conservatism of the Playford era in South Australia. It was also a time of growing assertiveness by the teachers' union. A few students, especially those training to be teachers of art, shared the mood, emboldened by radical ideas such as those soon to be contained in *The Little Red School Book*. The miniskirt was in fashion but there were restrictions: female students were not allowed to wear trousers and students signed attendance rolls, on and off, every day. The women's deans attempted to regulate for respectability. Pregnancy led to expulsion from the college and the loss of bonded Education Department allowances.

It was at Western that Jean met Peggy Mares, a fellow lecturer. They began conversations that lasted some thirty years, ranging over topics such as student selection and streaming, education and social control, the economics of education, funding for private schools, and structured learning versus a do-it-yourself curriculum.[5] Margaret Bearlin, a fellow member of WILPF was there too. Jean was on WILPF's South Australian executive in 1967, and soon after became its liaison officer. Margaret had a long involvement with the Student Christian Movement and she expressed an affinity with Jean's communist background because her two brothers were party members: 'For us, our work was politically engaged because we saw education as a political matter and we were both passionate about justice and the way schooling perpetuated inequality'.[6]

Together Jean and Margaret, with colleagues, taught a compulsory year-long course on schooling in society, organised around themes that had a sociological emphasis. This was well before the first sociology of education textbooks concentrating on Australian education were published.[7] Five hundred students took this course each year. Lectures were repeated five times because there was no lecture hall large enough to hold the students. Jean taught about one hundred students in this course, each allocated to one of her ten tutorials. For the most part, Jean found her colleagues and the students at Western stimulating. She enjoyed the experience.[8]

On holidays in the summer of 1967, Jean wrote to Susan: 'I am being revoltingly lazy, ignoring domestic tasks for reading in the periods I get alone … Am also reading in education – a confusing field if ever there was one'. Jean was continually self-educating. Her university studies in education, and now her lectureship required new reading of her. Her personal notes on works by Rousseau, Durkheim, Dewey, and Bruner survive. R. S. Peters was her 'pin-up educational philosopher'. Jean attended one of his lectures while he toured Australia. He confirmed Jean's view that in courses on education, 'the starting point is practical problems and that you lead into more theoretical depths as you go on'.[9] Jean was also a keen reader of *New Society*, a weekly magazine for the social sciences launched in 1956 as a companion to the *New Scientist*.

Jean found comfort in C. Day Lewis's confession in his autobiography that 'he was not up to much as an academic since he tended to agree with each person as he read'.[10] Yet, her stated affinity with Lewis belied her capacity for critical analysis. Certainly, she often agreed with, or at least empathised with whomever she was reading or conversing, but once she had formed a defensible position, based upon what she considered to be the best available evidence, she held firm. It was an essential attribute when Jean came to work on the South Australian Enquiry into education. If a solid body of relevant research existed, the argument was sure, and she would favour action over further research.

Jean's return to work in the 1960s coincided with a crisis in education in South Australia, resulting from overcrowded schools, large class sizes, inequalities in the resources available to students in different schools, limited curriculum choices, authoritarian relations between teachers and students, a lack of parental involvement in school decision-making, and discontent among teachers over their pay and working conditions.[11] These problems were long in the making, not just in South Australia but the nation as a whole. The increasing birth rate and immigration that followed the Second World War contributed to what W. F. Connell referred to as an 'education explosion' between 1960 and 1970. The population increased by 22 per cent from 10.4 million to 12.7 million, and the number of school students increased by one third, from 2.1 million to 2.78 million.[12] In addition, the proportion of sixteen-year-olds staying on at school rose from 22 per cent in 1956, to 40 per cent in 1964, and 51 per cent in 1970.

Anticipating what was to follow, in 1958 the Australian Education Council, comprised of the six state ministers of education, commissioned a survey to trace the gap between the rapidly growing demand for education and what they could provide. Their subsequent submissions to the federal government in the 1960s were aimed at securing more support for government schools. While the Menzies government contributed by funding the construction of science laboratories and the succeeding Holt government, school libraries, the general under-resourcing did not improve: 'the proportion of GDP devoted to education was well below that of major OECD (Organisation for Economic Co-operation and Development) countries: 3.9 per cent in Australia in 1969–70 compared to 7.7 in Canada, 4.5 in France, 4.2

in Germany, 7.1 in Sweden and 6 per cent in the United States'.[13] In South Australia, the gap between the needs of schools and the amount of capital and recurrent funding needed was estimated to be $200 million in 1970. 'There is little doubt that the problem was more acute for South Australia than for other states: it had 9.4 per cent of the Australian population but 11 per cent of school enrolments, while 86 per cent of its students were in government schools – the highest percentage in the country.'[14]

After 32 years in opposition, the Labor Party governed in South Australia from March 1965 until September 1979, except for the two years from March 1968 to May 1970. During this interregnum, the electoral bias that had valued rural over urban votes and had contributed to keeping Labor out of office for decades, was reformed by the incoming Liberal and Country League (LCL) government. Joyce Steele was appointed Minister for Education, the first woman elevated to a cabinet position in South Australia. Steele had been a long-time advocate of government assistance for the educational needs of children with disabilities. Although conservative, and 'out of sympathy with the more confronting aspects of second-wave feminism', while in the education portfolio, she ended the bar against married women trainee teachers.[15] She expanded the provision of schools and teachers, and established regional education offices. Even so, there was a large and growing gap between the state's educational needs and available funding. She was caught both by Treasury restraint and administrative resistance to reform.[16] Her main relevance for Jean's career was that it was she who implemented a key election promise of the new LCL government, to hold an enquiry into South Australian education.[17]

The Committee of Enquiry into Education in South Australia was appointed on January 29, 1969. Its terms of reference were:

To examine, and to report and make recommendations to the Minister on:

(i) the whole education system of the State in order to determine the most effective use of resources available to the State for education;

(ii) the organisation of the Education Department, including the organisation of teacher training;

(iii) means by which curricula and teaching methods of the schools of the Education Department can be kept under continuing review.[18]

Jean's contacts with University of Melbourne economics graduates living in Adelaide were influential in her appointment to the Enquiry. They included Peter Karmel, Vice-Chancellor at Flinders University, and Eric Russell, Professor of Economics and Geoffrey Harcourt, Senior Lecturer in Economics, both at the University of Adelaide. When Karmel was appointed to lead the Enquiry, he talked to Harcourt about who might work with him. Harcourt recommended Jean, knowing of her results in the Diploma of Education, and her other qualities.[19] It was Eric Russell who let Jean know that Karmel would request that she be released to work with him on the Enquiry.[20]

At this key juncture in her career, Jean's progress relied upon the recognition, respect, but also goodwill of males. James Richardson, the founding principal of the newly opened teachers' college at Bedford Park, down the hill from the not much older Flinders University, invited Jean in early 1969 to take up a lectureship there. The college was 'up the totem pole in that time'.[21] About six weeks after she started, the call came from Karmel. Richardson initially

Figure 6.2 Eric and Judith Russell, close friends of Jean.
Eric supported Jean several years earlier as she left the Communist Party.
He was an economist, one of three or four at the University of Adelaide,
without whose assistance Jean's national career may never have taken off. 1968.
Courtesy of Susan Blackburn.

agreed and then retracted once he realised that Karmel wanted Jean to start almost immediately. On Karmel's urging, Jean suggested a replacement to Richardson which he accepted. Soon after, Jean was seconded as a 'research secretary' to the Enquiry, commencing in April 1969 and continuing until the middle of 1971.[22] She could not surrender all her responsibilities at Bedford Park however. In a letter to Susan in August 1970, Jean wrote that she was marking essays and preparing for school visits, as well as finalising first drafts of chapters for the Enquiry's report.[23]

Jean's appointment to the Enquiry marked the commencement of a working partnership with Peter Karmel that became the defining collaboration of her career. Jean thought that Karmel was 'very brilliant'.[24] Karmel described himself in later years as 'not a hard-line economic rationalist type economist, more an old-fashioned Keynesian welfare-type economist'. He acknowledged that Jean did a lot of the writing for the subsequent report, and was influential because she was an 'extremely intelligent, balanced sort of person and writes well ... she wants kids to emerge from school who can read and write and reason. She's not a sort of "softie" at all, she's not all tears in the eyes and this sort of thing.'[25] The context of statements such as these are that the 1960s saw the beginning of a new phase of progressive and 'alternative' curriculum and school reform.

The Enquiry continued through June 1970 when Don Dunstan was elected premier in a new Labor government in South Australia. Hugh Hudson, another economics lecturer at the University of Adelaide, was appointed Minister of Education. Jean was happy: 'Now I am a member of a party in power. It feels great'.[26] Although Hudson indicated that no major moves would be made on education until the Enquiry had completed its report, this was not what happened. Along with a reforming Minister, there was a new reforming Director-General of Education, A. W. (Albie) Jones. Jean was soon writing that 'changes in the Department follow almost daily, mostly in accordance with what we were recommending, and the report will be old hat before it is printed'.[27]

Jean thought that the report was 'rather dull' but nonetheless important because it had revealed so much about schooling and the ways of the Education Department that had neither been collected nor made public before. W. F. Connell provided a similar assessment, describing the report as 'large, thorough, [and] indigestible'.[28] Jean encountered resistance from bureaucrats in the Department who 'hugged its information to its bosom', but over the course of the

Enquiry she developed some sympathy towards them, 'because over all those years of great defensiveness ... they were so hard pressed for staff and money'. Jean recalled: 'I rooted out ... every bit of information I could lay hands on and made it public, and that was good'.[29]

Some of the information that the Enquiry wanted was not hidden – it was simply not available, or only partially so. For example, when Jean was asked to estimate the number of children attending pre-school education in 1969, including the qualifications of staff and sources of funding, she only had access to figures for children in the 129 centres affiliated with the Kindergarten Union (KU), the organisation with responsibility for distributing government funds for pre-school education. However, there were 279 centres, both KU and independent, that were drawing free milk in South Australia, and Jean figured that if she could access the free milk lists, she could estimate the number of children enrolled in all pre-schools.[30] Universally provided free milk was a contribution by governments to child nutrition in this period. Not all families according to health professionals at the time could be relied upon to feed their children sensibly. The pre-schools not affiliated with the KU were each sent a questionnaire to gather additional information and so complete the data set required for the Enquiry.

Jean found these challenges 'exciting'. She enlisted the help of a young geographer to create a social ranking by occupation of Adelaide suburbs from census data, and then compared this ranking with retention rates, the award of Commonwealth secondary and tertiary scholarships by school, and the subsidies paid to schools. Such research built on the skills she had developed in the Department of War Organisation of Industry over twenty-five years earlier. Jean was aware of the research into social inequality in education undertaken in preceding years by James Coleman in the United States and Bridget Plowden in the United Kingdom.[31] Despite her careful planning, it was perhaps the novelty of the process that contributed to Jean's uncertainties about some of her conclusions in the writing. To Susan she wrote: 'Hope some pattern emerges'.[32]

The scope and pressures of the Enquiry were considerable. Karmel telephoned 'at odd times with some new idea to follow up'. Jean described Karmel as 'a great figures man' and herself as 'the theoretical analyst'.[33] They worked well together, appreciating each other's different skills. They shared similar values and strongly believed that 'public policy should benefit those who were least well off'. At the time, Jean described her work on the Enquiry in these terms:

> I write the descriptive stuff, present the evidence, raise the issues requiring policy decision and state pros and cons. When the committee has made its decisions and hacked my draft to bits I rewrite and seek out further material they think relevant.[34]

There were times when Jean relied upon Karmel's technical expertise to manage the data. In her usual self-deprecating way, she wrote that Karmel 'Makes me realise how fifth rate I am'.[35] But she also felt comforted that he occasionally struggled to get things right.

> I am still feeling rather incompetent about my work for the Committee of Enquiry. I seem to put in a lot of time and not get very far. I am drafting the chapter on class size and teacher qualifications. For such a publication you can't afford to make any mistakes. I am a bit cheered in a nasty way because the sophisticated calculations done by Karmel and Hirst [a consultant to the enquiry] predicting student numbers have turned out to be seriously at fault now we have, at last, the 1969 figure from the Department ... statistical techniques are only as useful as the assumption on which they are based.[36]

It was not only that Jean felt pressed with work, too slow and like 'a muddler', there was a huge amount of data to manage – in a time when personal computers did not exist. In 1970, she received on loan from Ian Hayward, a member of the Enquiry, a 'beautiful electronic desk calculator'. She wrote to Susan that she hardly knew how she had ever done without it. Her negotiations with the Bureau of Census and Statistics about the coding of occupations for the tertiary entrance study alerted her to the benefits of mainframe computers, and their potential to 'provide much fascinating information'. An example of the kind of information that she thought computers might organise were the qualifications of men and women teaching students in their final year of secondary school. Jean was interested in the degree to which teachers' qualifications matched the subject areas they taught.[37]

Figure 6.3 Working on the first of the Karmel reports, the South Australian Enquiry into education (1969–1970). Summer holidays in January 1969 were at Moana beach, south of Adelaide, but Jean – as researcher, writer and consultant to the enquiry – had little time to relax.
Courtesy of Susan Blackburn.

The Enquiry dealt with many submissions on a range of matters that Jean admitted to knowing little about. This presented a challenge, since Jean considered herself to be 'the grand scale argument type'.[38] She supplemented her professional knowledge by attending lectures given by visiting experts and continuing to read widely. School visits broadened her understanding of the constraints and possibilities of schooling, as did her efforts to support Hugh when the Unley High School administration was 'coming down on him for not very much'.

> I hate the whole establishment and am sad that there seems to be no alternative. Saw a tremendously exciting non-graded primary school yesterday. You don't have to teach kids in the way Unley does.[39]

The enquiry into education in South Australia broadened Jean's knowledge of schooling in ways that would later help to define her contribution as a schools commissioner at the national level: 'The Committee is regarding what goes on IN the classroom as beyond its terms of reference, and I am coming to the conclusion [that] nothing else matters much'.[40] She followed up:

> It's the spirit and attitude of teachers that takes first place ... Read Blishen's *Roaring Boys*. A more realistic, less sensational book about teaching in a slum school than *To Sir with Love*, which conveys a real concern and compassion without condescension and a wry awareness of the limited influence of schools and teachers.[41]

Jean ended up writing seven of the 18 chapters, as well as the summary of the final South Australian report. She had to rewrite another two chapters drafted by others. By the time it was almost complete, she conceded that she was 'Heartily sick of whole report'.[42] Paradoxically she also felt sad that it was over, mainly because she 'enjoyed very much working so closely with Karmel who is both a very able and a good man'. Jean knew that her future was in education, but she was not drawn to any return to teaching; 'the tedium of listening to all those half-baked ideas and complaints, and reading cartloads of mediocre material plays a large part in this'. She admitted that the experience of working on the Enquiry had reinforced something she had learnt about herself while working in War Organisation of Industry, 'that in spite of my constant self-distrust I have some ability in imposing structure on masses of material and I enjoy doing it'.[43]

The *Report of the Committee of Enquiry into Education in South Australia 1969–1970* was one of five reports in as many years prepared by committees set up by state and federal governments between 1969 and 1973.[44] They grappled with a range of issues, including balancing the demands on schools to prepare workers, citizens, and self-fulfilled individuals through to issues such as examinations and streaming. Two features distinguished the South Australian report from others: its scope, which covered pre-school to tertiary education, and its 'admirable chapter on equality of opportunity in education' which attempted to explain why 'many inequalities exist within the provision of apparently equal opportunities'.[45]

Jean was interested in demonstrating the very different outcomes obtained from schooling by children in different areas of Adelaide. She was aware that several members of the committee thought that the reason for this was self-evident. Then, as now, beliefs about success at school were based upon assumptions about the combined impact of factors deriving from genetic and socio-economic attributes, sometimes referred to as the question of nature versus nurture.

Jean described the situation at the time, when arguments about the influence of nature or intelligence (measured as IQ), held sway:

> You either had it or you didn't have it and you could tell very early whether you had it or not, that was pretty unvarying throughout life, so they said. I knew in my bones that that was wrong. Well after all, I guessed that I would have had an IQ of 50 or something, had I been tested at age five.[46]

Jean was determined to show that educational achievement was related to a child's circumstances and not determined by IQ alone. A clear correlation emerged in the mapping she conducted into the link between educational outcomes and socio-economic factors for different areas of Adelaide. It gave her the opportunity to argue for a new educational program in areas where there were high levels of disadvantage, which she did with Karmel's full support. The two shared the view 'that public policy should advantage most those whose private resources were least'.[47] While many of the Enquiry's recommendations were followed, some were not, notably a recommended disadvantaged schools program and an education advisory board, on which would have been parents, teachers, and community members.

Jean argued that the report was not 'educational' in the sense that it did anything much about big issues in education. It was mainly concerned with resources, the kind of resources that might support teachers to become more adventurous by lightening their workloads and providing them with more equipment and support staff. However, it did provide the detailed and carefully constructed statistical analyses that provided the rationale for the desperately needed redistribution of available resources, 'to bring about actual equality of opportunity where it does not now exist'.[48]

Reflecting on why the Enquiry took place two decades later, Jean cited the entrenched authoritarianism in secondary schools that contradicted more recent theories of child rearing and development. Over the course of the Enquiry, she amassed a great deal of material; she 'mostly did the ferreting out' of information for the report.[49] Karmel told her that she should have received an honorary doctorate for her work. She doubted that others would have found it as fascinating as she, and she still believed that she was 'much better at criticising than at being confident about what ought to be done'.[50]

Most of the recommendations that Jean felt strongly about were accepted by the Enquiry, but her efforts to change its social analysis failed. In her view, the analysis was 'crap'.[51] Jean admitted that she did not know how to find answers to lots of questions, such as for what size enrolment the state government should be obliged to offer full secondary courses in country South Australia.[52] This was an important issue because it cut to the heart of her concern about the impact of social disadvantage on educational outcomes. The conundrum appeared in the report.

> Given a certain sum of money, should it be spent on making more opportunities available to those now able to use them, thereby probably making more of their potential and, hopefully, benefiting society through the operation of their more highly developed skills? Or should it be spent on remedying the deficiencies of those now less able to use the opportunities, thereby bring more of the populations up to some designated level of proficiency but not developing the higher skills of others.[53]

The chapter 'Equality of Opportunity in Education' was written by William Radford, the Director of the Australian Council for

Educational Research (ACER). Radford emphasised individual differences and Jean conceded that it was 'the period of each to his full potential ... though they were all male'.[54] Even so, the report had recommended a disadvantaged schools program, arguing that success at school was due to a combination of hereditary and environmental forces. For the time, Radford provided a nuanced account of the influence of hereditary forces: 'Because a variable has a genetic component it does not imply that environmental influences cannot affect growth'.[55] However, 'genetic endowments' were assumed to explain specific variations in success at school, such as intelligence and reading ability, and social disadvantage was understood almost entirely in deficit terms. Jean railed against the 'blame' that was attached to parents, families and communities who experienced social disadvantage for the lack of success of their children at school.

Using the completed report of the Enquiry as his blue print, the Minister of Education, Hugh Hudson, introduced a policy of comprehensive secondary schooling. Unimpressed by courses of study followed by technical high schools as alternatives to the Public Examinations Board syllabuses, Hudson sought to create a single type of school that provided a range of courses allowing pupils to progress in different subjects at different rates.[56] South Australia and Victoria held on to their technical schools longer than other states and Jean would be involved in the demise of technical schools in both. For decades technical schools in Australia had struggled to provide young people with an education and credentials that were valued as highly as those in the high schools. The technical schools had their defenders, but by the 1970s there was a growing feeling that they provided working-class youth with inferior opportunities, if not always an inferior education.[57]

Jean's views on acceptable forms of secondary schooling for working-class children firmed up during her work for the Enquiry. They were possibly influenced by the 1957 Wyndham Report in New South Wales, which argued that the curriculum for the years of compulsory secondary education should be general, not vocational.[58] Fifteen years later, Jean's Victorian 'Blackburn Report' (1985) was consistent with her earlier thinking. Bipartite systems, especially the technical schools, functioned to reduce opportunities for disadvantaged and working-class children regardless of the potential for curriculum innovation, community links and the relationships with local employers that were sometimes a feature of these schools.[59]

Back at Bedford Park Teachers College, soon to become the Sturt College of Advanced Education, Jean became the staff representative on Council, head of faculty, and was promoted to senior lecturer. Though involved in restructuring the education courses, she was 'hard put to reply' to the question: 'What must teachers know?'

> Apart from some reasonably deep acquaintance with at least one discipline, I would want people to be able to recognise what questions were empirical questions, and proceed to test them, and how to cope with considering propositions that were not empirical. Beyond that I am pretty much of a pragmatist about teaching. You need to know what you are trying to do, and do what works.[60]

Jean was often frustrated: 'Our course is a dead loss ... Unless some radical change can be effected I shall look for another job. I am rather off teaching anyway. Sick of talking and listening and reading semi-literate muck'.[61] The frustrations as well as satisfactions come and go with teaching, but it was more than this with Jean. After the Enquiry she found it difficult settling back into college work.

In 1971, Jean attended a philosophy of education conference. She was 'very impressed by the tone of discussion among these philosophers – disagreement without imputing motives, attaching labels and all the rest'. She had come to the view that 'Most of the difficult things which bug me about education – nature of knowledge, basis for dividing it, status of knowledge claims, ethical questions – are all philosophical problems, and all are very interesting'.[62]

Responses to the report of the Enquiry ranged from very critical to praise. She met Hugh Stretton socially and he reassured her about some of the radical left criticism of the report. He said: 'the only thing wrong with me [Jean] was that I valued the advances in understanding that the efforts of men over a long period had made possible and bully for that'. But things were never simple for Jean. She was changing her attitude to compulsory schooling. It was possible that it had achieved too little and had been 'positively harmful in many ways'. At the same time, you could not leave children to the mercy of their family backgrounds. Deschooling society would likely serve few but the social elite.[63] Jean evaluated the contribution of the social sciences to such questions as they had developed during the 1960s. She was suspicious of sociology and except for explicit studies into particular questions, she found it mostly 'hog-wash'. She imagined that she agreed with Hugh Stretton on this. She had a similar lack of regard for political science; it made her appreciate her background in economics.[64]

One of Jean's colleagues asked her to collaborate on some research papers. Jean thought that together they could make a 'reasonable team' but her ideas about research were heading in a different direction:

> I am becoming more and more bored with the details of empirical study, and am not interested in research which seems to me

to be pedantic and futile, undertaken merely for qualifications. I should still like to do something on education of girls, but in-depth interview with a sample of early school leavers rather than through questionnaire, about which I am increasingly suspicious as a means of finding out what people think and feel.[65]

At the Bedford Park Teachers College, there were new and old colleagues. In 1972 Kevin Gilding from Western Teachers College and Tess Caust, one of Jean's earliest Adelaide friends, were on the staff. Jean was older than most of her immediate teaching colleagues, a senior figure to the mainly young men who taught with her. Dean Ashenden taught history at the college. He and Jean began to talk education and more, the beginnings of an enduring friendship. Jim Walker was there, Jean thinking of him as a 'special mate'.[66] Dean took Jean to a meeting to hear Humphrey McQueen: 'he was more rhetoric than rationality'. Dean tried to persuade her to attend a panel for the Radical Education Association on the report of the Enquiry. Her diffidence derived in part from receiving the association's latest newsletter; apparently 'schools existed to serve the capitalists'.[67] Dean and others like Ken Bridge were on the left, the New Left in terms of politics and education. Jean occasionally enjoyed the arguments, but she was not convinced of the new radicalism, the re-vitalised Marxist approaches to the world's problems. The generational differences, and sex imbalance gave her pause for thought:

> A lone middle-aged woman among twelve young men is somewhat difficult too. I find them rather childish in their perpetual chaffing. They are very kind and friendly to me, and always ask me to the pub with them afterwards, one thing which used to infuriate me at Western was the mysterious

disappearance of the men at various times, no woman ever being asked to accompany them.[68]

Dean remembered her as generous to the ratbags of the left. She liked that they were 'having a go'.[69] At some point in 1969 Jean was astounded to discover that an Old Left friend, Graham Smith, had received a half-time scholarship to complete his degree. He took a politics unit – on socialist ideas from the utopians, through Marx to the present. Not that many years previously Jean and Graham had been excoriated in the press for being communist teachers, and Jean had found it impossible to get an appointment in a public school. Now the Education Department was paying Graham to study socialism!

Jean looked on with interest as former Presbyterian Girls College students and some of her daughter's friends began making their reputations in the new feminism. Jean reported to Susan that Anna Yeatman, the daughter of Jean's doctor, was writing for the New Left journal, *Arena*. On occasion Jean met with Anne Summers, unhappy after leaving her marriage.[70] Jean's response to the new feminism was mixed. Women who had children should not be a problem for feminism. She thought that the 'sex war is the most bitter and futile of all wars ... I cannot help feeling that a lot of the contributions in *Sisterhood is Powerful* [a book she was reading], are nothing more than the outpourings of personal spite.'[71]

Publicity surrounding an old Unley High friend of Susan bemused her: Anne McMenamin's threat, only a threat, to publicly burn a live dog was a protest against the Vietnam War and no doubt, the use of napalm against humans.[72] Jean's economist friend Geoff Harcourt was at the centre of efforts in Adelaide to organise resistance to the Vietnam War. Jean was not that active, but she did go to some meetings of the Campaign for Peace in Vietnam, one of them to support Geoff Harcourt's bid for leadership.[73] ASIO noted her presence at other anti-Vietnam War meetings a little earlier as agents continued to follow Maud McBriar's activities, mainly in the meetings of the Women's League for Peace and Freedom. Judith Russell's activities were noted also.[74] Later, Jean felt torn as Bob Hall, a teachers college student refused to be conscripted for the war. She felt sorry for Eric Pfitzner, now Principal of Adelaide Teachers College, having to deal with the matter. Jean supported Hall in the end. She wrote about the moratorium campaign a year later. She marched in the great demonstration that occupied a city intersection, and after which many arrests followed.[75] The Labor Party had withdrawn its support for the event as the campaign was taken over by radical students. Jean wrote that they were 'more intent with smashing imperialism and capitalism than with winning support for stopping the war'.[76]

At home, Jean continued her exasperation with having to support Hugh in completing homework that reflected the 'most unimaginative' ways in which he was taught, 'mostly learning this and that by heart'. You should not 'subject your child to such rotten teaching'. She was tempted to send him to Scotch College where a new head was reputedly doing the kind of things that met with her approval.[77]

In the later part of 1972, Jean took an extended period of leave due to ulcers in her abdomen. It didn't stop her from reading and she declared herself a logical positivist after reading a Penguin book on positivist philosophy.[78] She had decided to study philosophy the following year, because she was 'more and more convinced of the limits of empiricism'. This period of intellectual ferment was reinforced by debates that raged over the South Australian Karmel report. The criticisms by radical educators and students that it had not gone far enough left her dispirited. She had little time for the claim that 'the system' should be 'smashed and schools dissolved'.[79]

In the early 1970s in Australia, about 80 percent of all children aged 5–14 were enrolled in public schools. The remaining included about 15 percent in systemic Catholic schools, and 5 percent in high-fee non-government schools. There were great disparities between and within these systems. Systemic Catholic schools were chronically underfunded, with their problems growing worse with the 'very rapid decrease in numbers of Catholic religious brothers and nuns, existing on a pittance, who had made their schools financially possible. The exodus was continuing, and costs were rising faster than the rate of inflation. If Catholic schools were to continue there was no obvious avenue of rescue other than Commonwealth government grants'.[80] The Goulburn school strike in 1962, where Catholic schools closed temporarily, sending their students to the local public schools was an early warning of the developing crisis.

Jean accepted that in comparison with similar nations, Australian schools were starved of funds.[81] Despite a tripling in Commonwealth and States spending on all forms of education in the ten years prior to 1972, inner-city public schools and many schools in rural areas remained deeply under-resourced. The issue of whether state aid should be provided to non-government schools had been a live issue in Australia from colonial times. It had led to a split in the New South Wales Labor Party in 1963, the same year that Prime Minister Robert Menzies had attempted to capitalise on the division by promising funding for science blocks for non-government and government schools alike. Funding for school libraries followed. In

1969, non-government schools received recurrent grants from the Commonwealth, and in 1972, government and non-government schools received capital grants. The Liberal-Country Party Coalition had resisted making recurrent grants to government schools despite a national survey commissioned by the states in 1970 that projected massive deficits for public and non-government schools alike.[82]

In his 1967 Curtin Lecture, Sam Cohen, who had attended the University of Melbourne at the same time as Jean and had been a student leader of the left, proposed an education policy which provided a basis for the reforms of the Whitlam government five years later. Cohen 'acknowledged the failure of the system to establish and guarantee equality of opportunity for every child'. He argued the need 'for a national enquiry into all aspects of primary, secondary and technical education, in both government and non-government schools', a policy for which the Labor Party had been unable to gain support while in opposition.[83]

Conflict over the ban on state aid to non-government schools had to be resolved if the Labor Party was to succeed in winning federal elections. Through the efforts of Gough Whitlam and his allies, the anti-state aid plank was removed from Labor's platform during its 1969 annual conference. There, the Party also resolved to create an Australian Schools Commission to assess the needs of students in all schools and make recommendations for funding based on their needs and priorities.[84] Jean described the process and its policy implications: 'Whitlam was a crucial influence in transforming sectarian issues in school funding into class issues of appeal to the ALP, and in associating the needs of public and Catholic schools as aspects of social justice'.[85] Improving the circumstances of children in parochial Catholic schools was part of the Labor Party's strategy of eliminating the continuing electoral damage posed by the Catholic-associated Democratic Labor Party (DLP). On reflection, Jean criticised the lack of forward planning that should have defined any ongoing responsibility of the Commonwealth for funding non-government schools once the immediate resourcing crisis was averted.

The national election on December 2, 1972 brought the Labor Party to government once more after 23 long years. Its electoral success was in no small part due to its education policies. The day after winning office, the new Prime Minister, Gough Whitlam, asked Peter Karmel to chair the promised national enquiry to be conducted by an Interim Committee for the Australian Schools Commission. Whitlam was reportedly impressed by Karmel's work on the South Australian report, including the attention it gave to the impact of socio-economic differences on schooling outcomes. Karmel accepted on the condition that Jean Blackburn was also appointed.[86] According to Kim Beazley Snr, the soon to be appointed Minister of Education, 'Karmel said he must have Mrs Blackburn'.[87] The phone call from Canberra was received, and Jean accepted the invitation to work with Karmel on the new report, this time it would be a national report on school education, its reform and funding.[88]

Jean had worked so hard for relatively little recognition on the South Australian Enquiry that she insisted on being appointed as a member of rather than a consultant to the Interim Committee. Karmel made sure that she was offered the position of Deputy Chair. Dick was supportive, recognising it as an acknowledgement of her work in South Australia. However, when Jean engaged a 'cleaning lady' in preparation for her absences in Canberra, she wrote to Susan saying that Dick seemed 'very gloomy' about it all.[89]

Other members of the Interim Committee were selected by Whitlam as initial Minister for Education, before the Labor caucus met to approve a ministry. There was no formal process of calling for nominations. Nevertheless, the committee was composed of people from various sectors, including state departments of education in New South Wales, Victoria and South Australia, personnel of the Catholic and other non-government schools, and a university dean of education.[90] They 'may well not have been the people that the organisations themselves preferred', but they were representative enough. This method of appointment gave them the advantage of not having any obligation to represent the views of nominating organisations.[91] Karmel and the government also benefited from this.

Jean was the only full-time female member of the Committee.[92] When she arrived in Canberra to begin work, she was asked to wait in a room on her own. An ASIO officer arrived and read aloud relevant sections of the Crimes Act. He asked her to sign a document saying that she was aware of the provisions in the Act. Jean inquired if this was a routine procedure. He responded, 'No, not to everyone. We're doing it to you because you know that in the normal course of events you would never have had such a job in the Government'.[93] The 'normal' course of events to which he was referring was the long period from 1949, the Cold War, when the vehemently anti-communist Liberal Party had been in government.

The Interim Committee was required to complete its report by the end of April 1973, so it would be available before the new government's first budget. During the four and a half months it took to complete the report, Jean was based in Canberra, returning home to Adelaide every second weekend. She worked seven days a week, waking at 4.30am to get started early. She was single-minded in her approach. While in Canberra, she stayed at University House.[94] The small team who produced the report worked in offices located in the Universities Commission and the Reserve Bank. They often worked into the early hours of the morning.[95] Since Karmel maintained his position as Chairman of the Universities Commission, the heavy work of the Interim Committee often fell upon Jean and the other full-time member, Greg Hancock, who had been recommended because of his expertise in financial costing.[96] According to Jean, 'Hancock was basically in charge of data collection and I was shut up in a room to write which I did. I stumbled my way through all the arguments about the values of the Committee, the discussion of equality of opportunity and I guess the main argumentation of the Report'.[97]

Karmel and Jean met each day in his office for lunch. Jean recalled, 'I would produce a draft and give it to Peter. And Peter would say "What do you think about it?" and if I said, "I don't feel I've got it right," he'd just give it back and I would have another go'.[98] Jean acknowledged that these kinds of projects were, in the end, collective endeavours, and that some very important ideas came from other members of the Committee.[99] At the same time, the burden of responsibility Jean felt for getting things right produced a kind of isolation. Dean Ashenden thought of her as 'an intellectually lonely figure ... Because basically she'd thought harder, more carefully, more scrupulously about most of those things [considered by the Interim Committee] than almost anyone else around the place'.[100]

The work of the Committee was not limited to Canberra. Its members visited government, Catholic and other non-government schools in metropolitan and country areas in every state, and the Australian Capital Territory: 91 metropolitan and 52 country schools.

They met and received submissions from many organisations and individuals. Jean recalled that the most impressive person interviewed was a Joan Kirner, the President of the State School Parents' Federation of Australia, and its president in Victoria. Jean thought that Joan and the Federation were alone in advocating that schools be more democratically run at the local level. Jean went on to develop a longstanding working friendship with Joan, a future premier of Victoria. Representatives of the anti-state aid organisation, Defend Our Government Schools (DOGS) also spoke with Karmel and Jean. The DOGS representatives were unimpressed; they knew the enemy when they saw it. Later, DOGS mounted a constitutional challenge to the new state aid to church-owned and run schools that the Interim Committee was about to recommend.[101] The Interim Committee compiled a nationwide database to compare the resources of schools of all kinds. Its terms of reference required that it set a target for improvement over a certain period and recommend to the Commonwealth government its allocation of funds. The committee decided that resources alone were insufficient, recommending the introduction of special purpose programs, such as for disadvantaged schools, innovation and teacher development. Jean recognised their significance; it was 'the first time in the history of Australian education that people other than bureaucrats [would be] empowered to make decisions and to be funded to get on and do it'.[102]

The Interim Committee's terms of reference presented a challenge to the newly established federal Department of Education. A Schools Commission would mean that it had fewer decisions to make and less influence to wield. This was not an unintended outcome. Jean's experience working on the South Australian report was that education bureaucrats had been defensive and secretive.[103] Karmel too considered that major changes in education policy were more likely to be produced by public committees and reports rather than by discussion papers from ministerial staff and bureaucrats, 'many of whom are generalists, who often don't know a great deal about it and who change their jobs pretty often'.[104]

There was sufficient 'give' in the Interim Committee's terms of reference for elaboration on the rationales for its funding proposals. While Whitlam had informally expressed a view that high-fee non-government schools should not receive government assistance, there were no formal directions as to what the Committee might recommend.[105] *Education in South Australia* had 'written off the private schools altogether and said they were private business'. Jean had thought there was no alternative in South Australia because so many schools, particularly parochial Catholic schools, were so 'monstrously underfunded' the state government could not afford to take responsibility for them.[106] Nationally though, it was possible to do something. Jean believed that the situation in many of these schools was intolerable: it 'was unfair to the kids and it was bad for the country'.[107] Jean described the conditions of inner-city schools in Sydney and Melbourne, many of them public, as 'disgraceful – class sizes were high, teachers' qualifications low, libraries poorly resourced, and there were many more students than could be adequately accommodated'.[108]

Jean believed that one of the significant achievements of the Interim Committee's report, *Schools in Australia*, was that for 'the first time schools of all kinds and everywhere were compared'.[109] The emerging approaches to funding and spending accountability wrought by the Interim Committee extended beyond the public system. The recommendations pushed Catholic education in Australia towards further systematisation as standardised data collection was required.

This could only occur with the establishment of offices at both state and national levels. Previously the administration and governance of Catholic schools had usually been located in diocesan offices and the provinces of the various religious congregations. 'The scattered and uncoordinated nature of these administrative units … made it difficult to collect and interpret comparable data on which to base a coherent account of the total "system" of Catholic education in Australia'.[110]

The terms of reference did not require the Interim Committee to comment on the quality of education or define equality of opportunity. Instead, it was to deliver on the Labor election commitment to fairer schools funding. 'The grip of resources in the political mind was absolute'. For teacher unions this was the core of the case for why new federal funding was needed for public schools. However, the Interim Committee was asked to 'work towards establishing acceptable standards for those schools, government and non-government schools alike, which fall short of those standards'.[111] This allowed the Interim Committee to make recommendations concerning the needs of particular groups of students, not just in terms of resources but also changed approaches to schooling.

When asked if an economist was 'indispensable' for the task set for the Interim Committee, Peter Karmel acknowledged that its recommendations were 'very resource-oriented and very input-oriented'. Hence, 'it was quite appropriate given this that they looked for somebody with some economic background because one thing economics is about is the allocation of resources'. Jean described the role of economists, and the commitment she believed she shared with Karmel, in similar but more political terms: economists 'could contribute to better distributions of wealth'. Jean believed that both she and Karmel were reformists, and that this was evidenced by their shared 'commitment to what later became the Disadvantaged Schools Program ... that meant having the smallest classes and best equipment and all the rest of it in the areas where the least advantaged kids were at school'.[112]

Jean believed that one of the reasons why Karmel was 'a terrific chairman' was that he never went into 'a meeting without mapping the agenda'. One of the most complex issues for these agendas related to the question of whether funding should address educational needs, or support parental choice of school. Karmel recognised that the Interim Committee's commitment to equality of opportunity meant that funds would be injected into all kinds of schools because it adopted the position that 'the kids who had least outside the school should have more within it', and it showed 'that kids who needed the best schools had the worst'.[113] Karmel accepted therefore, that a degree of school choice would be a consequence. Funding would go to non-government schools, thereby supporting the ability of some parents to choose these schools instead of a government school. Karmel knew that this was 'somewhat inconsistent with a commitment to try to equalise resources in opportunity terms'. It meant that there would be less money available to address the needs of children of parents who were not able to exercise such choice, perhaps due to their location or income.[114]

The Committee recommended that funding to well-resourced non-government schools be phased out. This was the position that Whitlam favoured – but the new minister, Kim Beazley viewed this as a broken election promise. According to Jean, the whole committee agreed to the phasing out recommendation and they thought that the draft was 'terrific'. At the same time, she also recalled that there were objections to a draft chapter, 'The Justification for and Limits of State Aid to Private Schools', and it did not appear in the report.[115]

The physical report ran to an economical 168 pages made up of three sections. Part 1, 'Background', outlined the existing Commonwealth commitment to education, summarising the contributions from government and private sources. The chapter 'Trends and Conditions' detailed the background to conditions of schools across Australia. It compared differences in enrolments, teacher qualifications and expenditure between sectors, states, and sometimes school levels.

The removal of the chapter that provided a justification for Commonwealth funding of non-government schools, as well as its limits, meant that the arguments concerning state aid were left to the chapters titled 'Values and Perspectives' and 'Equality of Opportunity'. They conveyed the Committee's rationalisation for its recommendations and described how it had assessed the financial needs of schools. The scale of the task was neatly summarised as occurring in 'a period of considerable educational uncertainty and ferment'. Indeed, the fabric of schooling, its patterns of control and organisation, and the outcomes it sought, and the methods by which schools should pursue them, were all in question.[116] The Interim Committee responded by asserting the importance of schools forging closer links with families and the world of work; of providing young people with the experience of belonging to a diverse group of people while also developing a sense of their own identity; and of building caring communities where both education and people were valued.

There were many differences between *Education in South Australia* and *Schools in Australia*. The most important concerned ideas about inequality. The South Australian chapter on equality of opportunity was mostly about the individual, catering for individual differences, whereas the chapter in the national report, written by Jean, dealt with broad social groups rather than the characteristics of individuals. Among Jean's many achievements, establishing new policy settings for addressing inequality in education in terms of the differences between groups was one of her most significant contributions to public policy. Its consequence was a new interpretation of the terms of reference of the Interim Committee, to give disadvantage a broad meaning that allowed resources to be allocated according to the needs of groups rather than the needs of individuals.[117]

The chapter on equality of opportunity in *Schools in Australia* provided the philosophical heart of the report. Jean argued that it was intended 'to move the focus away from the IQ ideology' as the major determinant for success at school.[118] *Education in South Australia* had attributed inequality in education to genetic endowment as well as the stimulating or inhibiting nature of the familial environment, but Jean was unhappy with how these arguments denied the impact of resources and disparities on and between social groups. The new chapter on inequality is replete with powerful, elegantly reasoned arguments about the effects of schooling and the curriculum, and the mechanisms beyond the school that contribute to inequality: 'More equal outcomes from schooling require unequal treatment of children'; 'The capacity to succeed in the skills of abstraction which are central to academic achievement is itself unequally developed [through schooling] in different social groups', and; 'To the extent that higher education is financed from taxes it has thus a somewhat regressive effect, poorer people contributing to the cost of education of a group in which the children of richer parents predominate and from which recipients can expect to draw higher than average incomes'.[119]

Jean placed schools at the centre of her reasoning about inequality in education, and this is reflected in *Schools in Australia*: 'schools should really take account of the people who came to them and make sure that what they taught connected in some way with the experience of the lives that those people led.'[120] The thrust of a recommended Disadvantaged Schools Program (DSP) would be to keep 'open the question of whether schools themselves operated in ways that actively contributed to the disadvantage of poor students'.[121] Jean argued that this perspective would produce a focus away from understanding *families* living in communities experiencing disadvantage *as the problem*. This approach would distinguish the DSP from allied programs elsewhere, such as Priority Areas in the United Kingdom, and Title One in the United States.

Part 2, 'Programs', was the longest section. The Interim Committee determined an index for the quantum of recurrent resources. It involved 'weighting the quantities of the various resources used within the schools by fixed salary and price weights'.[122] A school was classified as requiring additional resources if it fell below an agreed acceptable standard. The Interim Committee identified several standards, such as a minimum time for professional development for teachers, the provision of relief staff when teachers were absent from duties, the reductions in first year teachers' workload by ten per cent, and so on. It was in the articulation of these standards that the Interim Committee identified how it would deliver on the requirement to attend to 'need' in devising its funding formula. Importantly, the Committee stated that recurrent grants were intended to fund 'the general operations of schools and not to overcome special difficulties of particular schools; that is, the general recurrent grants assume a uniform mix of different kinds of pupils. Special assistance for disadvantaged and for handicapped children is provided under separate programs'.[123]

Perhaps the most controversial analysis related to the categorisation of non-government 'independent' schools (both Catholic and non-Catholic) into eight categories, A to H, according to the level of resources available in the school, 'A' being the highest. The Committee recommended raising the 'resource levels of all schools in six years to 140 per cent of the state school average for 1973 in the case of primary schools or 135 per cent in the case of secondary schools'.[124] The introduction of general recurrent assistance for public schools was a radical departure from previous Commonwealth policies that assumed that public education was almost entirely the responsibility of the states. The Interim Committee also recommended phasing out Australian Government support for the non-government non-systemic schools with resource levels already above the agreed targets: 'government aid cannot be justified in maintaining or raising standards beyond those which publicly supported schools can hope to achieve by the end of the decade'.[125]

The special assistance programs could fund the construction of libraries, particularly for primary schools, the upgrading of disadvantaged schools, the establishment of special facilities for children with a physical or intellectual disability, teacher professional development, and fostering improvements in quality and equality through innovation. Innovation would be supported by encouraging reflection and initiative among teachers, parents and local communities about the nature of the service being provided. They were to be premised on 'the grounds that those involved in practice were the best judges of what problems needed to be addressed and what kinds of assistance [were] most helpful in addressing them'.[126]

Schools in Australia dealt only in a cursory way with the initial education of teachers. Instead, it focused on support for the ongoing professional development of working teachers. Its recommendations for improvement included establishing education centres where teachers could find out about new ideas, and plan, implement and test curriculum changes. Before this, employer-provided teacher education was 'parochial, instrumentalist, behaviourist and minimalist' and mainly concerned with promoting 'high fidelity adoption of central initiatives'.[127] In contrast, professional and subject associations actively involved teachers in their own professional learning, but these had limited reach because membership was not high, especially amongst primary teachers. The creation of education centres was a direct challenge to academic and employer in-service providers who had largely ignored the working knowledge of teachers. Consequently, 'two distinctive bodies of knowledge about teaching coexisted in a state of mutual disrespect bordering on hostility. One was founded on the application of generic theories typically those drawn from psychology. The other was based in teachers' thinking about their work'.[128]

Part 3 of the report, 'Administration', contained a summary and the recommendations occurring through the report. These prepared the ground for the coming Schools Commission. The Interim Committee had strong convictions about the importance of primary schooling and how funds were to be distributed according to need and other priorities. Predictably state departments of education objected to the suggestion that they be told how to spend the money allocated to them. They requested global ('untied') grants but the federal Minister insisted that grants be spent as directed. Despite this win, the Committee's recommendations were not always implemented.

An example was the libraries program, which had previously been administered by the Department of Education and Science. Priority should have been for schools in greatest need, but the Libraries Committee interpreted 'need' as the 'readiness' of a school to receive a library. The Schools Commission subsequently had to insist that the intended purposes of funding be satisfied.[129]

This final part of the report outlined how the Schools Commission would function, its structure, staffing and mechanisms for consultation, accountability and data collection. There should be a chairman, three or four full-time commissioners and six part-time commissioners. The report proposed the creation of regional boards and other committees to oversee tasks such as the establishment of building standards, libraries and special projects. The Minister of Education, Kim Beazley, was unimpressed. He favoured using existing institutions, including the organisations of non-government schools and the state departments of education rather than creating a new national bureaucracy.[130] His other view, that funding to elite schools should not be phased out, was not supported by cabinet. It opted instead to remove funding from the best-resourced schools immediately.

We have spent some time on the report, *Schools in Australia*, because it was a crucial policy document that Jean Blackburn had a significant hand in writing: 'I did have a more varied mental equipment than most of them ... I'm a good word-spinner and that is a power of its own'.[131] The report also provided a map for her work over the next seven years as a Schools Commissioner though not before a brief return to work in Adelaide.

As required, *Schools in Australia* was ready in time to affect budget processes.[132] The Interim Committee was disbanded in May 1973.

This meant that the bill for establishing the Schools Commission and implementing the system of schools funding recommended by the Interim Committee had to be seen through by officers of the Department of Education. Labor did not control the Senate, so the chances of an easy passage for the bill were low. There were powerful interests within and outside of state and federal parliaments that would seek to effect changes. Looking back, Jean thought that handing over the report to bureaucrats was a 'fatal mistake' because they 'thought that we were interfering in an outrageous way with both the State systems and the private sector and were not sympathetic in that sense'.[133] The Treasury and Public Service Board took no practical steps to prepare for the Schools Commission prior to Ken McKinnon's arrival in Canberra to take up his appointment as chairman in September 1973. No premises or staff were authorised.

During the interregnum between her appointments to the Interim Committee and Schools Commission, Jean resumed her position at Bedford Park, in the now autonomous Sturt College of Advanced Education. She described it as rather dreary though she found the first-year students whom she taught as 'keen and interested'.[134] In this period she was also in demand to speak at meetings about her work on the Interim Committee. In the talks she gave, she reflected upon the task ahead for the Commission in the light of what had been recommended. She elaborated on ideas that had only been briefly introduced in *Schools in Australia*. For example, in an address to the National Conference of State School Parents Association, Jean reiterated the Committee's commitment to schooling and, more than this, schools that were responsive to their local communities: 'responsibility for enabling every child to acquire the basic skills [they] must have to operate in society rests with the schools. [Schools] can only discharge it by learning from the community they serve as well as teaching it.'[135]

As 1973 wound to a close, the passing of the legislation was running into difficulty. Supporters of government schools wanted guarantees of funding priority. Others fought for the right of every child to be supported in a school chosen by their parents. McKinnon thought that the 'political stakes vastly outweighed the educational considerations'.[136] Malcom Fraser, leader of the opposition, had amendments passed in the Senate to ensure that high-fee non-government schools retained their Commonwealth grants. He insisted that it was his fear of a new outbreak of sectarian conflict that led to this position rather than the alternative, a stricter needs-based funding model.[137] The struggle over these amendments lasted some months, reaching the point where a double dissolution of parliament could have been triggered. The bill finally passed both houses on December 13, 1973, when the Country Party detached itself briefly from the coalition with the Liberals and voted with Labor once assurance had been secured that there would be funding to all independent schools.[138] The Country Party wanted new funding for rural schools sooner, not later.

The legislation that implemented the report was divided into two Acts: the Schools Commission Act and the States Grants (Schools) Act. They received Royal Assent on December 19, 1973. According to McKinnon:

> The final [Schools Commission] Act contained separate unreconciled clauses each of which was claimed by one or other of the main protagonists as supporting their position, especially in discussions and negotiations in future funding ...

The ambiguity of the Act was one of the weaknesses in the formation of the commission. The core issue, was and remains whether public policy should be based on common schooling financing and conditions, forcing those that opt out to pay their own way, or, conversely, that governments should support the cost of education for all students irrespective of the type of schooling chosen. In short, should all students have access to the same amount of government funds no matter how well off their parents and their schools?[139]

Another difficulty was the appointment of members. The Interim Committee recommended that members of the Schools Commission be appointed on merit according to their expertise and background experience, and not as representatives of sectors. However, according to Karmel, Beazley 'couldn't live with that because he had pressure on him from the independent schools and the Catholic schools and also the teachers' unions'.[140] McKinnon recalled that the Minister gave his support to the appointment of David Bennett, Peter Tannock, Peter Moyes and Desmond Wood. On the advice of Peter Karmel, McKinnon gave his support to the appointment of Jean Blackburn and Greg Hancock as the full-time members. Other members were the nominees of interested organisations: Joan Kirner (Association of Council of State Schools), Ray Costello (Australian Teachers' Federation), Albie Jones (Directors-General of Education), Tony McNamara (Catholic parents) and Frank Martin (Catholic schools).[141]

Once established, the Schools Commission became the means by which the Commonwealth, the new Labor government, demonstrated its commitment to school education through increased funding. The Commission was to identify how these resources should be spent. It was an educational and economic challenge, and one that ideally suited Jean's background and intellect. Even so, when McKinnon asked Jean to be a full-time commissioner, she initially declined, among other reasons, because her home and family were in Adelaide. McKinnon assured her that arrangements could be made that would allow her to continue to live at home, but it was not a straightforward decision for Jean. Around this time, Dick wrote to Susan that Jean was 'worried by pressure to go to one job or another ... the College wants her badly but the heart goes with the commission job'.[142] It does not seem to have been a deciding factor but there was a stark difference in remuneration between these two options. Jean was earning about $6,000 a year working at Sturt CAE. As a Schools Commissioner, her salary would jump to $17,489.

Around the time that Jean was negotiating her role on the Schools Commission, Hugh's difficulties at Unley High were reaching breaking point. He was bored with his studies and was regularly in trouble. At one point he was suspended from school for a couple of weeks. Dick and Jean had both gone in 'to bat' for him. Jean was 'indignant' that the school was even more authoritarian than the schools she had experienced as a young person. She learned first-hand how powerless parents were when on one occasion she went to complain about the curriculum, and questioned what Hugh was being taught: 'I can remember the venerable Mr Giles looking at me and saying, I never studied any history in my life and I haven't felt the want of it'.[143]

Jean told an interviewer that she was 'furious about the education her own children received'.[144] Despite the difficulties, and much to Jean's delight, Hugh did well in the Leaving: 'I think I came top of the school in economics'.[145] The following year, 1974, Hugh went to Pembroke School, a newly amalgamated, non-government senior school with a progressive headmistress, Di Medlin. Hugh had a 'good year' and experienced a sense of liberation.[146] Jean had a good year too: 'the early Schools Commission, was in lots of ways a much more exciting body than the Interim Committee. Well, first of all it had Joan Kirner on it'.[147]

Between completing her work on the Interim Committee and taking up her position on the Schools Commission, Jean had the opportunity to reflect on her work on the two Karmel reports, including their reception. She believed she had been instrumental in challenging the tight, centrally controlled nature of the work of teachers in the state departments of education, the approach that ensured that at 'any minute of the day someone sitting in headquarters knows what every class will be doing'. Jean was concerned that this situation 'stifled the initiative and sense of responsibility of teachers'.[148] The special purpose programs were proposed on that basis; they were to 'tap grassroots' initiatives.[149] The programs were intended to 'break down the rigidity of the centralised control of public systems' and deliver more control and responsibility to teachers and school communities.[150] This was the Interim Committee's own radical and controversial suggestion at a time when systemic schools, both government and Catholic, were monitored and controlled by more or less efficient bureaucracies. In so doing, the Committee elevated the role of teachers and parents in policy making at all levels – though there were limits.

Jean did not believe that a participatory model of schooling meant that each school should decide its own curriculum, tailored to the perceived needs of its students, solely at the local level. Such an approach could result in 'effects which were pretty sad'. For example, some secondary schools allowed girls to opt out of mathematics, assuming they were not interested, or did not need this subject. Jean believed that an important role of schooling was to introduce students to a 'common culture', and that involved attention to curriculum.[151] One question that Jean found difficult to resolve was 'whether all should be initiated into the High Culture because it gives the language and the discourse, or whether, if they don't like it, kids should be able to pass it by. On the whole, I believe it is diversity of means rather than ends which should be sought in the years of secondary schooling'. She was prepared to stand by her judgement 'that some ways of understanding and operating in the world are more fruitful than others'.[152]

The late 1960s and early 1970s were years of radical ferment in education. Ivan Illich's book *Deschooling Society* was published in 1971 and was widely read in the 1970s. Schools were often portrayed as repressive institutions on a variety of grounds and members of the Interim Committee and the succeeding Schools Commission were affected by the arguments. In Australia the magazine *Radical Education Dossier* (1976–1984) promoted the new critical thinking. While few doubted the desperate need to improve the conditions in schools serving low-income communities, though not always the Catholic systemic schools, there was also a deep ambivalence among readers of the radical thinkers. Although Jean sympathised with supporters of Ivan Illich's ideas about deschooling and self-directed learning which were gaining some support at that time, she retained 'a commitment to work for better organisational forms (and people) rather than to abolish school'.[153] Jean wrote to her daughter:

> My feeling about school can never follow Illich, though I agree with many of his criticisms. I come from a culturally barren home and found in school a good deal to lift the mind and spirit.

This may be taking an 'uplift' view of the school, but the whole notion of education must involve some view about 'worthwhile' activities, even if people come to different conclusions. I do firmly believe that reflective and mentally disciplined responses to most problems are preferable to instinctual and uninformed ones – both because more workable and less egocentric conclusions are likely to result and because meaningful discussion is thus made possible between people who differ, discussion which should, if people try to keep themselves open to reason, lead to better answers. Also one has to consider that people don't live in a vacuum – TV, peer groups etc. influence. This does not mean that schools are good or that they ought not to care a great deal more about people, social and emotional development and growing autonomy etc. – but it is a commitment to work for better organisational forms (and people) rather than to abolish school.[154]

Jean waited for the Schools Commission to begin work. It had been a few short years, just over four in fact, between her appointment to the South Australian Enquiry, and finishing the national *Schools in Australia*. In that time, remarkably she had sped from being a lecturer in a teachers' college in Adelaide, to a figure already of significance in the making of national education policy. She had rapidly developed a capacity to write policy with arguments that persuaded, and much of the policy was radical for its time. Jean was in the middle of making an exciting if exhausting new life.

During this period, other lives came to an end however. David Caust died in 1968. He was an old comrade and friend, and occasional prescriber of medications to help with Jean's depression and other ailments. Claire Muir, Jean's mother died in July 1970, and her mother-in-law, Doris Blackburn the following December. These women represented contrary poles for Jean in what it might mean to be a woman, one at home confined by family and domesticity, the other abroad as a feminist, peace and social justice activist. Jean's relationship with both was difficult. In 1967, she had been writing to Susan: 'Nana [Claire] goes on and on about nothing. Granny [Doris] is so full of herself she gives no opportunity for audience participation, so the ego shrivels all round, and I am almost incapable of speech after 3 days'.[155] At the same time, we should not leave Jean's mother on too negative a note. She was a crucial supporter of Jean's early ambitions when it counted.

1968 was the year that Jean's daughter, Susan, met a Colombo Plan student from Sri Lanka, Dayal Abeyasekere. They wanted to marry but Jean and Dick wondered if they were too young. Susan was a bit shocked when Jean suggested they 'live together' for a while, but her

Figure 6.4 Family, from left to right, Dayal Abeyasekere (Susan's husband), Jean, Hugh (standing), Dick and Susan, the year that Jean joined the Interim Schools Commission, 1972.
Photographer Dayal Abeyasekere, courtesy of Susan Blackburn.

parents hosted the wedding. Eric and Judith Russell witnessed the marriage certificate. There was a non-religious ceremony held at the Registry Office in Adelaide.[156] Jean was intrigued as she met Dayal's mother, and learnt more about Sri Lanka and Buddhism. Jean's first child, Bill, was on the move also. He went with his employer to Sydney when the company left its factory in Adelaide. Initially at least, Bill found it difficult to settle. He endured problems with his mental health, causing Jean concern, but she could do little.[157]

Jean's world changed in other ways. Helen Palmer's *Outlook* folded in 1970. Like Jean, Helen both admired and distrusted the new, mainly student, radicalism.[158] Judah Waten and Hyrell Ross continued to turn up around the time of Writers' Week in the Adelaide Festival of Arts. Sometimes they stayed with the Blackburns, ate together – and argued. Judah and Hyrell left the Communist Party for the pro-Soviet Union Socialist Party in 1972. The age of the survivors of 1956 was giving way to new enthusiasms, the new feminism, and revivified socialist and revolutionary thought and action under the aegis of the New Left. Jean's Schools Commission years would be backgrounded by these changing personal and political circumstances.

Chapter 7

SCHOOLS COMMISSIONER: WHITLAM GOVERNMENT YEARS, 1974–1975

> [The] early years of the Schools Commission were just about the most exciting time that there has been in the history of Australian education ... the ideas were flying fast and furious and people were really alive and into the scene.[1]

> *Girls, School and Society* ... I perhaps shouldn't say so because I had a large hand in writing it, that that was one of the best things that the Schools Commission produced.[2]

It wasn't until the start of 1974 that Jean commenced full-time work as a Schools Commissioner. She was provided with an office and administrative support in Adelaide but was frequently away on Commission business. By that time, Susan and Bill had left home, and Dick no longer travelled as much for work. Jean decided that it was now her turn to prioritise paid employment. She rose at five in the morning, starting 'work then because there was always peace at that time of the day'. She also considered that it was her 'best time'.³ When she was working on a big report for the Schools Commission she only made it home to Adelaide every second weekend. Hugh recalled:

> she always put a lot of effort into being a mother and when she was there, cooking the meals and doing the housework, not that she always took kindly to it, because it was a load on her time which she found stressful. You could tell there was a lot of stress in her life because she was so busy. There was the coming and going, of being picked up in Commonwealth cars, being taken to the airport ... I don't really remember being alone or, being left alone. I was there with my Dad.⁴

The role of Schools Commissioner gave Jean the opportunity to develop her vision for schooling in a democratic society, but it would come at a cost. In the preceding years, she had felt 'oppressed by the pressure' of contributing to large-scale inquiries into schooling. She feared getting something wrong and producing an 'inadequate standard'. While working on the enquiry into education in South Australia, Jean confided in Susan that the 'pressure is quite killing, and I am debilitated by excessive anxiety. Obscurity and routine have compensations'.⁵ Despite these thoughts, Jean took up the new role with enthusiasm. It was a different kind of task; she would have many more resources to draw upon, and there would be other compensations.

As one of two full-time commissioners, Jean had a wide-ranging portfolio. She had a hands-on role in the development of the Disadvantaged Schools Program and centres for teacher development. She also contributed to the Commission's programs for the children of migrant families, children in rural areas, Aboriginal children, and the education of children with disabilities. In addition to her core responsibilities, her work included visiting schools, giving addresses to various national, state and other education organisations, and providing ongoing advice to the Chairman and other commissioners on their areas of responsibility. The files related to Jean's work on the Commission deposited in the National Library of Australia number in excess of 650. Most of these included multiple documents. This number does not include items related to *Girls School and Society* which were inexplicably destroyed.

This chapter focuses on Jean's work on *Girls School and Society* and her contribution to establishing the Disadvantaged Schools Program (DSP).

Jean's role as a commissioner involved conducting inquiries and formulating policy. The task was complex, and there were many competing interests to be taken into consideration. In her correspondence, she emphasised that the Commission was not running schools but was involved in a 'funding exercise'.[6] This exercise involved surveying the problem under question, identifying desirable directions for change and encouraging these changes through funding policies. Initially, the Schools Commission operated with a three-year funding cycle which allowed the steps, scale and pace of change to be staged over time. In a letter to David Bennett, Jean outlined her approach to special education, though the method reflects her approach more generally.

> I think there is an obligation not just to state views but to be prepared to attempt to convince people that they are tenable, not just on general principle but by being able to show that they work ... The power of the word is considerable in bringing about

> change … people should always feel that they have played some part in decisions that affect them (even if it is only that they have been listened to and that their arguments have been considered and rejected for reasons which are clear to them although they may not accept them) … you can't dragoon people into doing things, you can only make it possible for them to do them and attempt to persuade them they are good things to do.[7]

In the same letter, Jean acknowledged, perhaps wryly and at odds with some people's expectations of her, 'I have been known to change my mind when I came to know more about something!' The great challenge was to change people's minds, an educational rather than a funding exercise. She knew that she might be required in each local setting to repeat an argument that may have been thoroughly outlined in a previous report, or in educational research, 'in order to allow others to participate in the process of thinking it, or rethinking it'. As a commissioner Jean was a policy maker of national significance, but she never lost sight of the need to be an educator as well, which proved to be a tremendously important attribute for a schools commissioner.

Australia has long been plagued by problems associated with organising and funding its schools. The Australian constitution left responsibility for education and schooling as a residual power of the states of the Commonwealth. The federal government was not imagined as a provider of public education, or any kind of education except perhaps as it might be relevant to its named powers, such as national defence. The emergency during the Second World War saw the federal government assume the power to collect income tax, the major source of government revenue. The end of the war saw no return of the income taxing power to the states, but it did see a rapid expansion of population, and relative poverty for state governments expected to provide the infrastructure for new suburbs, including health services and schools. State governments could not do this satisfactorily without the assistance of the federal government. And so, a long struggle began. If federal governments were to provide substantial funding for schools, they would demand some control over the programs funded. The states resisted the loss of control.

The nature of Australian federalism emerged as only one of the obstructions to funding schools rationally. There were individual non-government schools and systems of non-government schools that claimed public funding, the most powerful of the systems being that of the Catholic Church. 'Need' and 'choice' emerged as counter-arguments to how the funding of schools should be organised. Should schools with poor facilities and with students, often from poorer families, whether in government or non-government schools, receive the lion's share of discretionary funding from state or federal governments? Or should the right of parents, rich or poor, to choose a school for their children, government or non-government, be supported by tax-raised government revenue? Policy relating to this contest between 'educational need' and 'right to school choice' increasingly populated the policy speeches of political parties as they sought election from the 1970s. Jean Blackburn and the Schools Commission entered this policy contest, initially with a strong needs-based approach.

The Australian Schools Commission was established early in 1974 and during its first years, it operated in an atmosphere of optimism and hope. Although some members represented particular constituencies, they were also committed to finding overall solutions, with compromise if necessary. As well as the work of the Schools Commission and its meetings, the commissioners also joined high level committees concerned with education in the different states. According to Ken McKinnon, some of the 'best and most energetic of educational thinkers' took part in deciding on priorities and assessing innovations applications. The Commission consulted widely and in an ongoing way with national and state organisations including annual meetings with the directors-general of state departments of education. 'Regular consultations made it normal for parents, teachers, state education officials, and other stakeholders, to civilly discuss the merits of different educational approaches'.[8]

Despite the atmosphere of hope and optimism, the Commission was bedevilled by funding issues. Most concerning to Jean was not that public money was provided to non-government schools, since she had seen first-hand the terrible conditions in poor Catholic schools, but that there were insufficient conditions placed on how the regular recurrent and capital grants would be spent in these schools. Prior to the establishment of the Schools Commission, the Minister, Kim Beazley agreed that Catholic diocesan school systems could provide system-wide rather than disaggregated individual school data, with the subsequent Commission funds to be distributed without close Commission supervision. Jean expressed the view that ensuring transparency and accountability in the expenditure of public funds was a fundamental aspect of social policy: 'it was the government's business to make those kinds of tough decisions'. In retrospect, Jean believed that determining the basis of need upon which funds would be allocated was 'a deeply [and] philosophically important piece of public policy' that should have been handled by the government because it was much more than a technical task.[9]

Initially, the increased level of funding to the states that was recommended by the Commission resulted in an improvement in government schools. In a relatively short period government schools reached and passed the targets for improvement set by the Interim Committee while systemic Catholic schools fell even further behind.[10] Jean suspected that the consequence of Beazley's agreement with the Catholic Church was that the new resources were often diverted from upgrading existing schools as intended, to expanding the Catholic school sector, the building of new Catholic schools.[11] Consequently in 1975 the Schools Commission established guidelines that placed a major emphasis on bridging this gap between government and the poorer, mainly Catholic, non-government schools. The core issue that remained unresolved, despite the Schools Commission's own commitment to needs-based funding, was whether all young people should have access to the same amount of government funds for the purpose of their schooling or whether funding should be allocated according to need.

The Interim Committee had outlined a number of values that were endorsed by the Schools Commission even though they were not all included in the Schools Commission Act. These values included the devolution of responsibility to the people involved in the actual task of schooling, community involvement in educational programs, and the special purpose of schooling in building 'a community where both education and people are valued, and where the influences of the market place do not dictate the price placed upon individual talents'. The Commission also supported recurrent education in the form of each member of society having an entitlement to a period of free public education that could be accessed after interruptions to schooling due to workforce participation or leaving school early for another reason.[12] In the absence of legislative support, it was left to the Special Projects Program established by the Commission to advance these values. Without the programs by which the Commission could support these ends, their achievement would have been like 'whistling in the dark'.[13] However, Jean observed that it was 'hardly going overboard for equality' since special funding was an 'insignificant proportion of the total sums recommended – $17.5m supplementary recurrent for disadvantaged schools in a program of $660m'.[14]

The Special Projects programs were designed to foster change and support innovation by engaging teachers in thinking about the problems they faced.[15] For example, the Innovations Program provided additional resources in the form of a network of innovation consultants, and grants from the Commission to individual applicants. Notably, approval of personnel with institutional authority, such as school principals, was not required nor did they have the right of veto. This approach was led by David Bennett, the commissioner with deep roots in the Labor Party and a background as a reforming school principal. Jean thought it 'was one of the most important means of teacher development … that we've ever had in this country'.[16] In terms of providing direct support to teachers for professional development this program remains an historically exemplary approach to reform in Australian education.

The first report for the triennium 1976–1978 was presented to the Minister at the end of May 1975, sixteen months after the Schools Commission was established. It picked up the tasks set down for it in *Schools in Australia*, but with the added burden of the compromises that had been required to permit the passage of the bills through parliament, which enjoined the Commission to reconcile two very different principles: the prime responsibility of governments to ensure that public schools are accessible to all and of the highest quality, and to support the right of parents to choose to have their children educated in a non-government school. Jean reasoned: 'To enable all parents to have a choice seems to require that no cost be associated with the choice; yet such a possibility could only become real at a public cost, which taxpayers would have to agree to meet'.[17] Subsequent federal governments shifted towards the prioritising of choice, especially the government of Malcolm Fraser (1975–1983). The succeeding government of Bob Hawke (1983–1991) did not re-establish 'need' as the pre-eminent objective of schools funding, though start-ups of new non-government schools were slowed.

The financial resources of federal governments made it difficult for state governments to resist their interventions, but federal governments have had their own incapacities. As the Schools Commission discovered, federal governments did not wish to set up government instrumentalities that assumed the detailed administration of schools or their funding. Nor could governments resist the politics of parental school choice and the demand of non-government schools to receive public funding, whether the schools were wealthy or not. The electoral cost of challenging the new right of parents to publicly funded school choice has continued to pose a great risk to the main political parties. Nor was the federal government through the Schools Commission for a time, the only player in seeking to make coherent national education policy. The meeting of ministers of education, federal and states, also had a significant role to play. Other interested parties included the Commonwealth Department of Education, each state and territory department of education, public school systems, non-government school systems and non-government independent, non-systemic schools.[18] One Schools Commission memo listed the frustrations when these diverse interested parties insisted on having their say. Federalism was not the only impediment to the rational funding and organising of Australian schools. After having served as a commissioner, Jean reflected on how it functioned: 'The Schools Commission represents, and always has represented, an unstable compromise between conflicting positions and interests more easily reconciled in a period of economic prosperity than adversity ... originally premised on the ideology of social democracy tempered in its purity, as ever, by the need to reformulate policies which would win support among a majority of the electorate'.[19]

Ken McKinnon talked about some of the consequences of these competing interests for the Commission. Getting the different churches and religious groups to work together, *with* rather than against the Commission 'was a complicated task involving several years of negotiations' to minimise religious dissension and the daily requirement of 'overcoming special pleading and grandstanding'.[20] For core recurrent and capital programs, planning and finance committees had to be established by the Commission in each state, as were Disadvantaged Schools Program advisory committees. The state government representatives on state committees had a right of veto, but they were reluctant to use it. Failure to spend Commission money could more easily bring a state government into disrepute rather than the Commission. At the same time a program, such as that for schools serving communities experiencing disadvantage, could look very different in each state as a result. In Queensland and Western Australia for example older approaches to literacy and numeracy education were implemented. There was less innovation.[21]

Important to keep on-side were the directors-general of education in each state. McKinnon recalled: 'while we met with State representatives in the State, including the Directors-General, annually the Commission also consulted the DGs as a group for two days each year in Canberra, a rare time for DGs to spend exclusively discussing educational ideas and needs. We met and discussed ideas with every group that had credibility and some that didn't. Overall, it was an approach that despite obvious success, in Canberra circles was sometimes criticised as being too radical, too expensive, and likely to raise expectations too high.'[22]

McKinnon had sought advice in 1974 from a leading constitutional lawyer on the legality of the Acts that established the Schools Commission and its intended activity. Section 96, which allowed the federal government to make grants to the states without specifying their purpose was the primary constitutional means by which Commission programs occurred. The Commission had to work through the states, but by doing so its direct control over funding and programs was limited.[23] For Jean, the frustrations arising from federalism were palpable; they often dictated the operation of the Commission structures and national education policy beyond. By the 1970s an effective national policy for education and schooling had become a necessity. Children and young people regardless of their state or region required an equal and fair chance for a good education. Australia seemed far from being able to provide it.[24]

In preparation for its first triennium report, the Schools Commission embarked on a community education campaign, distributing leaflets and information about the seven projects it would administer, promising a 'massive "shot-in-the-arm" for Australian education'. It encouraged authorities, organisations and individuals to 'place their views to the Commission to ensure that recommendations in the next report are realistically based'.[25] This involved a large-scale process of consultation. In its first 12 months, the Commission acquired a staff of about 70 for its secretariat. A little later, advisory boards were established in each state. Each board was composed of nine members including one of the Commission's full-time members as chairman; one member nominated by the state Director-General of Education, the Director of the State Catholic Education Office, the government school teachers' organisation, and the government-school parents' organisation; and four members appointed by the Commonwealth Minister for Education.[26]

The Commission itself usually met every four to six weeks, except when finalising reports, when two or three meetings might be necessary within a shorter period of time. It alternated regional meetings with those held in Canberra, combining meetings with consultations and discussions with a wide variety of interested parties in the state where a meeting was held, and with visits to schools. Between Commission meetings some commissioners might be involved in other meetings, or visits to organisations and institutions where educational activities were being funded by the Commission, or for which funds were being sought.

The general mode of working was to proceed by consensus on any matters which involved policy development. Proposals for financial grants not involving policy issues were usually resolved by the votes of a majority. McKinnon reasoned that to function successfully, 'serious efforts' had to be made to develop policy positions acceptable to all its members.

> Internally the practice of forming teams comprising commissioners, staff and outside experts, developed staff, built teamwork and encouraged rapport. The consequent unity of purpose and civility of dealings among people of different world-views made communication and debate more effective. For instance, country communities were surprised and impressed that members Joan Kirner ... and Fr Frank Martin (Director of Catholic

Education in Victoria), ostensibly on opposite 'sides' could team for consultations in country areas.[27]

The preparation of Commission reports was an extended process of consultation and refinement that provided the commissioners with 'their strongest input into policy development'. McKinnon recalled that they had to 'use persuasive skills to win through on particular points of view'. The process included the preparation of papers by members of the secretariat on relevant topics, summarising statistics and current practice, and outlining possible options for advice to government. A 'Commission view' sometimes emerged from discussion of these papers. Often it took several drafts for a version to emerge that everyone could support.[28] Many of Jean's files in the National Archives are a consequence of this process, especially her drafts of Commission reports in her key areas of responsibility, the Disadvantaged Schools Program and Special Education.

As a commissioner with the support of a permanent secretariat, Jean was able to call up information when required. For instance, her instructions on the task of investigating 'The School in the Community' were detailed, demonstrating a clear direction for the secretariat or a person commissioned by it. It was the kind of groundwork that Jean probably would have done herself in her previous roles, but the new scale of her responsibilities meant that she had to outsource research. Nevertheless, she provided the analytical framework, and key questions detailing the information that was required about existing practices in Australia and overseas, and stipulating the need for a checklist by which the degree of community participation in schooling might be judged. She also provided suggestions about whom she thought might do a good job.[29]

The Interim Committee for the Schools Commission had recommended that about 80 per cent of the funds that the Commonwealth provided to schools should be spent on two big programs, which were under the control of state departments and non-government school organisations. These were the general recurrent and capital works programs. It reserved about 20 per cent of the funds for special purpose programs, which made funds available to 'people at the grassroots'. The Disadvantaged Schools Program (DSP) was the flagship special purpose program of the Schools Commission. It was closely aligned with the Innovations Program. The aims of DSP were to support: more effective learning, more enjoyable and meaningful school programs, and greater contact between parents and the school.

According to R. W. Connell, the Interim Committee's overall 'equality program' was intended to address manifest problems in how schools were funded, in three ways – by levelling up, providing compensatory education, and stirring the pot.[30] Levelling up required the Commonwealth to use its financial power to reduce disparities between schools by introducing needs-based funding, and by urgently 'refurbishing inner city schools serving, by and large, the poorest populations, a high proportion of them immigrant. The physical condition of these schools, especially in Sydney and Melbourne, shocked the Committee sufficiently for it to call them a national disgrace'.[31] Levelling up was to be achieved through the general recurrent grants and general building grants programs. Compensatory funding was intended to deal with some failures of the welfare-state model, by compensating specific groups who experienced disadvantage. This form of funding targeted facilities and teacher training for children having 'difficulties in specific aspects of learning as to require specialist attention on a withdrawal basis'.[32] Compensatory education was the primary focus of the special education program. Connell's third category, 'stirring the pot', was to be achieved through the Disadvantaged Schools Program (DSP) and the Innovation Program. Funding would be based on the needs of groups rather than individuals, and it would focus on changing the ways schools functioned.

Jean's ideas on equality and opportunity were clear-cut: 'I dislike the whole "compensatory" thing'. She emphasised the need to situate a problem within groups, not individuals. In the early days of the Schools Commission, Jean was asked to comment on a pamphlet being prepared by the Australian Teachers Federation to provide members with information about the Commission. Jean rewrote the questions to reflect the Commission's concerns about equality and opportunity:

- Should the least well provided for schools have first claim on increased resources?
- What is the 'opportunity' which school should aim to make more equal?
- How can the resource needs of different schools be fairly compared?[33]

The philosophy underpinning the DSP was based on the Interim Committee's approach to funding resource levels. The Committee had taken the view that those schools that have the least should get the most, to ensure that all young people in whatever kind of school should have access to educational provision of an adequate standard. Beyond the minimum agreed standard of funding, the DSP provided additional funds to schools based on the socio-economic characteristics of the population they served *and* plans for the use of funds that demonstrated community engagement. Unlike similar programs overseas, such as the Priority Areas in the United

Kingdom or Title One in the United States, the DSP kept open the question of whether the schools themselves operated in ways that actively contributed to the disadvantage of students in low socio-economic communities.

Drawing upon ideas developed in the English Plowden Report,[34] the DSP was not established to compensate for presumed innate differences in the intellectual capacity of young people due to their membership of different social groups or presumed social differences due to differing cultures and parenting practices. Such explanations for educational inequality were based on deficit understandings of low-income families and children that resulted in an assumed mismatch between the intellectual demands and culture of schools and the intellectual capabilities of these children and the cultures of their families. While such a social explanation can move the 'blame' for inequality in education away from individuals and families, Jean believed that it seldom does. Instead, rejecting such assumptions, the DSP adopted the explanation that 'the school plays an active part in the production of unequal learning chances', and that resources alone would not bring about the kinds of changes that were required to improve the educational outcomes for children growing up in disadvantaged communities.

The program developed a model of collaborative critical reflection.

> Teachers had to be committed to the students and their families and believe in their capacity for learning. Teaching somehow had to relate better to who those people were, how they saw themselves, what they had to contribute. No known model existed, and even if they did, it was also part of the Commission's ideology if you like, that it was only when the people collaborated to identify and tackle their own problems that the kind of commitment necessary for effective action

could develop ... Above all, but concentrating on the school rather than on individual 'disadvantaged' students as the unit of action, the Program pointed towards institutional change.[35]

The DSP channelled Commonwealth money through special committees direct to school communities to do what they decided was needed to improve community relationships in their schools. Both the DSP and the Innovations Program provided small grants to support proposals that were worked out at school or district level by teachers, or teachers and parents. These programs were intended to provide alternative sources of income to support different approaches to those common in the schools that belonged to the large bureaucracies of education. The Interim Committee hoped that this kind of funding would stimulate a radically different approach to schooling since, 'people engaged in the problem were exchanging notes with each other and seriously trying to work the situation through'.[36] These small programs were intended to move 'responsibility for making decisions nearer to the point of action' in order to empower people at the local level to take responsibility for their practices.

Jean was closely involved in the operations of the DSP, attending weekend workshops with the program's consultants for example.[37] There was no shortage of advice on how the program should operate. Peter Tannock, a co-commissioner, but also professor and dean of the Faculty of Education at the University of Western Australia, had proposed the formation of an evaluation unit. Jean provided a considered response. She thought:

> that evaluation cannot be a *post hoc* external process. My view that only those engaged in the action are competent to evaluate it, is not, as it may have appeared, a dismissal of evaluation. It is rather that evaluation has to be built in to all

stages of planning and action, to sharpen up objectives and to participate in evaluating alternative paths in action as it develops. Hence I am keen to see people who could assist this process incorporated into task forces in, say, the Disadvantaged Program.

However, there is also an urgent need, which, on reflection I acknowledge, for a group of people, not necessarily engaged in the action, to work on the sophisticated and difficult theoretical tasks of models and methods of evaluation. I don't feel madly hopeful, since considerable effort, far greater than we could mount, has been put into this matter in other countries, resulting in as much argument about what constitutes appropriate assessment as about the programs themselves. However, since a significant part of the problem relates to inadequate specification of objectives, some initial advances could be made in Australia on this issue at least.[38]

Evaluation was an ongoing issue for the DSP, and it was made doubly difficult because it was not just a program about improving learning outcomes, which could be measured by a variety of means, it was also about making children's schooling experiences more enjoyable and satisfying. These latter intangible qualities were difficult to assess systemically.

Less than a year after penning her response to Tannock, and on the day of the Whitlam government's dismissal by the Governor-General in November 1975, Jean wrote to John Keeves from the ACER inviting him to attend a planned meeting for December to talk about the DSP, but specifically to discuss definitions and issues surrounding the measurement of educational disadvantage, educational need and equality, their relationships to cultural diversity and the possible delineation of "competency" in outcomes of schooling'.[39] Other people invited included Don Edgar, Jim Walker,

R.W. Connell, Barbara Falk, Margaret Vickers, Peter Musgrave, and Doug White. It was a gathering of some of the brightest Australian minds at work on the issues surrounding inequality in education at that time. Much of the best work of the Commission was conducted by getting people together to talk, to identify the difficulties and to plan further action.

Early on, there was considerable confusion and disagreement about the concept of disadvantage and the objectives of the DSP.[40] Pat Thomson observed that the 'arbitrary statistical "cut off" for the program and lack of formula transparency bewildered and angered schools that were deemed ineligible, even though they were only marginally different from those which received funding'.[41] Jean was often called upon to justify how the funds were distributed.

> The Disadvantaged Schools Program is essentially a neighbourhood program, few non-systemic schools could be expected to qualify. It should be made clear that 'disadvantaged' minorities within schools do not constitute qualifying circumstances and that it is *concentration* of relative poverty affecting total conditions of upbringing we are on about. Schools charging substantial fees, even if they have a number of relatively poor families in them, cannot, by definition, qualify.
>
> The Program is not a welfare program – the socioeconomic factors used to identify schools are those known to be associated, *on average* with relatively low success in *learning*. We are not interested in two working parents, single parents or family breakdown as such. There is no evidence that these factors *of themselves* are associated with low learning outcomes …
>
> The emphasis then is neighbourhood, *total* school population and occupation/income (assuming this is also associated with parental education).[42]

Even for those schools that were eligible for funding, extra funds were not automatically guaranteed. The whole staff of the school, assisted where practicable by parents, and supported by the DSP field consultants, analysed their local situation and proposed ways of improving its educational offerings. The purpose of involving parents was not limited to supporting their participation, which Jean acknowledged would be difficult due to 'mutual distrust', for example. Parents were to be involved so that professional educators might learn from them 'about the way of life, the hopes and expectations of the group from which the students come so that the school is able to draw on the actual experiences of children and to act with rather than on the local communities'.[43]

Jean argued that when this process worked well it 'engendered commitment ... and many imaginative responses to a challenging situation ... which may be more important than funds in improving the schooling of children involved'. Proposals from schools were assessed by a Task Force in the system. It determined whether the project constituted 'a reasonable attack on the difficulties seen'. The funding mechanism in DSP required 'committed reflection'.[44]

A recurring question posed to Jean was what constituted disadvantage.

> When we speak of educational disadvantage we are talking about children who, because of some ascribed characteristic of birth related to a position in the social structure which their parents occupy are likely, on the grounds of statistical association, to be less successful than average in their schooling.

Jean asserted that it was 'necessary to frame the definition in a way which emphasises that it is a sociological and not a psychological concept'. To this day, confusion persists about this distinction, and

Jean's clear thinking still has much to contribute to understanding both the problem itself and what constitutes an adequate response in educational terms. Jean was forthright in her conviction that the nature and purpose of schooling had a 'unique and central function' related to a child's intellectual development. She was unimpressed by the debate over whether young people from different social groups required adjustments to what they were taught because they learn differently, or because they lacked what it took to learn.

> I am critical of good time social adjustment approaches as ends in themselves, or approaches which begin from the assumption that some kids can't learn traditional skills and the concepts central to organising information about the physical world. This does NOT mean that more drumming of literacy and so on should be the core of programs ... How the child views himself as social being and as learner is crucial to learning. He builds this view on how others value him. An essential part of this view is the value he sees others place on his cultural difference from them – especially when those others are powerful and he is not.
>
> However, for schools, valuing social difference does NOT mean valuing illiteracy equally with literacy, leaving prejudice, assumptions and limited perspectives undisturbed.[45]

Jean insisted on the need for a 'compulsory core' curriculum, one that was structured in such a way across the years of schooling so that each year should be somewhat more demanding and sophisticated than the last.

In her view, progressive schools, were 'a rort so far as kids are concerned'. She had visited 'a number of progressive schools which were lovely and where everybody was very happy and it was very nice, but you know, each teacher made the curriculum in the classroom'. Jean never forgot the fortuitous nature of the events that had enabled her to receive an intellectually challenging education at University High. She wanted all children to have access to the kind of knowledge that would open up opportunities, and not prematurely close them due to the circumstances of their birth and upbringing.[46] She developed the view that the curriculum should function in ways that closed any gap that might exist between students and the culture of school.[47] Curriculum determination should not rest with teachers as individuals, and schools had larger responsibilities than their possibly idiosyncratic decisions.

In her DSP files housed in the National Archives, Jean emerges as a collector of relevant and high-quality research, opinions and reviews, reports, and more, which she used to develop and hone her arguments. They provided the foundation that converted policy into practice. She then supported ongoing analysis, indeed evaluation of the practice, especially by getting people together to talk, to isolate difficulties and to plan further action.[48] Jean emphasised that it is better to do something decently in a few schools, and to regard that activity as a pilot operation, than to smatter indifferent programs over a larger number of schools.[49] These files also document some of Jean's many visits to schools across Australia, which provided her with first-hand experience of the conditions of schooling on site. The files demonstrate that Jean was an excellent field worker – making detailed notes soon after her visits and, later, reflecting further on the experiences.

In September 1974, Lyndsay Connors, a later schools commissioner (1983–88) but who was described then as 'a former teacher of English, now a housewife in Canberra', wrote in *The Canberra Times* that one disappointing implication of *Schools in Australia* was the message that 'Girls can wait'. She was disappointed that the report had drawn attention to the fact that, except at the highest socio-economic level, girls are educationally disadvantaged, but had failed to make any specific recommendations to deal with this situation.[50]

Jean acknowledged that there was some ambivalence among members of the Interim Committee about 'whether it was a good thing to be channelling a lot more resources into this rather dubious enterprise which was very class biased ... we didn't think about it being biased against girls or ethnic minorities at that time ... That came later'. Jean's 'old Marxist background and Peter Karmel's economic preoccupations' meant that disadvantage was seen as arising primarily from socio-economic difference. Jean acknowledged that she was 'largely ignorant' about the emergent 'new feminism', and that many feminists were 'indignant' about the statement in *Schools in Australia*, which she had penned, suggesting that 'girls are only disadvantaged when femaleness is also associated with low socioeconomic status'. At that time, she extended this logic to the children of 'migrants who had educated parents' since, according to Jean, they 'didn't have any trouble in coping with the school system'.[51]

The Commission established a group to assist it with the development of policy related to the schooling of women – *Steering Committee for the Enquiry into Social Change and the Education of Women*. The Committee included well-known feminists – Elizabeth Reid, the Adviser to the Prime Minister on women's affairs, Susan Ryan, the Executive Officer of the Australian Council of State Schools Organisations, Professor Jean Martin, a pioneering Australian sociologist based at the Australian National University and author of an important essay on girls and their education,[52] and Cathy Bloch, a teacher unionist. Bill Thiele, a student counsellor at the University of Queensland, and David Widdup, a mathematician and gay activist were also members of the Steering Committee. Eva Cox, Anne Summers, Clare Burton, Wendy McCarthy, Lorna Hannan and other leading Australian feminists of the mid-1970s were either consultants and/or hired to do specific research.

Jean and Ken McKinnon interviewed Daniela Torsh for the job of executive officer. Torsh, previously as Dany Humphreys, had been Women's Officer for the National Union of Australian University Students. She was a leading feminist and wrote a column for *The Australian* newspaper. She came into the job in the middle of her doctoral studies and the bibliographical work developed for her dissertation would provide an essential foundation to the work of the Committee. During her first conversation with Jean, Jean told her that working for a government instrumentality such as the Commission might be difficult.[53] Jean had herself known the frustrating politics of producing public reports that were required to be acceptable not only to their committees and chairs but also, down the track, to government. It was inevitable that compromise and frustration would be part of the process.

After a couple of meetings of the Steering Committee, Ken McKinnon thought that 'it looked like going mad'. So, he decided to chair it. He wanted something that would be 'adequate for government purposes … It had to meet the test of a government document of standing and authority'. He also asked Jean to be involved: 'I said to Jean … you'd better come in on this one Jean, they'll pay attention to you. They'll see me as the policeman and you as the positive. Which was true'. According to Dean Ashenden, Jean appreciated McKinnon for his 'political smarts', and Ken appreciated Jean for her 'intellectual and political integrity'.[54] Their relationship commonly involved a division of labour.

Dany presented a first draft of the Committee's report to McKinnon in February 1975. Only the first chapter of this first draft survives.[55] It began with a discussion of a lecture that Virginia Woolf once gave, on whether, had William Shakespeare an equally clever sister, Judith, she would have received the education and opportunities to achieve as had her brother. Woolf thought not. It was a nice start, but it disappeared from the report. McKinnon felt that the draft was not 'capable of being published in our name'.[56] He believed that a Schools Commission report needed ideas and vision certainly, but that it had to be based on facts and figures and an inexorable building of a case for achievable policy change and action. A different genre of writing was required. There was an ideological issue as well. The report would be reformist, innovative and daring but not radical in the way that some on the committee, such as Widdup and Torsh, might have wanted. Its brief would not be expanded to encompass gender relations and identities more broadly. Schools and teachers *would* be considered capable of reform. This was the kind of argument and writing that Jean Blackburn was good at.

Around this time, the workings of the Commission were challenged by a transition from triennial to annual budget planning. The changes made feasible by a three-year planning cycle were under threat, and with it a key rationale for the existence of the Schools Commission itself. In a renewal of her correspondence to daughter Susan, which had waned during her work on *Schools in Australia*, Jean commented: 'I have the enormous job of largely rewriting and of editing the draft of our girls report over the next couple of weeks. The fate of the Commission hangs in the balance'.[57]

It took the rest of 1975 to produce the report, *Girls, School and Society*. There was conflict. Dany was on the radical side, not only in feminism but in her approach to schooling. Lyndsay Connors had written about Dany's disenchantment with schooling because sexism was deeply embedded in its structures and practices.[58] Jean was also concerned about sexism, but she took a different approach to overcoming its impact on girls, maintaining a belief in the equalising potential of schooling. In Dany's words, 'Jean was much more devoted to the possibilities of "the school"'. Jean acknowledged that she and Dany 'fought and fought in the committee. But it was a productive kind of fighting and that was very good'. From Dany's perspective, she thought that she had 'a very good relationship with Jean … she always made me feel she respected me, and my views – she didn't agree with them. We had what I would call a civil disagreement'.[59] Dany told us, her interviewers:

> The biggest issue that I had with Jean [Blackburn] was that I wrote a draft, and then she came along and rewrote it all, and she didn't just 'rewrite' it, it was a complete change of, not focus, it was a complete change of style and analysis and politics. And, of course, I wasn't very happy about it.[60]

During the period in which Jean was working intensively on *Girls School and Society*, she was also worried about her son Bill's mental health. He was living in Sydney and had told her that 'he had had great difficulty resisting the urge to kill himself and had gone and deposited all pills at the chemist to remove the possibility'. Jean was in contact with his doctor, and arranging for family and friends to provide a 'backstop' for Bill. 'I have found that I don't want to talk to anyone about it, but was getting pretty neurotic myself writing the damn girls report'.[61]

Figure 7.1 Jean in the early Schools Commission years, with her youngest son, Hugh, who was still living at home. Jean was often in Canberra working on the Disadvantaged Schools Program and towards the report *Girls, School and Society*. 1975. *Photographer unknown, courtesy of Susan Blackburn.*

Problems also arose because the Committee had to manage the perception that, by putting emphasis on improving the success of girls at school, it was criticising schools for not intervening in the situation. Some also thought that the Committee was denigrating women who wanted to marry and stay at home to look after husbands and children. Jean told Peter Biskup:

> we considered that very carefully for a long time, and I think we all advanced our thinking about it and that what we said in the end was, OK, people had to have in fact the option, with some full understanding, and the options shouldn't be constructed by sex. And, in a way, some of that stuff was very advanced for its time, because it was saying that this thing was about changing boys as well as about changing girls.[62]

Another point of contention arose about the teaching of sexuality. Jean observed that the Committee 'got into some trouble down the track about whether in teaching about sexuality ... you should teach about homosexuality, we nearly all fell to bits over that issue; we wouldn't say it because it would jeopardise other things that we wanted to say. I didn't know that I supported it, anyway'. David Widdup argued for a policy that included a recognition of homosexuality, and the problems that gay and lesbian youth had with schooling and education.[63] He lost the argument, and Jean, with the backing of McKinnon led the opposition. McKinnon highlighted the role of Jean Martin in matters such as this, and the importance of her advice on the writing of the final report.[64]

The published report was far-reaching, as was required by its terms of reference:

1. to examine the extent of underachievement by women and girls in education and its contribution to the inferior status of women;
2. to examine the reasons for this, including community attitudes and implicit and explicit discrimination against women and girls in schools;
3. to examine the ramifications of the increasing participation by women in the labour force on Australian education;
4. to recommend any program projects and the necessary funding to assist girls so that they have as many careers and life choices open to them as do boys.[65]

The report covered many aspects of schooling but was not limited to it since 'social realities beyond the school and social changes going on in the society clearly have relevance for schools'.[66] The Committee conducted original research, but also received and analysed submissions from schools, parents and teachers. This 'showed that social class was more significant than sex in determining who stayed how long in school, but that in *post school* educational participation sex was more significant than social background'.[67] Recognising that all girls were not equally disadvantaged meant that new questions needed to be asked about their specific disadvantages. A different set of policy responses were anticipated as a result, different for example to those developed for young people from socially disadvantaged backgrounds in general, who were not well served by schooling. The report recognised that schooling contributed to patterns of inequality for girls beyond school and drew attention to what both girls and boys learnt in school about their futures.

Jean did not necessarily support the setting up of girls' units in departments of education to educate teachers in the ways in which schooling did not perform as well for girls as for boys, especially when girls' participation to the end of secondary school surpassed that of boys. She argued that the emphasis needed to be on eliminating sexism – the kind that not only limited opportunities for girls but limited boys as well. It was not a popular argument, particularly among those feminists who considered that the curriculum, both its content and how it was taught, was not inclusive of girls' experiences, and their differences. Jean was not very sympathetic towards this view.

Lyndsay Connors added the following explanation of Jean's position: 'she wasn't against feminist analysis or anything like that but, in the end, she wasn't buying the idea that women were some innately superior race'. Jean believed that 'there is always a tension between equality and difference, which one sees in all directions of public policy'.[68] Connors 'found her very inspiring as a feminist ... She believed sincerely that a world that was better organised for girls and women would be better for men as well. It was a sort of uncomplicated view in a way ... Yes it did attract some hostility'.[69]

The group analysis that Jean had applied in making the case for funding based on socio-economic disadvantage was not as useful in describing girls' experiences of schooling. Being a girl did not require 'special' treatment but girls' differences, both between themselves and compared to boys, needed to be better understood and addressed. At the same time, the report did recognise that some groups of girls and women did have special needs due to limited access to educational opportunities that may also have involved the effects of racism and isolation. The needs of girls and women from a migrant background, those who were Aboriginal and those living in country areas were highlighted.

Girls, School and Society criticised the limiting function of currently existing male as well as female norms, its explanatory power resting on sex role socialisation theory.[70] Published during International Women's Year, the report reflected the growing influence of the Women's Movement, and an expansion and elaboration of feminist analyses. There was favourable reference to the new feminism which had 'opened up new ways of looking at education as part of the process through which differing expectations are passed to boys and girls growing up', going beyond a simple comparison of differences in participation and achievement to a recognition of the impact of 'social arrangements and differing perceptions of possibilities among boys and girls. The Women's Movement was redefining the issues and the ways which they were to be confronted'.[71] There was concern with the educational, career and life impacts of low *self-esteem* among girls, and a strong discussion of sexism as its cause. Sexism was about 'the expectation that individuals will be different kinds of people occupying different social positions merely because they are female or male [and] is very like racism which generalises in similar ways from characteristics acquired by birth.'[72] There was a recognition that masculinity and femininity varied in different societies, which strengthened the argument against allocating too much responsibility to nature or genetics for perceived differences between girls and boys.

The report argued that children learned to conform to particular 'sex stereotypes' or 'sex roles' through 'sex role socialisation'. Occasionally boys got the worst of it: 'Deep seated fears of homosexuality in our society, and stronger condemnation of it among males, undoubtedly play a part in what appear to be more severe early sex role shaping of boys than girls'.[73] The report surveyed the overt and 'hidden curriculum' that operated in schools. Equal treatment of boys and girls was the aim. It identified multiple inequities and discriminations that existed in schools and were capable of reform. It was strong on such recommendations. On the necessity of sex education for example, it recognised that some communities might be offended in its implementation. As in all the reports associated with Jean, the impacts of social class, and then migrant and Indigenous circumstances conditioned the argument. The report established 'principles for action in schools – and knew its own significance. It was the 'first national consideration of the education of women and girls in Australia'.[74]

Despite the controversies, Lyn Yates assessed the Report to be 'probably the best one that was done on this area world-wide in the 70s'.[75] Denise Bradley recalled, 'I remember reading that report and being stunned ... It was such a revolutionary document'.[76] Jean Martin's biographers assessed it as an 'epoch-defining document both for educational policy and the emerging feminist movement'.[77]

Girls, School and Society was a foundational document that underwrote efforts in state education departments and schools to reduce inequalities by improving and expanding the education of girls. The Schools Commission argued that if the issue of sex role socialisation was viewed as a discrete issue that was only of relevance to girls, to be addressed through a discrete program, then 'this may tend to absolve people from the need to think about it in context'. Instead, it argued that 'since girls are a part of all education, their special needs should be considered in the development of all programs'. The Commission supported an integrated approach to addressing the needs of girls, but it exercised its influence through its special programs. To be successful, this integrated approach would need to be taken up in all its programs.[78]

The Australian Schools Commission set out three phases in its 'program' for girls: first, an analysis of the issues and a consequent increase in the individual and social consciousness of the impact of sex role socialisation; second, the recognition of the implications of this new consciousness for the various facets of education; and third, a translation of intellectual commitment into action. It acknowledged that the final phase was the most difficult, and the Commission did have difficultly following through. But without the foundation of the first and second phases, the efforts of the states and of feminists working in education may not have been possible or as well targeted.[79]

Soon after *Girls Schools and Society* was published, the Commission established a regular standing committee of the Commission tasked with advising it on particular topics, conducting relevant research, monitoring national action and reviewing legislation. Its terms of reference included: 'to recommend action research projects related to the education of women and girls for funding by the Commission', and, 'To stimulate at all levels in education study and action designed to encourage awareness of sex role socialisation and sex stereotyping and to promote the development of vocational advice which is not based on sex differences'.[80] A further advisory group established in support of the policy was made up of a broad selection of people including those involved in the different levels of education, unionists, journalists, academics, and so on. The advisory group differed in composition and purpose from the committee that had produced *Girls Schools and Society*. It was more representative of those who could implement its recommendations. The executive officer was Pam Cahir, who had been hired by the Commission as an advisor on girls' education.

Susan Ryan was an active Labor Party and Women's Electoral Lobby member in the Australian Capital Territory. Before the Committee had finished its work, she was an elected Senator to the Australian parliament. In her biography, Ryan wrote:

> *Girls, School and Society* ... would irrevocably change the debate about gender and education. The executive officer to the committee, Daniela Torsh, was a cutting-edge researcher into gender issues in schooling. When released in 1975, this report set out within a clearly described economic and social framework all the ways in which schools had limited girls' opportunities and reinforced artificial and damaging divisions between the sexes. [...] directed by Jean Blackburn, one of Australia's best education thinkers, and supported by the excellent work of the path-breaking sociologist Jean Martin, the working group had comprehensively examined curriculum, organisation, performance of teachers' assessment methods and relevance to the labour market. The report made a convincing case for change in all these areas and set the direction for reform strategies for the next twenty years.[81]

People who knew Jean say that they can see her influence and recognise her ideas in all the major reports that she worked on, but she herself was careful to acknowledge that these were collective efforts. In 1975, she wrote to Barry Hill, the education journalist at *The Age* to thank him for the 'nice things' he said about *Girls School and Society*, and to ask him to not refer to her as its 'principal author', nor for *Schools in Australia*.[82] Jean knew well the experience of writing reports for committees. When providing feedback to Dany Torsh on her first draft of *Girls, Schools and Society*, Jean commented: 'It is luxurious to be cast in the role of critic rather than creator! However it is hacked about, all honour goes to the one who first has the courage to enunciate a framework'.[83]

Jean continued to experience Commission work pressure as 'quite killing'. Shirley Randell, then a policy adviser in the School Commission's secretariat and subsequently the Director of the Disadvantaged Schools Program, recalled how she supported Jean when she was writing drafts for the Commission's Report for the Triennium 1976–8:

> Jean was a huge self-critic, and at the end of a day she'd sit in her room and write, and write, and write ... she'd drink Scotch, I think she even smoked ... can't remember ... she sat in that room and she'd furiously write. At the end of the day I'd go in and ask how it was going. And she'd say, 'This is rubbish', and screw it up and throw it in the rubbish bin. 'I'll start again tomorrow'.
>
> So I would pull the stuff out of the rubbish bin and type it up. And have it there for her the next day.[84]

In the middle of 1974, Jean attended the World Congress of Comparative Education Societies in Geneva to inform herself and the Commission about problems and directions of change in other industrialised countries. During this trip, she also visited the United Kingdom, and met with people involved in similar programs to those funded by the Commission. Although she was frustrated that some of the people she planned to meet were unavailable, the trip provided her with the opportunity to reflect on the work of the Commission. In her written report on the trip, Jean spelled out what it would take for the Commission 'to establish a right to exercise leadership within a framework of agreed values'. Her reflections suggest a maturing of her understanding of the 'funding exercise' that the Commission was undertaking. There was no doubt that it had responsibility for overseeing school funding, but the right to exercise educational leadership was something it would have to earn.

> In order to exercise the power latent in good ideas, the Commission has to demonstrate that it has them, that they are feasible in the real world and that they have support in a forward moving body of opinion which has considerable following among people working in the field of education and/or among the public generally.[85]

Perhaps more than any other commissioner or policy maker since, Jean's vision for schooling was intended to release the power latent in good ideas. She undertook this task in collaboration with her peers, with those in the profession of education, and also with members of the Australian population who shared her concerns.

Jean was appointed to the Schools Commission because of the quality of her prior work with Peter Karmel. As a commissioner, she stepped out of Karmel's considerable shadow and established herself as one of Australia's foremost and creative educational leaders. The Commission, under Ken McKinnon's leadership and with a number of remarkable commissioners including Jean, along with Greg Hancock,

Joan Kirner, Peter Tannock and David Bennett, had more than met the expectations of the Whitlam Labor government's education policy. But by 1975 the oil shock had occurred, and the last Labor budget prepared by the new Treasurer, Bill Hayden, retreated from its big spending predecessors. The economic turmoil exacerbated the political turmoil that too often engulfed the Labor government. Their combined effect would not only rebound on the Schools Commission but national education policy more generally.

Chapter 8

SCHOOLS COMMISSIONER: FRASER GOVERNMENT YEARS, 1976–1980

> We asked Jean Blackburn if she considered the possibility of a [school] council and parents … marching the school back to the worst of 19th century educational practices. 'That's a hard one,' she said. She got up from her chair, paced a bit, sat down again. She has an easy face to watch – open, fresh, marvellously animated. The smiles and raised eyebrows that punctuate her talk vanished: 'Well, if that's what they want, – if they can't be convinced otherwise – I have to say it's their right. Of course, they would need solid backing from the community'.[1]

Soon after winning the election at the end of 1972, Australia's new Labor government recognised the Peoples Republic of China, opening the way for visits to China by different groups. Many educators were keen to see the impact of the Cultural Revolution on students, teaching and schools, an interest that was linked with the educational turmoil in the West arising from the student revolt, deschooling and alternative schooling movements and New Left thinking about education. Deirdre Jordan, a lecturer in educational sociology at the University of Adelaide was desperate to go. She engaged her contacts, among them Hugh Hudson in the South Australian Labor government, then through Hudson to Mick Young, one of the architects of the 1972 Labor victory. Jordan and a friend recruited for a tour for January 1976. Jean Blackburn and Maureen Linskey, both from the Schools Commission, signed up. Susan, Jean's daughter, joined the trip as well. Jean told her not to worry about the cost. She would have plenty of money since she was holding 'a document signed by the Gov Gen [Governor-General] and Minister' extending her appointment for six years, 'if I last that long'. Jordan held meetings of the group in late 1975, introducing Jean to her co-travellers as 'big-time'. The description embarrassed her.[2]

Jean avidly read up on China, but she was anxious. She never quite knew how her ASIO file might affect foreign travel, and in this case, to a communist country.[3] In the end there was no trouble. Via Manilla, Hong Kong and Guangzhou, the group flew into Beijing on the evening of January 5, 1976. It was a momentous time to be setting foot in China. Three days later, Zhou Enlai died and the trip was conducted amongst universally worn black arm bands as mourning gripped the nation. Mao Zedong was in his last few months of life, as was the Cultural Revolution. The power of the Gang of Four was slipping away.

The Australian group visited universities, technical institutes, infant, primary, middle and secondary schools – and re-education camps for error-prone comrades and citizens. Despite being told many times that it was impossible to learn to grow rice on a blackboard, much of the pedagogy the group saw was conservative, but with the addition of practical classes such as students practising acupuncture on one another. There were factory annexes attached to schools. The aim was to inculcate a pro-worker socialist culture. Students learnt to labour as they were educated. There would be no false distinctions made between mental and manual work. Like others in the group, Jean was captivated by the performances put on by tiny children through to older youth. The song and dance routines were intensely colourful, patriotic and Maoist.

Jean was interested in more than education. One of her fellow travellers, Judith Redden, was on the trip. She knew Jean through Schools Commission activity in South Australia's Catholic schools. Judith told the story: 'Jean was fascinating in China. [...] we'd missed out on a visit to the street committee, and so Jean and Deirdre and I managed to wangle our way to have a special visit. [...] to sit down with these women in the street committee.' As the women talked about managing the community's housing, marriages, indeed, fertility – under what circumstances having a child might be allowed, 'Jean was ... right into the situation and thinking through ... the consequences of what might happen as a result of this [social engineering]'.[4]

In the mid-1970s Westerners were rarely seen in China, so on ascending the Bell Tower in the centre of Xi'an for example, the group attracted a crowd of thousands. Bicycle and foot traffic in central Xi'an came to a stop as the crowd stared. From Beijing and Xi'an, the group travelled by train and air to Zhengzhou, Wuhan and back to Guangzhou. They were away 23 days in all.

Jean's experience of the trip in China gave her new perspectives on several issues. Speaking to a special education conference on 'parents and professionals' in September 1976, she told the participants that China was interested in reducing the isolation of schools from the rest of society:

committees of workers, peasants and soldiers, along with CP [Communist Party] cadres and teachers run the schools, with considerable local autonomy, relying on the binding force of a shared view of the purposes of the operation, and a determination to end the gap between mental and manual labour.

Parents, she informed the conference,

were a non-category so far as the governance of schooling is concerned. I was greeted with incredulity when I asked about their role. I was told that workers, soldiers, peasants and teachers are also parents, so there was no need for parents to be separately represented.

Jean went on to say that the apparent consensus about schooling may have been 'imposed' but at least there was clarity about 'the integration of schooling into the general purposes and life of the society'. In Australia of course, things 'were very different and a great deal more complicated'.[5]

In later years the tendency of educators like Jean to view education reform in China during the Cultural Revolution sympathetically was sharply revised, as evidence of the violence inflicted on the educated, including teachers, professors and other 'bourgeois' intellectuals, and the setbacks to schooling and higher education that had occurred, became undeniable. Dean Ashenden remembered Jean relating the Chinese experience with deep scepticism, but that may have come a little later.[6] Within a fortnight of arriving home, Jean asked Susan if she had yet managed to make sense of China: 'The more time passes the more impressive the whole bit seems to me – especially the degree of local initiative, even if it is within a dictated framework.'[7]

It was in Hong Kong, on the way home, that Jean learnt that she had been included in the Australia Day honours list for 1976. She would be an 'Officer' of the Order of Australia, and Peter Karmel, a 'Companion'.[8] By the time she got back to Adelaide there were congratulatory letters, 'which I presently need to keep up the spirits'.[9] (Like many of her co-travellers, Jean experienced illness during and after the trip.) Among those who congratulated her were Susan Ryan and Margaret Bearlin. Ruth Hoadley wrote that the official citation

> won't say the things I would like to say – You have enriched my life, and ... everyone who has the privilege of coming in contact with you, even briefly, by your dedication, your lively appreciation of society, your vision of what could be, and your willingness to work prodigiously hard to bring it to reality, your scholarship which is tied so firmly to the needs of people – but perhaps most of all by the loving kindness that flows from you. Just by being you, you are an inspiration. Thank you.

Dick reported to Susan that Jean and he were feeling 'the clutch of the Establishment about us'.[10]

Receiving an Order of Australia was always going to be fraught. The Governor-General had dismissed the Whitlam-led Labor government less than three months previously and soon enough the new Prime Minister, Malcolm Fraser, reintroduced imperial honours. Not only Jean, but H. C. Coombs, Jean's old colleague in the wartime federal public service, and the writer, Patrick White, resigned their honours.[11] Jean wrote to John Kerr as Governor-General, telling him she would never have considered accepting what had now become an 'imperial award', nor be a member of an order that awards titles, 'setting people apart in everyday life'. The 'false position' she had been placed in required her to resign.[12] Jean was angry, and it made her even less enamoured of working, though one step removed in the Schools Commission, for a Liberal-Country Party coalition government.

For most in the Schools Commission there was apprehension on returning to work in early 1976. It was not even certain that the Commission would survive, given the hostility of the Liberals to its establishment. By 1976 however, opposition had lessened. Country Party support for the Commission continued, and Catholic Church support had grown, along with the more predictable support from those committed to public education. The Commission had 'delivered' to more than public schools, and, with the passing of the federal budget through the Senate following the Whitlam government's dismissal, the plans of the Commission for 1976 were secure. Nevertheless, even if the Commission survived, there were lobbies that expected policy changes following the fall of Labor. Jean wrote on the Disadvantaged Schools Program a fortnight after the dismissal: 'the main thrust in 1976 is to keep up the impetus begun and to extend it through continuous re-appraisal of action.'[13]

Margaret Guilfoyle held the education portfolio from 11 November 1975 until just before Christmas. She appeared to have little sympathy for the Commission.[14] One of the lobbies that had great expectations after the change of government was the Headmasters' Conference of Independent Schools. A letter written to Guilfoyle welcomed the probability that 'the doctrinaire elements might be taken out of the Schools Commission charter'. It looked forward to new policy that would encourage parental school choice, the end of 'equality of outcomes', easing the burden of parents' investment in private schooling and further development of a voucher system to fund schooling.[15]

Schools Commissioner: Fraser government years, 1976–1980

From late December 1975 through to the end of 1979, John Carrick, a powerful figure in the Liberal Party, was the Minister of Education. Though the Commission would re-orient itself under his direction, he was not as averse to the Commission as others on the right of politics. He appeared to trust that the presence of Peter Tannock on the Commission would protect the interests of non-government schools.[16] Nevertheless, a period of tension and reappraisal of the philosophy and work of the Commission was inevitable. As Minister for Federal Affairs as well as Education, Carrick was flummoxed when a set of grants for individual schools under the Disadvantaged Schools Program arrived on his desk for approval. He would not approve them, sending them off to the relevant state ministers of education for advice. Presumably, since the Disadvantaged Schools Program was not abandoned by the Fraser government, Carrick came to understand the rationale behind DSP grants to individual schools.[17]

The new year began badly for Jean. After China she spent some time at home, ill with chronic bronchitis. She wrote to Susan:

> I cannot feel any enthusiasm about working for the Fraser Government. The Schools Commission will be made over to be useless as an independent force (if it is not abolished). The new triennial report (due at the end of next month) has not had a word written yet and I don't want to write any. In short, I shall, whether by the decision of others or my own decision, not be long in the SC as I see it. I don't really know how to think about it.[18]

When Jean returned to work, she responded with energy, if not optimism, to the challenge of defending and extending the work of the Commission. She was the main drafter of chapter 2 in the Commission's report for the rolling triennium, 1977–1979 which recapitulated 'basic positions' discussed in previous reports. The subheadings were: 'Equality of opportunity', 'Equality and outcomes' and 'Openness and participation'.[19] The essays under each heading were not necessarily what the new government wished to read. Jean, no doubt seen as responsible for many of the 'doctrinaire elements' of the Commission, knew there was trouble ahead. Over the next few years she put effort into thinking through a viable Commission plan, indeed national plan, for funding Australian schools under the new political circumstances.[20] It became an impossible problem, and Jean – indeed, the Commission under McKinnon – eventually lost the capacity to influence funding decisions.

In September 1976, fellow-Commissioner Joan Kirner sought Jean's help in getting some arguments together for a presentation she was due to make. Jean told her not to panic – she would know what to say – but then Jean listed the following issues: despite declining recurrent funding 'it is vital that national responsibility for adequate standards remain', the crucial importance of federal funding if school buildings are to be improved, the essential work and impact on improving parental involvement and the devolution of decision-making, the role of national intervention in drawing attention to populations with special needs (migrant, Aboriginal, disadvantaged, girls and the handicapped), and the role of federal policies in causing improvements to 'the ways State bureaucrats operate (in supporting good people embedded in not very supportive environments)'. Jean wrote about parents, how they would be 'ineffective until such time that a funded national secretariat employing researchers can be put together on behalf of parents' and that 'power requires knowledge in the educational sphere'. Jean thought that Joan would have thought of these points, but she agreed that defensiveness now characterised the argument. It would be up to Joan if she wished to point to the present government's susceptibility to the non-government, non-Catholic schools' lobby.[21] Jean signed the letter with love.

The Fraser government communicated its changing priorities to the Commission. The 1978 directive by Minister Carrick is representative:

> The Government wishes to encourage choice and diversity in education and to assist parents to exercise the right of choice of schooling for their children in either government or non-government schools. Its programs of grants towards running costs recognise this principle and also the expectation that the States and the non-government schools will continue to make reasonable contributions towards the operating costs of their schools and systems.[22]

McKinnon, chair of the Commission, had little option in re-orienting the direction of the Commission, even if Jean may have wished for a stiffer resistance.

Jean had written earlier of the combined effects of the government's new limits on schools funding, and the directive that 'payments to non-government schools should be increased in specific ways'. The effect would be a transfer of 'some $13 million of Commonwealth funds in 1978 from government to non-government schools'. The consequence would be that 'the Commission's consultations with State and non-government authorities and with teachers and parents have little credibility, since who is to gain and who is to lose is already known, and the Commission is unable to influence policy'. The reports of the Commission were in danger of becoming little more than 'an academic exercise', 'the confirmation of an already decided allocation of funds'. Jean argued that the Commission was being deprived of its responsibilities as set out by the Act, and that a consequence would be a new outbreak of 'prejudice and bigotry' between government and non-government school sectors as the 'needs principle' in funding policy was displaced.[23]

New warfare did break out. The government schools' lobby was increasingly alienated from the changing direction of the new government, and therefore the Commission. In 1980, David Widdup, having moved on from the *Girls, School and Society* exercise, was acting Secretary of the Australian Teachers Federation (ATF). On behalf of the ATF, he wrote that recurrent grants were a huge problem as the backlog in government schools' building programs mounted and areas of disadvantage were left unaddressed. 'The continuance of the nexus between government school running costs and private school recurrent grants … allows the Government to channel more funds to rich private schools while funds to government schools are frozen.'[24]

The Defend our Government Schools (DOGS) organisation, which had never reconciled itself to the Commission, began a new round of campaigning against state aid to private schools.[25] For the Commission itself the argument could not be as simple as government versus non-government schools funding. In August 1977, Jean wrote to John Keeves (Director of the ACER) that in some areas the effect of Commission policies was better than expected because state governments had unexpectedly invested more in schools as well as the federal government. But there was a continuing problem because, despite improvements, the gap between the resourcing and resources of parochial Catholic schools and Commission targets was increasing. It presented the 'ticklish situation' where the needs approach suggested a transfer of funds from government to this group of non-government schools.[26] At one point, Jean thought the answer had to be the transfer of the parochial schools into the public system, as had occurred in New Zealand. Otherwise there was simply too little capital to effect 'acceptable standards'.[27]

Jean tried to point out the consequences of the Fraser government's policies, but there was little response, especially as the efforts of non-government schools, rich or poor, to secure a greater share of federal government funding came to coincide with the beginnings of a shift in government policy to neoliberalism, or economic rationalism, as it was called in Australia. The difficulties of the Commission were exercised in a paper reviewing its report for the triennium 1979–1981 produced by the Parliamentary Library. Its first sentence was calculated to alarm: 'The Schools Commission Report can be viewed as an attempt to re-establish its own priorities in the face of the Government's policies.'[28] In mid-1978 the phrase 'choice and diversity' had entered the governmental discourse about what was expected from federal schools' policy.[29] It increasingly displaced the 'equality and needs' discourse.

The successes of the Schools Commission had rested in part on the capacity of its members to work together, to unite the parties which were most affected by its decisions, and the fact that the Commission stood 'apart from the responsibility of operating schools and is therefore less constrained by a need to defend the status quo, more open to alternative possibilities'.[30] The Fraser government prepared to make changes in both these areas. The government's 'new federalism' as well as choice and diversity approaches would see a shift in power from the Commission to school systems and state governments.

One of Jean's allies on the Commission had been David Bennett. He had charge of the Special Projects (Innovations) Program which was devoted to teacher development and changing school cultures. His expectations of what Australian schooling might look like in the future, and of what teachers might be capable, often coincided with Jean's views. Though a little younger than Jean, David's path through the University of Melbourne, labour, socialist and education politics probably resonated with her. He was one of the architects of Labor policies in education for Victoria and the nation from the late 1960s. He was an obvious person for Minister Carrick not to reappoint when his initial term on the Commission ended in January 1978. He, Joan Kirner and Jean were identified by observers as the heart of the social democratic vision as it existed in the Commission.[31]

Like Jean, Kirner was an old scholar of University High. She had been sent there when her private school could not offer senior science subjects. On the Commission, she soon formed a strong relationship with Jean, and in later years wrote about it:

> it was on the Schools Commission that I met one of the most important influences of my life – Jean Blackburn: intellectual and educational thinker and writer extraordinaire. It was Jean who told me about the early feminist battles, who showed me how to work from the facts and the research, who made the connection between economics and social justice, who made me argue and write professionally. And in return I linked her with the importance of community ownership, participation and networking.[32]

Jean was impressed with Joan, a 'skilled politician', the 'most skilled politician I have ever had anything to do with'.[33]

As a full-time commissioner, Jean continued to work on existing and developing programs. She travelled often and widely, accepting invitations to speak at many conferences and seminars. Along with the meetings of the Commission itself, she was an active member of committees that had responsibility for receiving submissions for school improvement projects and the spending of funds, especially those in South Australia and Victoria. She accepted appointments to South Australian education-related committees and authorities, notably the Tertiary Education Authority (TEASA). For the SA Education Department, she reviewed papers for the Tanunda conference on planning for the 1980s. There she argued for the radical reform of teacher appointments and promotions. Appointing the right staff for local circumstances was a priority, and work with the teachers' union was essential if such a goal was to be realised.[34]

There was a new Commission initiative in country Victoria, a program that ran parallel to the main Disadvantaged Schools Program. Joan Kirner fostered it and Don Edgar, a sociologist specialising in family policy, was involved. In reporting to McKinnon, Jean talked about the planning committee, government and Catholic school representatives working together. She believed the program had generated community interest, and participation: 'it acts as a learning experience for both professionals and community, bringing them together in consideration of what the students should get out of school and in the consideration of the quality of community life'. It spread an understanding that schools could not be solely responsible for educational experiences and outcomes. 'The format of the program expresses the belief that responsibility for and control over the allocation of funds is a central aspect of real community participation in the work of the schools.'[35] Such summary statements expressed Jean's view of what an ideal Commission program or project might attempt and achieve. A potential problem for the program was its vulnerability to criticism if money was spent, say, on a local swimming pool rather than a literacy teacher. People in the Commission could usually see the significance for education of this kind of community development, but its legality was marginal.[36]

One rural issue that occupied lobby groups and the Commission during this time was whether the Commission should fund boarding schools as a solution to some forms of rural disadvantage. Jean spoke bravely to one lobby group, arguing that there were unacceptable impacts on local schools within commuting distance when families abandoned them. A handwritten note to herself reminded Jean of a basic position: 'public funds should not be used to maintain or increase inequalities of circumstances of upbringing between children'.[37] There was a more sympathetic response to families in genuinely isolated circumstances.

The Disadvantaged Schools Program remained at the heart of her work. Her memories of school visits from the late 1960s had convinced her of the program's crucial importance:

> We went to a shocking school on Monday – Kilburn Primary, where the kids have nits and the Head is too stupid to see the problems. He is well equipped he says – with the (latest?) old library where the kids are all below their chronological age in reading etc. They surely are deprived kids. More than half the school has only one parent for one reason or another.[38]

Jean's files on the Disadvantaged Schools Program in the National Archives are prodigious in number and size. They include material on relevant academic research along with her papers and contributions to administration. One of her best papers is titled 'Future of Disadvantaged Schools Program'. It concluded:

Our Program is a challenge to schools. We should not try to conceal that. It is not a destructive challenge, as I believe the American compulsory public disclosure of test results ... is. It is a challenge the schools concerned can meet on their own terms. It challenges educators to accept responsibility for the part they play in accentuating or diminishing the negative consequences for some children of an unequal society. That, basically, is what I believe the Program is about. It does not attempt to impose answers, but rather to engage people in the power and responsibility of finding their own.[39]

The DSP occupied a large part of Jean's time. She continually asked the question: 'Where do we go from here?'[40]

Figure 8.1 One of the many Disadvantaged Schools Program committees that Jean attended on behalf of the Schools Commission.
Seated from third on the left, Shirley Randell (Director of the Program), Judith Redden (South Australian Catholic Schools DSP representative) and Jean Blackburn, c1977.
Courtesy of Shirley Randell.

Jean talked to children and parents on her school visits. Parents also wrote to her. One long letter from a mother passed on to Jean discussed the positive role of the DSP in her working-class suburb, and the frustrations. Too many of the local secondary teachers refused to believe working-class children and their parents were as ambitious for their futures as the more affluent. The consequence was low expectations for the children, a denial of quality education.[41] How were parents understood in terms of the Disadvantaged Schools Program?

> The emphasis is on school change, not client blame. This perspective has proved difficult for many professional educators and teachers to accept. The tradition of educators is to blame parents for lack of interest in their child's schooling, to feel that their obligation to children does not extend to varying their own approaches to teaching to suit learners, or to examine their own assumptions.[42]

Jean did not overestimate what the Commission and its programs could achieve. In a recorded talk on educational disadvantage for the University of New South Wales in March 1976, she argued that schools could not by themselves 'bring about a more equal society', but they could be more effective, especially with children 'whose social background does not mesh so neatly with that of teachers and bureaucrats as does that of the children of middle-class well-educated parents'. Irrespective of background, children needed to have the 'capacities required to allow them to be full citizens'.[43]

Schools already involved in the program had to be challenged to think better about what they were doing. The Commission's 'National Project for Dissemination and Communication' published two papers, one from Don Waters and the other, from Jean. They contrasted their approaches to the role of the teaching and learning of 'basic skills'. Waters argued that it was a good thing that the DSP sought social objectives, making for happier schools and students, and schools better embedded in their communities though he was not sure that there would be any 'pay-off' in terms of increased basic skills. Jean argued that school students had a lot of things to do, not just reading, writing and arithmetic. 'To be good at them at the cost of becoming dependent, passive, remaining ignorant about oneself and the world and being unselfconfident and downgraded would be senseless'. Teachers 'make the decisions which determine this – and without reasonable competence in the 3 R's it is difficult to become any of those other good things either'.[44]

Funding from the federal government through the Schools Commission for the DSP continued, but there were no new funds. The program began to do less, and new initiatives declined. Program accountability remained a pressure point. Were claims that the program improved children's learning justified?[45] The pressure to reliably define and measure disadvantage was unremitting. Jean was aware of competing approaches, such as the meritocratic, which was concerned with the variable participation of different social groups in post-compulsory education, or a standards-based approach, which looked at the 'failure to meet some basic minimum educational standard'. There was also the 'character of the neighbourhood' argument and its relationship to school achievement. She would argue that the competing approaches needed to be brought into the open.[46] Another question that did not go away was how schools were selected for participation in the DSP. The level of disadvantage was not always the primary criterion for selection. Resourcing, in Jean's words, 'in most systems is made on the basis of judgements about the quality of educational proposals put up by school staffs in collaboration with parents, to the degree that they can be achieved. [The] additional resources [are] an inducement to self critical analysis of school operations and proposals for improvement.'[47]

The distinctive character of the DSP was defended and publicised, and the successes celebrated. Shirley Randell as federal Director of the DSP visited Adelaide in April 1979. In South Australia the DSP was strongly supported by senior Education Department directors, John Steinle and Jim Giles. Randell observed: 'Very effective State Task Force with quality principal participation, however still no parental involvement at State level. Best programs I have seen in operation in Australia at Mansfield Park Primary and Junior Primary schools – both principals on the Task Force. Staff are specially selected at both schools; good retention, but four years work "burns out" teachers: high level of community involvement and support'.[48] Such memos point to the support that Jean and the program were receiving not only from Shirley Randell herself, but significant numbers of school teachers and principals, and state and Catholic education bureaucrats.

At the same time, Jean recognised that the DSP could cause conflict within schools. It was probably rare that teaching staffs were united in their attitudes. On a visit to Lalor High in Victoria in 1979 she discovered that:

> the principal and senior staff are opposed to the Program. They are opposed on ideological grounds, but also, I gathered, because of the way in which the Program works. There is a DSP committee in the school which receives and vets applications for funding under the program from faculty groups and individual teachers. Maths individualisation, remedial literacy, excursions etc. are funded under the Program, but there is not what could be called a considered school program. This is the more

remarkable in that many of the staff feel that the curriculum is unsuitable for most students.

In this case the principal wanted grants spent on building maintenance, resenting the right of groups other than the school council, to initiate the spending of funds. The principal and deputies believed that the school's capacity to teach the academic curriculum had been impaired as a result of new, more participatory decision-making. Jean thought that the school leadership was in opposition to its students. They seemed to believe that parental expectations that their children should qualify for more than similar employment in low-grade factory work were unrealistic. Jean concluded: 'it is hard to feel reassured about this school' with its irreconcilable differences in educational philosophy. She wondered if the air of frustration she often noticed in Victorian schools encouraged the teacher union militancy she observed there.[49]

Though Jean believed heart and soul in the DSP, she was not unconscious of the program's deficiencies, and not just because of its funding problems. In 1981, a year or so after leaving the Commission, she wrote that much 'of the rationale now appears simplistic and some aspects of it have given rise to minimum competency tests and other unhelpful devices' and maybe the word 'disadvantage' was one of the problems, becoming an 'excuse for all sorts of perversions of [the program's] original intent. At the same time, she stood by its original social justice justification, 'its main drift'.[50] The program had pioneered the identification of social group as opposed to individual characteristics as a basis for analysing educational experience and outcomes.[51]

Interest in the Disadvantaged Schools Program remained strong for many years. In 1989 Jean was asked to write a paper on its policy ideas for the Commonwealth Department of Employment, Education and Training. In doing so she argued that the program had unique importance in Australian educational history. It had disrupted the idea that all schools should be resourced equally, regardless of social inequality. 'It pioneered in public systems the notion of whole school participatory decision making'. As it evolved it 'became the most effective form of teacher development in our history', focused as it was on 'better learning approaches and higher achievement in schools located in poorer communities'.[52]

The DSP lost repute by the end of the century, especially as instrumentalism, including the precise measurement of student learning gained authority. Lyndsay Connors, a later Schools Commissioner, was angry with this development:

> No program has been more subject to misrepresentation. Most galling have been the many damaging conclusions that have been drawn by particular researchers, based on a false assumption that it was possible to compare stable populations over time within this Program. In fact, in NSW, the schools originally in the DSP were often those serving the children of the poorest working families in areas of inner city decay. Now they are mostly in different areas of the State, serving the children of those who have paid the price for economic re-structuring.[53]

It had been both a virtue, and source of frustration for some, that the DSP worked differently in different schools, education systems, sectors and states, and changed its character over time.

The most comprehensive assessment of the DSP was undertaken by R.W. Connell, Viv White and Ken Johnston. The claims that Jean made for the program were mainly supported in their conclusions, though the program's deficiencies were not underestimated either. 'Over its lifetime the DSP has been the venue for some of the most imaginative work in Australian education. Change has been incremental but it has happened.'[54]

> The DSP succeeded, as few other initiatives in Australian education have, in tapping the energy and inventiveness of classroom teachers and parents. It managed not only to mobilise a great deal of local action but also to sustain it over a decade and a half of erratic support from the centre. The decentralised design of the program has been crucial in this.[55]

Of all the practical legacies of Jean Blackburn's work for Australian education, this program was the most significant.

Jean's thinking in education covered multiple domains. She was one of the Commission's most reliable and articulate defenders and publicists. She was always alert to new argument and new research. She made sure she attended the conference in Sydney in June 1976 organised around Samuel Bowles and Herbert Gintis, and their newly published *Schooling in Capitalist America*. In seeking permission to attend the conference as a member of the Commission, she told McKinnon that it would demonstrate 'that we are not afraid of ideas!'[56] Jean led one of the conference discussion groups. However, it is unlikely that she was over-impressed by Bowles and Gintis's argument and view of the working-class school, that it mainly functioned to deliver compliant factory workers to industry. Jean met up with Jim Walker at the conference. He was developing his own argument about working-class schooling and work and would later refer to the Bowles and Gintis argument as 'crude reproductionism'. Jean and Jim talked at the conference about their shared admiration for the Jurgen Habermas book, *The Legitimation Crisis*. Later, Walker sought Jean's help in developing a research project based on critical theory, using Habermas in particular.[57] Jean insisted she was 'not on the Frankfurt tram', but that did not mean she was not interested, or willing to take up particular insights.[58] It remained true that following her 1940s and 1950s experiences with Marxism, she was not likely to become a devotee of any particular school of thought. Jean's friendship with Dean Ashenden meant that several of the papers that he and Brian Abbey wrote at this time, developing their Marxist analyses of education, appear in her files. She was interested, but there is not much evidence that they affected her thinking to any degree.[59]

Jean remained in touch with Peter Karmel. At some point he asked her for advice on a proposed questionnaire on 'Essential learning about society'. Jean told him that it was ill conceived, framed in a way that dissenting from any of its propositions 'would be tantamount to advocating wife beating'.[60]

Jean was also involved in assessing research proposals for the Education and Research Development Committee (ERDC). She assessed one proposal as having a too strong and outdated social-psychological orientation. 'There are many issues other than social mobility that alienate younger generations from parents. Ethnic identity, sexual mores and the social roles of the sexes are some which spring to mind.'[61] Jean also advised the Australian Council for Education Research (ACER) on occasion.

There was one project at this time about which she was enthusiastic. She was a referee in March 1976 for the funding from the ERDC of R.W. Connell and Dean Ashenden's, 'Class inequalities in schooling'. This project eventually led to more than one book, but the first, *Making the Difference* with two more authors, Sandra Kessler and Gary Dowsett, was a timely and historically significant sociological analysis of Australian schooling. Jean advised the proposed principal investigators on how to correct weaknesses in their application.[62] A few years later she had a little involvement in a project put together by Peter Fensham on youth alienation from school and transitions from school to employment.[63]

Jean reviewed materials sent out in the name of the DSP and Commission, a task that helped her clarify her curriculum thinking. She found a proposed 'Do-it-yourself' activity sheet being prepared for schools had too loose a discussion of class and culture. There was no such thing as a single 'migrant culture'. 'What is important for teachers is the view of the world kids have in their heads, how to get access to that view and how to enable them critically to examine it.' One section came across as pure propaganda. 'It is not possible to push a position down people's throats, especially one which assumes a level of social and political sophistication which most teachers lack.'[64] In another paper reviewing drafts for a report on student assessment, she began in typical form, trying to understand what the term 'progress' might mean. She reviewed the work of schools historically, especially the compulsory years, and their clear attachment to the 'social control' function, the governing of the unruly lower classes. The range of issues she surveyed as relevant to the making of assessment policy included the devolution of assessment authority to schools and the changing character of what should constitute the curriculum in a period of new social pressures.[65]

Jean wrestled with the idea of 'competency' based approaches to learning. Like other approaches, they too often concentrated 'on performance tested in pencil and paper ways', underplaying the 'extent to which learning is an interactive process in which the learner has to be engaged with the problem and to incorporate new information and insights into transformed mental structures which are his creative act'. A consequence of arguing that 'Knowledge consists in having good reasons for believing something to be the case', required a recognition that learning required more than restricted and formulaic approaches to content.[66]

Occasionally Jean 'let loose' publicly. One example is a talk Kevin Gilding asked her to give as part of the centenary celebrations for the Adelaide College of Advanced Education, the hundred years since the foundation of the former Adelaide Teachers College and its predecessors. The introduction to the subsequent publication described it as 'an unprepared and spontaneous expression of thought and feeling', with all the 'characteristic vigour of the speaker's style'. 'Unprepared' of course, it was not, but Jean did allow it to survive as a polemic. The target was older, assimilationist approaches to the education of non-English speaking migrant children. 'During the 1950s teachers tended to see migrant pupils as a nuisance' – how could they be taught if they did not already know English? She quoted Harold Wyndham's refusal, as Director-General of Education in New South Wales, to even collect statistics on such children, asserting that once they turned up in public schools they were 'Australian children'. She went on to look at the history of research into literacy, and the early ignoring, by the ACER for example, of the 'sociological ranking of their sample'. Pedagogy alone did not explain or solve the illiteracy dilemma. Her third example 'of wilful evasion of a difficult problem' related to state aid to non-government schools.[67]

Later, in the 1990s, Jean held forth on the effects that the old bureaucratic authoritarianism of public education departments had had on schools and teachers. It enabled the retreat from any local responsibility for what was going on in schools. Excuses for inaction were easy: 'They will not let us do it ... We have no control'. She related her experience in the early 1970s of hearing directors-general of education in Western Australia and New South Wales speaking to principals of their schools 'in a way that you would think some emperor kicking around slaves might speak'. Jean admitted however that the devolvement of authority to schools, the decentralisation question, was not straightforward. Sometimes you needed a strong centre to get things done.[68] Her thinking shifted over time and circumstance, on this as on other questions.

In April 1979 Jean travelled abroad on behalf of the Commission. This time she was seeking an understanding of developments in education policy in the United States, as well as attending an OECD forum in Paris for which she had to write a paper ('If I can subdue my body long enough to write ...').[69] Greg Hancock, her fellow full-time Schools Commissioner, had been seconded to the OECD, and he met her in Paris. Jean's paper for the meeting was on the financing and governance of education for special populations. It was revised and distributed by the Centre for Educational Research and Innovation (CERI), an education arm of the OECD. It began with typical clarity: 'In all public education systems, students benefit unequally from resources provided. Many of the decisions which bring about this result are either so traditional that they are unexamined or are made by professional educators within flexible budgets without being publicly visible or justified'.[70] There followed an identification of the different groups requiring differential funding, discussions of how this should be determined, and the politics of achieving good funding outcomes. Later she reflected on the Paris meeting, telling Alice Day from the Commission that:

> A mountain of research has not revealed anything not able to be deduced from common sense about such things as the effects of divorce, working mothers etc. on children. The answer is always – 'It all depends'; nothing can be attributed to the factor under study in isolation. The methodological problems of such studies, to put it mildly, are immense. I also find studying people in their most intimate lives as objects in this way distasteful.

She wondered if another kind of research might be more useful, research into:

> what schools appear to assume about families, about what can be left to families, what views teachers have of working mothers, unmarried partners, single parent families etc., at how well schools enable students to appreciate what is happening to families and have changed their own operating assumptions to respond to changes in societal patterns, [and] the implications those patterns may have for the schools' responsibility to young people.[71]

Regardless of her doubts about some of the research sponsored by CERI/OECD, Jean's participation meant that the Schools Commission was being noticed internationally.

From Paris, and after a distressing trauma at Charles de Gaulle airport – her booking from Paris had been cancelled – Jean flew to Washington.[72]

Her task in the United States was to examine the Title I program, a nationally funded effort aimed at improving schooling in poorer communities, but also schools 'in which special action for disadvantaged students is operating'.[73] Unlike the Australian DSP almost all its funds were to be used for 'withdrawal remedial instruction for low achieving students'.[74] She was organised for an impressive range of meetings with officials of the Division of Compensatory Education in the Office of Education in Washington and the Congressional Committee on Education, the National Institute of Education and the Institute for Educational Leadership. Then, after a day free in New York, it was on to California. She was to spend several days at Stanford University meeting education staff, and at least another day with officials of the State Department of Education in Sacramento. She was to meet representatives of the Friends of Public Education, the Coalition for Fair School Finance and the California Teachers Association. She visited schools in both Washington and Sacramento. She was away close to three weeks.[75] After arriving home she wrote to her host at Stanford:

> The trip was very valuable to me, reducing my insularity somewhat and informing my view of the US better. It is not unreasonable that in such a large population there should be so many people of the quality I talked with, but it impressed me greatly, nevertheless. So also did their generosity in giving time and willingness to engage, and their high seriousness. In retrospect, I recognise the degree to which I was incapacitated by nervousness. I am not really cut out for the establishment round.[76]

Self-deprecation was never far from Jean's interactions with the world. Nevertheless, she was pleased to affirm, after examining the California School Improvement Program, that her approach to DSP administration in Australia was supported 'by American research on school change – that the most effective action is that based on the analysis, and reflection of people who will carry out the action and for which they take responsibility.'[77]

Jean's trip to the United States was made under the auspices of 'The Australia/US Policy Project', founded in 1977 with Ford Foundation,

Commonwealth Department of Education and Schools Commission sponsorship. Peter Karmel, Ken McKinnon, Peter Tannock, Ken Jones and other Australians formed the local committee. McKinnon, who had studied for his doctorate at Harvard, had contacts within the Ford Foundation and with significant administrators and academics in government and Stanford. He had advocated the project and insisted that Jean's Title I work was about the US policy makers wanting to see how Australia dealt with disadvantaged students and schools, as much as Australians trooping off to the US to be told how to do it.[78]

In examining the Title I material from her US trip, Jean, not unexpectedly found its objectives and assumptions very different from those of the Commission, but she also recognised the contextual demands of a very different political system and society, and the consequences for thinking about poverty, disadvantage, and what schools might contribute to correcting the problems. She was pleased that the Title I Program 'has never supported, and does not now support, a client blame approach'. Importantly it 'directs the school to look at its own shortcomings in relation to its students and their parents'.[79] Jean wrote a report that was later published by the Commission and then the Curriculum Development Centre.[80] Its analysis was balanced. For example, though she criticised Title I for its intimidating compliance protocols she showed that she understood the reasons that had led to them. She also did not hesitate to expose the problems that the DSP in Australia had with project evaluation and accountability in the spending of funds. She thought it praiseworthy that Title I spelled out the rights of parents in seeking support under the program. This report is one of the few longer publications that appear under Jean's name as sole author.

By the late 1970s Jean was increasingly involved in work for a new Commission project on the schooling of 15 and 16 year-old youth, but her general responsibilities as a full-time Commissioner continued, including the two-day meetings every six weeks of the Commission in Canberra. Jean arrived some days ahead, to work with Shirley Randell on the DSP, consult with McKinnon, and prepare material for the Commission meeting. As pressures on the Commission increased it became more difficult to secure unanimity for its work. Jean was often engaged in trying to negotiate agreed wordings and policy.[81] Occasionally she would be the recalcitrant: 'I find myself unable to accept the decisions taken by the Commission at its last meeting'.[82] McKinnon worked hard to resist damaging dissension and factionalism within the Commission, and in this he was remarkably successful, though it became more difficult during the Fraser years.[83]

A major part of Jean's final year and a half on the Commission was taken up with the school visits that the Commission committed to in preparation for its project on the education of 15 and 16 year-old youth. She was constantly struck by the enormous diversity in the ways schools did or did not respond to the changing circumstances of the economy – and of youth. Her school visit reports constitute a remarkable archive of a moment in the history of Australian secondary schooling in the late 1970s. For example, on St James Christian Brothers College in Queensland, a non-systemic school that probably should have been in the Disadvantaged Schools Program, Jean reported that the school was unable or unwilling to cope with pressures arising from growing youth unemployment and the need for curriculum reform. The boys Jean talked to argued that 'the heavy dose of religious doctrine (5 periods a week) is counterproductive.' They told her that they were not getting enough of an education that would prepare them for the labour market.[84] At the other end of the scale was the Huntingdale Technical School in Victoria, earlier described as a 'lighthouse of alternative possibilities for education and society'. Jean praised the 'civilised relationships among and between staff and students'.[85]

In 1979 she turned up at Unley High, the school that her children, Bill, Susan and Hugh, had attended, and where Hugh had had such trouble. She noted its traditional characteristics, the academic expectations which made it difficult for the school to respond well to individual differences. The inflexibility of the school in responding to the needs of individuals was emphasised in her meeting with the school's mothers' group.[86] Jean was unlikely to have been surprised. At Henley High, also in South Australia, she noted the school's perplexity over 'how to succeed in running a school which prided itself on its academic reputation, without casting out the lesser breeds'.[87] The term, 'lesser breeds' was a sarcastic comment by Jean on the prevailing attitudes. At Port Adelaide High she noted the multiple problems in this working-class school: 'God knows what to do – I don't'. But having said that she made an astute analysis of the curriculum and how it might be improved.[88]

A few months later Jean was attempting to summarise what she had learnt from her dozens of school visits: 'The schools are highly organised, highly disciplined formal institutions in which problems of student apathy are more evident than active resistance to the school's regimen and characterised by high levels of organised task involvement'.[89]

Part of Jean's work included negotiation with community groups such as the Australian Greek Welfare Society over how Commission programs and their governance would affect them. Not everyone could get what they wanted. She found the single-minded 'chauvinism' of many of the ethnic organisations difficult to deal with.[90] She firmly resisted, for example, the idea that funding for multicultural education should be committed solely to the teaching of community languages, and that the state committees recommending on project funding should be dominated by such groups. Multicultural education was an issue for more than the community organisations. She worried that migrant and multicultural education were insufficiently distinguished.[91]

As she thought her way through the question of education for the 'handicapped' her responses to the demands of organisations were similar. She drafted a letter to David Bennett at one point, offering a plan about what kind of research should precede project funding, and why it was important, politically and tactically to keep the interested lobby groups engaged with the process.[92] She was prepared to question first principles. At a conference of the Special Education Association in 1976, she asked:

> Did we make a colossal mistake when we segregated our children from the general life of the community in schools? Did we build upon this initial folly in thinking that an activity which is essentially based on human interaction could be modelled on the impersonal rationalistic bureaucratic model of mass production with its input-output nexus, its pecking orders and rigidities?[93]

The Commission would fund the training of special education teachers, but it would also seek their placement in regular schools.[94] Jean argued against many of the historical consequences of traditional educational psychology: 'Diagnostic labels may be used as a means of evading the responsibility to teach as well as be a means to improved teaching'.[95] She was also critical of those advocating the various forms of separation of 'gifted and talented' students in schools. Privately she was scathing of a proposal for funding the 'gifted' as a new disadvantaged group.[96]

Jean had less to do with projects concerning Aboriginal education within the Commission. Nevertheless, she acknowledged how much she learnt from Ken McKinnon as he established an Aboriginal advisory committee whose members were nominees from Aboriginal communities. Ken or Jean only attend their meetings when invited. Jean told an interviewer:

> Because I tend to be a bit quick on the draw, and when they were all going on, you know, I would think, 'God, that will never work!' And I wanted to say 'No, no, no, that's not the way'. And Ken just said to me, 'You just shut up, you just don't say a word'. He said, 'They'll work it all through in the end.'[97]

It was a different approach to dealing with other groups working with the Commission.

Once *Girls, School and Society* was published in early 1976, there was follow-up work to do, though much of it occurred in the state education departments as women's advisers and units were established.[98] Jean incorporated girls into the wide range of her policy work and speeches. In May 1976, she gave a lecture at Monash University on 'Girls', and later that year opened a 'Sexism in education' conference at the Wattle Park Teachers Centre in South Australia. In the Monash lecture she publicly asked herself why there was no dedicated Commission program on girls and their education. Her notes for the talk suggested that 'Promotion of sex equality through schooling and assistance in coping with options in society not just a "girls" question'.[99] In May the next year she was organising a 'sex roles' seminar within the Australian College of Education annual conference. In 1977, she was commenting on a Tasmanian DSP report. She thought the treatment of girls was disappointing but agreed that the 'disadvantage' framework was limiting, obscuring the underlying issue.

> If girls undervalue their own capacities as a result of general social influences (and there is considerable evidence that they do) there may be a need for the school to confront this and counter it. In this framework, retention rates, subject choice and so on are only part of the picture. How confidently prepared are early leaving girls to make their own significant choice? What things regarded as given in their lives do they in fact have a choice about? What are the implications for boys of the changing social role of women?[100]

Jean's argument in this area was reinforced by Millicent Poole's research showing 'that social class was more significant than sex in determining who stayed how long in school, but that in post school educational participation sex was more significant than social background'.[101] In 1979 Jean opened the Australian Women's Education Coalition (AWEC) conference, talking about technological change and its coming impact on girls in the labour market.[102] A side issue was single-sex schooling, increasingly advocated on feminist grounds in the late 1970s. Jean was far from convinced. Coeducation for all its dangers to many girls was preferable to seclusion.[103]

Later Jean worried about a backlash against non-sexist education, somehow tied up with growing youth unemployment, and hindering the equal opportunity argument. Some patriarchal sections within the Catholic Church were angry with the approach of *Girls, School and Society*. On the other side was the AWEC, which Dany Torsh had played a role in founding. It pressed for more action from the Commission in implementing the recommendations of *Girls, School and Society*. Torsh had been disappointed with the Commission's relative quiescence following the report and the want of a strong feminist appointment to follow her in the post-publication phase.[104] As Jean prepared to leave the Commission in 1980 there was more activity, but Jean herself was not a major player in those efforts.[105] A continuing problem was the populist criticism of women competing with men in a difficult labour market. Jean composed a letter to *The Advertiser* newspaper: women had always worked, often in low-paid or unpaid jobs. They were not to be blamed for the current unemployment statistics. Continuing exclusions from paid labour put women at risk of poverty, especially in old age.[106]

Jean appeared as an expert witness before the Sex Discrimination Board in South Australia in 1979. She found the experience 'somewhat unnerving, as the judge (Robyn Layton) knows as much as I do, and I got rather bored even with myself'.[107] Involvement in girls' and women's issues continued through her last year with the Schools Commission when she played a role in advocating a Women's Studies Department at the University of Adelaide. In March 1980, she was on the street in Adelaide on International Women's Day. Jean's association with that event stretched back forty years.

On a more personal level Jean was ruminating about marriage and sex, following a couple of marriage breakdowns among her colleagues in the Commission.

> Spending time in Canberra I find myself the recipient of all sorts of gossip and confidences which make me wonder whether there is such a thing as a happy person. We had a fierce discussion over dinner ... about what sisterhood means when women are

competing for men ... There is a plethora of marriage breakups, with the new partners often drawn from the office staff and over which the original wives – non-office – are considerably hurt. None of us knows these women well and some of them appear to have no supportive networks in Canberra, having been dragged there with husbands and not working. We tend to sympathise with our colleagues, but one wonders. If marriage is to become increasingly sexually unstable; and this seems inevitable, the only sensible thing over the long-run would seem to be to take sexual encounters as only a special form of the friendships which people have outside marriage and to accept that long association and children may continue to be important to people while not sexually exclusive. While this may be rational, there must be some doubt, however, about whether people can handle it.[108]

In thinking about this question Jean was not only being a sexual radical but thinking about her own marriage. While there is no evidence of extra-marital relations on her or her husband's part, the significance of children as a reason for a continuing marriage was an issue for her. She was fascinated by the impacts of the new feminism. She met one couple who had 'just read *The Women's Room* (the mother is doing an MA under Anna Yeatman and is an intense feminist) and the father was overcome with the guilt of being male. Yet he supports his wife, two daughters at university and two more at private school in a very comfortable manner which they ... take as their due. Makes me wonder'.[109]

It was in this period that Jean's acquaintanceship with Denise Bradley developed into friendship. Denise, a dynamic and ambitious feminist, was the women's adviser in the South Australian Education Department. She and Jean had more than education policy as a mutual interest; they were feminists, both with boys as children.[110]

In these years from late 1975 to 1980 there were deaths among Jean's circle of friends. In February 1977 Eric Russell died, then a few weeks later, Cecil Teesdale-Smith. In 1979 Helen Palmer died. How well the relationship between her and Jean was repaired after Helen's 'vicious' letter concerning Jean's role in delivering state aid to Catholic schools is not known.[111] One of Helen's final publications was a study of the history of elitism in Australian schooling, a fine essay, most of which Jean would have approved.[112] Deaths like these contributed to Jean's feeling that she was growing old. She ruminated that taking a package tour on a coming trip to India might be more advisable than she and Dick trying to get around independently.

Jean's eldest child Bill continued to have his troubles. In the late 1970s he suffered a short period of mental illness, but he recovered and went on to marry Margaret (Meg).[113] By 1979, Jean's younger son, Hugh, was feeling good about his engineering course at the Institute of Technology, something that pleased Jean greatly, even if the garage at home had been overtaken by a car Hugh was attempting to restore. The anxiety she had felt about Hugh in earlier years dissipated. Dick continued work at the CSIRO, and attended CPA (Communist Party) branch meetings and conferences. By this time the CPA was rather different from what it had been twenty years before. Those members with strong attachment either to Chinese or Soviet Union versions of socialism had split from the party, leaving a membership more interested in the social movements, or in Dean Ashenden's words – he was also a member of the Party at the time – when it was 'a kind of hippy collective. Poor old Dick and a couple of others – were still there, loyally plodding on'.[114]

Schools Commissioner: Fraser government years, 1976–1980

Both Jean and Dick continued to enjoy performances at the biennial Adelaide Festival of Arts. In one letter Jean wrote of a fine gamelan performance at Monash University in Melbourne.[115] Susan, while developing her career as an historian of Indonesia, brought her parents into contact with Indonesia and its cultures. Jean's relationship with Louisa, Dick's sister remained strong – and Tess Caust was still arranging beach holidays south of Adelaide in which Jean and Dick participated.[116] There were new friendships as well, some made with employees of the Commission. Pam Cahir was one of these, Jean occasionally staying with her on trips to Canberra. Margaret Vickers, educational researcher and activist, a niece of Jean's old friend from university days, Jessie McLeod, was another with whom Jean occasionally met and stayed.

Figure 8.2 End of year holidays, Jean and Tess Caust (right), 1979. Jean is increasingly occupied by the Schools Commission study of educational needs of 15–16 year old youth.
Dick Blackburn photographer, courtesy of Susan Blackburn.

Figure 8.3 Jean and Louisa Hamilton, Jean's sister-in-law.
They had been friends from the 1940s. It was Louisa (Blackburn)
who had taken Jean home when Jean had been expelled from her own home
by her father while a university student. 1980.
Courtesy of Susan Blackburn.

Figure 8.4 Jean with her father in Canberra in 1980.
Jean did not give up on the relationship though there
had been painful difficulties from her childhood.
Les Muir reached the age of 101, dying in 1991.
Photographer unknown, courtesy of Susan Blackburn.

In 1979 Jean made a small commitment to the broader labour movement. In that year, the Evatt Memorial Foundation was established, and Jean joined its Education and Grants Committee. Other members included Manning Clark and Joan Kirner. Jean and Joan spoke against suggestions that the Foundation provide scholarships. They were elitist, assisting a very small group of young people. Jean was against any 'welfare' orientation for Evatt foundation projects. The committee united behind the idea that interest in labour movement history and values be fostered.[117]

Jean also became involved with the Australian College of Education (ACE). It provided an independent voice and a meeting point for professional educators. It was composed of 'members' and 'fellows'. Jean would receive a medal from the ACE a few years later. She was part of the movement to increase the involvement of women in its activities and leadership.[118]

Jean had finished at the Schools Commission by the time *Schooling for 15 and 16 year-olds* was published in late 1980. The Commission chair, Ken McKinnon was reluctant to see Jean go before the report was substantially complete. It bears the marks of her input. Jean had written in early 1980 that she had decided to retire in July, but 'Ken translated my "mid July" statement into when the 15/16 study is complete'. A major reason for Jean 'wanting to get out' was that 'I don't want to do it'. Part of that was to do with the tide turning in terms of educational funding; education was a predicted casualty as the government sought to finance reductions in personal income tax. There was also:

> widespread disillusionment about the individual and social payoffs from education – so nothing expansionist looks credible.

> I began working from the other end, pointing out the social penalties of not attempting to fashion a school system which better serves all students – but that argument seemed to be leading straight back to selective schooling, as I would still want those whom the school can succeed in interesting in academic matters to get that.[119]

Jean wanted to work on a major publication on school improvement. This was an idea she had discussed with McKinnon as early as 1978 while negotiating her workload. Such a project could outline lessons learnt on effecting school and educational reform from the collective experience of the Disadvantaged Schools Program.[120] As things turned out, it was the 15 to 16 year-olds study that would occupy her instead. She knew the potential significance of such a report, telling a national parent conference in 1978 that 'Parents could no longer protect children from unemployment', and that 'the youth unemployment crisis was not short-term'.[121] Schools had to rethink their operating assumptions. She had argued that the intended Commission report should be brief and readable rather than encyclopaedic, and this was the format in which it appeared.[122]

There was every reason at this time for the Commission to work on the 15 to 16 year age group and its schooling. In the late 1970s there was no escaping rising youth unemployment; it would continue to rise as technological change and the loss of working-class jobs profoundly affected the labour market for all youth, but especially those who left school at fifteen. The view of secondary schooling that had informed the Wyndham scheme in New South Wales in the early 1960s for example, was no longer viable. Though hailed at the time as an advance for universal secondary education, it had suggested that the compulsory years of secondary schooling, Years

7/8–10 needed to deliver a comprehensive curriculum, suitable for all youth, but that the post-compulsory years (11 and 12) could focus on the academic subjects in preparation for the entrance requirements of universities and other tertiary education colleges.[123]

As the Schools Commission report pointed out, in 1980 only just over half of young Australians were remaining at school into their sixteenth year, although this was changing. The contracting youth labour market was producing increased retention in senior secondary classes, and the question had to be asked: 'What kind of schooling should be offered the age group, many of whom had no intention of tertiary study?' The Schools Commission was certainly not the only group attempting to provide answers. State systems of public education worked on the problem and were coming up with a range of different approaches. In these circumstances, a good Commission report would be useful. It could present the problem as a national problem. It could collect and disseminate useful research results from within and outside Australia. It could collect information on what systems and schools were doing, especially those that were doing it well, and publicise those approaches. It could suggest not only policy but provide an analysis of the circumstances required for systems and schools to reform their practice.

The report's preface argued that there were deepening tensions being felt by youth. There was a heightened demand that schools prepare young people for work. These years of adolescence, 15 and 16, were bringing new problems for the transition of young people from childhood to adulthood.[124]

The Commission decided that its full and part-time members should visit one tenth of Australian schools that worked with the 15–16 age group. This was a massive impost on all the commissioners' diaries, including that of Jean, who visited schools especially in Tasmania, Victoria and South Australia.[125] The reports written by Jean and others following each visit are remarkable for their insights. They were certainly useful in the documenting of good, and bad, practice. No doubt they helped lead to one of the stronger statements in the report, that there were too many difficulties in the way of both counselling and, if necessary, getting rid of poor school principals.[126] Submissions were invited, and a program of consultations was undertaken with business leaders, trade union representatives, parents, teachers and hundreds of school students themselves.

The report documented the dissatisfactions that too many young people had with their schooling. But Jean refused the proposition that the solutions focus on individual students and their problems: 'The world is such that excessive individualism, excessive preoccupation with private benefits and individual perspectives court social disaster'. Alienation of youth needed to be met by stronger attention to 'interpersonal understandings'. School curricula could not ignore the necessity for 'helpful guidance in health and life patterns, in sex roles, in social expectations and in responding to crises'.[127] More 'applied' knowledge was required in schools if the needs of the young were to be met. This had to lead to substantial curriculum reform. Some schools were doing well, but most were 'lagging'. The report did not gloss over social differences and the different schooling expectations of different social groups: 'There are structures of power and reward which affect all social groups, some more favourably than others'.[128] Its approach to resolving the inequality problem was never going to be enough, but at the very least there needed to be a commitment to democracy, discussion, the outlawing of violence as a means of social change, openness, the right to organise, equality before the law, equal opportunity and opposition to 'discrimination on the basis of race, sex, belief'.[129] Nor should schools uncritically endorse values and beliefs either of majority or minority groups.

The learning process for young people had to be more active and practical. It should also enable

> the recognition of fates made common by our common humanity and by the sharing of social positions – as males or females, as members of ethnic groups, as members of an industrially advanced society, as people raised in and moving into socio-economic groups.[130]

From here the report moved to the strongest of its curriculum proposals, ideas that Jean would develop through the coming decade. 'Work', broadly conceived, could become the basis of the post-compulsory curriculum. New curriculum should not centre on sporadic work experience placements, nor should it focus on individual career counselling, though it could incorporate both. It should include a study of technological change, past and present, and how it might affect the future. It might involve study of the organisation of paid and unpaid work and the significance of qualifications. How did apprenticeships and other kinds of training operate, or the sexual and ethnic division of labour? It might involve the study of decision-making as it occurred in different kinds of employing organisations, including the possibilities for worker participation. Also included should be the history and function of trade unions, how investment decisions were made, how the demand for labour operated, and the dynamics of employment and unemployment more generally. The 'frameworks through which students come to view the world using observation, experience, general ideas and theories drawn from the disciplines' were to be engaged.[131] This would be a curriculum that clearly rested on the social sciences, including economics, history and sociology, with the capacity to frame work experience and career counselling programs. If done properly it could not be a 'soft option'; it had the potential to engage all young people regardless of their social differences and post-school intentions.

The report also developed a critique of credentials, the way they were used, and the phenomenon of 'credentialism'. Credentials should not be used to close off pathways through school (and life). There needed to be a single Year 12 certificate, more descriptive in character than current state certificates, a certificate that recorded pre-vocational experiences and achievements. A major argument was developed for the 'adaptive' school. Secondary schools could not refuse their responsibility for working with students who had not 'mastered the basic operations of reading, writing and calculation'. That would certainly require working with primary schools as their students transferred into secondary. Nor could schools refuse their responsibility for 'redressing or moderating the effects of social class and accidents of birth'.[132]

The report discussed much more than these issues, and of course, many more people than Jean Blackburn had a hand in its writing. Nevertheless, Jean's influence was obvious as with so many of the Schools Commission reports during her era.[133] This can be seen in the encouragement for schools to engage more directly with their communities (the want of which, for example, could make work experience placements especially difficult). Though supportive of school-based curriculum development there was an insistence that this did not mean teachers should develop curricula independently. There were dangers in this. Centrally or regionally based support services needed to be funded and engaged by teachers and schools.

Jean was not uncritical of the report, both during the period of its writing and after.[134] In 1983 she was arguing that it had not satisfactorily solved the problem of suggesting a core curriculum that could apply to all students given their substantial social differences – class, gender, ethnic and more. Issues raised such as individualist approaches, common culture, the impact of social hierarchies and structures needed much more work.[135]

The report made a tentative move towards recommending Year 11 and 12 colleges, separate from schools devoted to the students who were completing compulsory education. Such propositions would reappear several years later, in a stronger form, in Jean's recommendations for Victorian secondary schooling.

From as early as 1976, early in the first full year of the Fraser government, Jean actively considered the timing of her finishing up with the Schools Commission. In 1978 she was writing that the Commission was 'in a mess'. She was rethinking her position on the correct relationship between government and education and was frustrated with the blockages in the way of radical improvement in the education offered in Catholic parochial schools. 'All this seems to add up to saying it is time to go'. She talked about it with Peter Karmel who thought the University of Adelaide would likely accept her as an honorary fellow and provide her with office space. There was also a faint possibility she might become the South Australian Commissioner for Equal Opportunity.[136] In August 1979 she tried to submit a letter of resignation but was talked out of it. 'I get the general impression that Ken is apprehensive about who might replace me and [is] willing to let me write my own ticket.'[137] There were also personal factors, such as Dick and Hugh wanting to see more of her.

At one point there was the nebulous possibility of a senior post in the South Australian Education Department.

In fact, Jean remained at the Commission through to mid-1980. It was not unusual for her to have strong doubts about the worth of what she and the Commission were doing. Arguably such tension, despite its disabling effects, encouraged Jean's thinking, helping her to clarify arguments and positions. Nevertheless, the process, documented for the preparation of a paper for a meeting of the Australian Council of Educational Research, caused her great anxiety.

> On the one hand, I am very trad[itional] about ed[ucation], and afraid of the anti-intellectualism now taking over; on the other I feel hopeless about the possibility of fundamental change and about the possibility of valuing people for their intrinsic humanity in a stratified society. Yet I cannot see any complex society operating except in a rational/bureaucratic way. My mind and spirit are too feeble for this stuff. I am also nauseated by most educational talk – much more interested in sociology and history – perhaps because you can qualify everything by so many nuances that you don't have to say anything too crude with which you feel uncomfortable.[138]

With the public announcement of her resignation, there were many messages thanking her for her work. Some of her correspondents who had worked with her in the Disadvantaged Schools Program were quite distressed. Colin Thorpe wrote of seeing her at a national school councils meeting much earlier, in 1973: 'on the stage was this frail looking woman saying some of the most sensible and quietly radical things I had heard at that time. I remember I couldn't take my eyes off your face – transfixed by the words and the sincerity'.[139] There were messages from senior public servants in state education departments. The letter from Jim Giles, the Deputy Director in South Australia, suggests the depth of feeling her resignation evoked:

> The fact that you are retiring from your position as a full-time Commissioner ... is one I find particularly unpalatable. The combination of rationality and idealism which you have brought to bear on education in this country has resulted in programmes which have permanently changed the way people think about schools. This must remain as a significant memorial.
>
> Personally, I regret your departure from the position more than I can say. I know as a fact that a whole number of people, including myself, have gained continual inspiration from your ability to retain a sense of high purpose amidst a plethora of detail and your refusal to be weighed down by the merely mundane. Would you please accept my most grateful thanks for your work, my sincere admiration and my very best wishes for your future?[140]

Jean's resignation took effect on July 18, 1980, eighteen months before the formal end of her third contract. She told one interviewer that she was pretty well worn out.[141] A contributing factor to her resignation was that she had begun to disagree with McKinnon more often, though their mutual regard and affection remained. He was more inclined to promote 'choice and variety, and I never entirely approved of that. For reasons that it was very hard to know how to get it into a framework which also included equality'.[142] McKinnon himself knew what he was losing. He wrote of the significance of Jean's contribution, 'it has been a tremendous importance to me to have you as a colleague. Your intellectual integrity, capacity for hard work and enthusiastic co-operation has meant a great deal to me. We have been much stronger as a Commission because of it'.[143] Jean's last

Commission meeting occurred in Canberra from July 14 to 18. It was followed by several farewell dinners.

Ken McKinnon did not long outlast Jean on the Schools Commission. He was not reappointed as Chair when his seven-year term came to an end in January 1981. He and the new Minister for Education in the Fraser government, Wal Fife, were not working well together.[144] As McKinnon prepared to move to a new job with UNESCO, *The Canberra Times* ruminated on the failure to reappoint, obviously contacting Joan Kirner and Jean in the preparation of its story.

> The Government apparently wanted the commission to 'quietly administer election promises'. Dr McKinnon had shown in the past that he was not prepared to merely have the commission implement unacceptable government-funding 'guidelines'. In the past three years, two of the original four full-time commissioners have not been replaced, leaving only 11 commissioners instead of the original 13. Dr Jean Blackburn, a full-time commissioner who resigned earlier this year because she felt that the social philosophies on which the commission was founded were no longer being followed, said last night that she was 'mad with rage'. While she had not always agreed with Dr McKinnon, he had worked well beyond the call of duty in stimulating discussion and thought about education.

According to the news item, Jean went on to say: 'It is the end of an era ... in which we thought education could contribute something very significant to the enlightening of society'.[145] Three years later Jean was arguing that the Schools Commission had played an important part in revitalising Australian schooling, but that recently it 'had run into the sand'. Federal support had fallen for public schools, but risen dramatically for non-government schools, causing considerable alienation among public school supporters. Inflexibilities in funding patterns along with directives from government had caused the Commission to lose the initiative in education policy. Jean's analysis of why the Commission was failing was more substantial than just these points, but they were at the heart of her argument.[146] Some years later, Susan Ryan, Minister of Education in a new Labor government, appointed Lyndsay Connors to the Commission, specifically, though unofficially, to advocate for public schools. Commenting on Jean's experiences with the Commission in the light of her own, Connors remarked:

> she [Jean] had ended up with the feeling I think, and I ended up with a similar view, that we'd just really been co-opted into a body that was just there now to make it look respectable to funnel so much public money into private schools. I think, well it sounds a bit churlish to say you felt used, I mean I was terribly pleased and excited to be appointed to the Schools Commission, and it was a wonderful experience and it was for Jean too. I don't want to say I was 'used', but I felt ... and she felt the Schools Commission had turned into a way of legitimising one of the most bizarre schools funding policies that's ever happened in any country in the world really.[147]

Chapter 9

CURRICULUM THEORIST AND EDUCATIONAL ACTIVIST, 1981–1989

Jean Blackburn's hesitant voice and pensive face belie the fact that her mind is working overtime. Best known as the main author of the controversial Blackburn Report ... Ms Blackburn, 64, has had a crusade to battle this year. And while she has come through a little weary, Ms Blackburn has not thrown down her ink-stained gauntlet. Being torn between criticism and praise of her revolutionary report has not been easy, but as the one-time Schools Commissioner admits, life in education is never simple.[1]

I saw her quite often during this time, just about in tears, was very upset by the personal attacks which effectively questioned her integrity. But as well as that whole nest of questions around the two types of school, unions – and so on – I mean, education politics in Victoria were still then very intense. It is still the case that education talk, which is just politics by another name, is in Melbourne like nowhere else in Australia.[2]

Jean had retired from the Schools Commission, but she was far from finished with education policy. People in many educational agencies and institutions knew her work and they sought her advice and contribution. Her thinking about girls and women drew her into the emergent field of women's studies as well, but there was one more major job for government on the horizon. There was pressure in Victoria for a rethink of its post-compulsory schooling arrangements in an era when youth unemployment and school retention were both rising, and when curriculum had to adapt to the changing circumstances of youth.

In 1981 Jean noted the Fraser government's decision not to reappoint Ken McKinnon as chair of the Schools Commission, and the government's 'razor gang' cuts to the Commission's budget.[3] Peter Tannock took over as chairman. Her relationship with Tannock had been good, he was very personable. At the same time, Jean felt vindicated in her decision to leave. She had had a stronger personal and policy affinity with McKinnon. McKinnon would go on to a vice-chancellorship at the University of Wollongong and more significantly for Jean, he would accept the chairmanship of a newly formed Victorian State Board of Education.

Jean was 61 in 1981. A priority was to secure a base for her post-retirement activities. In early 1981 Kevin Marjoribanks, professor in the University of Adelaide's Department of Education, offered Jean a research fellowship. Marjoribanks' own research addressed the sources of unequal educational outcomes and as Jean had form in this area she accepted the fellowship. Jean remembered her 'output' as a research fellow mainly in terms of giving speeches: 'I thought that I would enjoy that, being able to say what it was that *I* thought ...

rather than sort of running the line of some body with which I was associated'.⁴ Jean's fellowship also supported her work on the senior secondary school curriculum, linking it more closely to 'the world of work'.⁵ Marjoribanks secured Jean's services for the *Australian Journal of Education*. She was an advisory editor from 1981 to 1985.

Jean shared an office at the university with tutors in the department, two of whom, Judy Gill and Alison Mackinnon, would be of future significance for her.

> Judy Gill painted a picture of her, striking in a red and black caftan, presenting papers on educational policy – 'Awe inspiring!' Judy was also impressed by her refusal to be overawed by even the most prestigious visiting speaker ... her ability to cut through to the core of an argument and her, at times, devastating honesty about a speaker. One of her pithy statements, delivered within earshot of the speaker was: 'It is easy to be clever, when you don't have the burden of being original!'⁶

There was also the continuing paradox. Alison Mackinnon remembered being 'astonished' that this 'famous person' did not seem to have much confidence in herself.⁷

Historically this was the period when the argument for women's studies in tertiary institutions gathered strength.⁸ At the University of Adelaide a group including Jean and Alison Mackinnon supported the argument for women's studies though it was the professor of geography, Fay Gale, who was the driving force.⁹ In December 1981 the University issued its report on women at the university. It referred to research supervised by Jean for the Tertiary Education Authority of South Australia (TEASA) on women's employment in tertiary education.¹⁰

A group of women chaired by Jean began the campaign to secure funding for women's studies at the university. Jean's preferred option, a unit that would teach undergraduate subjects, was supported neither by existing departments within the Faculty of Arts nor by students. Most students seeking to do honours or masters degrees in women's studies were loyal to their originating disciplines and departments.[11] A research centre was the viable alternative and in May 1983 Susan Magarey was appointed as its full-time head.

Jean participated in the new Women's Research Centre, attending its seminars and joining the editorial board of its journal, *Australian Feminist Studies*, but her involvement had its limits. Denise Bradley believed that in the end, 'She didn't want to be sitting round talking about the issues which interested all those academic women, and she wasn't a women's studies person, she was an education policy person. She liked them all, was grateful for their company socially but not much interested in the work they were doing or the issues they were debating.'[12] Jean found it difficult sometimes not to have too much say, to resist completing sentences for people as they talked. She had little respect for much of the research and writing associated with 'the postmodern turn'.[13] Susan Magarey went to some trouble securing republication rights for an article by Donna Haraway: 'A Manifesto for Cyborgs'. A discussion of the article at one of the research centre seminars became difficult: 'Jean thought it was the most god-awful nonsense, so she kept interrupting and telling us what to think, which effectively sabotaged the discussion'.[14] Despite the patchy reception of Jean's contribution, her second university fellowship from 1986 was with the Women's Research Centre. She chaired its advisory committee from 1987 to 1988.[15] Late in 1985

Magarey invited Jean to launch her biography of Catherine Helen Spence, South Australia's pioneering feminist.[16]

Jean was closely engaged with the Third Women and Labour Conference which took place in Adelaide in June 1982. She helped plan the post-conference publications and was one of a collective of women who met regularly to edit two books containing the better papers. Margaret Allen's dining room table was the usual venue around which planning took place. The challenges of postmodernism and radical feminism were also on the agenda here.

> Jean, steeped as she was in Marxist analysis, was very impatient with some of the radical feminist writing, describing it as 'piffle'. We never thought of Jean as not one of us, although she was some 30 years our senior. Around that table, she spoke of her great loneliness when a young mother and her pleasure in seeing how a number of us were able to combine motherhood, work and an intellectual life.[17]

Figure 9.1 The collective of women who produced and edited two volumes of papers in 1984 (*All Their Labours*) from an earlier Women and Labour Conference. The adults, left to right, Margaret King, Carol Johnson, Margaret Allen (and daughters), Jean Blackburn and Alison Mackinnon.
Margaret Haselgrove photographer, courtesy of the photographer and Margaret Allen.

Margaret Allen recalled the collective as a 'feminist discussion group'. The first of the volumes was mainly on women and work, the second on more cultural topics, 'embroidering the framework'. Sue Bellamy's paper caused the greatest dissension, along with the cover illustration. Jean was the most opposed. Jean had little sympathy for many of the arguments and positions of radical feminism. Even though much of the collective considered itself 'socialist feminist', in the end the majority felt that the published papers had to include a representative range of feminist research and writing.[18]

During this period, Jean continued her association with the TEASA. This was a statutory-based commitment, dating back to the end of 1979. Though TEASA's responsibilities looked impressive, 'coordinating post-secondary education in the State', there were problems, the main one being a lack of power in relation to the universities. Kevin Gilding, a former vice-principal and colleague of Jean at Western Teachers College, was its chairman. The original colleges of advanced education (CAEs) could be supervised fairly closely, but as amalgamations occurred this became more difficult.[19] In the 1979 to 1982 period, Deirdre Jordan and Jean, part-time members of the TEASA board, visited the CAE staffs to talk about amalgamation into larger institutions. Jordan remembered that 'it was really very unpleasant ... We had to go out and ... persuade them that this was a good idea. And they were very resentful ... I can remember very hostile receptions'.[20]

With the end of the baby boom, TEASA was involved in reducing the number of places available in teacher education. TEASA recommended that the Sturt CAE, Jean's former institution, enrol no more students from the beginning of 1981. Both Jean and Deirdre were signatories of the report recommending Sturt's closure.[21] From quite early on Jean had concerns about the role TEASA might play, specifically 'with the hatchet jobs for which it [TEASA] is to be the agent. Students and resources applied to preservice teacher education are to be reduced by 25% by 1984, but we can get no reassurance that overall tertiary participation will be preserved.'[22]

Gilding consulted Jean about establishing a sub-committee to look at women in tertiary education and from 1980 Jean chaired TEASA's Advisory Committee on Post-Secondary Education of Women and Girls. Early members included Denise Bradley, then Women's Adviser in the South Australian Education Department, Kay Iseman (later Schaffer) from the Salisbury CAE and Peggy Mares from Adelaide CAE. Other appointments followed. In 1981 the committee funded Kay Iseman to look at educational and employment opportunities for mature-aged women in tertiary education and to develop strategies assisting 're-entry' after long absences. Jean's personal history of re-entry into educational study meant her support for the work. Iseman wrote *Moving Women In* following a research trip to North America.[23] The committee also worked on reorganising the institutional arrangements for research and teaching in women's studies across South Australia's tertiary institutions and campuses.

In 1982 a report by John Keeves, Director of the Australian Council for Educational Research (ACER), into education, was published. It had been commissioned by the South Australian government. It was the first major report into South Australian school education since Peter Karmel's 1969–1971 effort.[24] As a significant author of the Karmel exercise, Jean took a keen interest in Keeve's work – and she was not impressed with the result. The report was 'neo-conservative'. 'Scientism stamps the whole approach to teaching and learning …

The human element is ignored (and by implication deplored).'[25] Jean had dealt with Keeves during the Schools Commission years when ACER and the Commission were usually, but not always cooperative.

Jean had the responsibility of drafting a response from TEASA to Keeves' proposals concerning the education of women and girls. She was scathing in her assessment, writing that the arguments about encouraging girls into technological and science studies were conceived in terms of 'deficits in girls'. The 'human norm assumed is that of technological man'. The report failed to address early school leaving by girls. Keeves was uninterested in setting targets for women in promotion positions or increasing the limited range of vocational opportunities for young women. Curriculum reform was mainly conceived as a management issue, rather than 'content, method or relationships in learning'. When Jean was invited by the South Australian teachers' union to speak at its 'Who owns the curriculum?' conference, she spoke not of the deficiencies of Keeves, but selected another target. The Education Department's latest curriculum guideline 'was devoid of firm social commitment of any kind'.[26] The defects Jean identified in the South Australian reports and guidelines influenced her review of Victorian education two or three years later.

Jean and the TEASA committee were keen for the universities and CAEs to produce accessible statistics on the ratios of male and female in staff appointments and promotions. Jean's economics background usually led her to demand 'hard data', crucial if persuasive cases for reform were to be made. Jean and Gilding visited the CAE principals and university vice-chancellors to discuss the issues and request statistics. Peggy Mares remembered the difficulties: 'That sort of thing was not easy to do because they [the university vice-chancellors especially] felt very strongly that they were in charge of their own fiefdoms ... But she got it, she got it done. And the figures were astonishing when they came out.'[27] Recommendations included the encouragement of affirmative action, but not the more contentious 'positive discrimination' in favour of women.[28] Jean wrote an article for *Australian Feminist Studies* about some of the issues involved.[29]

In October 1982 Jean resigned as chair of TEASA's committee on the education of women and girls. Gilding's response was affectionately sharp: 'I certainly do not thank you for your letter ...'; nevertheless, he recorded her 'stimulating' contribution, arguing that it had 'been rather in excess of your own summation of it'.[30] They had got on well together, and Jean continued her involvement with TEASA as a consultant to a review of a South Australian school to work transition program. The report revealed problems that were familiar to Jean: the program had been too hastily introduced and funding from federal and state governments was ill-coordinated. Poor definition of both intended purposes and possible action had caused problems. There was a lack of clarity about 'the terms on which upper secondary schooling should be restructured'. Too few 'sections of the community' had been involved.[31] Jean would have an opportunity to think further about these issues in her coming Victorian education enquiry.

Jean's address to the 1979 conference of the Australian Women's Education Coalition (AWEC) drew attention to pressures 'now potentially pushing back the limited gains women have achieved over the recent period'.[32] In 1981 she was invited once more to talk about girls' education. Dale Spender, a prominent Australian feminist often remembered for her arguments that boys monopolised teacher attention in coeducational classrooms, was the other keynote speaker.[33] Jean was reported by *The Canberra Times* as arguing that schools continued to fail girls in dealing with 'dilemmas presented by social realities'. Teaching, or lack of teaching about 'procreation' (sex education) was only one of the failures. She was alarmed by increased federal funding for non-government schools: 'it might not be too alarmist to suggest that the public schools are being progressively assigned the responsibility for preparing students for jobs of "other rank", while subsidised schools progressively become the recruiting grounds for higher education'. She argued that too many feminists still operated on the assumptions of an era, 'when economic growth, full employment and détente between the great powers were taken for granted'. The argument for sex equality needed to address questions about 'humanly desirable traits and the kind of society in which they might better be more highly valued and more freely be exercised'.[34]

Jean's presentation at this AWEC conference was controversial. It drew less support than Spender's address. Drawing on her peace movement experience, Jean said she was unimpressed by uncritical arguments about women's right to participate equally: 'Promoting a female elite within patterns set by men can hardly command much of our enthusiasm. A neutron bomb made by women is no better than one made by men. An environment despoiled by female operators does not thereby become less despoiled'. Jean argued for a better, more human society, and it was this that caused the problem. The sex inequality question was but one part of a bigger question. The inseparability of the fates of women and men needed recognition, an understanding that a world which was better for women would also be better for men and for children. Women did contribute in significant ways to the culture, they were less likely, she thought to be violent, addicted to power and acquisitiveness, and these were approaches that were 'humanly' valuable, less likely 'a threat to the human race'.[35]

Jean's position was criticised for not being feminist enough. According to Denise Bradley, her argument about the long-term common interests of men and women went 'down like a lead balloon':

> there were hostile questions, but it was also just the failure ... to give her adequate respect ... a complete failure to accept that this was a perfectly reasonable argument from somebody who ... had a great deal more form on this issue than anybody else in the room ... Now many of them wouldn't have known that ... it upset her very badly ... but she didn't think she was wrong. And that was always the case with Jean. She could go into the foetal position about the lack of support, but that didn't mean that she'd say: 'I give in and I was wrong'. I've never known her to say that in her bloody life. Once she'd come to an opinion, I mean she would worry away about things but unless a very good argument was raised against her she would not back down because people she liked disagreed.

Lyndsay Connors and Pat Thomson gave similar reports of the speech and its aftermath. A not insubstantial issue for Bradley, Thomson and Connors, as well as Jean herself was that each of them had boy children. She argued that boys were not to be separated from feminist visions of the future.[36] Jean's more general social justice *and* feminist imaginations were at work in the argument.

Jean continued to make time for reading. She admired the writing in Shirley Hazzard's *The Transit of Venus* but had difficulty in working out what it was about 'beyond the people and their relationships'.[37] A couple of years later she was reading Drusilla Modjeska's *Exiles at Home*, and Christina Stead's *For Love Alone*. 'I am "into" Christina Stead at the moment, and enjoying the encounter greatly.'[38] She went with Tess Caust to see *My Brilliant Career*, 'easily the best Australian film I have ever seen'.

She was fascinated by the observations of Deirdre Jordan and Judy Redden after they returned from a second journey to China. According to Jean, Deirdre told of a decline, the beginnings of a black market, a commercialisation of tourism. In their view, China had lapsed from being a 'moral society'. Jean thought that Deirdre's 'reactions are very much coloured by her previously idealised view of it all'.[39] A visit to Peter Newnham, one of Jean's Diploma of Education teachers, saw her come away with a copy of Kolakowski's *Main Currents in Marxism*, dealing with, among others, Lukacs and members of the Frankfurt School.[40]

> Good stuff in drawing attention to the dangers which arise when people despise empiricism and logic in their theoretical schemes. He gives voice to a number of the objections I expressed to the Teachers as Researchers movement led by [Stephen] Kemmis of Deakin [University] (a charismatic character if ever there was one) and based on the work of Habermas.[41]

Figure 9.2 Deirdre Jordan was Chancellor of Flinders University, advising Jean to make the job her own when she was offered the chancellorship at the University of Canberra in 1990. Jordan, a Mercy sister, had organised the travel to China in which Jean participated in 1976. This photo, 1986.
Courtesy of Susan Blackburn.

Jean remained engaged with developments in socialist thinking and remained suspicious of a number of popular trends in educational progressivism.

In this period, recurring unhappiness, indeed, 'misery' and depression continued to dog Jean's emotional life. At different times her friends, Dean Ashenden and Denise Bradley, and probably others, recommended that she see a psychiatrist or seek medication. She had been a smoker for many decades so there was nothing new there, but she was drinking more heavily, increasingly spirits, which may have helped sometimes, but not at others. The drinking was likely a source of tension with Dick.[42] There were plenty of indications that old age was going to be a trial.

Like most citizens in South Australia Jean had watched on as Don Dunstan's life after government was subject to public gaze. The impending publication of the *It's Grossly Improper* book threatened to make public an explosive narrative of a feckless male lover and possible corruption. When it appeared in bookstores, Jean refused to read it, but Maud McBriar, one of Jean's oldest friends from University of Melbourne Labour Club days, did. Maud told Jean that she thought that some of it was plausible. Jean wrote to Susan that it was no-one's business what Dunstan's or anyone's sexual preferences were.[43]

In 1982 Jean's son Hugh completed his engineering degree at the South Australian Institute of Technology. His picaresque progress through the University of Adelaide, then public service and Institute had caused Jean some anxiety. She felt she had made a mistake in pushing Hugh towards university enrolment immediately after school. After graduation, Hugh worked as a consulting engineer for a couple of years before beginning a doctorate at Monash University.[44] He met his partner Helen Barraclough, in 1984, and she and Jean got on well. By this time Jean's friendship with Deirdre Jordan and Judith Redden, both sisters in the Mercy order, had grown. Their affection was mutual.[45] Jean had an interest in the inspiration and work of these women whose educational leadership occurred in and beyond Catholic institutions. But Jean's interest was leavened by Hugh's partner, Helen. She had endured unhappy experiences at the Goodwood Orphanage in Adelaide, an institution run by the Sisters of Mercy.

A trip to India had marked the beginning of Dick's retirement from the CSIRO.[46] Jean planned a visit to Sri Lanka in 1981, the interest arising from Susan's marriage to Dayal Abeyasekere. Dick and Jean invited Dayal's mother to accompany them on their travel. Susan explained that she was:

> [a] very devout Buddhist and meditator whose reactions to things would take us by surprise ... She often explained things by reference to what people did in previous lives. She also tried to get Jean to meditate, saying 'It will stop your hair going grey', which was not the right approach with Jean. But like everyone else Jean and Dick grew quite fond of her and they later stayed with her on a visit to Sri Lanka'.[47]

There was movement too with Bill Blackburn and his family. In 1983, Jean became a grandmother. Bill and Meg's daughters, Naomi and Robyn were born in 1983 and 1986 and whenever Jean was in Sydney, she would visit them along with friends like Lyndsay Connors and Ken McKinnon. Earlier, in 1982 there was a less than successful visit to her elder brother Allan, living in Victoria, for reasons that may have stretched back to their childhood years. There was a happier relationship developing with her younger brother, Les Thomas Muir. Jean and he would meet when she was working in Victoria. Les, working for the Albury-Wodonga Commission, had the fun of introducing her to a meeting at the trade union training college in Albury. He and Jean shared an interest in government policy and its implementation. Les recalled that Jean gave a terrific talk: 'I had to thank her on behalf of all the union people there, "and as a matter of fact, she's my sister". It was nice. And the next morning she flew away on a little two-seater plane somewhere for the next one'.[48]

There were also deaths to contend with. Tess Caust, comrade and friend from times as early as the New Housewives' Association in the late 1940s, died two months after Judah Waten, both in 1985. A coincidence saw Judy Gillett (Goss) replace Tess as director of the Education Department's reading centre. Judy had lived with Jean for several months in 1952, one of the two daughters of Joe Goss, newly arrived from London.

Figure 9.3 Jean with friends dating back to her earliest years in Adelaide, still with plenty to talk about. Margaret Ward (a South Australian public school headmistress and sister of David Caust), Jean Blackburn and Tess Caust in 1981.
Courtesy of Susan Blackburn.

In 1988, Jean's father, Les, celebrated his 98th birthday in a nursing home in Canberra. Jean was there with other extended family, along with Bill, Meg, Naomi and Robyn who came south from Sydney. Les seemed to enjoy the occasion though he was convinced he was living in Perth rather than Canberra.[49] By 1988 the trials of old age and illness were pervasive. Jean wrote to Susan:

> Age is a bugger. When I observe the inanities of my contemporaries I see that quitting the scene is a social benefit. I cannot hope that I don't share such a prognosis. Dick has a disturbing and persistent cough, Elliott [Johnston] has just had a by-pass operation, Elizabeth [Johnston] has broken ribs and a leg ulcer; other friends inhabit a world closing in. Resisting the idea that there is no way to go except down consumes a lot of energy, along with keeping up the confidence involved in doing anything beyond the back yard. It's not as bad as that really, but this is My Chance to Moan.[50]

By the late 1980s Susan and Dayal's marriage was failing. Dayal had found an academic position in Queensland and Susan went with him to contract employment. However, there was no prospect of tenure for her and she soon left for a senior lectureship in politics at Monash University. There she joined the well-regarded centre for Southeast Asian Studies, 'replacing' the retiring professor, Herb Feith. Her marriage ended. She suspected that Jean was not too disturbed by this course of events. Susan and Dayal divorced in 1993, just a couple of years before Dayal's untimely death from a heart attack.[51]

By the end of the 1980s then, Hugh and Helen, and Susan (having reverted from Abeyasekere to her original surname, Blackburn), looked as if they were settling in Melbourne permanently. Jean played with the idea of leaving Adelaide and returning to Melbourne to live, but there were lots of arguments against. That Dick was quite opposed was one.

Figure 9.4 Friends growing old, 1988.
As Rivkah Brilliant, Rivkah Mathews had met Jean at University High in the 1930s. They were comrades as undergraduates in the University of Melbourne Labour Club.
Hugh Blackburn photographer, courtesy of the photographer.

The Blackburns and Johnstons, and others including Effie Best formed a party that took theatre subscriptions together. These and other friends were organised by Ruth Fletcher for a trip to the Kimberleys in Western Australia for June in 1988. The trip lasted five or so weeks, its participants mainly staying in motels, camping, and touring in a minibus. Maud McBriar and Peggy Mares were in the party. Peggy remembered a discussion as Dick Lang, the tour leader, opined on the importance of men in Aboriginal society, and how a want of completed initiations was causing social breakdown. Peggy challenged him – was it not women 'who had actually maintained the genealogy and a whole lot of the social fabric'. Jean spoke up. Elliott Johnston was interested since he was in the middle of his work as a royal commissioner into Aboriginal deaths in custody. When the Queen's Birthday holiday arrived, Maud announced her admission to the Order of Australia for her contributions to conservation and the environment.

Effie and Peggy thought that Jean was not always at ease socially at this time, even with old friends. She was sometimes impatient and brusque. Peggy thought it was because she was so 'committed to getting things done' that time spent socialising could seem a waste of time. Jean was not unaware of this, at times appalling herself and being sorry a little later.[52] Then there was her phone manner. A number of our interviewees commented that the phone would ring and very few if any niceties would be exchanged before discussion of the matter at hand. Then 'clunk', the business over, there was no winding down or goodbye. The first time was a shock, then it was affectionately 'just Jean'. But she was not always so concise.

> She could be very, very full of circumlocution and agonising, and being very, very slow ... but then on other occasions she'd ... just suddenly see what was wrong. And then she'd say it. Often very, very directly ... [I] never found it offensive and I wouldn't have thought most people did, if they knew her ... I can imagine the first couple of times she did it to a couple of Directors of Education. They might have been a bit surprised, but she wasn't being rude. She'd seen the answer and she'd now tell you what it was.[53]

Other friendships continued from the Schools Commission years and before. In Dean Ashenden's case there was mutual admiration and affection. Denise Bradley thought Jean was a major formative influence on Dean – they 'had a great relationship'. It certainly prospered despite differences they may have had on education reform.

When Dean worked for Susan Ryan, Minister of Education in the newly elected Hawke Labor government from March 1983, he would occasionally sound Jean out for her views on policy.[54]

In 1982 the Cain Labor government was elected in Victoria.[55] Robert Fordham became Minister of Education, quickly moving to establish an advisory State Board of Education with Ken McKinnon as chair. Its members represented several of the constituencies concerned with education. The Board was soon 'looking for something to hang its hat on' and discussed the possibility of a review of post-compulsory education. McKinnon was in touch with Jean as the discussion progressed.[56]

There were many reasons why a review was needed, including a renewed consideration of the changing educational needs of students in years 11 and 12 in the light of their employment prospects and social circumstances. There were two kinds of public senior secondary school in Victoria, the high and the technical, with the technical schools recently expanding their role into Year 12 education. Technical and Further Education (TAFE) was also playing a part, providing up to 15 per cent of the age group with its courses. Year 12 accreditations were multiple and confused, which did not always help students as they competed for jobs and tertiary places. Non-government enrolments stood at near 30 per cent of the whole, which, with a falling school-age population and the decreasing size of many public schools, caused problems for the breadth of curriculum able to be offered.

The issues around educational reform in Victoria were highly politicised. The so-called 'five organisations' consisting of the three teacher unions covering public schools and two parent and school council organisations, were powerful, and they often worked together. They had a long history of conflict with Liberal governments and expected better from the new Labor government. Later Jean thought that the new Labor Minister, Robert Fordham, even 'took instructions' from the 'five orgs' at one stage, though Helen Praetz doubted this. The difficulties in managing the portfolio were real and Fordham's interest in reform genuine.[57] The universities, often in opposition to the demands of the five organisations, threatened independent processes to assess student qualifications for university entrance.[58] One might wonder at Jean's decision to march into the middle of all this. The probability of producing a report that achieved fair support across the competing systems, institutions and organisations was low as she was not unaware. As Schools Commissioner she had written of the difficulties in different states, her reports on school visits in Victoria constituting a remarkable portrait of public and Catholic schooling in the late 1970s.[59]

According to *The Age* newspaper: 'She was confronted by a fragmented schools structure which helped enforce a restrictive curriculum, and a clash between vocational and theoretical education.'[60] Hedley Beare wrote: 'Blackburn was called by the Cain government to tackle one of the toughest issues in education and one that has dogged governments around the world: how to make an effective certification process that marks the end of secondary schooling. The complication comes from the fact that the Year 12 certificate is used for many purposes.'[61] Jean was qualified to take on the task. She knew about rural and urban differences, government and non-government school systems and the national and international policy contexts.[62] Some schools she had visited had suggested solutions. In 1979 for example, she wrote to the deputy principal of Kyneton High School:

'I was most impressed in the technical/academic combination which the school uniquely represents in Victoria'.[63] She could see the potentially negative consequences for young people as they navigated a fragmented system.

McKinnon invited Jean to a two-day meeting of the State Board to plan an 'enquiry into the upper secondary school'. Joan Kirner, now in state cabinet supported Jean's involvement. The meeting had another purpose, to assess Jean's suitability as a leader of the enquiry. That Jean had credibility with the teacher unions was a factor in her favour.[64] Back in Adelaide, she was telephoned by Fordham and asked to chair the review.

> I felt honour bound to do it because he said I was the first Australian woman who had ever been asked to chair a major education enquiry ... So, I thought, for the honour of the sex I should do it. And also I have to say I have an insatiable interest in public business ...

This decision took care of the next two years of Jean' life, from 1983 to 1985. If she had not completely grasped the system-wide problems when she took up the appointment, she was soon cognisant of their magnitude. Later she used the word 'shambles' to describe Victoria's Year 12.[65] As Lyndsay Connors recalled about Victorian public schooling: the high levels of school autonomy and devolution were 'heaven for teachers' but schools were often so small that their senior levels could not provide a minimally broad curriculum. There was also the problem of 'an assortment of "alternative" curricula and credentialing provisions'.[66] Denise Bradley remembered Jean as knowing in advance that her efforts would attract criticism, sometimes from old friends on the left, but she was determined, in Bradley's words, that she *would* make 'sensible decisions' about 'all these boutique bloody little schools [that] weren't actually offering children choice'.[67]

Victoria stood out for the number of men and women across the universities, CAEs, the teacher unions, and indeed schools, who were deeply engaged with the question of what constituted a good education. An indication of this was the strength of alternative schooling in Victoria. Many of these intellectuals and activists were on the left and their relationships with the teacher unions often made them a force. They included Bill Hannan of the Victorian Secondary Teachers Association (VSTA) who wrote about curriculum in a way that had never been seen in teacher union publications, the focus of the union broadening beyond the perennial issues concerning wages and conditions. Among those in the universities were Stephen Kemmis and Doug White. Kemmis's *Towards the Socially Critical School* (1983) had wide circulation, while White wrote on education for the new left journal *Arena*. Marie Brennan had been involved in the production of progressive Education Department policies on democratic schooling and curriculum just prior to the Blackburn report.[68] There were others like Gerry Tickell in the Technical Teachers Union of Victoria (TTUV) who put educational and curriculum issues at the forefront of industrial campaigns. Ron Tandberg's cartoons in teacher union magazines focused on the shortcomings of educational practices and relationships in schools and systems. All would be critically interested in Jean's efforts on school reform in Victoria.

One of the first difficulties that Jean faced was the question of to whom she was reporting. The Education Department opposed the idea that it be the State Board of Education. Jean had her concerns as well. The review was likely to be more effective if it reported directly to the Minister of Education, that is the government of Victoria, instead of an advisory body. It was resolved that she should work to the Minister of Education not the Board.

A second difficulty was that Jean could not work with the officer assigned by the Education Department. He had no enthusiasm for the review and Jean decided to make it a condition of her continuing that she choose her own staff. She had noticed a paper of Helen Praetz which exposed major flaws in the unemployment statistics for 15–19-year-olds. Helen joined the review, and she and Jean found Marion Russell, who would be the executive officer. Jean reflected: 'in a working life stretching over some thirty years, I have never enjoyed such a mutually supportive and productive working relationship'.[69]

A potential difficulty lay in Jean's decision to remain based at home in Adelaide, commuting regularly to Melbourne. In Melbourne an enviable suite of offices was found in the main Education Department building and a flat was rented for her sporadic use. Managing from Adelaide was easier now that Hugh had left home. Dick occasionally came to Melbourne with her.[70] When rounds of commitments in Melbourne concluded, Helen and Marion packed her 'off into a taxi', and 'we'd think "Oh that's it for a while!" But no ... she worked inordinately hard. It worked out okay because occasionally I [Helen] went to Adelaide ... to do stuff there ... because when she came to Melbourne it was flat out the whole time. So the thinking – she did a lot of her thinking and reading ... in Adelaide.'[71]

The review was supported by a Coordinating Committee that included the Director-General of Education, the Director of the Catholic Education Office who also spoke for the non-government sector, the Chair of the Technical and Further Education Board, Chair of the State Board of Education (Ken McKinnon), and the Chair of the Victorian Institute of Secondary Education. Helen Praetz was a member, and Marion Russell the executive officer. Jean could not understand why the teacher and parent organisations were not represented. Fordham explained: 'You wait till you get a little way down the track and you'll understand'. She did: 'there were agendas which couldn't be spoken ... the big fight in the end was around the question of the separate upper secondary colleges'.[72]

Though the coordinating group worked well, there was a less happy relationship with the Working Party. It included representatives from the same organisations as the Coordinating Committee but was prone to dissension from early on. Gerry Tickell from the TTUV, though nominated to the Working Party by the State Board of Education, not unexpectedly kept a brief for the teacher unions. The possibility of an end to the split system of public secondary schooling was on the table. If that happened it would affect not only schools but teacher careers and, in all likelihood, the future arrangement of the unions themselves. Praetz talked about the Working Party as 'made up of the second level people all of whom fulminated and carried on'. Jean reminded its members that they were 'the second level'. The 'first level' was the Coordinating Committee which provided her with 'support and enthusiasm and energy ... whereas the others were really not helpful'.[73]

The review produced a discussion paper in April 1984.[74] The Minister was happy enough, though the broader reception was mixed.

> Mr Fordham said, 'I'm very excited at the prospect. The changes would be more radical than anything known in our lifetime'. Leading educationist Ms Jean Blackburn ... said the aim of the discussion paper was to make education at the senior school level 'more adult orientated, with a better understanding of society itself ... The paper will be distributed to all post-primary schools

and TAFE colleges. It will be translated into 10 languages: Chinese, Croatian, Vietnamese, Turkish, Spanish, Maltese, Italian, Serbian, Arabic and Greek.'[75]

Jean's review was to be a model of community outreach and fearlessness in facing difficult facts. With optimism, she argued that the review would be informed by the best available thinking about giving young people a chance in a changing world.

Jean argued that extending the years of compulsory school attendance was not a consideration. Yes, young people must be encouraged to stay on at school but attempts 'merely to reduce labour supply by keeping young people out of the work force could have destructive effects'. Curriculum change was required, but the economic circumstances of young people had to be considered as well, especially when unemployment benefits were higher than student allowances. Simple vocationalisation of post-compulsory schooling was no answer: 'general education at its best enlarges horizons'. Jean's previously rehearsed educational views were being imprinted on the enquiry: 'There is no reason why an education which is "liberal" in the sense that it feeds informed reflection on the human condition and on how people live their lives should be abstracted from that condition and those realities or from the productive activities of the society'. A division between 'academic' and 'non-academic' was to be avoided.

A chapter of statistics describing what 15–19-year-olds were doing in Victoria was followed by a description of the existing organisation of the post-compulsory school curriculum: 'There is a progressive narrowing of the purposes of secondary schooling across Years 10, 11 and 12 until at Year 12 tertiary selection becomes, by default and in practice, its overwhelming purpose'. A new curriculum rationale was required for the post-compulsory years, and it had to include the concept of an 'extended general education'. It was unacceptable that only the students in the academic curriculum should have access to serious encounters with the ideas and concerns of their time and culture. Mathematics, science and technology, humanities and arts, and the study of society should be 'pursued in some form by all'. Another chapter exercised the credentialing issues, and what criteria should enable the creation of a universal Year 12 certificate. Then there was the question of what kinds of schools might meet the requirements. The possibility of senior schools, separated from junior secondary, was canvassed.

Responses to the discussion paper were invited. In Jean's view, the discussion paper 'put into the realm of public debate much which had previously been concealed', including the fact 'that all forms of Year 12 certification did not have equal purchase for tertiary entry'. She argued that many subject options supposedly available within the Higher School Certificate were actually phantoms for most students. Too many schools were so small that a fair range of subjects simply could not be offered.[76] A curriculum capable of increasing student retention was therefore unavailable.

Almost 400 written submissions were received, and Jean and Helen Praetz travelled Victoria speaking to public meetings. In one month alone, Jean addressed over 80 meetings. It was exhausting work. Jean and Helen learnt to manage by developing a 'Box and Cox' approach, setting up a public dialogue: 'she'd say, I'd say'.[77] Jean later remarked: 'There was an enormous amount of discussion ... I come from Victoria ... but I still find Victoria the most fascinating Australian State because you can get an argument about anything or nothing in Victoria [*laughs*]'.[78]

> In most places there was opposition. Well you can imagine, you go to one country town which is smaller than the next one … and they fear that if there's going to be an upper secondary thing it'll be in the other town … Reasonable enough fear. In the cities people carried on about how they'd have to take the train three stations or something or other and what a terrible tragedy that would be …[79]

Helen Praetz described the program of meetings:

> after the Discussion Paper when everybody blew up and carried on, couldn't believe the numbers and so on … people would storm into the hearing and say things. Jean would just listen to them. She'd say 'I can see you don't think much of what we've said. What would you do?' There'd be just a deathly silence. Because it's easy to say 'blah blah blah', but actually 'What was the proposal?' And there were none.

> Boy did we have morning teas, go and talk to the local high school. Of course, it was in the days when you had a high school and a technical school, Catholic school. And they'd all come along to, say … Wangaratta … People and local press. It was all big deal, and they all yacked on and often people who'd been doing terrific things in the classroom really felt as though they were recognised. It was great. Jean would say, 'Oh that's wonderful what you are doing here.' … when people talk about technical schools in the country, we looked at lathes calibrated in *inches* – you know – they had no equipment. There were these people battling on, and doing such good works … and the Catholic schools were often doing terrific stuff. You know, they were picking kids up – but they kept on saying – 'but you know, they're not going to get any qualification out of this'.[80]

Jean was well-known, sometimes from her Disadvantaged Schools Program visiting days.

Oh ... they loved her. Big deal ... Jean coming! ... the invitations absolutely tumbled in the door ... dying to see Jean ... she was just so lovely with people, and applauded their work. She could do better than anybody ... somebody would ask what amounted to a pretty dumb question. And she would transform it into something else ... She'd listen to them, and she'd say: 'Now it seems to me, you are asking something very interesting'. And then she'd reframe, so in fact it *was* something very interesting. And the person would say, 'Oh yes, that's right' ... and then she'd deal with that ... she was always so respectful of other people's views, and attended to them so thoughtfully and – then we'd go away, and say, 'Well! What did we get out of that?' Then we'd list what we got out of it, and you know, that's why we had a lot of credibility, because we were not just talking about it in general.

Some activists in the technical teachers' union were abusive. At times it came close to stalking: 'Two intimidating teachers followed me around several Melbourne meetings, repeating a standard interjection and question suggesting that I was in league with the forces of darkness'.[81]

Along with the meetings and submissions there were a further 29 consultations with groups that included teacher and parent organisations, universities, employers, non-government schools and their teacher associations, equal opportunity units in government and the principals of the colleges of advanced education.

Both McKinnon and Kirner let Jean get on with the job. Having been such a warrior for the Victorian Federation of State School Parents' Clubs in the 1970s and early 1980s, Kirner was now in government as Minister for Conservation, Forests and Lands. For her it was time to step back from education.

Following the publication of the discussion paper, Jean initiated three new working parties with about 20 members each to review responses, submissions and to develop proposals. Their briefs were curriculum, credentials and structures of schooling. They were chaired respectively by Peter Fensham, John Scott and Jean herself. Jean singled out her co-chairs for thanks in the final report, but she found the work of John Scott, Vice-Chancellor of La Trobe University and an Englishman, particularly valuable. He was disinterested where others were not: 'he had the advantage of not thinking that everything that was made in Victoria is perfect'.[82] Jean and Helen attended the meetings of each group. To reduce conflict, the fractious Working Party remained marginalised.

Opposition to reform developed as proposals for re-casting the organisations offering a senior secondary curriculum were being formulated. The most suspicious was the VSTA, the union of the high school teachers. Anne Borthwick, Bill Hannan and Graham Marshall from the union were involved in the review's sub-committees. They came to consider that VSTA policies were failing to register to a sufficient degree.[83] Bill and Lorna Hannan would later argue that Jean, Helen and Marion isolated themselves from the practicalities of possible reform.[84] This was not true. 'Isolation' was not the reason why Jean came out against some policies of the VSTA.

The Blackburn Report was released on May 1, 1985.[85] It made 45 recommendations, each of them supported by argument and evidence. Some of the fiercest critics of the specific recommendations acknowledged the strength of the report's philosophical framework. New targets were recommended for increased participation in post-compulsory schooling. There were proposals for better financial support of young people. The number of education systems providing post-compulsory education, including TAFE, were to be reduced. A two-year course of study with semester length units was envisaged. The curriculum was to be broadened for more students in terms of subject choice, with a mix of theoretical and activity-based units. There would be a compulsory subject examining 'work in society'. The two years were to be arranged to provide a 'general education'. Jean later wrote:

> I think that it has some of the best curriculum statements that have appeared in any Australian educational reports and a lot of other people think that too ... It set everyone thinking about how better to combine intellectual development and technical and office and computer and all sorts of other kinds of skills.[86]

A new credential, the Victorian Certificate of Education (VCE) would be awarded by a new credentialing authority and entrance qualifications for tertiary institutions would change as a consequence. Existing technical and high schools were to come together as comprehensive schools. Where possible separate post-compulsory schools or senior colleges should be formed. The Report concluded:

> While following the recommendations here will not bring the best of all possible worlds into being, the Committee believes that the changes it has recommended will be a considerable improvement on present arrangements. They will provide a basis for many young Victorians to participate more fully in their society and will contribute to the development of all young people as knowledgeable, skilful and caring citizens.

With the release of the report, Jean returned home to Adelaide, and shortly after left Australia for a three-month trip to Europe. Susan took long service leave and travelled with her parents. Recuperation was the object, and Jean needed it. Susan recalled Jean in Greece:

'she was escaping from the aftermath ... there'd be times even when you were in some place like Delphi which is just magic as far as I am concerned – she just went to bed – and she didn't get up for a couple of days. She also had illnesses ... ongoing stomach problem'.[87]

There would be limits to the extent that Jean could walk away from Victorian education and its problems. Jean was well aware of the firestorm that broke out with the publication of the report, and the ways in which its recommendations would and would not be implemented over the next few years. Helen Praetz and Marion Russell, especially Helen, would remain at the centre of efforts to implement it.

The Blackburn Report as it came to be known was broadly accepted in Victoria despite some opposition.[88] It developed national significance, influencing reform in South Australia where Kevin Gilding led a similar enquiry in 1988. Western Australia, Tasmania and the Northern Territory also took note.[89] In Victoria, not everything proceeded as the report intended and many small secondary schools survived with their limited curriculum offerings. In later years Jean admitted a faint regard for the Kennett Liberal government's success in closing many small secondary schools, though she had little time for the rest of its agenda.

Just before the report's release, Robert Fordham was replaced by Ian Cathie as Minister of Education. Cathie was more independent of the teacher unions, especially the VSTA, which augured well for the report's reception. The government accepted the general thrust of the report and immediately accepted twelve of its recommendations. A working party was planned to work through the curriculum and assessment recommendations. A Ministerial Unit on Postcompulsory Schooling which included Bill Hannan, Helen Praetz and Marion Russell was established to monitor the implementation of the report.[90]

The VSTA vehemently opposed the report. In Jean's words, the report had argued 'that the only way to get the kind of spread of curriculum that was needed which would include vocational subjects as well as academic subjects was to establish separate senior high schools. That's what I fell out with the VSTA about. They half won in the end.'[91] On publication of the report the VSTA newspaper was rushed to members. The headlined blared: 'Blackburn Out – Black Burnout: Everything you didn't want and more'. Pages of critique followed. According to Graham Marshall, deputy president of the VSTA, the report 'represents a tragic waste ... high expectations held by teachers, parents, the wider educational community and the government itself have been hopelessly dashed'. Another column was headlined 'Shonky processes, shonky results'.[92]

Much of this opposition was simply about VSTA policy not becoming the report itself but the union followed up with a more considered rebuttal.[93] Bill Hannan helped with the case against: 'They didn't show enough knowledge of the system and the forces in it to work really. The senior colleges weren't going to work. So, coming out with the grand idea that you'd have senior colleges everywhere ... It wouldn't work.' When asked why, Hannan replied: 'Probably the unions; the teachers anyway. The teachers, as articulated by the union.' He agreed that it was mainly about the old problem of teachers feeling that they would be stuck in a junior or senior school, their careers damaged. Hannan also argued that once the initial heat of the report's reception died down, the VSTA 'probably did more than anyone to pursue what I would think of as a reasonable interpretation of Blackburn'. Senior school campuses, if not senior stand-alone schools, were eventually established in Victoria.[94] Jean's thinking about two-year post-compulsory colleges had had a long gestation, well preceding the Victorian review.[95]

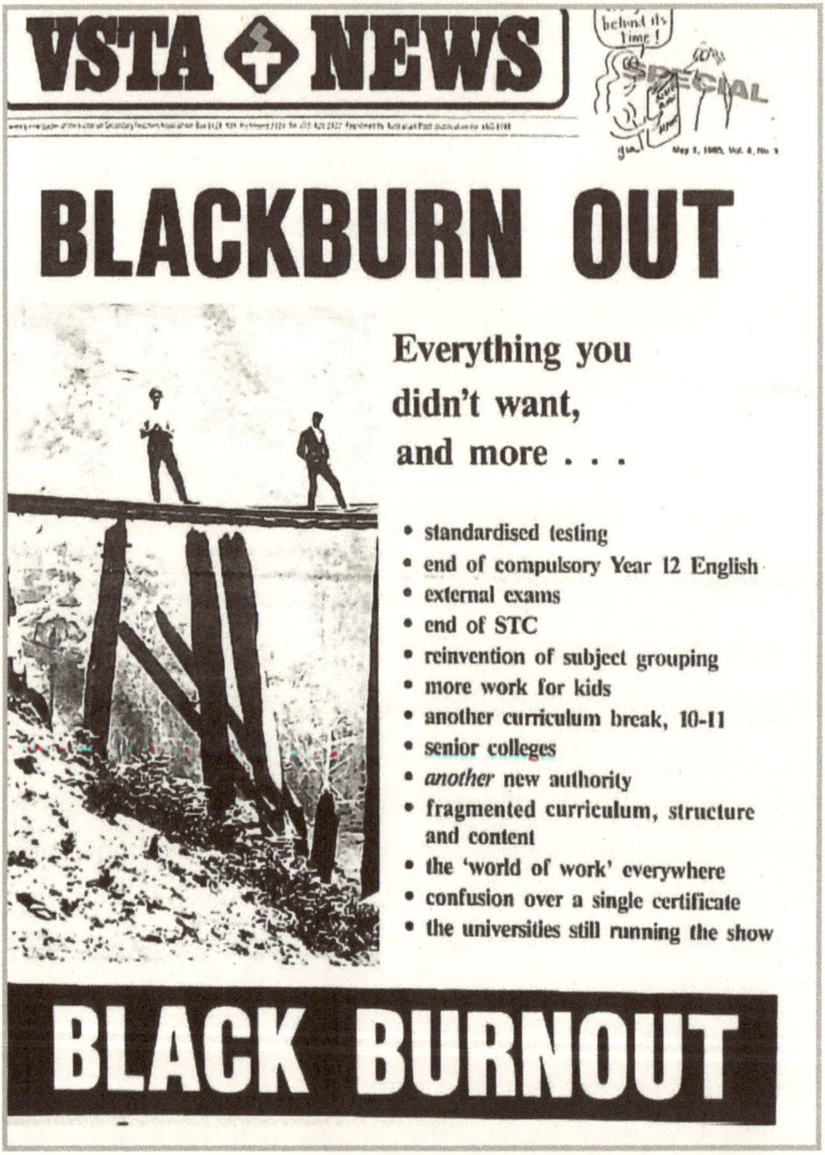

VSTA NEWS

behind its time!

SPECIAL

BLACKBURN OUT

Everything you didn't want, and more . . .

- standardised testing
- end of compulsory Year 12 English
- external exams
- end of STC
- reinvention of subject grouping
- more work for kids
- another curriculum break, 10-11
- senior colleges
- *another* new authority
- fragmented curriculum, structure and content
- the 'world of work' everywhere
- confusion over a single certificate
- the universities still running the show

BLACK BURNOUT

Figure 9.5 Front page of the emergency edition of the VSTA newspaper, 1 May 1985.
The VSTA was one of the more powerful teacher unions in Victoria.
It became less antagonistic towards Jean's report on
post-compulsory schooling in later years.
Image from newspaper collection, State Library of Victoria.

The TTUV developed a more positive response to the report, and earlier. 'Blackburn has provided an opportunity to put into place a comprehensive secondary education system that can reflect those aspects of technical school organisation and curriculum delivery that have allowed many technical schools to progress towards a comprehensive format over the last fifteen years'.[96] Many years later there was substantial nostalgia for the old technical schools, but by the1980s they were already becoming more comprehensive institutions as the kinds of employment available to young people changed. Fazal Rizvi argued that the report did not anticipate the degree to which the service economy would displace manufacturing in Victoria. Nor could the extraordinary changes in information technology in the 1990s through the 2010s be accurately anticipated. However, Jean had pushed secondary education in the right direction.[97]

There were controversies around the kind of curriculum that Jean's report recommended. Gwyn Dow, another old Melbourne friend, supported Jean's argument concerning the essential place of the humanities in the curriculum. Dow supported the 'work in society' approach to bridging school knowledge and broader social engagement. She was not so impressed by a lesser place for English in the new post-compulsory curriculum.[98] Catholic and other non-government schools and universities rejected Work and Society. Eventually a subject titled Australian Studies did get through, implementing some of Jean's original intentions.[99] Lyn Yates argued that 'the two main lines of attack were either that it was a Marxist plot or that it was mickey mouse, which would be a long way from what she was intending by it.'[100] Teachers educated in the 'disciplines' disliked it. Praetz argued that Jean believed that work was a common destiny for most young people after their early education, 'so they ought to understand the dynamics, the main drivers of it, the personal requirements of it'. Praetz argued that even if, as a school subject, it had a limited life, the argument had an effect on the later Mayer Committee's thinking about key competencies that should be achieved by schooling.[101]

The Blackburn Report and its surrounding politics addressed many issues, only a few of which can be addressed here. Non-government schools were not as opposed to the report as might have been anticipated, partly because Jean never advocated an undemanding curriculum. Many of her recommendations about tertiary entrance were acceptable to the universities. Jean herself was not responsible for later problems with subjects in the VCE. She disapproved of one development:

> a lot of the units required enormous initiative on the part of students. Big research projects and all of that … which for my part I feel was inappropriate because in the first place it advantages enormously the students who have well educated parents and well stocked homes. That's not what teaching is about. Teaching is about taking the message to everyone so to speak. So the students felt/were very overburdened by all of this, the numbers of projects they had to do and yet the training in independent work is obviously very important at that level.[102]

Some blamed Jean for the continuing drift to private schools, but this tendency and its causes were nationwide, not just Victorian. Lyn Yates argued that 'there were a number of things going on that made many parents feel their children wouldn't have as competitive a chance in public schools'. The public system was being built around an ethos of inclusiveness while 'the private schools were being left free to spruik naked competitive advantage'. Post-report developments 'fed the drift because it was so clear that the private schools had an advantageous parent community that could underpin the research-based components of the [assessment tasks]'. She thought the VSTA influence on the Board of Studies after the Blackburn Report was significant in this development.[103]

How much of a difference did Jean make to secondary schooling in Victoria? By the late 1990s schools were very different from what they had been in the 1970s.[104] The technical schools did close. For a time, a common Year 12 certificate was produced and there was an increased number of senior campuses if not separate senior colleges. School retention increased and the drive towards rethinking the curriculum for contemporary circumstances was advanced. At the same time, Jean's report was but one stage of a continuous process of change and reform that began in the 1970s and continues through to the present day. Writing for *The Age* newspaper in 1991, Geoff Maslen reviewed what had happened since the release of the report. 'Few people realised when the Blackburn report was published … that it was a 68-page packet of potential dynamite … Despite the initial outcry, it is now clear that Jean Blackburn had a remarkable grip on educational trends, as can be seen by the transformation of the state's secondary school system.'[105]

After finishing her Victorian work Jean had more capacity for interventions in national debates, usually in education. Jean's accomplishments were sufficiently well-known for several universities to confer honorary doctorates on her. The speeches she gave in receiving these and other honours were often publicised, giving her one avenue for continuing her public engagement in policy debates. The honorary doctorate that meant most to her was conferred by her own university, the University of Melbourne, in 1988. Jean's frustration that she had not achieved a doctorate had never quite disappeared. The Professor of Education, Kwong Lee Dow, made sure the honorary doctorate was specifically in 'education'. That was important to Jean. She spoke at the ceremony for only a few minutes, but 'I talked about myself as a woman of my generation'. A luncheon followed the ceremony:

> And I said to – it was quite a genuine question, to a number of … they were the wives of chancellors and things, with whom I happened to be speaking. I said, "One thing I've never worked out … is do you call yourself Doctor when you've got it or not?" … And one of them said in rather cold tones, "It used to be considered vulgar, but people do it now".[106]

Jean decided to use the title, not all the time, but when it suited her and her message.

In 1986 Jean gave the Curtin Memorial Lecture at the Australian National University. The lecture had been initiated with a gift from John Dedman, and of all the government ministers she had worked for, Dedman remained Jean's favourite. She reflected on the history of Commonwealth government involvement in education, spending time on the roles that 'need', equality and disadvantage played, especially from the 1970s. She worried that non-government school expansion, and within the public system, curriculum diversity and increased school autonomy, were reducing the capacity of public schools to make an impact on those families and schools that were in the most trouble. Social residualisation, that is increasing levels of parental unemployment and poverty concentrated in some school communities, was increasing. She finished by quoting Nugget Coombs who had talked about John Curtin in a lecture in the same series. He had spoken of the importance of seeking broad consensus in the making of public policy, and that consensus was to be built around 'the light on the hill of greater equality and compassion for those in need'.[107]

In 1988 the Australian College of Education conferred its medal on Jean.[108] Shirley Randell, former colleague of Jean and now President of the College, asked Dean Ashenden to write in support: 'To say that Jean Blackburn is our finest living practical theorist of education is to understate the case, since it is hard to think of anyone else who really fits the category', and, 'She has a moral authority in the eyes of literally thousands of people in and around Australian education which is, so far as I know, unique. This position derives from ... a combination of fierce social commitment with an equally fierce scepticism and critical intelligence.'[109] At the award ceremony Jean reflected on the accidental nature of her career, but also of the experiences that led her to understand the material character of injustice and poverty in schools.

> I shall never forget the heroic efforts made by teachers in the inner city schools of Melbourne and Sydney in conditions shameful for a society of Australia's wealth. I remember particularly a teacher in one such Sydney school guarded by a ten foot fence beyond which migrant mothers waited for their children. When I asked her what she would think of first if the school were better resourced, she replied, 'Something beautiful here, perhaps a fountain in this industrial desolation'. I understood and did not find the reply frivolous.[110]

Over the next few years Jean was invited to give graduation addresses at universities that included La Trobe and Adelaide. Joan Kirner as Minister of Education in Victoria hosted a party in her honour in 1989. Jean was in danger of becoming a national treasure, but not perhaps in South Australia, where a vaguely promised job in the Education

Department failed to eventuate – and there would be a shocking humiliation in the early 1990s. Nor in her own eyes had she achieved the status: 'I am presently writing the La Trobe graduation thing and getting more pompous by the minute. Was cut out to be a lay preacher; pity the religious basis disappeared'.[111]

In her writings on girls, women and education, new themes competed with old. She noticed the argument in the book, *Making the Difference*, by authors well-known to her, including R.W. Connell and Dean Ashenden. There was 'no longer a single model of masculinity and femininity in Australian society' and there were educational consequences.[112] Jean launched the book: 'It was at the Inner City Education Centre in Stanmore. And the joint was packed. She gave a wonderful speech.'[113] Connell dedicated a follow-up study from the same project to three outstanding teachers, Jean Blackburn was one of them.[114]

In writing about curriculum, Jean thought it 'entirely too much to expect that any and every school community of teachers, parents and students can alone construct the curriculum'. This in part was a comment on the influential school-based curriculum development (SBCD) movement from the 1970s. Jean advocated a model of curriculum development that would see negotiation between teachers and schools, their communities, and centres of curriculum expertise. The expertise needed to be based on access to the best research and thinking available, and an understanding of broader educational contexts than the local alone. The school curriculum also had a responsibility to counter the haphazard acquisition of manipulated knowledge through the mass media. The school 'potentially represents a counter-culture stressing reason and human continuity and the commonality of the human condition'.[115]

In 1984 the Australian Teachers Federation published in its magazine a 'Manifesto for a Democratic Curriculum'. This was put together by Dean Ashenden, Bill Hannan, Doug White and Jean. Hannan coordinated the effort and wrote the first draft. Ashenden recalled that 'We scarcely changed it ... we met around at Bill's place mainly; all three of us were a bit bowled over. It was fantastic. Looking through it you could see it did come from a conversation.' There was a little federal funding to help with airfares. 'It was a terrific experience for the four of us'.[116] The manifesto began with the statement that 'Australia's schools still mirror the tension between an ideal of schooling for all and a practice of schooling which reflects and consolidates social divisions'.[117] There were discussions about the changing definitions of equality in education, the kind of 'common' education that would enable active citizenship, and the importance of such education as 'public' education. There were arguments about reconstituting what might be thought of as literacy and 'basic skills', and about Australian studies. A new grouping of curriculum fields was suggested, one of which was 'institutional knowledge'.

The manifesto was produced before Jean's Victorian post-compulsory review was published, and several of the arguments in the manifesto affected or coincided with the argument of that report. There were responses published in *The Australian Teacher* three months later. Many were supportive, including that of Brian Crittenden but he also had concerns that 'significant individual differences in ability and interest' were not addressed, and the relationship between the knowledge and skills described in the manifesto with the academic disciplines was unclear. Ann Junor of the New South Wales Teachers Federation thought the manifesto lacked urgency. It failed to 'address the reality of the coming struggle to achieve an extension of universal public education, in the face of powerful forces undermining this right.'[118] Whether in support or not, the reactions identified the manifesto as a significant intervention in Australian thinking about curriculum and the democratisation of schooling and social equality.

Though Bill Hannan and Jean had different views on the post-compulsory report she had produced for the Victorian government, their disagreements were mostly to do with structures and the industrial consequences for teachers as a result of her recommendations. Their approaches to curriculum questions and the social equality responsibilities of school systems were close enough for them to cooperate on the manifesto.

By the end of the 1980s the force of the manifesto had diminished in the face of neoliberal inspired reforms. Jean noted the effects of a growing uncertainty about curriculum content in response to changing ideas about 'knowledge' itself. Social diversity and a growing legitimisation of choice within a market of schools reduced the interest of government education systems in social justice-oriented reform. Many non-government 'private' schools embodied 'individualistic conceptions of social life'. By emphasising individual differences and benefits from education they denied the associations of schooling with the 'quality of social life'.[119] Such trends made it difficult for governments seeking a 'national curriculum' over the next twenty years. In 1989 Jean was supporting the introduction of a national 'core' curriculum. She thought Australia was returning to the themes it had rejected in the 1970s. 'A common core curriculum is going to require a great deal of hammering out ... I do see it as an important national program. I have always been devoted to the idea of common important learnings and I do not understand how equity can have meaning in education without a notion of that kind.'[120]

National curriculum agencies in Australia had a chequered history through the 1970s and 1980s.[121] It was for one of these, the Curriculum Development Centre (CDC), that Jean developed her ideas for a curriculum about work and society. Jean wrestled with well-established educational polarities: mental versus manual labour, vocational versus general academic, and then technology and science versus the liberal arts, and preparation for work versus citizenship development. Jean wrote papers advocating a common work and society curriculum.[122] In the monograph published by the CDC in 1987, Jean worked her way through the historical and contemporary connections between school and work, including the ways that schooling socialised young people, training them in work-appropriate habits, attitudes and personality characteristics as well the teaching of literacy and numeracy. Because schools aided youth employment, they needed to go beyond individualised approaches as commonly occurred with career guidance:

> the rise of credentialism, and the drying up of satisfactory alternatives to prolonged schooling and post-school training, have changed the situation which prevailed for so long. In these circumstances equal access to understandings relevant to the making of informed choices about study and work have become a basic school responsibility for equity and other reasons.[123]

Girls in particular had needs in the area given the troubling nature of their access to the labour market over a very long period.

In the monograph Jean argued that work was profoundly affected by the ways gender operated. At the same time there were the effects of the historical development of work, technology, living standards, industrialisation, labour organisations and wage fixation, economic policies and the generation of wealth, and the relationships between work and leisure for the 'way of life'. There was a need to imagine possible futures in all of this. Jean believed that the curriculum she advocated had the potential to be an exemplar in terms of active learning and investigation. She went on to discuss curriculum focuses and approaches to developing relevant materials, whether the subject should be a core or elective study, and when it might be studied – and the possible place of work experience for young people in such a subject or study.

> Whether engagement with the experience of work is through work experience or research involving interviews, workplace visits and the study of related documentary material and historical and contemporary accounts and analyses, it is obvious that the study will involve the close involvement of employers and trade unionists as well as of teachers, students and scholars.[124]

Jean did not advocate a prescribed syllabus. Any syllabus had to respond 'to local decisions and possibilities', but there had to be attention to changes over time and 'research', whether by a class, student groups or individuals. A good textbook and a handbook guiding students to sources and containing relevant statistics were essential. Jean did not share 'the currently fashionable view that the existence of a basic text and supporting documents and points of reference constitutes a limitation of professional initiative'. This kind of statement was typical of Jean. She was progressive and democratic in her curriculum thinking, but she always maintained that local initiative needed to be guided by substantial central initiatives. Working-class children especially were in danger without such an approach.

Jean remained deeply interested in federal education policy through the remaining years of the Fraser government. She monitored the growing marginality of the Schools Commission, as it became a 'less progressive influence on Australian education'.[125] Her Victorian report was written in resistance to a number of its directions. She spoke against the additional state resources that were directed towards 'ruling class schools'. She spoke of the growing difficulties of youth from low-income families undertaking full-time higher education.[126] She noted the decreasing support for both comprehensive schooling and a common curriculum.[127]

Through working for the Tertiary Education Authority in South Australia and finding herself based in a university, Jean was often invited to contribute to conferences and seminars. She reflected on the kinds of contributions academics made to education policy and governance. 'The Australian academic tradition is one which stands aloof from engagement with immediate problems facing governments, and even to a considerable degree from research which might clarify options in public policy.' She contrasted this with what occurred in the United States 'where social scientists and lawyers move in and out of academic pursuits, engage in policy relevant research and are on hire to advocacy groups and governments on a scale not yet evident in Australia', though a possible exception had been what had occurred in the Second World War. Jean wanted to see more of this cross-fertilisation between the academy and government.[128] She repeated the theme many times. She was disappointed with what the universities had offered in the Schools Commission years and after. In the secondary schools she had visited there was no question that 'it is the best practitioners who are streets ahead of Australian [university-based] theorists in education'.[129]

In 1983 the Fraser government was defeated, and the Hawke Labor government came to power. Susan Ryan, an old colleague and friend of Jean was appointed Minister of Education. Would it be possible to set the Commonwealth government on a course in education that resumed some of the agendas of the early Schools Commission? Ryan was of a mind to do so despite the different economic and political circumstances of the mid-1980s. In Dean Ashenden's words, 'the whole ALP mode of thinking then was beholden to Karmel. Which is to say, Jean, in many ways.' Jean did some behind the scenes work to get Dean Ashenden introduced to Ryan and appointed to a job in her office.[130] In the end, however, Jean would have little official involvement in Hawke era education policy. Her main effort was with Victoria, and not long after she had finished there, Ryan lost her portfolio to John Dawkins. His take on education policy contradicted the older Karmel/Blackburn settlement.[131] The Schools Commission was abolished in 1988 and 'Education' was absorbed into a new ministry that included employment and training in its title. Jean saw the changes as indicative of the growing influence of the economic rationalists. In her words, they focused 'on the economy rather than the society, saw education as the means of advancing Australia's position in a competitive global economy, with a more instrumental curricular emphasis'.[132] She was sensitive to the changing meaning of the word 'public' in education in these circumstances.[133]

By the end of the 1980s Jean had been outflanked on education policy, though there were yet two appointments for her in the area in the early 1990s. As Brian Hill had done a decade before, many people continued to listen to her: 'I'll come out of the woodwork anytime to hear Jean Blackburn speak because I treasure her clarity of utterance, her creativity of suggestion and her concern for people'.[134] Joan

Kirner was also concerned to acknowledge her impact and historical significance.[135]

Denise Bradley noted Jean's significance as a 'shining example of leadership in policy advice' at a time when there were so few women in really senior executive positions, when 'mentoring' was virtually unavailable.[136] Jean put effort into referee reports that helped women, and on occasion men also, to get jobs. Denise Bradley's own appointment as first Vice-Chancellor of the University of South Australia was supported by a reference from Jean. Margaret Allen, Julie Marcus and Lyn Yates were also beneficiaries.[137] Jean's impact on Helen Praetz's professional life was transformative. 'People took me seriously because Jean thought I was [good] – a whole lot of people were so open and friendly and respectful because of Jean … You always knew with Jean – if she thought you were wonderful she told everybody.'[138] Jean could even admire natural enemies if they were clever. Ken McKinnon invited Jean to speak at a seminar at the University of Wollongong. She was at the podium with the darling of the right in the 1980s, Lauchlan Chipman: 'Oh Ken, the most awful thing. I cannot really bring myself to totally hate someone who is so clever'.[139]

By the end of the 1980s there were trips to the Adelaide Central Market on Friday or Saturday mornings for coffee and meeting with friends.[140] Jean continued to write papers, but Dick wrote to Susan, 'Jean suffers physically in generating another paper for a conference; I hope the tension eases soon.'[141] Her wit, and her intolerance of pomposity held, as Ailsa Zainu'ddin's description of her behaviour at a conference in Adelaide, or one of Lyndsay Connors' stories, confirmed: 'I heard this awful, horrible sort of snort behind me, and a low growl, and it was Jean who said something like "Well, that's a load of crap for a start" – in a quite audible voice'.[142]

It may be that Jean in this period was losing some of her inhibitions about expressing herself when she was unhappy about what she was hearing. Several of our interviewees remarked on her increasingly direct commentaries. There is no single explanation: discontent with her health problems, the increasing absence of policy work to engage her, her alienation from the postmodern turn and the rise of neo-liberal economics and its effects on public policy, were all likely to have played a part.

Jean held to her views of what good schooling should be and do. Certain kinds of teacher behaviour were a problem:

> her whole orientation was towards the social order, and its comprehension and improvement, so psycho-babble wasn't her thing at all. She temperamentally did not like it, and she thought it was politically counter-productive … we were visiting a couple of schools … There was a young woman there who was a teacher. She was getting into the touchy-feely sort of stuff, sort of made her [Jean's] skin crawl … it wasn't what schools could or should do. What the schools were about above all else was … you treat people decently and … the first duty is to teach them about how the world works.[143]

In 1989 the Soviet Union collapsed, and in 1991 the Communist Party of Australia was dissolved. Jean Blackburn had left the party 45 years before, and in 1991 the Party left her husband, Dick. Jean and Dick both had roughly another decade to live, and little of it was going to be easy.

Chapter 10

FEMINIST MATRIARCH, 1990–2001

Jean seemed to me to be living an almost over-examined life. I mean everything had to be examined and re-examined … I admired it, but it drained her terribly, and I think it affected her health adversely. It was long after she was on the Schools Commission, that she was diagnosed with an intestinal problem and she relayed to me in conversation what the doctor had said to her about her condition. I think she quite liked what the doctor had said to her: 'This is part of being *you*. This is the down side of what makes you so remarkable, and if you were a dull person just sitting around not caring less about anything, you wouldn't have it.' And I thought it helped her bear it a bit better.[1]

Despite Jean's difficult relationship with her father, the foundations of which were laid in childhood, a rather tortured love, respect for his achievements and perhaps a sense of duty meant that she remained in touch. Several years before she had performed a remarkable service for him. After the death of Jean's mother Claire, Les Muir discovered that he really needed another woman to do what he thought women should do for men. He determined on a candidate, and asked Jean to approach her, to propose an arrangement. Jean agreed to be the go-between, and the intended responded favourably, performing as expected until an illness intervened. Later, whenever Jean was in Canberra, she made time to visit her father at his nursing home. On one occasion Dean Ashenden drove her there. Jean began talking about Les, quickly becoming enraged by his treatment of her and her brothers when they were children. At the same time, she could provide an analysis of its causes: 'I think her position was that he was absolutely a man of his times, he was very poorly educated himself and saw little value in it for anyone but particularly for a girl.'[2] Jean attempted to write an autobiography in her 70s but reflecting on her childhood was always a problem.

Her father turned 100 in April 1990 when Jean was 70. There were celebrations. A notice was placed in *The Canberra Times*: '100 years old today. With loving wishes to Leslie Allan Muir, of Kankinya Nursing Home, Canberra. From his daughter Dr Jean Blackburn of Adelaide, his sons Allan of Melbourne and Les of Canberra and from his 8 grandchildren and 19 great grandchildren in Canberra, Melbourne, Sydney and Southport Q'ld.'[3] Jean met relatives whom she had not seen since the 1930s. She was startled by the story of cousins whose parents Les had assisted during the Depression. Without him, their families would have been in dire poverty. The knowledge improved Jean's assessment of him, although her younger brother, Leslie Thomas, remembered the assistance in terms of Les having guaranteed a loan for a brother, who nevertheless went bankrupt.[4] Les lived another year and a half, dying in December 1991 and Jean composed the death notice for *The Canberra Times*. Allan, Leslie and Jean inherited equal shares of the estate. Jean was better off by some $270,000.

Although Jean received appointments to public authorities of significance in the early 1990s, one way or another her thoughts were turning towards her own life story. She had presented a paper on the New Housewives Association and her role in it to a Labour History seminar in Adelaide in 1987. The 1990s saw the growth of interest in oral history, and there were institutions and persons keen to record Jean's story. Two extensive interviews were conducted, the first on behalf of the National Library by Peter Biskup in 1990 and the second, the Australian College of Education by Tony Ryan in 1994. There were others, including one with Wendy Lowenstein in 1994. Lowenstein, with her own communist history, evoked some unique responses to questions that others would not have asked. Jean could be defensive. On another occasion Jean wanted to know what the interviewers, authors of a history of International Women's Day, were going to say about her. Possibly as a consequence, they ended up saying very little.[5]

As Jean's wider responsibilities wound down, several people encouraged her to write her autobiography, especially in the period following Dick's death in 1999. Judy Gill, a friend of Jean and an academic at the University of South Australia, worked with her. Alison Mackinnon helped with establishing a relationship with the Hawke Institute at the University of South Australia while Jean and Judy plotted the outline of a book. Judy commented on drafts that Jean wrote about her early life, mainly up to entering the University of Melbourne as an undergraduate.[6] Janet McCalman's social history of working-class Richmond in Melbourne inspired her.[7] The proposed book was given a couple of titles: *Jean Blackburn: A Very Public Commitment* and another, *Jean Blackburn: A Woman of her Time*.[8] Jean began writing but two, maybe three things went wrong.

The first was that her old problem of never being satisfied with a particular piece of writing was particularly intense. There exists in

Jean's private papers many brief drafts of autobiographical reflection, but she accepted none as final. The second problem was that Jean was having to confront a period in her life which she remembered as deeply unhappy. Depressed already with the ailments of old age she depressed herself further as she turned over the experiences. She talked with friends. Not long before Jean died, Lyndsay Connors wrote to her: 'it would be wonderful to have your account of your own life, or aspects of your life and how your thinking developed. But not at the cost of making yourself tired or ill'.[9] A third problem we suggest is that concentration on the self as opposed to working on public policy for example, was difficult for Jean. One of the themes of Jean's life was a fear of domestic entrapment. It recurred as she found it ever harder to walk and to escape home. Finally, the attempt to write 'the self' became impossible. She would not countenance one suggested way through, a 'stream of consciousness' approach. In 1999 Jean had speculated on whether to write a policy-oriented memoir, but she thought she should try the more personal approach, despite noting elsewhere, 'An autobiographical approach – NO – too painful on the one hand & too ego centred on the other'.[10] She never quite solved the problem of the different approaches. At another time, when the idea of a public policy focus was in the ascendant, she wrote: 'I do however have quite strong feelings about preserving what I regard as private from public view, and that by the same token, my own remarks about people with whom I have worked should relate to disagreements about policy and not be hurtful to them.'[11]

Dean Ashenden saw her whenever he went to Adelaide. 'We'd go and have dinner or something ... it would often be the first thing she'd say – "Can't write, can't write, can't write".'[12] This autobiographical crisis came at the end of the 1990s. Before then, at the beginning of the decade, there were still planes to catch to Canberra and Melbourne in pursuit of public duties, and even a job in Adelaide as the centenary of women's suffrage in South Australia drew close.

The first of Jean's 1990s appointments was to the Council, and then the chancellorship of the new University of Canberra.

The creation of the unified national system, 'the Dawkins revolution', meant unprecedented turmoil for higher education in Australia. Existing CAEs would either form new universities while some, in parts or as a whole, would amalgamate into existing universities. For a period, there was a plan to unite the Australian National University (ANU) and the Canberra College of Advanced Education but there was strong opposition in both institutions. On one side there was a fear that the research prestige of the ANU would be diminished, and on the other, that the commitment to professional education, especially teacher education would be downgraded. Opposition to the amalgamation was too strong and in 1990 the Canberra CAE became the University of Canberra, a stand-alone university. The new university partnered with Monash University in Melbourne, its role to assist the new university through its foundation period. The principal of the college, and now the university's first Vice-Chancellor, was Roger Scott. He and his Council urgently required an inaugural chancellor.

Scott was very aware of Jean's work in the 1970s and 1980s through his academic interest in public policy in education. He had heard Jean speak and was 'impressed, as everyone else was, by her grasp of issues and command of language'. For the position of chancellor, Scott had in mind 'someone with mainstream experience in education to help manage the transition – a serious scholar and not a celebrity', so it was unsurprising that:

> Jean was my first choice ... I have always been a believer in positive discrimination to overcome disabilities suffered by women in every area of Australian public life ... I thus welcomed the input from several female Council members ... I almost certainly consulted Mal Logan, VC [Vice-Chancellor] of our sponsoring university [Monash]. I was also aware that Jean was held in high regard by some of the key players within the ANU, especially Karmel, and inside the federal education bureaucracy, so the appointment was likely to be free from external criticism.[13]

Jean was appointed first to the new university's Council on February 15, 1990, and elected chancellor less than two weeks later. With her father in Canberra, the appointment suited her. She consulted Deirdre Jordan and Roma Mitchell, two of three pioneering women chancellors of universities in Australia. Jean was to be the fourth. Each of them encouraged her, though Mitchell warned that there were negative aspects to the role – the way academics 'talk on and fight about everything'. Jordan was more positive, telling her that she could craft the role to make it her own.[14] *The Australian* newspaper announced Jean as the 'New first lady of Canberra'.[15]

Within weeks, Roger Scott resigned as Vice-Chancellor to take up the post of Director of Education in Queensland. Jean had to lead the search for a replacement. At the same time the Council of the University was in dispute with the federal Minister of Education, John Dawkins.[16] He had not wished to see a University of Canberra separate from the ANU. Dawkins objected to the nominations to the University Council of members from the assembly of the Australian Capital Territory, an early problem for Jean to contend with. Though publicly describing the failure to accept the nominations as 'absurd',

Jean had to negotiate with Dawkins, but he was not for any quick resolution.

Don Aitkin was quickly identified as the most eligible candidate for the Vice-Chancellorship.[17] At the time, Aitkin was completing his term as leader of the Australian Research Council and he was reluctant to return to his substantive position at the Australian National University. He anticipated conflict there as he was unimpressed by some of the plans for its future. A family commitment meant he was unable to pursue possibilities at Stanford and Harvard in the United States, but he was unwilling to submit a formal application to the University of Canberra.[18] The Council's selection committee that included Mal Logan, Jim Walker and Lyndsay Connors brought Aitkin in for consultation – in many respects a *de facto* opportunity to assess his potential as Vice-Chancellor. The committee was impressed, and the next morning Jean telephoned him to offer the job. He accepted, and the University of Canberra was to have its new Vice-Chancellor from the beginning of 1991. In the meantime, Judith Brine held the position in an acting capacity. In announcing Aitkin's appointment Jean said that his 'wide background in higher education, and involvement in the development of higher education policy, made him an "outstanding appointee" for the position. She referred specifically to his role within the development of a unified national system for higher education.'[19]

Jean was formally inaugurated as Chancellor by the Governor-General, Bill Hayden, on April 19, 1990. In her inaugural address she spoke of what the new universities could offer as part of 'the responsibility of higher education institutions to the society which owns and funds them'. She argued that:

Figure 10.1 Jean as foundation Chancellor of the University of Canberra. c1990. *Photographer unknown, courtesy of the University of Canberra.*

> one does not have to endorse an education-led economic recovery to welcome the new emphasis being given to applied studies and research. It may also be seen as correcting a traditional imbalance in the prestige rankings of studies and activities in higher education. More importantly ... it recognises that all higher education has always been vocational. Academic work is itself one such employment. Vocational and liberal education, practice and theory, pure and applied research are not oppositional categories. Vocational education may also be liberal, extending intellectual horizons and the imagination, advancing knowledge, focusing theory and involving the development of moral, cultural and social judgement.

Elsewhere in the speech, she reflected on some of the negative consequences of the binary system of higher education that proceeded from the Martin report to the Menzies government in 1965. New universities such as Canberra had an opportunity to increase the access and opportunity that students were sometimes denied in the older universities. She warmly noted the foundation program for Aboriginal students.[20]

For friends like Margaret Bearlin and Lyndsay Connors, it was a wonderful thing to see Jean accepting and occupying the role of Chancellor. Bearlin was an academic at the predecessor CAE and now the university. Connors, who had studied with Bearlin some years earlier, was unexpectedly overtaken with emotion as she watched Jean assume the chancellorship:

> And for some ghastly reason ... I just suddenly found myself in floods of tears, as I looked at her talking there. The abolition of the Schools Commission was one of the worst periods of my life. It was horrible. It was a death by a thousand cuts. And it was done in a horrible way ... But when I saw her standing there ... I just felt this dreadful grief at the casting aside of

everything, in a way, the vision that had underpinned the Schools Commission, the vision that Jean had had of it, and it had all been swept away ... the move to some economistic view of schooling ...[21]

There is a significant co-dependence in the relationship between chancellors and vice-chancellors, which, if it breaks down, can have disastrous consequences, but Jean and Don Aitkin worked well together. Aitkin would collect Jean from the airport from time to time, on occasion taking her home for dinner and taking her to wherever she was staying, sometimes with her brother, Les Thomas. Aitkin remembered the period positively. Chairing Council meetings, one of Jean's tasks, could be demanding, but Jean was happy to accept Aitkin's guidance in order to get the business done.[22]

More challenging was the early problem of the new university's debt. In 1990, the foundation year, the Faculty of Communication had over-spent its budget, reportedly by more than half a million dollars, a substantial amount for a young university without the sources of income enjoyed by the 'sandstone' universities. Judith Brine secured the resignation of Bill Mandle from the Communications deanship, though he retained his continuing academic position. He was unhappy, arguing that the university had failed to give him the training required to manage faculty finances. He appealed to the Chancellor. This was not the kind of business in which wise chancellors intervene. Chancellors can receive appeals if there is a strong case that an injustice has occurred, but Jean decided that in this case intervention was not warranted. Mandle decided that Jean's reputation as a 'social justice' advocate was flawed.[23] Jean stood with Brine as sections of the university felt threatened by possible debt-reducing measures.[24]

Towards the end of 1991 Jean decided she would not continue as Chancellor. She appears to have had her doubts about her success in the role though there is little to suggest that she had not done a good job. Doubt was endemic to Jean. The major reason for her decision was her health. A surgical procedure had gone wrong in June 1991, leaving her with the condition known as 'femoral neuropathy'.[25] She was operated on for an internal growth. The procedure had its risks and the surgeon was unable to avoid severing the femoral nerve running from the pelvis down the leg, cutting off control of the main leg muscles. 'She had a long struggle to overcome the pain and to recover movement. Initially she was told she would not walk again but she seemed to develop alternative muscles to compensate and after some time was able to walk with a stick: she was a very determined woman'.[26]

When Jean rang Aitkin to tell him she could not go on, she said the best thing she had done for the University was to appoint him Vice-Chancellor. This was true. The University of Canberra had had a difficult foundation, and its leaders had been short-term or temporary for some time. Aitkin remained as a successful Vice-Chancellor for twelve years. Following Jean, he arranged the election of Donald Horne and then Wendy McCarthy as successive chancellors. At the end of the last Council meeting over which Jean presided, Aitkin drew attention to the fact that this was Jean's last meeting. 'Council members indicated by acclamation their thanks to Dr Blackburn for her service to the University as Chancellor'. Council then received visitors, including Peter Karmel as an emeritus professor of the ANU. Karmel and others presented a gift commemorating the inauguration of the university in 1990. It was a gavel for the use of the chancellor conducting council meetings. It 'joined gifts of mace from the government of the ACT and the chancellor's chair from the Australian National University, all of which had been crafted at the Canberra Institute of the Arts'.[27] Peter Karmel's presence would have meant a great deal to Jean.

In February of 1991, before the disabling operation, Jean accepted appointment as Chair of the State Board of Education in Victoria. This was the outfit for which Ken McKinnon had been foundation Chair a decade earlier and which had initiated the 1980s enquiry into post-compulsory education. By the early 1990s the Board was losing its relevance and was considered moribund by many.[28] Adding to the problem was the increasing perception that the Labor government was on a downhill slide. Joan Kirner had been Premier of Victoria from August in 1990. Barry Pullen and Neil Pope were the last Labor ministers for education, and Jean would work with them before Jeff Kennett's Liberals swept to government in September 1992.

Jean's predecessor as Chair was Bill Hannan who had endured criticism for being too close to the teacher unions. He then assumed two posts, one inside the education ministry as general manager of school programs and chief executive officer of the Board. Jean was aware of the charge that the Board was too close to the ministry. She said: 'I realise that it does seem to have become an arm of the ministry and I can understand that people might fear that ... I don't intend to be a rubber stamp for anyone.'[29] Jean expected to be in Melbourne for the week preceding each meeting of the Board.

As Chair of the State Board Jean was a member of a taskforce led by Ivan Deveson on accelerating links between the education sector and industry. The position gave Jean a chance to continue the arguments about vocational education she had begun nationally and

Figure 10.2 Jean while Chair of the State Board of Education in Victoria, with the Labor Minister for Education, Barry Pullen, and Chief Executive of the Education Ministry, Ann Morrow, c1992.
Courtesy Public Records Office Victoria, Item 14518-p001-000009.

in Victoria years before. Jean saw the initiation of the VCE following her review as historically significant, but it had evolved in ways that concerned her. Its purpose as a school completion certificate was not about 'selection' but opening future employment and education opportunities to an ever-increasing proportion of young people.[30] One VCE change which she had to accept was the decision by the Minister in 1992 to make the compulsory Australian Studies unit optional. The subject had loomed as an election issue and needed to be 'neutralised'. Much of Jean's argument about linking understandings of work, economy and society had rested on this subject. Its role in the curriculum was to be a unifying, citizen-making, compulsory study. She was disappointed, considering it a scandal that students could emerge from their schooling 'without a structured knowledge of the country, the world of work, and economic history'. The hostility of the Liberal opposition, and many of the non-government schools had been consistent. The Liberals had thought it 'politically motivated and ideologically driven'.[31]

The election of the Kennett government in September 1992 signalled radical change in Victorian education policy. Anxieties about schooling, tertiary entrance and employment had increased as the pressures arising from neoliberal economic reform, and especially in Victoria, the growing pressure on working-class jobs in manufacturing increased. An article in *The Age* newspaper reviewed the previous ten years in education. It discussed the successes and failures of Jean, Bill Hannan and other progressive educators. Brian Crittenden was reported as criticising the 'naive egalitarian view: a will to believe that significant differences in ability, background learning, interest etc., either do not exist or can be camouflaged'. Some of this criticism was aimed at changes that occurred after the Blackburn Report. The report itself, according to Crittenden, 'did not envisage anything like the total reconstruction undertaken by the [later] Victorian Curriculum and Assessment Board'. The article's author, Luke Slattery concluded that by the 1990s: 'The community's anxieties about senior school education ... have imploded around tertiary selection and related issues. In a different environment it is possible to imagine the VCE, with its emphasis on broad skills, marrying theoretical and practical studies, and links with further training and work, receiving a more generous reception. But in the early 1990s the only thing Year 12 students and their parents cared about was securing one of the coveted places in the state's five universities'.[32]

The incoming Kennett government disbanded the Board of Education in October 1992. Her work for the Board was Jean's last government appointment in education. There had been some pleasant aspects to it. Much of the antagonism following her report had passed. Jean was described by a Ministry of Education official as an 'eminent Victorian' and 'a positive role model for youth'.[33] On a personal level it had enabled her to keep in close contact with her children, Susan and Hugh, both living in Melbourne.

In 1894 the South Australian government led by Charles Cameron Kingston legislated for women's suffrage, and not only that, but it established the right of women to stand for election to parliament. It was the first Australian colony to do so, and one of the first jurisdictions in the world. There was good reason to mark the centenary. The history of the struggle to achieve women's suffrage deserved to be better known, especially the efforts of women such as Mary Lee. It would give government and communities the chance to develop projects of contemporary relevance to women. The women's movement in South Australia embraced the possibilities. The first task was to secure a commitment and funding from the state Labor government led by John Bannon.

Susan Magarey of the University of Adelaide, the biographer of Catherine Helen Spence, was one of those who began talking to various women's groups about the impending centenary, among them women of the Liberal Party. Jennifer Cashmore, a Liberal member of parliament became enthused with the possibilities. From 1991 she was asking questions in parliament and writing, seeking a commitment by government. At the end of 1992 a meeting with Premier Bannon was convened by the Women's Adviser to the Premier, Jayne Taylor. Anne Levy, a Labor member of parliament, Mary Beasley, a senior public servant, Jean Blackburn and Jayne Taylor attended.

The first job was to appoint a chair for the steering committee. Taylor wondered about Jean, but there was also a lawyer, Lindy Powell, who had begun her career with Elliott Johnston's firm. She was younger than Jean and Taylor thought she might be more active and effective in inspiring younger women.[34] Nevertheless, at age 72 Jean was appointed to the role. Roma Mitchell, the Governor of South Australia, was appointed patron. The Steering Committee included representatives of three political parties: Labor, Liberal and Democrats. The Women's Electoral Lobby (WEL) and the Women's Christian Temperance Union (WCTU) were also there. Mary Ann Bin-Sallik and Natasha Stott-Despoja were to represent Aboriginal and young women respectively and Susan Magarey for women's studies and the universities. Mary Beasley was appointed Deputy Chair. Seven committees were formed – three more than had been formed to run the Blackburn Review in Victoria a decade before. Jean chaired executive and finance committees; Beasley, sponsorship and marketing. The historical committee was chaired by Magarey. There were two committees for events and their planning. Coordinating all seven and acting on their decisions rapidly became a major problem.

Jean knew that there would be a lot of work involved. In accepting the appointment, she wrote 'I shall need to rely heavily on the assistance and experience of the Women's Adviser'.[35] Some help came from the adviser but for too long Jean had too little support, trying to run her committees and coordinate from home. Eventually there would be an office established with an experienced public servant, Loine Sweeney, in charge, but even then, the ill-staffed office could not keep up with the proposals being generated by the committees. The funding from government for the year was both minimal and late in being provided.[36] Jean was disadvantaged especially in

Figure 10.3 At Government House, Adelaide, before it went sour for Jean. Key players in the preparation for the Centenary of Women's Suffrage in South Australia (1894–1994). From left to right, Anne Levy, the Minister for the Status of Women, Mary Beasley (public servant and Deputy Chair of the Steering Committee), Jean Blackburn (Chair of the Steering Committee) and Roma Mitchell (Governor of South Australia), 1993.
Rosey Boehm photographer, courtesy of the photographer and the State Library of South Australia.

comparison with the resources that Mary Beasley as a senior public servant brought to the work as Deputy Chair. Beasley often referred to the work her office did to support her centenary responsibilities. At one stage her executive assistant worked nearly full-time on it.[37]

There were other problems. Members of the Steering Committee had different priorities. Beasley and Jennifer Cashmore were enthusiastic in their wooing of businesses to sponsor events. Jean was more interested in community initiatives, and the program of these for 1994 was impressive. Early on, Susan Magarey worried that getting Jean's ear seemed more important than initiating a clear process of calling for and assessing submissions for funding projects, but that issue was ironed out once an office was established.[38] At one point, an ankle injury hampered Jean's mobility, but more significant trouble was brewing.

Two members of the Steering Committee began to undermine Jean and her work. The motivations for this are somewhat indeterminate, though an ambition to replace Jean as head of the Committee and therefore the centenary celebrations is likely to have been part of the mix. Loine Sweeney was approached by two members of the Steering Committee. The meeting, in her words:

> quickly descended into what I can only describe as a string of incoherent allegations about Jean's performance as Chair and what they suggested was her declining capacity. I was astonished to be asked by them to cut Jean out of 'the loop' in their quest to build a case to the Government to have her removed as Chair. As I sat mutely listening, they told me the best approach was to avoid liaising with … her or [to] send her any information. I was again shocked when they followed this advice with more: to similarly avoid keeping the Minister for Women, Anne Levy, informed about progress in planning the celebrations.[39]

Sweeney was in a difficult position, but she decided in favour of continuing her responsibility to liaise with Jean, and a little later, warning her of the hostile activity. She would suffer as result, eventually losing her job mid-way through the centenary year. On Jean's reaction to the news, Sweeney wrote:

> As Jean's centre of gravity was integrity, respect and valuing collaboration and friendship, she was hurt and loathe to dwell on not being treated likewise. However she didn't seem totally surprised and trusted the advice. I could see that she felt diminished by the lack of confidence in her it implied. But we

had a good laugh about both being in the same boat. She had confidence in me and I in her, so we would put the dragon to one side and keep working together to keep the year on track!⁴⁰

For Jean, part of keeping the 'year on track' was accepting opportunities to talk wherever she could about the year and its plans. She 'had the informed enthusiasm that the historic occasion of the Centenary needed, understanding only too well that it provided a rare public platform to highlight and engage with the community about women's history, equality and South Australia's history as an innovator'.⁴¹ Jean herself embodied fifty years of feminist experience.

Jean wrote a well-researched and adaptable speech. One of several women's clubs Jean visited was the 'Minerva Group' which she addressed in March 1993. She told the story of how the suffrage came to South Australia, with reference to an old interest of hers, the married women's property acts. She castigated the historiography that portrayed the suffrage campaigns as inconsequential in the face of men's 'gift' of the suffrage, or the portrayal of suffragists as wowsers and kill-joys. She welcomed the belated recognition by many second-wave feminists that the first wave were indeed 'admirable fighters for the advance of women'. She acknowledged the crucial interventions of the Women's Christian Temperance Union, a group that Jean had engaged with in the 1940s. She acknowledged the Working Women's Trade Union in the struggle. She acknowledged defects in the nineteenth century campaign as it related to Aboriginal women.

Towards the end of her speech she outlined the developing program for 1994. Anne Levy as the responsible Minister had announced the major events in December 1992. They were to include the launch of Australia Post stamps, a booklet on Mary Lee, an Art Gallery exhibition of women artists, special events in Writers' Week and the

Figure 10.4 Jean at work during the lead-up to the South Australian women's suffrage centenary. She gave many speeches in the 1993–1994 period, insisting that the history of women was important, and that women need to continue writing and making their own history, c1993.
Rosey Boehm photographer, courtesy of the photographer and the State Library of South Australia.

Adelaide Festival of Arts, a re-enactment of the 1894 parliamentary debate extending the suffrage and the commissioning of a tapestry for the parliament commemorating women's contribution to society. Towards the end of the year an international conference with the theme 'Women, Power and Politics' was planned. Glenda Jackson, celebrated actor and Labour member of the House of Commons in the United Kingdom, was one of the invited speakers. There were more events than these in the central program. Then there was a great range of community and corporate sponsored events. Hills Industries, the South Australian manufacturer of the iconic Hills Hoist, part of the lives of most suburban women in Australia for many decades, sponsored a 'major exhibition on one hundred years of housework'.

T-shirts, tote bags, a women's diary and calendar were to be produced. Jean concluded with an appeal not only for support but an encouragement to the Minerva women to write their own history as a contribution to women's history more generally. 'When we look back over the hidden history of women it becomes increasingly clear that at least one of the reasons why it has been so consistently bypassed is that women are shy about writing their own lives and the story of their organisations.'[42]

In the historical committee chaired by Susan Magarey, Jean proposed that there be a 'a major exhibition of working women and the women's movement over a 100-year period'. It was not surprising that women and work should have been a focus for her. There were approaches to the universities. Would Kevin Marjoribanks, now Vice-Chancellor at the University of Adelaide consider honorary degrees for more women? He replied that gender would not be a criterion, but that Fay Gale was already listed for an award. Deirdre Jordan, now Chancellor at Flinders University, developed a project that was indicative of the kinds of local activities that developed throughout South Australia:

> And so one thing that we did was to plant trees joining the Hall of Residence with the University. So there's a path ... and a bridge that you cross, so we invited any kind of women's group or girls' schools, or anywhere where you might get women, to nominate someone whom they thought should be remembered and to say why ... And then planted trees, and had little plaques on them to celebrate that.[43]

Jean's 'Suffrage' notebook detailed contacts, events and other planning including the radio interviews and attempts to involve women living elsewhere than South Australia, including Joan Kirner of course, Anne Summers and Susan Ryan. Jean was delighted that her suggestion that Glenda Jackson participate in the big conference came to fruition. The pressure was unceasing through 1993 as planning and publicity intensified.[44]

And then Jean was removed from her position as Chair. This occurred just days before the launch of the centenary year, slated for 1 January 1994.

The Labor government in South Australia was in dire straits during 1993. John Bannon resigned as Premier; the collapse of the State Bank was an event for which his government could not escape some responsibility. After a disastrous year, Labor was voted out of office on December 14, 1993. A new Liberal government was formed with Dean Brown as Premier and Diana Laidlaw the Minister for the Arts and Status of Women. Before the first fortnight was out, Jean lost her position. The conversations that led to the action are mainly unrecorded, though Loine Sweeney was tipped off late in 1993 that 'that the person I knew to be Jean's key underminer and a close associate were having private meetings with a Liberal Shadow Minister and that as part of these meetings, they were mounting a case as to why the incoming Government should dismiss Jean Blackburn from her role as Chair'.[45] A set of existing connections also provides clues to likely course of events. Mary Beasley had worked with Brown in an earlier Tonkin Liberal government. She had worked closely with Jennifer Cashmore, a leading Liberal member of parliament through 1992 and 1993 on centenary committees. When the new government moved to put its stamp on the centenary committee, it quickly replaced Jean with Mary Beasley as Chair and appointed Jennifer Cashmore as the new Deputy Chair.

Jean was called into Dean Brown's office. She spoke of the meeting:

Premier was rather nice actually. He is, and so is Diana Laidlaw. Anyway they said they wanted to strengthen the committee and they were going to bring on – I approved of what they were going to do in lots of ways – bring on someone from local government and a couple of other areas which I thought was quite good. They said to me, and we want you to be the vice patron. I just laughed. I said if I were to become the vice patron that would be saying publicly that you consulted me about these changes that you're making and I approved of them. So I don't want to do that, thank you. So it was all quite amicable.[46]

The offer of vice-patron was a clumsy 'kicking upstairs'. Jean formally rejected the role in mid-January, informing both Premier and Governor, Roma Mitchell. Jean became instead the 'inaugural' or 'founding' Chair of the centenary committee.

Many people were outraged by what had happened. Susan Magarey resigned both as chair of the historical committee and member of the Steering Committee. She wrote to the Premier protesting against the 'conversion of a politically bi-partisan program into a partisan staging of the events planned for 1994'. She wrote of Jean's status and achievements, declaring that her appointment had 'ensured interstate, indeed international as well as local recognition and respect for [the] ... program of activities'. Magarey was particularly disturbed that Mary Beasley had replaced her: 'To replace her with a salaried bureaucrat (who should – officially – have no choice but to do the behest of her political employers), and to make that bureaucrat's deputy a member of the Liberal Party, is to make a nonsense of the politically bi-partisan nature of the 1994 commemorative activities'. She finished: 'Your removal of Dr Blackburn from the leadership of the Women's Suffrage Centenary Steering Committee after all the hard preparatory work has been completed, but before the major commemorative activities could have allowed public acknowledgement commensurate with her (entirely voluntary) labours, cannot appear as anything but an act of ingratitude and, I regret to say, of political opportunism'.[47]

That the sacking occurred just before Christmas meant there was limited press attention, but *The Australian* took it up: 'A row over the removal of the chairwoman of the Women's Suffrage Centenary committee cast a shadow over the start of celebrations commemorating the 100th anniversary of the granting of parliamentary voting rights to women in South Australia [sic] ... Retired academic Dr Jean Blackburn said she believed her removal as chairwoman might be linked to her association with Labor politics. "They didn't tell me that. I just surmised that," Dr Blackburn said yesterday. But the new Minister responsible for the status of women, Ms Laidlaw, denied that changes in the committee – now controlled by public servant Ms Mary Beasley – had been politically motivated'.[48] There was also an item in a gossip column:

> The good Dr Jean Blackburn worked like a dog all last year, chairing and preparing the calendar for the SA Women's Suffrage Centenary steering committee, whose celebrations start today and carry on through this year. But Jean's fellow committee members and various key feminists are astonished that the Brown Man has suddenly axed her, handing the job to Mary Beasley ... opening the year on a miserable and disharmonious note. Ken Pearce, Di Laidlaw's PR flak, has surprised one and all, and perhaps even the hale and hearty doctor herself, by suggesting it was Blackburn's 'fluctuating health' that led to the Beasley coup.[49]

When parliament convened two months into 1994, Anne Levy, now on the opposition benches spoke to the event. She was 'saddened and angered' by Jean's dismissal. She believed the sacking occurred for 'blatantly political reasons', the incident 'leaving a very nasty taste in the mouths of many people, including me'. It 'reflects poorly on those who made the decision to denigrate Dr Blackburn'. Levy referred to the many protests that had been received by the government.[50]

After the sacking, Jean continued with several pre-planned engagements. She attended the launch on New Year's Day. 'She arrived subdued but with her characteristic dignity and was heartened to see a big, happy crowd turn out – women, men, families and community grantees – all bedecked with the celebratory balloons provided in purple and gold – South Australia's historic suffrage colours.'[51] She spoke, drawing attention to the work of Loine Sweeney in organising the day's events, and was photographed with the Minister, Diana Laidlaw, and the new Chair, Mary Beasley. At some point something remarkable took place. There could be no glossing over Jean's presence and the work she had done for the centenary. The crowd launched into a great demonstration of affection, support and, for many, anger at her treatment. The clapping and acclamation went on and on, embarrassingly 'on' for the new minister, Laidlaw, and the new chair, Beasley. It was a symbolic, but welcome part reparation. At the first meeting of the Steering Committee following the sacking, the minister, Laidlaw, turned up, expressing 'her appreciation to Mary Beasley for taking on the responsibility of the chair of the committee and to Jennifer Cashmore for agreeing to fill the deputy chair position'.[52] Laidlaw's presence may have stifled potential disturbance in the committee.

Later in the year Jean launched an exhibition celebrating the contribution of Barbara Hanrahan to the arts in South Australia. She praised the State Library's effort in collecting oral histories from women. Jean herself was interviewed on her role in the centenary celebrations, and her memories of International Women's Day over the decades.[53] She wrote to her daughter, Susan, about the wonderful contributions that so many organisations had made to the year. She began to recover from the effects of her dismissal. 'I have been especially heartened personally by public demonstrations of affection and support, not only from the Women's Movement, but by public agencies such as the State Library and History Centre, the YWCA, the WCTU etc. repudiating my displacement. Removed from responsibility, in this sense I have enjoyed the outcome, and lost the initial pain of repudiation.'

Figure 10.5 At the launch of the Suffrage Centenary. Jean (fourth from left) has been sacked as Chair by the new Liberal Minister for the Status of Women, Diana Laidlaw (far left) and displaced as Chair by Mary Beasley (next right). Standing in front of Jean is Loine Sweeney, principal organiser of the year's events, and next right Natasha Stott Despoja, who represented younger women on the Steering Committee, 1 January 1994.
Rosey Boehm photographer, courtesy of the photographer and the State Library of South Australia.

She wrote of the Flinders event where Deirdre Jordan 'spoke simply and movingly about the suffragists, linking the dead and the living in a "long-running saga"'. Jean was introduced by Jordan as one of those for whom a plaque had been made, for her 'outstanding contribution to education' and 'development of social justice policy'.[54] There is no record of Jean attending the South Australian Jockey Club's race day in honour of the centenary, a social event celebrated by the new centenary Chair, Mary Beasley. Beasley recorded later that the launch itself had been difficult for her to get through, recognising that the women's movement in South Australia had been split. The interviewer, Allison Murchie was sympathetic, remarking that it was 'old thinking' that you had to be left-wing to be a feminist.[55] But that was not quite the point.

Despite protestations to the contrary, Jean worried about what had happened. 'I didn't do it as well as some other people could have done it ... We were bugged all the time ... people ... had plenty of grand ideas but we ... had damn all money. That was a big problem.' In Loine Sweeney, Jean eventually had an executive officer who could work with her as Shirley Randell, Helen Praetz and Marion Russell had in the past, but the want of an adequate budget and united support from her committee in the context of a failing and failed Labor government brought her to grief. Jean's son, Hugh, thought that the experience for Jean was 'shattering ... I don't think she really got over it ... Especially if it's your last engagement in public life. It seem[ed] pretty unkind'.[56]

1994 was a busy year for Jean with continuing obligations to centenary celebrations. She gave a major speech to the Australian College of Education which she had persuaded to meet in Adelaide as part of the year's events. Towards the end of the year there was a last effort for the University of Canberra. The Council wanted a portrait of Jean as the foundation chancellor. She agreed to sit for the South Australian artist, Robert Hannaford. He had previously painted a study of Jean's friend Hugh Stretton and later painted Lowitja O'Donohue.[57] The portrait was hung in an administration building of the University of Canberra. Jean both admired and was disappointed with it, thinking that it made her look sad. Others, including Don Aitkin thought it was an honest representation of Jean in the mid-1990s. If she did look sad, there were good reasons why Hannaford should have painted her so. Jean's health was poor and her tendency towards depression was not improved by the suffrage centenary sacking. In the 1990s she was often on medication to help deal with depression.

Right at the end of 1994 came a joyous event. Dean Ashenden married Sandra Milligan at a ceremony at Smith's Beach, Yallingup, in the Margaret River region in Western Australia. Jean and Dick were invited along with many others whom Jean knew. She had a lovely time over the days involved. As Dean described it:

> Turned out to be just a great week. Everyone except Dick had a good time. And Jean had the best time of all. And also she would get on the turps. We'd provided plenty of wine and beer and so forth, but of course, she and Dick … so they snuck off to get the bottles of whisky … they'd get rid of one of those a day I'd say … it was great having her there because everyone liked her, because she was having such a fantastic time and so on.[58]

Lorna Hannan remembered: 'a whole lot of us went and occupied a row of – was it a motel? – some place like that … And [Jean] was there – very keen on gathering the gossip. That was the kind of occasion when it was grand to be with her. And she had a ball.' According to

Lorna though, 'when she got to the wheel-chair stage she was sick of it. She didn't want to be in the wheel-chair. She didn't exactly want to be dead. But she didn't want to be in the wheel-chair'.[59]

Jean had more honorary degrees conferred on her in the 1990s as well as university graduation ceremonies to attend as speaker. In April 1992 she became a Doctor of Flinders University. In May 1993, the Vice-Chancellor of the University of South Australia, Denise Bradley, composed the citation for the honorary doctorate from her university.

> She has had a most distinguished career as an educational theorist and policymaker. Her contribution to the development of a distinctively Australian response to the educational challenges of the latter decades of the twentieth century is generally acknowledged to have been profound.
>
> She has always worked from the position that education is a right, a right which a just and democratic society will ensure is available to all citizens.
>
> Her particular contribution to the public debate about opportunities for women is outstanding. Particularly from the 1960s, she with another remarkable woman, Edna Ryan, has placed the issues in this debate in an historical context and connected them to the broad quest for social and economic justice for all citizens.
>
> Her heart has always been with those groups disadvantaged by the circumstances of their class, gender or racial origin but in her work to improve their position it has been her powerful intellect which has been at their service. Unlike many who write or speak in this area of educational policy she has never had recourse to poor argument or to emotional appeals for some vague and undefined form of just treatment.[60]

Bradley finished, averring her 'tenacity' and 'honesty'. Deirdre Jordan and Judith Redden attended the ceremony with other guests. As Redden recalled: 'it was a big occasion. And, Lyndsay Connors had come over to it, and I can remember I was with them, and as we left, I can remember us driving down Wakefield Street, and Jean had broken her leg, and so she was very unhappy, and she was saying "Oh, I know now that I'm mortal." And "I'm not enjoying this, I'm not accepting." ... It was very sad.'

And then there was a second 'gong'; one that she would keep as opposed to that of 1976. In the Australia Day honours list for 1995 Jean was awarded the AO, Order of Australia, by the Keating Labor government. In 1997 the deans of education schools and faculties recognised her work with an award, and then came an honorary doctorate from the University of Canberra in 1999. Such awards and graduation ceremonies allowed her to reflect on a range of educational subjects including the authoritarianism of the old centralised government departments of school education and the promise of the newly autonomous colleges of advanced education, their transformation and merging into universities.[61] At Victorian graduation ceremonies she spoke about the historical and social significance of the expanding access to higher education, to which she had contributed.[62]

The arguments that Jean developed in the 1980s about the relationships between higher education, school and curriculum reform, and youth unemployment continued to be made in the 1990s.[63] Her visions of improved social access and justice remained germane, but the policy discourse had shifted. The education policies of the Hawke and Keating governments, especially after the removal of Susan Ryan from education, were dispiriting enough.[64] John

Howard's Liberal National Coalition, elected in 1996, confirmed the commitment of federal education funding in support of parental choice of schools for their children, especially schools in the non-government sector.[65] For Jean:

> The major issue of the present moment in Australian education is the dual threat to the quality and social comprehensiveness of public school systems arising out of reduced resources from state governments on the one hand and federal action on the other. Behind both these developments is the policy desire to treat schooling as a market where competing products are academic scores and the price is determined by fees payable. Parents as consumers shop around for the best deal in this scenario.

Federal governments were 'subsidising parents to move their children out of public school systems'. Not only had enrolment share declined, but with it the capacity of public schools to effectively meet the needs of the populations left behind: 'government schools are losing middle-class achievers, and in this sense are "residualised" ... the trend is away from socially comprehensive schools.' She acknowledged that as a 'long retired person' there was little she could do about it. She noted the new energy of the Anglican church, alongside the Catholic, in establishing low-fee schools, supported by substantial state funds.

> I brood about whether it is too late to redefine a public system as one substantially funded from public funds, within which schools of varying religious or other philosophical affiliations may exist provided that they follow an agreed national curriculum and promote values emphasising the shared commitments which make our multicultural political democracy possible, and themselves follow an equitable distribution of educational resources favouring those students whose families have least private resources over the period of compulsory schooling.

To members of the audience who heard this speech, Jean concluded: 'I pass the baton to you'.[66]

With Helen Praetz, Jean made one last attempt to write a very substantial account of school policy in Australia, and what might be done to improve it. The draft paper, 'Divided schooling in a federal context', was never published. It provided an exploration of how schools had changed, and the consequences of 'the public/private division in provision in the light of our belief that governments retain ultimate responsibility for the outcomes of school systems as long as they use tax revenues to support them'. It included analysis of recent school choice policies and their impact on the 'half-forgotten arguments supporting the establishment and maintenance of public schooling, arguments in which "common citizenship" loom[s] larger than "markets" and "public choice theory" in identifying core values, and social justice plays a role in arrangements promoting equality of opportunity'.[67] Some of the argument appeared in an article Jean wrote for *The Australian* in July 1996.[68] She co-wrote a chapter in a book with Judy Gill and Ann Morrow on public education policy around the same time. That chapter worried about the 1996 federal States Grants Act that removed the funding ceiling on the establishment of new non-government schools and increased the pressures on existing government schools that resulted from the trend towards privatisation.[69]

The argument about 'what to do' in the paper with Praetz foundered on the problem that the Commonwealth government had the funds to affect schools' policy, but in fact controlled no sizeable school systems. The chances of an agreement between federal and state governments that would allow the Commonwealth to bring most non-government schools into the public system under special arrangements, as had occurred in New Zealand, were unlikely. Jean found herself in an 'immobilising fit of anxiety' over it all.[70] At the same time she would insist to the last that a reversion to simplistic and polarising arguments about public and private schooling had little future. She preferred to base her argument on the question of what might constitute good educational provision in a democracy. Karl Popper was a useful starting point.[71] Jean put effort into trying to define the commitments and responsibilities that publicly funded non-government schools should assume. Nevertheless, she was coming to a dead end; of necessity she was having to hand the 'baton' on.

One of the baton holders had received it long before. As late as 2000, Lyndsay Connors was reporting for the Victorian government, post-Kennett, on reforms there. Jean was one of those from whom she sought comment on her analysis.[72]

Jean's children and friends remained a source of comfort. Hugh had married Helen in 1992 and completed his doctorate at Monash in 1993. There was a new man in Susan's life, Roger Spegele, an academic at Monash University whose field was international relations. He and Jean found plenty to discuss. There continued the occasional visits to Sydney, to see Bill, Meg, Robyn and Naomi, though worryingly, Bill briefly lost his job in 1997 – but quickly found a better one. She continued to visit Lyndsay Connors and Ken McKinnon when she was in Sydney. In January 1997 there was a family gathering at Mallacoota Inlet in the East Gippsland. Susan organised another gathering for Christmas the following year, but by then the frailties of Jean, now 79, and Dick, 81, were all too apparent. There was also Bill. While recovering from a surgery he developed motor neurone disease, and Jean, who had worried about Bill from his childhood, had more to concern her. Jean tried to talk to her children about Dick's declining health; if they wanted to talk to him about anything, they would not have much longer.[73] There were significant deaths. One was Rivkah Matthews (Brilliant) whom Jean had befriended at University High in the 1930s.

Women friends, including Effie Best, continued to meet at the Adelaide Central Market for coffee, talk and shopping in the 1990s. Jean developed a friendship with Liz Alpers and she and Jean invited ten women, their friends and acquaintances, 'to meet regularly to discuss a book we have all agreed is challenging and worthwhile'.[74] Woe betide the book, and even the person who recommended it, if Jean thought it was hopeless.[75]

Liz and Jean audited lectures in ancient history at the University of Adelaide. This was an old enthusiasm resurrected from Presbyterian Girls College teaching days. There were still visits to the theatre with Elliott and Elizabeth Johnston and other friends. Time was spent with Kevin Gilding and family at Easter in 1996. That was 'great'.[76] Alison Mackinnon asked Jean to read drafts of the new history she was writing, the work that became *Love and Freedom: Professional Women and the Reshaping of Personal Life*.[77] Jean had read with approval Anthony Giddens', *The Transformation of Intimacy: Sexuality, Love, and Eroticism in Modern Societies*.[78] Jean engaged Alison in more than one tough discussion, to the point that Alison wondered:

> It might have been the bits at the beginning, it might have been a bit too post-modern, it might have been too much about middle class and privileged women or ... [S]he went straight down the line and I walked out reeling ... So, her critical faculties were still sharp and I don't think her critical faculties were ever very

tempered by the sense of "Maybe I won't say it quite like that" [laughs] "and hurt her feelings".[79]

Jean herself wrote that she had enjoyed the encounter 'though we have many disagreements'. Thinking about the books by Giddens and Mackinnon helped her to make sense of her own life, especially the conjunctions of motherhood, marriage and professional career.

Jean had formally begun thinking about public policy and old age in 1990. In one speech she recognised that she was new to thinking about the field, but the structure of her talk was familiar. There were statistics about the issues, including the adequacy of the ways that older, poorer citizens were supported by governments. She had positive things to say about new superannuation policies. She wondered about the wisdom of separating the value of the family home from pension determination, especially when there were no longer any inheritance taxes to speak of. As she had argued the previous twenty years in education policy, she believed that 'need' should play a stronger part in government provision and that governments had to make good rules, indeed bureaucratic procedures, that ensured public accountability and a fair distribution of resources – not that she was against more 'consumer power' to challenge misguided administration. She concluded with a critique of policy as it affected women. She believed that an earlier retirement age for women than men rested on an assumption that women had been economically dependent on men throughout life and would need earlier economic support as their husbands died. There was also the problem of continuing assumptions about women as natural carers: 'what are we saying as a society willing to pay $500 a week for un-means tested care in nursing homes and allowing $42 a fortnight as a rebate to women caring for the dependent old in their own homes?'[80]

In 1998 Jean flew to Sydney for a conference organised by the Australian Education Union. It was a big affair, chaired by Phillip Adams. 'Speakers included Joan Kirner, Don Dunstan, Kim Beazley, Stewart Macintyre. (I had just finished reading his *The Reds*, vol. 1) and talked with him about it.' She stayed with Bill and Meg, enjoying their company, 'and that of the girls – now up to good conversation and very impressive'. In October of that year, there was another conference in Sydney honouring Peter Karmel and marking the twenty-fifth anniversary of *Schools in Australia*.[81]

Jean and Dick were well-enough off not to have to struggle with many of the issues Jean had discussed in the 1990 speech on old age policy. They had several investments, mainly in government instrumentalities, recorded for 1991, and a short list of donations, to the Jessie Street Library, Salvation Army and Community Aid Abroad.[82] Nevertheless old age was a trial. She and Dick were thrown more on one another's company. Prickly patterns of behaviour were longstanding. Jean did not hold back her criticisms of the book Dick was writing on the history of irrigation in Australia.[83] At the same time Jean wrote that she was 'lonely, despite my lovely, practically supportive, but mentally pre-occupied husband'.[84] Jean had trouble with various medications prescribed for her depression. At one stage Prothiaden seemed to be the best of them.[85] She wrote about her friend Ellen, probably Ellen Christensen, and how depression especially:

> overtakes the reflective old – and perhaps especially those retired women whose lives have not been confined to second-hand retailing of the business of others, or practical pursuits

and domestic detail, but which have enabled them to work with their intellectual peers – male and female. Their 'retired' position is thus not unlike that of professional men who have also been engaged in collective public business, rather than in individual research. I'M WORKING ON IT![86]

In the middle of a notebook Jean kept for managing her tax affairs there is a startling entry made some time in 1998:

> Just recording that I am LONELY and BORED. Don't care about money – and feel I have accumulated in a fit of absence of mind on the one hand and limited ideas about spending it associated with my history on the other (now that I cannot travel and dreams of a more expensive and beautiful house were long ago given the thumbs down by D).[87]

In 1996 Dick was diagnosed with leukaemia. He had had serious bronchitis and emphysema a year or so before and became progressively more ill before dying on 6 August 1999. Apart from their common University of Melbourne and communist histories – and the significant sexual attraction that lasted many years – they were very different people, who often appeared not very compatible to those who knew them. Dick was reserved, Jean open, Dick with few words, Jean with many, Dick the loyal communist, Jean critical and adaptable, and so it could go on. But there were other things that kept them together: their shared life in their house and garden, their joint friends, and of course, the children. The straightforward virtue 'loyalty' also explained their longevity as a couple. Susan wrote in early 1997 of:

> [the] restaurant dinner with Hugh and Helen for father's birthday … Parents behaved themselves remarkably well, always a source of worry when they both drink and then sometimes start finding

fault with one another. This morning as I was taking mother to do some shopping she remarked on how well she and father now get on: "Better than we have for years really. Of course it's partly because we don't have sex now: that's always a source of tension."[88]

Susan and Hugh never doubted the love of either of their parents, but Dick was more of a mystery to them than Jean.[89] At one point Susan, despairing of learning more about her father, exchanged letters with him on the significance of communism in his life. Dick was worried, for example, that knowledge of the importance of the Communist Party in opposing the White Australia policy from very early in the twentieth century, through to the protection of the environment with the green bans, was slipping away.[90]

Figure 10.6 Survivors, Dick and Jean at Separation Creek on the Great Ocean Road in Victoria, at a family gathering, 1998. Despite the name of the creek and other difficulties, Jean and Dick's marriage lasted 56 years.
Courtesy of Susan Blackburn.

The list of speakers for Dick's funeral included his sister Louisa Hamilton, Elliott Johnston, Maud McBriar and Ted Jackson. Judy Ferguson (Goss) also spoke, recalling Dick and Jean's kindness to their family in the 1950s. Jean's notes for what she was planning to say included the following: Dick 'took his responsibilities very seriously', and his world view changed little over the years. He lived simply but was not much fun. His caring nature was experienced by friends and colleagues – and Jean herself. Dick cared for her 'after my disablement in 1991', and she could not imagine life without him: 'But no one witnessing his physical decline over the last years could want [to see it] continued.' She said that his decline was a terrible thing; there had been no relief from his respiratory problems. She remarked on the support that her children had given her before and after his death.[91]

Some time after the funeral Susan and Jean went through Dick's possessions – including the bundle of letters that Jean had sent him over many years. Jean decided they were not for preserving. As they talked Jean reflected on sex. She appreciated the fact that, unlike during her youth, it was now possible for women to talk about sex, rather than having neither the words nor the confidence to talk about physical responses. She reflected on the frustrations of the early years of her marriage when Dick was away on fieldwork: 'I was really on heat then: I felt as though I could have had sex with any man who appeared at the door.' With the writings of the new feminism in the 1970s she was not alone in discovering more about her own body and sexual response. Jean said that early on she had been insecure about Dick. At some point, Ted Jackson reassured her that Dick was absolutely loyal.[92]

Following Dick's death Jean spent time in Melbourne with Susan, Roger, Helen and Hugh. They wanted her to come and live in Melbourne. She resisted: 'I love them all dearly, as they do me, but their lives are so busy and their time so committed that fitting Mother into it would, however they disclaim such a possibility, be pretty hard and ultimately resented, however well disguised'. The other issue was that her old Melbourne friends were now few. Some were dead and others dispersed. Instead of Melbourne Jean decided a better option was a pleasant retirement home in Adelaide but arriving back in Adelaide following Dick's death caused fresh woe. Dick had always looked after the bills, and now there was a pile awaiting her with bold red 'overdue' statements printed on the envelopes.

This was part of another problem. Jean could never get Dick to talk about what might need to be done when he died. She had to work out how to carry on without his briefing on their investments, about which Jean knew little, as well as family finances more generally. It upset her greatly.[93] Money, its accumulation, management and spending were a cause of lifelong problems for Jean. As she had been surprised in her youth by the wealth of her father, then she was astonished in turn by the wealth Dick had accumulated on their behalf. They 'could have splurged on all kinds of pleasant things but they didn't indulge themselves beyond some overseas trips and a little house renovation like new carpets and revamping the kitchen'. Initially this was Jean as much as Dick, though according to Susan, Jean in later life 'got used to a more expansive way of living. I noticed then that she wore more expensive clothes and began drinking whisky: previously my parents didn't drink spirits, just beer and wine'.[94]

At some point after Dick's death, Jean made a will leaving her estate equally to her three children, after bequests. The four beneficiaries of bequests were the Don Dunstan Foundation, the University of South Australia Foundation (for the Bob Hawke Centre), the International Women's Development Agency and the Smith Family. These agencies promoted social democracy, gender equality and the alleviation of family poverty to varying degrees.[95]

Susan worried about her mother's drinking, and she remonstrated once or twice. Jean was temporarily penitent, but then she said she needed it: it helped her sleep, it made life less boring. Sometimes she forgot to eat as a result. At some point in her last few months she brooded over her marriage. She'd been to dinner with younger friends who were apparently very happily married. She wept when she came home: 'It was seeing the two of them together and thinking about how lucky they were to have an emotionally and intellectually intimate life, she said, that made her think again about what a bad marriage she had had, and how she should have ended it earlier.' It seemed difficult to focus on the better parts of her marriage and life. This was also the period when she was trying to write her autobiography and she was brooding over her childhood as well.[96] There is little doubt that Jean was often unhappy, even miserable, in her last few years of life – unless she was out and about, and there was less of that as time went on. She would say to Denise Bradley and Lyndsay Connors when they were together that she had nothing *real* to do. Denise and others worried enough about her depression to suggest that she see a psychiatrist, but that was advice she chose not to take.[97]

Several of her women friends regularly dropped in to visit as she declined, among them Judy Gill, Liz Alpers and Alison Mackinnon – which Jean appreciated. But it was not quite the *real* thing that she had talked about with Bradley and Connors. Jean made a last entry in her 'condensed biography' some time in 2000. She noted her honorary position with the University of South Australia, and then the final entry: 'But cannot write'.[98] Judy Redden noted Jean's distinctive conversation style, constant always, despite age: 'The thing I loved about Jean was that if she walked in here now, she'd sit down. She'd immediately go into an intense discussion about something that she'd been thinking about, or that she'd read, and she wouldn't notice anything. It would just be this intensity.' In congenial company, even with all her troubles, according to Judy Gill, 'she still really enjoyed conversation – so long as it was real conversation! And was great fun to be with. She had a capacity to laugh at herself and to send herself up'.[99]

By mid-2001 Jean decided she could no longer manage the house. She was interested in the collection of townhouses and apartments in the city, Christie Walk, where Effie Best lived, but building was proceeding too slowly there. Instead, following the sale of her house in September, Susan and Hugh helped Jean shift into a two-bedroom unit in the Victoria Grove Estate at 254 Greenhill Road, Glenside. She was not to be there long.

A few days before her death, Jean attended a party organised by Effie in Adelaide's parklands, a first outing since breaking her hip weeks earlier. Judy Gill took her on to the launch of Suzanne Franzway's book, *Sexual Politics and Greedy Institutions*. Jean was in her element – greeting old friends and discussing politics and policy, 'leaning on her walker with a glass of wine in her hand'. She spoke to her children Susan and Hugh on the next Saturday. She was in good spirits.[100] She telephoned her brother Les Thomas, rambling a little, but saying how she'd loved meeting up with him and his family in

Canberra in recent years. She said that after so many years, she felt that she had an extended family at last. She rang her other brother, Allan, as well, but failed to reach him.[101]

Jean died in her sleep on Sunday December 2, 2001, aged 82. Her cleaner found her in the morning when she came to the unit. Jean's doctor told Susan and Hugh that it was a heart attack. A post-mortem was not needed according to the doctor because he knew of her heart problems.[102]

Jean's funeral service was held four days later on December 6 at the Heysen chapel in Centennial Park, Adelaide. Her brother, Les Thomas, spoke as did Dean Ashenden and Hugh Stretton. Dean spoke of her as a 'woman of the left, she hated cant, loved tough thinking, and insisted absolutely on open debate and hard facts … [She] experienced the best and worst of public life in Australia'.[103] Susan Blackburn concentrated on Jean's history, her personal influence, and especially her feminism. 'To me, Jean is my mother, a very loving and fallible person, someone with a strongly pronounced ability to enjoy and suffer in life. Through her I learned what burdens women have to bear, but also and increasingly, what women can do. She has been an inspiration to me in many ways'.[104] Denise Bradley spoke of her significance as a force for more equal educational provision, especially for children without the advantages that some class, gender and racial origins gave them. For four decades Jean was 'Australia's most powerful and persuasive advocate in national debates about educational opportunities'.[105] The service included the singing of *La Marseillaise* as Jean had requested.

Dean Ashenden and Ken McKinnon wrote obituaries for *The Australian* newspaper, Bill Hannan for *The Age* and *The Canberra*

Times and Miles Kemp for the Adelaide *Advertiser*. Margaret Allen wrote for *Australian Feminist Studies*.[106]

The three cities in which Jean had worked hardest, Canberra, Melbourne and Adelaide, each saw memorial gatherings over the next few weeks. Lyndsay Connors spoke at the Canberra gathering on March 25, 2002, observing that: 'A deep sense of morality was matched, in Jean's case, by a beautiful mind', and 'I never thought of Jean as a social radical. She was in many ways a conservative when it came to education, reminding us of our responsibility to teach what was well validated and to stick with understandings about the nature of knowledge that had served us well until we could be sure we had something demonstrably better to replace them with.'[107] In Adelaide, Judy Gill organised a gathering of some 25 women. Peggy Mares talked about Western Teachers College days, and the progress of conversations with Jean that started in the 1960s lasting into the 1990s. Claire Woods spoke of her memories of Jean as her teacher at school, Maureen Dyer about working with Jean in Schools Commission projects, Alison Mackinnon on Jean's work for women in higher education, and Judy Gill recalled the story of Jean and the Women's Suffrage Centenary. Louise Bywaters talked about a speech Jean had given at a recent meeting of the Australian College of Education.

The Canberra gathering initiated a memorial fund while the Adelaide group decided on an annual Jean Blackburn lecture.[108] At the New International Bookshop in Melbourne on December 17 there was another gathering. Susan and Hugh spoke, as did Dean Ashenden, Helen Praetz and others. Bill Hannan read from Wordsworth, one of Jean's favourite poets. Everyone sang *La Marseillaise*.[109]

Susan collected the letters she received from people who had known and loved Jean. Marjorie Pizer recalled their undergraduate student days in the late 1930s. Judy Gill recalled Jean's last days, and in a later letter expressed interest in writing her biography. John Legge, an old friend from university days and much later a colleague of Susan at Monash University, recalled Jean as an impressive student leader in the 1940s. He and Maud McBriar had been together recently, talking about Jean. Peter Karmel wrote of his sorrow at Jean's death. He thought that her contribution to schools in Australia was 'tremendous'. Elliott Johnston wrote of the great regard he and his wife Elizabeth had for both Jean and Dick. Ted Jackson wrote of a half century of friendship. Julie Marcus wrote of the help Jean had given as she began her academic career.[110]

Jean Blackburn's death was a symbolic as well as personal event. She had been a central figure in the transformation of the way Australian schools and schooling had developed from the 1950s and 1960s. From the 1980s, markets, competition, international comparisons, narrow measures of educational success, and the emergence of children and parents as consumers of educational 'products', had overtaken the equality of opportunity discourse. Equality and opportunity had been at the heart of Jean's influence and thinking on education. Her death signified the dimming of a light, the diminishing power of the justice in education argument to change the policies of government.

CONCLUSION: THINKING ABOUT THE LIFE

Jean Blackburn certainly had a major impact on the transformation of Australian school education over the final three decades of the twentieth century. Arguments and policy that she made remain full of insight, and often relevant in the twenty-first century. But Blackburn was more than an educational reformer, she was a creative intellectual who engaged forcefully in broader public debate and policy making from the 1940s through to the 1990s.

Her life may be thought of as representative of a particular generation in the first half of the twentieth century for whom communism provided an alternative to the several devastations of capitalism and war. She was sufficiently independent as an intellectual, a woman, and a feminist to leave communism behind as the worst of its Stalinist history was revealed, but her 'darkness at noon' did not lead her to embrace the Cold War or right-wing conservatism. In the history of Australian feminism, she was one of several women whose personal experience actively joined earlier feminist thinking and action to the 1960s 'second wave'. This history was responsible for another continuity, the joining of the post-war reconstruction thinking of the 1940s to the reformism of Labor governments in the 1970s. As a social democrat Jean embraced the possibility that governments could improve the lives of working-class and disadvantaged populations.

Conclusion: Thinking about the life

Jean Blackburn's life did not fulfil the expectations of her parents, especially the demands of her father. There were plenty of obstructions in her early life that threatened any realisation of her potential and there were many more to come. These may well be responsible for a paradox. The articulate, apparently confident maker of educational policy, a person whose influence on people, communities and organisations could effect change, was often subject to debilitating self-doubt and bouts of severe depression.

Arguably the 1970s were as important as the 1870s had been in the history of Australian education. In this second period federal governments converted their hesitant interventions into schooling into the permanent and transformative. The older settlements of the 1870s on the state aid issue, no assistance to schools owned and governed privately or by churches and other organisations, was comprehensively overturned. The emergence of state or public education systems as highly authoritarian and centralised, with prescriptive curricula and remoteness from parental and local community influence, was also substantially revised in the 1970s. The ways that 'equality' and 'opportunity' were imagined and delivered through schools were altered, and in some cases redefined altogether. The overwhelming influence of assimilationist thinking in the schooling of Indigenous and migrant children, the lack of questioning about schooling for the separate and unequal fates of most girls and boys – these were challenged, and schools could not be the same thereafter.[1] Jean Blackburn was a powerful actor in each of these transformations.

We could write much about the continuing relevance of Jean's educational thinking for the present. Her frustration that too few academics in education in Australian universities engage sufficiently with the practical reform of schools and broader education policy remains relevant.

Though we concluded our last chapter by describing the new economic and educational policies that displaced those that Jean advocated, there are many elements of the 1970s reforms that remain. Jean Blackburn was a contributor to the idea that differential funding for disadvantaged students should occur, though in the twenty first century these disadvantages are likely to be defined in narrower terms, of deficits in skills acquisition, numeracy and literacy, rather than in broad social terms. The extremes in times past of authoritarian and parent-excluding regimes of school governance have not been resurrected, though one could argue about the effectiveness of contemporary arrangements. Schools now attempt to be more humane institutions, though again, the demands of schools competing in markets for parent customers may be an impediment to a fuller realisation. Senior school curricula and assessment regimes have become more responsive to the needs of youth in general, not just the more conservative entrance requirements of some universities.

It is unlikely that there will be a more substantial return to the kinds of policy advocated by Jean any time soon, but as the Gonski reviews of Australian education for the federal government in 2011 and 2018 demonstrated, the issues raised by Jean do not go away. If we consider the new fear, that unequal access to high quality education, and the creation of fragmented and hierarchical school systems diminishes Australia's global economic competitiveness, then that approach seems far from Jean's thinking. She had no great regard for anything very useful arising from educational reform dependent on the creation of school markets, or the market imperative in education and life more generally. Nevertheless, in contemporary education policy debate there is a continuing critique of inequality, fragmentation, hierarchy and the destructive effects of unequal and numerous school systems. Jean Blackburn had strong ideas about how governments might reduce the prevalence and ill effects of these phenomena.

Jean's educational thinking developed over the years from well before, but especially following her education studies at the University of Adelaide in the 1960s. As the different reports and programs that she worked on presented a range of challenges and issues, some of which were new to her, she thought through viable explanations and possible resolutions. She worked from a set of assumptions and principles about what schools could be and should do. The 'principles' suggested the answers. She developed an internalised focus on producing practicable, social democratic, equalising and opportunity-producing policies, capable of transforming institutions and lives. Her version of the socially responsible and responsive school informed both her policy writing and her criticisms of inferior alternatives. With the process came careful listening, but also advocacy and persuasion.[2]

There was also a kind of serendipity involved in Jean's career, an alignment of circumstances that allowed her to be effective and powerful. It included working for new Labor governments that had been out of office, sometimes for very long periods of time. In South Australia, the local Karmel report was received by a reforming Dunstan government after the barely interrupted socially conservative Playford years. Nationally the Whitlam government was determined on a 'crash through' approach with its huge range of social and other policies, including what Karmel's Interim Committee for a Schools Commission prescribed for education. A decade later in

Victoria, the Cain Labor government, after the years of the Bolte and Hamer Liberal governments, also had the necessary store of frustration and energy for reform. Ken McKinnon thought about what such circumstances meant for the early years of the Schools Commission federally. He had never seen in education 'equivalent optimism and hope'. It was sufficient to overcome the ideological and other differences of the first appointees to the Commission.[3] The contingency of Jean's availability to Labor governments intent on reform helps answer the question: 'Why was Jean so successful?' There was a fortuitous coming together of Jean's personal talents and experience, her availability and readiness for work, with the political circumstances, national and international, that brought an end to the worst of the Cold War, helping to overthrow long entrenched conservative governments.

Jean was subject to many setbacks in her life and career which required great effort to overcome. At the same time, she had a capacity to read existing social and political circumstances and the determination to seize opportunities. She had courage, strength, perspicacity, persistence and fortitude if occasionally at the expense of an easy sociability. There was also the depth of her practical wisdom, her ability to turn ideas, visions and philosophical ideas into policy that could be implemented.

By the mid-1980s of course, it was becoming much harder for Jean as governments, Labor and Liberal, were increasingly attracted to neoliberal approaches to reform. The trend was clear, federal funding in education was used as much to build non-government school systems and even 'entrench advantage' in place of the correction of inequality.[4] If Jean's years of contingent luck had run out, her argument continued unrestrained:

Conclusion: Thinking about the Life

> Those who have 'made it' have no right to deny others similar possibilities. At a quite elementary moral level, there remains for me a good case for saying that children to whom the social structure ensures the worst deal should have the best schools – even if that does nothing to change the social structure or to affect the social composition of hierarchies.[5]

In the 2010s, the observer most likely to call on Jean's past statements for relevant comment on contemporary education policy was Dean Ashenden. He often quoted her with intent:

> Twenty years after Karmel, one of its architects looked back in dismay at what had been wrought. 'We created a situation unique in the democratic world,' wrote Jean Blackburn in 1991. 'It is very important to realise this. There were no rules about student selection and exclusion, no fee limitations, no shared governance, no public education accountability, no common curriculum requirements below upper secondary ... We have now become a kind of wonder at which people [in other countries] gape. The reaction is always, "What an extraordinary situation"'.[6]

Lyndsay Connors, a later Schools Commissioner, and also an official enquirer into Victorian public education, called on Jean as well.[7] Bill Hannan reflected on Jean's legacy. It was very much tied up, not only with the advocacy of equity in education, but with the 'final expansion of universal secondary education' in Australia.[8]

Jean had never been swept up by many of the popular enthusiasms in education that attracted many reformers and radicals. Alternative schools, deschooling and 'revolutionary' approaches were not a part of her approach, though she could learn from them. Her radicalism was the kind that could speak directly to governments and the directors of school systems, teachers and parents. Through the Schools Commission, she was able to convince many if not all, that schools educating the clear majority of Australian children were not only capable of reform, but that there was no other institution capable of implementing what needed to be done in education. She was often confronted by what she saw in schools, but even if on occasion, despair overtook her, school reform remained the necessary object. A newspaper journalist, Geoff Maslen, argued it astutely: 'As a high achieving, hard headed intellectual, she dismissed the progressive educationist view of a child-centred, permissive school environment. Instead, she is a firm advocate of disciplined, structured learning with an equally firm belief that all students, not just an elite few, must have access to "high culture".'9

Though no-one could doubt Jean's commitment to effective public education and the responsibility of government schools for educating most of the population, she would have had a very short career without coming to terms with the necessity of funding struggling Catholic schools with government, tax-raised, revenue. That funding was not delivered nearly as justly or efficiently as she wished, but that it was required was beyond doubt. This meant that Jean was able to work with those parts of the Catholic Church, or perhaps more accurately, persons within it like Frank Martin, or at the Disadvantaged Schools Program state level, Judith Redden, who shared a commitment to social justice. By the 1970s Labor governments reconciled themselves to the Roman Catholic Church and its demands for a share of public revenue for its schools. Without it, damage to the electoral fortunes of the Labor party from the splits of the 1950s would have continued interminably.

Denise Bradley once argued that Jean was born into the 'wrong generation'. She was 'old' before she got started; there were the 'wasted years' of the mid-1940s to the mid-1960s. Jean often agreed with the sentiment herself, but her experiences and intellectual formation through the 1930s to the 1960s also prepared the way for her unique contributions in a later period.[10] Out of frustration, Jean, like the new Labor governments of the 1970s, used the Cold War decades to build the energy for reform and embraced its urgency when the opportunity finally came. Jean's policy career did start late in life. Though it may be interesting to speculate on what she might have achieved had she begun earlier, there is little to be gained in the effort.

We have introduced the idea of Jean's life as 'representative' of her times. Jean's trajectory through her opportunities, many of them self-made, was highly individual, but her story resonates with several familiar tropes. One is the clever student from an unpromising background who makes use of early twentieth century merit-based opportunities to enter an academic high school – and excel. These sorts of opportunities in selective-entrance state post-elementary schools barely existed in Australia in the nineteenth century. Another trope is the young person who becomes a socialist as the Depression pointed to the failures of capitalism, and the Spanish Civil War pointed to the incapacity of the democracies in the face of fascism. In the 1930s and 1940s Jean was a young person swept away by the promise of Bolshevism, and like many in her generation, she also came to the bitter realisation that the promise was mainly false.

Jean was also representative of the many women who were employed in the Second World War in good jobs, who after marriage and children in the succeeding peace, were suburbanised and separated from paid, skilled and professional work. She shared the frustrations that many women felt, that they were demeaned for being thought useful solely as wives and mothers.

But from this point her story becomes less representative. Few women of her generation found work in government, making a new national schools' policy. Few women were able to marshal their gendered experience and long-lasting feminism into the creation of one of Australia's most significant government policy documents on sex inequalities and a program for their correction. In later years she was one of the first female chancellors of an Australian university, and the first woman to conduct a major government enquiry advocating substantial educational reform.

Jean composed her own reflections on her generation. In the mid-1980s she met with 'the group of men' who were then vice-chancellors of Australian universities. 'All of them were the first in their family network to go to university, as I had been in 1938.' She thought this was a good, if rough, class-based test of the existence of some equality of opportunity though she added the caveat, that the same hardly held true for the great majority of married women who were also mothers.[11] Jean Blackburn's was a twentieth century life, uncommon in many respects, but enriched by possibilities that had not existed in the nineteenth century. Contemporaries of Jean, men such as Nugget Coombs, benefited more easily from these possibilities than any woman could, but their careers belonged to a similar set of historical circumstances.[12]

Part of this generational complex of possibilities derived from what it meant to be on the left in politics. Jean moved from being a revolutionary, a communist, through to reconciliation with the existence of the state, despite capitalism. She became one of those – like Coombs, and the first Labor minister for whom she worked, John Dedman – who believed that the state, despite capitalism, was capable of engineering better lives for more people. She was one of those who planned for Australia's post-war reconstruction and while the post-1949 Menzies years displaced much of that planning, several public servants and intellectuals survived the hiatus to influence governments in the 1970s. Women in government were rare survivors of the gap, but Jean was one of them.[13] She continued as a socialist of the evolutionary kind, remaining committed to the labour movement. She also opposed Australia's participation in the Vietnam War, retaining her longstanding commitment to 'peace'.

We asked a number of our interviewees about Jean as an intellectual, about where she 'stood'. Dean Ashenden replied in this way:

> On the face of it, she was a social democrat working to civilise capitalism etc., but she didn't like having to settle for that. She was much more acutely aware of the workings of power than most social democrats (Peter K[armel], for example), and had a much more acute sense of unfairness and exploitation, and really knew that in some fundamental way the whole set-up was rigged. *But* she also knew that no one intellectual system could capture that, and that the cure could be worse than the disease.[14]

A dominating issue for Jean's feminism was an argument about 'dependence'. Without education, women were more likely to be dependent on others, usually men, as fathers and husbands. If in paid work, they would usually be dependent on low-waged, often 'unskilled', employment. Without a labour movement committed to equal wages and employment opportunities, they were likely to be poor. Without commitments by governments to equality, including the establishment of the conditions for genuine equality of opportunity including the use of affirmative action, women would continue to suffer.

After her days in the Communist Party Jean had resisted neat labels and attachments to specific schools of thought. This applied to her feminism as well as her politics more generally. Her feminism was pragmatic at times, as was required if governments were to be engaged in making and implementing policy. Elements of Marxism remained in her analysis and she occasionally came across as a socialist feminist, but we have never seen evidence that she described herself as such. At the same time the significance she attached to equality, social justice, social class, and the labour movement in her thinking is evidence of her leftist commitment.

Jean has been described as belonging to a special group of women on the Australian left, including Madge Dawson and Edna Ryan, who had an impact on the emerging social movements, or on the distinctive strength of feminism in Australian sociology for example. They served 'as models and mentors not only for younger women', but young men as well, for example in Green politics.[15] Among the women who acknowledged Jean's influence are Denise Bradley, Lyndsay Connors, Joan Kirner and Susan Ryan, and they are only four of the better known. The feminist vision of Jean Blackburn encompassed men and women; it was an Enlightenment project – with a demand for strong argument based on evidence – and a social justice vision.

Dean Ashenden once made the argument that Jean Blackburn shared similarities with Simone de Beauvoir, though the ways in which she was not similar were many as well. They were both 'full-on intellectuals, of the left, increasingly critical of the left, increasingly despairing of whether there was any way out or forward. Very similar ... And both very obviously charismatic. De Beauvoir very much larger scale, but Jean was the same with people who knew her.'[16] There is perhaps another parallel; Jean worked as an equal with men. There is little evidence of any acceptance of an inferior or subordinate role in those working relationships. Acknowledgements of her parity, intellectual strength and influence are numerous, and there is little doubt that Peter Karmel and Ken McKinnon relied a great deal on her thinking and writing in the decade and a half that they worked with her. Jean was an engaged intellectual, arguably from her late high school years. Her daughter wrote about her continual reading in literature and history along with politics and educational philosophy. She also read biographies, and perhaps unsurprisingly, there was a strong interest in Simone de Beauvoir.[17] She was a writer as well, for government, academic journals and newspapers. She advocated reform.

It was not our intention to traverse the domestic dimensions of Jean Blackburn's life in any detail. She was certainly a passionate person, not only in relation to ideas. In many respects her husband appeared the opposite. Jean's command over language and ideas were substantial, and the public performance could contrast dramatically with her inner anxieties. Her expressions of low self-confidence often surprised those who heard them. That did not stop her from summary judgements on others and what they had to say, though if she had been assertive the night before, there was occasionally regret in the morning. There is little doubt that she could enjoy social gatherings but at the same time she grew frustrated with the small talk that often greased the interactions. 'She liked to get down to the bone.'[18] As a mother, her children were assured of her love and commitment. The letters she wrote to her children are the evidence, as well as what her surviving children have told us. As a friend she was loyal, though certainly not to the point of suppressing disagreement. Friends she made at high school and university in the 1930s, as well as many from Communist Party days in Melbourne and Adelaide, and others from the 1950s, remained lifelong friends.

As Margaret Bearlin put it, for Jean '[t]here could not be a democratic society unless all children had access to the finest liberal education that you could give them' so being an educational reformer was to be a social reformer.[19] Lyndsay Connors drew our attention to something Hannah Arendt once argued, and which reminded her of Jean:

> Education is the point at which we decide whether we love the world enough to assume responsibility for it, and by the same token save it from that ruin which except for renewal, except for the coming of the new and the young, would be inevitable. And education, too, is where we decide whether we love our children enough not to expel them from our world and leave them to their own devices, nor to strike from their hands their chance of undertaking something new, something unforeseen by us, but to prepare them in advance for the task of renewing a common world.[20]

If the memory of Jean has diminished in recent years, there are those who are determined that it should not disappear. The inaugural Jean Blackburn Oration of the Australian College of Educators took place in 2014.[21] This biography also argues that her educational influence should continue because she decided early in her life that she loved the world enough to assume responsibility for it. Her contribution was to use the opportunities given her to create educational policies that had the potential for 'renewing a common world'.

NOTES

Introduction

1 Based on the story in Jean Blackburn, interview by Peter Biskup, September 27 & November 13, 1990, National Library of Australia.
2 Michael Pusey, *Economic Rationalism in Canberra* (Cambridge: Cambridge University Press, 1991), 281.
3 Susan Magarey and Kerrie Round, "From Autobiography to Biography," *Australian Feminist Studies* 19, no. 43 (2004): 99.
4 See Alison Mackinnon, *Love and Freedom* (Cambridge: Cambridge University Press, 1997).
5 Jean Blackburn and Ted Jackson, *Australian Wives Today* (Melbourne: Victorian Fabian Society, 1963); Committee on Social Change and the Education of Women, *Girls, School and Society*, (Canberra: Schools Commission, 1975).
6 Barbara Finkelstein, "Revealing Human Agency," in *Writing Educational Biography*, ed. Craig Kridel (New York: Garland, 1998), 46.
7 Barbara Caine, *Biography and History* (Basingstoke: Palgrave Macmillan, 2010), 46.
8 See Select Bibliography for interviews.
9 Susan Blackburn [SB], *Maurice Blackburn and the Australian Labor Party, 1934–1943* (Melbourne: Australian Society for the Study of Labour History, 1969); "A Golden Age for Children's Reading in Adelaide: A Memoir," *Journal of the Historical Society of South Australia* 38 (2010); "Children of the Revolution," (2011); "Food," in *Growing up in Adelaide in the 1950s*, ed. Susan Blackburn (Sydney: Hale and Iremonger, 2012).
10 Jean Blackburn [JB], "Quality Is Not What It Was," in *Quality of Australian Education* (Canberra: Australian College of Education, 1978).
11 Notes associated with Jean Blackburn's address to the Australian College of Education annual conference, Personal Papers of Jean Blackburn (hereafter cited as JB Personal Papers), M728: Item 13557806, National Archives of Australia (hereafter cited as NAA).
12 Lyndsay Connors and Jim McMorrow, interview by Craig Campbell and Debra Hayes, December 8, 2015.
13 Raewyn Connell, "Kartini's Children: On the Need for Thinking Gender and Education Together on a World Scale," in *Rethinking Gendered Relations and Resistances in Education*, ed. Jessica Ringrose, (Oxford: Routledge, 2014), 19.
14 "2014 Jean Blackburn Oration". https://www.austcolled.com.au/events/event/2014-jean-blackburn-oration. Accessed 22 September 2016.
15 Dean Ashenden, interview by Craig Campbell and Debra Hayes, June 7, 2016.
16 David Gonski, "Inaugural Jean Blackburn Oration," (2014).

Chapter 1. An unsatisfactory childhood, 1919–1932

1. [Autobiographical Fragments 2], c. 1995, Private papers of Jean Blackburn [JB Private papers].
2. Jean Blackburn [JB], [University High School], 2001, JB Private papers.
3. The Harvester Judgement of 1907 from the Commonwealth Court of Conciliation and Arbitration produced this gendered determination of the basic wage.
4. See, for example, Michael Gilding, *The Making and Breaking of the Australian Family* (Sydney: Allen & Unwin, 1991); Alison Mackinnon, *Love and Freedom* (Cambridge: Cambridge University Press, 1997).
5. Marriage certificate, reproduced in "Muir Family Reunion," 1992, 23, in possession of SB.
6. JB, "Early Life," JB Private papers; Jean Blackburn, interview by Allison Murchie, May 14, 1994.
7. Les Muir, interview by Susan Blackburn, May–June, 1981.
8. The Victorian Education Act allowed exemptions for children whose families faced hardship.
9. Muir, interview.
10. JB, [Family and Youth], c. 2000, JB Private papers.
11. Muir, interview.
12. Muir, interview.
13. Jean Blackburn, interview by Peter Biskup, September 27 & November 13, 1990.
14. "Early Life"; Muir, interview.
15. "Background," c. 2000, JB Private papers; "Memoirs, Chap 1, Early Life," c. 2000, JB Private papers.
16. See *Australian Dictionary of Biography*, s.v. "Wagstaff, Ernest Edward (1870–1965)."
17. Muir, interview.
18. JB, [Memoirs 1], c. 1980, JB Private papers.
19. [Memoirs 1].
20. "Memoirs, Chap 1, Early Life"; Susan Blackburn, interview by Craig Campbell, May 22, 2014, transcript, in possession of Debra Hayes.
21. Jean Blackburn, interview by Tony Ryan, May 12 & 19, 1994.
22. JB, [Autobiographical Fragment], JB Private papers.
23. "Memoirs, Chap 1, Early Life."
24. Muir, Les Thomas and Pryor, Janet, interview by Craig Campbell and Debra Hayes, April 15, 2015.
25. [Autobiographical Fragments 2].
26. Muir and Pryor, interview; Louisa Hamilton, interview by Susan Blackburn and Hugh Blackburn, November 20, 2013.
27. JB, "My Apprenticeship: First Draft (April 12)," c. 2000, JB Private papers.
28. "Memoirs, Chap 1, Early Life."
29. See Ann Morris, "Gendered Dynamics of Abuse and Violence in Families," *Child Abuse Review* 18 (2009).

30 [Memoirs 1].
31 JB to SB, 30 January 1968, in possession of SB.
32 [Memoirs 1].
33 [Memoirs 1]; S. Blackburn, interview.
34 S. Blackburn, interview; [Autobiographical fragment].
35 [Autobiographical Fragments 2].
36 Blackburn, interview by Ryan; [Memoirs 1].
37 Blackburn, interview by Biskup.
38 JB, "Myself When Young," 1999, JB Private papers.
39 "Memoirs, Chap 1, Early Life"; Muir and Pryor, interview.
40 S. Blackburn, interview.
41 Blackburn, interview by Murchie, May 1994.
42 [Autobiographical Fragments 2].
43 "Memoirs, Chap 1, Early Life."
44 "Early Life."
45 On the New Education, see R. J. W. Selleck, *The New Education* (London: Pitman, 1968); Christina Stead, *For Love Alone* (Sydney: Angus and Robertson, 1990). Stead wrote an alarming, though likely biased, description of early twentieth century elementary teachers.
46 "My Apprenticeship: First Draft (April 12)."
47 Blackburn, interview by Ryan.
48 "Background."
49 "Primary and HE-on to UHS," c. 2000, JB Private papers.
50 "Background."; Blackburn, interview by Biskup.
51 JB, "Occasional Address, Melbourne University Graduation Ceremony, August 1988," JB Private papers.
52 "Background."
53 "Primary and HE-on to UHS." See also "Early Life." For a systems view, see Richard Teese, *For the Common Weal* (Melbourne: Australian Scholarly Publishing, 2014), 9–18.
54 JB, "To University via Primary School," c. 2000, JB Private papers.
55 "Primary and HE-on to UHS"; "Early Life."
56 "My Apprenticeship: First Draft (April 12)."
57 [Memoirs 1].
58 "Background."
59 "To University via Primary School."
60 Muir and Pryor, interview.
61 "Background."
62 Blackburn, interview by Biskup.
63 [Family and Youth].
64 "Into University," c. 2000; JB, "Political Radicalism," c 2000, JB Private papers.

Chapter 2. School and the independent girl, 1933–1937

1. "When I set out to Lyonnesse", poem by Thomas Hardy.
2. Jean Blackburn [JB], [Autobiographical Fragments 2], c. 1995; JB, [University High School], 2001, JB Private papers.
3. [University High School].
4. Jean Blackburn, interview by Peter Biskup, September 27 & November 13, 1990.
5. Carole Hooper, "Opposition Triumphant," in *Toward the State High School in Australia*, ed. Craig Campbell and others (Sydney: ANZHES, 1999).
6. See Craig Campbell, "Arnoldian School Culture," in *Dictionary of Educational History in Australia and New Zealand* ([Sydney]: ANZHES, 2014).
7. Wendy Law Stuart in Eleanor Peeler, *Lawrie Shears* (Melbourne: Hybrid Publishers, 2014), 272; JB, "University High School," c. 2000, JB Private papers.
8. [University High School]. See also Peeler, *Lawrie Shears*, 269ff. There are two histories of this school: Alice Hoy, *A City Built to Music* (Melbourne: University High School, 1961), and Carolyn Rasmussen, *'A Whole New World'* (Melbourne: Australian Scholarly Publishing, 2010).
9. JB, "To University via Primary School," c. 2000, JB Private papers.
10. [University High School].
11. Hoy, *City*, 22–23.
12. [University High School].
13. On Ada Knowles, *Argus*, March 5, 1937; April 11, 1938.
14. Hoy, *City*, 27.
15. JB, "Memoirs, Chap 1, Early Life," 2000, JB Private papers. Blackburn, interview by Biskup; Jean Blackburn, interview by Wendy Lowenstein, July 1, 1994.
16. "Memoirs, Chap 1, Early Life."
17. [University High School].
18. "University High School"; [University High School].
19. "University High School."
20. *University High School Record* 15 no. 2 (1936): 16.
21. Les [Thomas] Muir, "LTM Address at JEB Ceremony 06.12.01," 2001, JB Private papers; Blackburn, interview by Biskup.
22. [University High School].
23. Rivkah Mathews, "Rivkah Mathews," in *More Memories of Melbourne University*, ed. Hume Dow (Melbourne: Huchinson, 1985).
24. Susan Blackburn [SB], [Personal diary, extracts, 1963–2001], entry December 17, 1963, in possession of SB.
25. JB, "To University Via Primary School [2]," c. 2000; "Memoirs, Chap 1, Early Life," JB Private papers.
26. Jean Blackburn, interview by Allison Murchie, May 14, 1994.
27. Muir, Les Thomas and Pryor, Janet, interview by Craig Campbell and Debra Hayes, April 15, 2015.

28 Blackburn, interview by Murchie, May.
29 Muir and Pryor, interview.
30 JB, "Into University," c. 2000, JB Private papers.
31 "Into University."
32 "To University via Primary School."
33 "Memoirs, Chap 1, Early Life." For further insight see Amirah Inglis, *Amira: An un-Australian childhood* (Melbourne: Heinemann, 1983). Inglis was Jewish from refugee parents though sent to MacRob, not University High. On social backgrounds of girls and teachers at University High, see Rasmussen, *Whole New World*, 53–55, 56–61.
34 Rasmussen, *Whole New World*, 53–55, 56–61.
35 "Memoirs, Chap 1, Early Life." The book was *Fascism and Social Revolution* (1934). Rajani Palme Dutt was a journalist and theoretician within the Communist Party of Great Britain.
36 Blackburn, interview by Lowenstein.
37 *University High School Record* 14 no. 2 (1935): 33; Jean Blackburn, interview by Tony Ryan, May 12 & 19, 1994.
38 Blackburn, interview by Biskup.
39 JB, "My Apprenticeship: First Draft (April 12)," c. 2000, JB Private papers.
40 [University High School]. See Richard Teese, *For the Common Weal* (Melbourne: Australian Scholarly Publishing, 2014), chs. 2–3.
41 "University High School."
42 Hoy, *City*, 64, 69.
43 University of Melbourne, "Examination Registers," 1934–1937, University of Melbourne Archives.
44 "To University Via Primary School (2)."
45 "To University Via Primary School."
46 "To University Via Primary School."
47 "Memoirs, Chap 1, Early Life."; [Autobiographical Fragments 2].
48 Jean Blackburn, interview by Kirsten Marks, December 13, 1993.
49 Christina Stead, *For Love Alone* (Sydney: Angus and Robertson, 1990 [1944]); for the social history of the unmarried woman teacher, see Kay Whitehead, "The Spinster Teacher in Australia from the 1870s to the 1960s," *History of Education Review* 36, no. 1 (2007).
50 [Autobiographical Fragments 2].
51 Louisa Hamilton, interview by Susan Blackburn and Hugh Blackburn, November 20, 2013; JB, [Notes Towards Planning a Memoir], c. 2000, JB Private papers.
52 "Into University."
53 "To University via Primary School."
54 "To University via Primary School."
55 "To University via Primary School."

Chapter 3. University, communism and war, 1938–1941

1. Jean Blackburn, interview by Tony Ryan, May 12 & 19, 1994, National Library of Australia.
2. Jean Blackburn [JB], "Background [2]," c. 2000, JB Private papers, held by Susan Blackburn [SB].
3. JB, "[Autobiographical Fragments 2]"; also, JB, "To University Via Primary School," JB Private papers.
4. "To University via Primary School."
5. "[Autobiographical Fragments 2]."
6. "To University via Primary School"; JB, "Into University," JB Private papers.
7. P. W. Musgrave, *From Humanity to Utility* (Melbourne: ACER, 1992); R. J. W. Selleck, *The Shop: The University of Melbourne 1850–1939* (Melbourne: Melbourne University Press, 2003).
8. Diana Dyason quoted in John Poynter and Carolyn Rasmussen, *A Place Apart: The University of Melbourne* (Melbourne: Melbourne University Press, 1996), 32.
9. Stuart Macintyre and R. J. W. Selleck, *A Short History of the University of Melbourne, 1850–1939* (Melbourne: University of Melbourne Press, 2003), 86.
10. Louisa Hamilton, interview by Susan Blackburn and Hugh Blackburn, November 20, 2013, in possession of Susan Blackburn.
11. Macintyre and Selleck, *Short History*, 89.
12. University of Melbourne, "Jean Edna Blackburn: Student Record (1938–1940)," in *Student Records*, University of Melbourne Archives.
13. [Autobiographical Fragments 2].
14. Jean Blackburn, interview by Wendy Lowenstein, July 1, 1994, National Library of Australia.
15. "History of Economics at Melbourne University," University of Melbourne, http://fbe.unimelb.edu.au/economics/who/history. Accessed 23 February 2014; Poynter and Rasmussen, *Place Apart*, 55–57.
16. Blackburn, interview by Ryan.
17. Jean Blackburn, interview by Peter Biskup, September 27 & November 13, 1990, National Library of Australia.
18. Ian Turner, "My Long March," in *Room for Manoevre: Writings on History, Politics, Ideas and Play* (Melbourne: Drummond, 1982), 141.
19. Manning Clark, *The Quest for Grace* (Melbourne: Viking, 1990), 44–45; B. A. Santamaria, *Santamaria: A Memoir* (Melbourne: Oxford University Press, 1997 [1981]).
20. Clark, *Quest*, 45.
21. [University High School]. The meaning of the phrase "what she meant" is not clear, though rather easily imagined.
22. Blackburn, interview by Biskup.
23. Raymond Priestley, *The Diary of a Vice-Chancellor* (Melbourne: Melbourne University Press, 2002), 46, 84, 123 & 291.
24. "G", "Culture and Society," *Melbourne University Magazine*, 1938.

25 [Join the Labour Club], *Farrago*, March 4, 1938. Also, March 15, 22 & 29; April 4 & 26, 1938.
26 *Farrago*, May 3; July 12, 1938.
27 *Farrago*, July 18, 1939, 1.
28 *Farrago*, July 11, 1939, 1.
29 Jean Blackburn, interview by Kirsten Marks, December 13, 1993, State Library of South Australia.
30 Blackburn, interview by Biskup. On the impact of the Non-Aggression Pact on the Communist Party, see Stuart Macintyre, *The Reds*, (Sydney: Allen & Unwin, 1998), 384–399.
31 Blackburn, interview by Biskup.
32 [Autobiographical Fragments 2].
33 *Farrago*, October 2, 1939, 2.
34 Rivkah Mathews, "Rivkah Mathews," in *More Memories of Melbourne University: Undergraduate Life in the Years since 1919*, ed. Hume Dow (Melbourne: Huchinson, 1985), 57–60.
35 Melbourne University Labour Club, "Minute Book, Committee and General …", 1931–1943, University of Melbourne Archives. See also Patrick O'Brien, *The Saviours* (Melbourne: Drummond, 1977), ch. 3.
36 "Friendship with Russia," *Argus*, December 10, 1940, 2.
37 *Farrago*, March 29 & April 23, 1940.
38 *Farrago*, May 7, 1940.
39 Poynter and Rasmussen, *Place Apart*, 63.
40 *Farrago*, April 29, 1941, 2.
41 *Farrago*, August 7, 1941, 3.
42 Mathews, "Rivkah Mathews," 64.
43 Hamilton, interview.
44 Blackburn, interviewed by Biskup.
45 "Social notes," *Age*, May 6, 1940, 3; *The Dandenong Journal*, May 29, 1940, 13.
46 Jean Blackburn, interview by Allison Murchie, May 14, 1994, State Library of South Australia.
47 Hamilton, interview.
48 Hamilton, interview.
49 Hamilton, interview.
50 SB, [Personal diary, extracts], entry February 27, 1965.
51 From *The Guardian*, November 7, 1945, reproduced in Australian Security Intelligence Organisation, "Blackburn, Gerard (Dick)," [ASIO file], National Archives of Australia.
52 SB, *Maurice Blackburn and the Australian Labor Party, 1934–1943* (Melbourne: Australian Society for the Study of Labour History, 1969). See also the same author, *Australian Dictionary of Biography*, s.v. "Blackburn, Maurice McCrae (1880–1944)."
53 O'Brien, *Saviours*, 51–54.
54 *Australian Dictionary of Biography*, s.v. "Blackburn, Doris Amelia (1889–1970)."
55 Susan Blackburn, interview by Craig Campbell, May 22, 2014.

56 Joy Damousi, *Women Come Rally* (Melbourne: Oxford University Press, 1994).
57 Carolyn Rasmussen, *The Lesser Evil?* (Melbourne: History Department University of Melbourne, 1992), 27.
58 See C. M. H. Clark, "Faith," in *Australian Civilization*, ed. Peter Coleman (Melbourne: Cheshire, 1962).
59 Hamilton, interview.

Chapter 4. Wartime public servant, and marriage, 1942–1950

1 Trevor Swan's verse in response to Jean's marriage in Jean Blackburn [JB], [Autobiographical Fragments 2], c. 1995, JB Private papers. (*Il y avait une fois*: There was a time; *je ne sais quoi*: I know not what.)
2 Australian Security Intelligence Organisation [ASIO], "Blackburn, Jean Edna," [ASIO file], National Archives of Australia.
3 [Autobiographical Fragments 2].
4 Paul Hasluck, *The Government and the People 1939–1941* (Canberra: Australian War Memorial, 1952), 369, 393–396. Quotation: p. 519.
5 See A. D. Spaull, *John Dedman* (Melbourne: Hyland House, 1998), 18–48.
6 Paul Hasluck, *The Government and the People 1942–1945* (Canberra: Australian War Memorial, 1970), 246–247.
7 Spaull, *Dedman*, 51–52.
8 *Australian Dictionary of Biography*, s.v. "Dedman, John Johnstone (1896–1973)."
9 Spaull, *Dedman*, 57ff. On Labor and post-war reconstruction, see Stuart Macintyre, *Australia's Boldest Experiment* (Sydney: New South, 2015).
10 Jean Blackburn, interview by Tony Ryan, May 12 & 19, 1994.
11 Jean Blackburn, interview by Peter Biskup, September 27 & November 13, 1990.
12 Blackburn, interview by Ryan.
13 [Autobiographical Fragments 2].
14 Blackburn, interview by Biskup.
15 Jean Blackburn, interview by Kirsten Marks, December 13, 1993.
16 "Clothes Can Be Smart but Simple," *Argus*, September 1, 1942.
17 ASIO file, "Blackburn, Jean Edna." On women and the referendum see Stuart Macintyre, "Women's Leadership in War and Reconstruction," *Labour History*, 104 (2013).
18 *Australian Dictionary of Biography*, s.v. "Swan, Trevor Winchester (1918–1989)."
19 Macintyre, *Australia's Boldest Experiment*, 278.
20 Tim Rowse, *Nugget Coombs* (Cambridge: Cambridge University Press, 2002).
21 Rowse, *Nugget*, 99–104.
22 Jean Blackburn, interview by Wendy Lowenstein, July 1, 1994.
23 Blackburn, interview Lowenstein; *The Woiker* (Melbourne: Office Committee of the Commonwealth Temporary Clerks' Association in the Department of War Organisation of Industry, 1943–1944).

24 *Woiker*, March 10, 1943, 1.
25 On the Communist Party and this phase of the war see Hasluck, *Government and People 1942–1945*, 138–9, 250, 364, 537, and Stuart Macintyre, *The Reds* (Sydney: Allen and Unwin, 1998), 412.
26 *Woiker*, April 19, 1943, 2.
27 *Woiker*, October 25, 1943, 5.
28 *Woiker*, October 25, 1943, 6.
29 *Woiker*, October 25, 1943, 6.
30 *Farrago*, September 10, 1942.
31 [Autobiographical Fragments 2].
32 Blackburn, interview by Marks.
33 Mollie Bayne, ed. *Australian Women at War* (Melbourne: Left Book Club of Victoria, 1943). Aims of CWWW, p. 73; see also Blackburn, interview by Lowenstein.
34 Kathleen Fitzpatrick, "Introduction," in *Australian Women at War*; see also Elizabeth Kleinhenz, *A Brimming Cup: The Life of Kathleen Fitzpatrick* (Melbourne: Melbourne University Press, 2013).
35 Bayne, *Australian Women*, 68.
36 See Marilyn Lake, *Getting Equal* (Sydney: Allen & Unwin, 1999); Macintyre, *Australia's Boldest Experiment*; Rowse, *Nugget*, 103.
37 Macintyre, "Women's Leadership," 75; Joyce Stevens, *Taking the Revolution Home* (Melbourne: Sybylla Cooperative Press, 1987), 91.
38 This story occurs as comment by Susan Blackburn [SB], in Louisa Hamilton, interview by Susan Blackburn and Hugh Blackburn, November 20, 2013.
39 Story of Hyrell Ross and Dick reconstructed from SB, [Personal diary, extracts, 1963–2001], entry May 12, 1996, in possession of SB, and Hamilton, interview.
40 State of Victoria, "Certificate of Marriage," 1943, JB Private papers.
41 "Funeral of Mr Maurice Blackburn," *Argus*, April 3, 1944.
42 Jean Blackburn, interview by Allison Murchie, March 26, 1994.
43 JB, "Into paid work," nd, JB Private papers.
44 [Autobiographical Fragments 2].
45 Hamilton, interview.
46 JB, "To Adelaide," JB Private papers. See also Judith Gill to Debra Hayes (email), 12 November 2017.
47 SB, [Personal diary, extracts], entry February 12, 2000.
48 [Autobiographical Fragments 2].
49 Blackburn, interview by Biskup; Blackburn, interview by Lowenstein.
50 Blackburn, interview by Ryan; "To Adelaide"; Blackburn, interview by Biskup; Myrdal, Alva, and Viola Klein, *Women's Two Roles* (London: Routledge & Paul, 1956).
51 JB to Ted Jackson, 30 September 1999, JB Private papers.
52 JB to editor, *Advertiser*, May 20, 1946.
53 JB to editor, *Advertiser*, March 29, 1947.

54 JB to editor, *News*, September 17, 1947.
55 "Referendum Talks Tonight," *News*, May 19, 1948.
56 See Bernard O'Neil, Judith Raftery, and Kerrie Round, eds., *Playford's South Australia* (Adelaide: Association of Professional Historians, 1996).
57 See Winifred Mitchell, "A Pilgrim's Progress," in *Against the Odds*, ed. Madge Dawson and Heather Radi (Sydney: Hale & Iremonger, 1984).
58 Blackburn, interview by Biskup.
59 See Judith Smart, "The Housewives' Associations 1915–1950," in *Consumer Australia*, ed. Robert Crawford, Judith Smart, and Kim Humphrey (Newcastle upon Tyne: Cambridge Scholars, 2010).
60 JB, "The New Housewives and the Communist Party's Conception of the Role of Women in the 1940s," c. 1988, JB Private papers. Also, Blackburn, interview by Lowenstein.
61 Australian Women's Archives Project, "New Housewives' Association (1946–1950)," in *The Australian Women's Register* (National Foundation for Australian Women).
62 JB, "The New Housewives Assoc – the LM and Women in the Late 1940s," 1987, JB Private papers. Also, Blackburn, interview by Lowenstein.
63 JB, "Conversation with Winifred Mitchell Aug 9th," nd., JB Private papers.
64 Blackburn, interview by Biskup.
65 See also Blackburn, interview by Biskup. There Jean explained that 'bringing it off' referred to women 'taking something every month' to avoid pregnancy.
66 "New Housewives – the LM."
67 "New Housewives – the LM."
68 ASIO file, "Blackburn, Jean Edna."
69 See Tom O'Lincoln, "Against the Stream: Women and the Left, 1945–1968," (1980), https://www.anu.edu.au/polsci/marx/interventions/rebelwomen/against.htm.
70 "New Housewives – the LM." See also Blackburn, interview by Marks.
71 "Conversation Winifred Mitchell."
72 Mitchell, "Pilgrim's Progress," 213.
73 "New Housewives and Communist Party's Conception." For a more favourable, brief semi-official history of the Communist Party in South Australia and mention of the New Housewives, see Jim Moss, *Representatives of Discontent* (Melbourne: Communist and Labour Movement History Group, 1983).
74 Joyce Stevens, *A History of International Women's Day* (Sydney: IWD Press, 1985).
75 "To Adelaide."
76 Stevens, *History*, 18.
77 ASIO file, "Blackburn, Jean Edna."
78 *News*, February 26, 7; and March 8, 1948, 5.
79 Blackburn, interview by Marks.
80 Letter from neighbour, in ASIO file, "Blackburn, Jean Edna." Dick Blackburn did not go to Woomera contrary to rumour.
81 Blackburn, interview by Ryan.

82 See SB, "Notes for Talk at Jean Muir Celebration, Melbourne 17/12/01," in possession of SB.
83 [Autobiographical Fragments 2].
84 Mary Ryan, *Beyond the Glass Ceiling* (Melbourne: Collins Dove, 1993), 71.
85 See Barbara Caine, "Mothering Feminism/Mothering Feminists: Ray Strachey and the Cause," *Women's History Review* 8, no. 2 (1999).
86 JB, "Launching CHS (Catherine Helen Spence)," 1985, JB Private papers.
87 "Notes for Talk at Jean Muir Celebration."
88 J. B. Miles, "Work among Women," (Sydney: Communist Party of Australia, 1943), 2–3. See also Lyn Finch, "Could 'Winnie the War Winner' Organise Women? Problems of CPA Women During World War II," *Hecate* 10, no. 1 (1984).
89 Stevens, *Taking the Revolution*, 27.

Chapter 5. Suburban life and beyond, 1951–1966

1 *Sunday Mail*, December 16, 1961.
2 Jean Blackburn [JB] and Ted Jackson, *Australian Wives Today* (Melbourne: Victorian Fabian Society, 1963), 24.
3 Muir, Les Thomas and Pryor, Janet, interview by Craig Campbell and Debra Hayes, April 15, 2015.
4 Australian Security Intelligence Organisation [ASIO], "Blackburn, Gerard (Dick)," [ASIO File], National Archives of Australia.
5 *Australian Dictionary of Biography*, s.v. "Miles, John Bramwell (Jack) (1888–1969)."
6 Jim Goss to Joe Goss, 25 September 1950. In possession of Judy Ferguson.
7 Judy Ferguson, interview by Craig Campbell, March 13, 2016; H. R. Gilmore, "Summary: William Blackburn, Aged 11," 1956, JB Private papers; Susan Blackburn [SB] to Craig Campbell (email), 30 November 2017.
8 Ferguson interview.
9 ASIO file, "Blackburn, Jean Edna."
10 Susan Blackburn [SB], "Children of the Revolution," 2011, in possession of SB.
11 See D. M. Horner, *The Spy Catchers: The Official History of ASIO, 1949–1963* (Sydney: Allen & Unwin, 2014), 211–213; Penelope Debelle, *Red Silk: The Life of Elliott Johnston QC* (Adelaide: Wakefield Press, 2011), 77–79.
12 Ian Turner, "My Long March," in *Room for Manoevre* (Melbourne: Drummond, 1982), 128.
13 Jim Moss, *Representatives of Discontent* (Melbourne: Communist and Labour Movement History Group, 1983), 37–42.
14 Jean Blackburn, interview by Peter Biskup, September 27 & November 13, 1990.
15 Jean Blackburn, interview by Kirsten Marks, December 13, 1993; Jean Blackburn, interview by Wendy Lowenstein, July 1, 1994. The connected politics of peace movement, nuclear disarmament and communism are complex. Jean Blackburn's account of her disillusionment is but one perspective.

16   ASIO file, "Blackburn, Jean Edna."
17   JB to editor, *Advertiser*, August 6, 1953, 4.
18   *News*, May 5, 1952, 7.
19   Judy Ferguson to Craig Campbell (email), 29 October 2016.
20   Blackburn, interview by Lowenstein.
21   Blackburn, interview by Biskup.
22   JB, "To Adelaide," JB Private papers; [Autobiographical Fragments 2], c. 1995, JB Private papers. See also Susan Blackburn, interview by Craig Campbell, May 22, 2014.
23   [Autobiographical Fragments 2].
24   SB to Craig Campbell (email), 15 December, 2015.
25   Blackburn, interview by Marks.
26   "To Adelaide."
27   SB, [Personal diary, extracts, 1963–2001], entry March 31, 2001, in possession of SB; on the forgery issue, Blackburn, interview by Lowenstein.
28   SB, [Personal diary], entry March 31, 2001.
29   "To Adelaide."
30   SB, "Children."
31   Dean Ashenden, interview by Craig Campbell and Debra Hayes, June 7, 2016.
32   Blackburn, interview by Lowenstein.
33   John McLaren, *Free Radicals of the Left in Postwar Melbourne* (Melbourne: Australian Scholarly Publishing, 2003), 133–137.
34   Ian Turner, "The Long Goodbye." In *Room for Manoevre*, 141–49.
35   *Australian Dictionary of Biography*, s.v. "Palmer, Helen Gwynneth (1917–1979)."
36   Editorial, *Outlook* 1 no. 1 (1957): 1–2.
37   David Bennett who was close to Jean on the Schools Commission in the 1970s had a 1950s *Outlook* history. Race Matthews, "David Bennett," (Melbourne: Australian Fabian Society, [1985]), 14.
38   JB, "'Shine, O Shine Them Pots!'," *Outlook* 3, no. 4 (1959), 12.
39   Respectively, JB, "Changes Brewing," *Outlook* 5, no. 4 (1961) and Palmer in *Outlook* 5, no. 3, 1961.
40   ASIO file, "Blackburn, Jean Edna."
41   Blackburn, interview by Biskup.
42   JB, "Adelaide Festival," *Outlook* 4, no. 2 (1960): 6. Ken Inglis, historian and friend of Jean helped make the case a cause célèbre.
43   *Outlook* 6, no. 4, 1962: 20.
44   E. A. Russell, "The Disarmament Debate," *Outlook* 1, no. 4 (1957).
45   SB, interview. Comment on the conversation closing strategy, Hugh Blackburn to Craig Campbell (email), 17 July 2018.
46   G. C. Harcourt, "E. A. Russell, 1921–77: A Memoir (Draft)," 1977, JB Private papers.
47   Geoffrey Harcourt and Joan Harcourt, interview by Craig Campbell, March 21, 2016.
48   "To Adelaide"; Peter Karmel, interview by Carl Green, June 12, 1992, in Carl Green, "Karmel, Labor and Education" (Honours thesis, University of

Sydney, 1992), Appendix C.
49 [Autobiographical Fragments 2].
50 Blackburn, interview by Biskup.
51 Jean Blackburn, interview by Tony Ryan, May 12 & 19, 1994.
52 Hugh Blackburn, interview by Craig Campbell and Debra Hayes, June 8, 2016; SB to Craig Campbell (email), 30 November 2017.
53 Harcourt and Harcourt, interview.
54 Blackburn, interview by Biskup.
55 Blackburn, interview by Lowenstein.
56 John Sendy, *Comrades Come Rally!* (Melbourne: Nelson, 1978), 102.
57 SB, "Children."
58 Graham F. Smith, *Speak up, Reach Out* (Adelaide: Wakefield Press, 2015), 62–64.
59 McBriar, Elizabeth Maud, interview by Bernard O'Neill, September 30, 1992.
60 JB to SB, 29 December 1966. In possession of Susan Blackburn.
61 Gilmore, "William Blackburn."
62 SB, "Reminiscences of Bill as a Boy," 2002, in possession of SB.
63 Susan Blackburn, "Children," 5.
64 Blackburn, "Children."
65 ASIO file, "Blackburn, Gerard (Dick)."
66 Blackburn, interviewed by Ryan, 1994.
67 SB, "Children."
68 SB to Craig Campbell (email), 25 May 2014. On reading and the relationship with libraries see SB, "A Golden Age for Children's Reading in Adelaide," *Journal of the Historical Society of South Australia* 38 (2010).
69 SB, "Children."
70 SB, interview.
71 SB to Craig Campbell (email), 25 May 2014.
72 SB, "Notes for Talk at Jean Muir Celebration, Melbourne 17/12/01," 2001, in possession of SB.
73 SB, [Personal diary 1963–2001], entry October 26, 1965.
74 Hamilton, Louisa, interview by Susan Blackburn and Hugh Blackburn, November 20, 2013, transcript, in possession of SB; SB interview.
75 Judy Inglis quoted in Rani Kerin, "'Mixed up in a Bit of Do-Goodery': Judy Inglis, Activist Anthropology and Aboriginal History," *History and Anthropology* 18, no. 4 (2007): 436.
76 See Kerin, "Mixed up", and Jean Blackburn, interview by Peter Read, July 21, 1988. For Dunstan's involvement see Don Dunstan, *Felicia: The Political Memoirs of Don Dunstan* (Melbourne: Macmillan, 1981), 45, 68–70.
77 See Rani Kerin, *Doctor Do-Good* (Melbourne: Australian Scholarly Publishing, 2011), 146–148.
78 ASIO file, "Blackburn, Jean Edna." For the conference see Judy Inglis, 'The assimilation of poisoned flour', *Nation* (May 19, 1962): 7.
79 ASIO file, "Blackburn, Jean Edna."
80 Blackburn, interview by Read.

81 Kerin, *Doctor Do-Good*, ch. 6.
82 SB, interview by Campbell.
83 Jean Blackburn, interview by Allison Murchie, March 26, 1994.
84 Norman MacKenzie, *Women in Australia* (Melbourne: Cheshire, 1962).
85 JB, "'I'm All Right, Jill …',' *Outlook* 7, no. 2 (1963).
86 Gisela Kaplan, *The Meagre Harvest* (Sydney: Allen & Unwin, 1996), 1–22.
87 Myrdal, Alva, and Viola Klein, *Women's Two Roles* (London: Routledge & Paul, 1956).
88 JB, *Australian Wives*, 15.
89 *Australian Wives*, 20.
90 *Australian Wives*, 23.
91 *Australian Wives*, 31.
92 *Australian Wives*, 35.
93 *Australian Wives*, 25.
94 [Autobiographical Fragments 2].
95 Peggy Mares and Effie Best, interview by Craig Campbell, February 15, 2016.
96 Jessie McLeod, [Review of] *Australian Wives Today*, *Outlook* 7, no. 6 (1963): 19.
97 Blackburn, interview by Lowenstein.
98 [Judy Gill], [Western Teachers College], c. 2000, JB Private papers. Also, Jean Blackburn, interview by Jack Cross, August 28, 2000, [Notes]; "Jean Blackburn: Timeline and Summary of Our Discussion," 2000, JB Private papers.
99 Peggy Mares to SB (email), 3 January 2002. In possession of SB.
100 Denise Bradley, interview by Craig Campbell and Debra Hayes, October 9, 2015.
101 SB, "Children," 3.
102 'She joins the comrades', *Sunday Mail*, December 16, 1961, 27.
103 SB to Craig Campbell (email), 25 May 2014.

Chapter 6. Career at last, 1967–1973

1 Jean Blackburn [JB], interview by Tony Ryan, May 12 & 19, 1994.
2 JB to Susan Blackburn [SB], April 20, 1971. In possession of SB.
3 Jean Blackburn, interview by Jack Cross, notes, August 28, 2000.
4 Jack Cross, "Western Teachers College," 2000, Jean Blackburn Private papers.
5 Peggy Mares to SB, 3 January 2002.
6 Margaret Bearlin, interview by Craig Campbell and Debra Hayes, July 20, 2015.
7 Alan Barcan, *Sociological Theory and Educational Reality* (Sydney: New South Wales University Press, 1993).
8 Bearlin, interview; Blackburn, interview by Cross.
9 JB to SB, 24 January 1968; quotation, JB to SB, July 20, 1969.

10 JB to SB, 13 February 1967.
11 Pavla Miller, *Long Division* (Adelaide: Wakefield Press, 1986).
12 W. F. Connell, *Reshaping Australian Education 1960–1985* (Melbourne: ACER, 1993).
13 Miller, *Long Division*, 293.
14 Bernard Hyams, "Education," in *The Dunstan Decade*, ed. Andrew Parkin and Allan Patience (Melbourne: Longman Cheshire, 1981).
15 *Australian Dictionary of Biography*, s.v. "Steele, Joyce (1909–1991)."
16 Hyams, "Education."
17 A. W. Jones, "Peter Karmel," in *A Broader Vision*, ed. Erica Jolly (Adelaide: the editor, 2001).
18 Peter Karmel (Chair), "Education in South Australia: Report of the Committee of Enquiry into Education in South Australia 1969–1970," (Adelaide: Government of South Australia, 1971).
19 Jean Blackburn, interview by Allison Murchie, March 26, 1994.
20 JB to SB, 15 March 1969.
21 Jean Blackburn, interview by Peter Biskup, September 27 & November 13, 1990.
22 JB to SB, 15 March 1969; Blackburn, interview by Murchie, March.
23 JB to SB, 3 August 1970.
24 Jean Blackburn, interview by Wendy Lowenstein, July 1, 1994.
25 Peter Karmel, interview by Carl Green, June 12, 1992.
26 JB to SB, 6 June 1970.
27 JB to SB, 31 August 1970.
28 Connell, *Reshaping*.
29 Blackburn, interview by Biskup.
30 Blackburn, interview by Ryan.
31 Coleman, J. S., et al., *Equality of Educational Opportunity* (Washington: U.S. Dept. of Health, Education, and Welfare, 1966); Central Advisory Council for Education (England), "The Plowden report: Children and their Primary Schools (1967). Retrieved July 17, 2016, from http://www.educationengland.org.uk/documents/plowden/plowden1967-1.html.
32 JB to SB, 10 July 1969.
33 Blackburn, interview by Murchie, March.
34 JB to SB, 9 November 1969.
35 JB to SB, 10 July 1969.
36 JB to SB, 15 June 1969.
37 JB to SB, 1 July 1970, 31 May 1970.
38 JB to SB, 22 October 1969.
39 On Unley High at this stage in its history, Craig Campbell, *Unley High School* (Adelaide: Wakefield Press, 2010), 185–187.
40 JB to SB, 17 July 1969.
41 JB to SB, 27 June 1970.
42 JB to SB, 26 October 1970.
43 JB to SB, 3 December 1970.

44 Connell, *Reshaping*.
45 Connell, *Reshaping*; also, Karmel "Education in South Australia," 255.
46 Blackburn, interview by Ryan.
47 Blackburn, interview by Ryan.
48 Karmel "Education in South Australia," 357.
49 Blackburn, interview by Lowenstein.
50 JB to SB, 27 May 1971.
51 JB to SB, 11 May 1971.
52 JB to SB, 27 May 1971.
53 Karmel "Education in South Australia," 357.
54 Blackburn, interview by Ryan. The 1960s was still a period when male pronouns were supposed to include females.
55 Karmel "Education in South Australia," 358.
56 John Steinle, "Today Students Can Pursue Academic and Vocational Subjects with Equal Rigour," *Broader Vision*, ed. Jolly.
57 Steinle, "Today."
58 Connell, *Reshaping*. See also Craig Campbell and Geoffrey Sherington, *The Comprehensive Public High School* (New York: Palgrave Macmillan, 2013), 48–57.
59 See chapter 8.
60 JB to SB, 11 May 1971.
61 JB to SB, 13 April 1971.
62 JB to SB, 4 September 1971.
63 JB to SB, 22 November 1972.
64 JB to SB, 13 April 1971. Jean approved of Stretton's book, *The Political Sciences* (1969), especially its critique of structural functionalism; and the intellectually detrimental effects of much Marxist argument. JB to SB, 2 November 1969.
65 JB to SB, 1 February 1972.
66 JB to SB, 1 February 1972.
67 JB to SB, 20 April 1972.
68 JB to SB, 13 August 1970.
69 Dean Ashenden, interview by Craig Campbell and Debra Hayes, June 7, 2016.
70 JB to SB, 27 June 1970.
71 JB to SB 23 August 1971. Jean was responding to Robin Morgan, ed. *Sisterhood Is Powerful* (New York: Random House, 1970). On the relationships between feminism, the Vietnam War and social change from the late 1960s, see Gisela Kaplan, *The Meagre Harvest* (Sydney: Allen & Unwin, 1996), 23–27.
72 JB to SB, 19 July 1969.
73 JB to SB, 30 July 1969.
74 Australian Security Intelligence Organisation [ASIO], "McBriar, Maud," [ASIO File], National Archives of Australia [NAA].
75 JB to SB, 16 November 1970.

Notes

76 JB to SB, 15 September 1970.
77 JB to SB, 27 May 1971.
78 JB to SB, 5 November 1972.
79 JB to SB, 22 November 1972.
80 Ken McKinnon, "The Schools Commission: A Review," in *Schools Commission Seminar* (Melbourne: University of Melbourne, 2010).
81 Blackburn, interview by Ryan.
82 Simon Marginson, "The Whitlam Government and Education," in *It's Time Again*, ed. Jenny Hocking and Colleen Lewis (Melbourne: Circa Books, 2003).
83 Cohen, Samuel. "Education in the 1970s." The John Curtin Centre, http://john.curtin.edu.au/jcmemlect/cohen1967.html.
84 Don Smart, "The Accelerating Commonwealth Participation 1964–1976," in *The Commonwealth Government and Education 1964–1976*, ed. I. K. F. Birch and D. Smart (Melbourne: Drummond, 1977).
85 JB, "The 1972 Education Programs," [1992], JB Private papers.
86 Blackburn, interview by Ryan.
87 Kim E. Beazley to Carl Green, 21 September 1992, in Carl Green, "Karmel, Labor and Education" (University of Sydney, 1992).
88 Blackburn, interview by Biskup. See Introduction of this book, p. 1, for the story of the invitation.
89 JB to SB, 10 January 1973.
90 Dr G. Hancock, Principal Research Officer, NSW Education Department; Mr E. Jackson, Director of Technical Education, Victorian Education Department; Mr A. Jones, Director-General, South Australian Education Department; the Reverend Father F. Martin, Director, Catholic Education Office, Melbourne; Dr P. Tannock, Dean, of the Faculty of Education, University of Western Australia; Mr M. Thomas, division of guidance and adjustment, NSW Education Department; Mr W. White, teacher liaison officer, Department of Education, Adelaide; and Dr Alice Whitley, recently headmistress, Methodist Ladies College, Sydney.
91 Weller, Patrick, "The Establishment of the Schools Commission," in *The Commonwealth Government and Education 1964–1976*, ed. I. K. F. Birch and D. Smart (Melbourne: Drummond, 1977), 55.
92 "Urges One-Year Scheme," *News*, February 5, 1974.
93 Blackburn, interview by Biskup.
94 Bearlin, interview.
95 Karmel, interview.
96 Kim E. Beazley to Carl Green, 1992.
97 Jean Blackburn, interview by Carl Green, August 21, 1992, in Green, "Karmel, Labor and Education."
98 Blackburn, interview by Green.
99 Blackburn, interview by Green.
100 Ashenden, interview.
101 Jean Ely, *Contempt of Court* (Melbourne: Dissenters Press, nd.), 119–121.
102 Blackburn, interview by Lowenstein.

103 Stephens, Andrew, "Battle Lines Don't Stop a Crusader," *The Sun*, August 9, 1985.
104 Karmel, interview.
105 Karmel, interview.
106 Blackburn, interview by Biskup.
107 Blackburn, interview by Biskup.
108 JB, [Interim Committee], 1981, JB Private papers.
109 Blackburn, interview by Green.
110 [Federal Catholic Education Office], 1973, "The Organisation of Australian Catholic Education", M734: 13599101, Jean Blackburn Personal Papers, National Archives of Australia. See also Helen Praetz, *Building a School System* (Melbourne: Melbourne University Press, 1980).
111 JB, [Interim Committee].
112 Blackburn, interview by Green.
113 Blackburn, interview by Green.
114 Karmel, interview.
115 Blackburn, interview by Green.
116 Karmel, "Schools in Australia," 10.
117 Blackburn, interview by Green.
118 Blackburn, interview by Ryan.
119 Quotations from Karmel, "Schools in Australia," 18, 19, 20 & 21.
120 "Schools in Australia."
121 Blackburn, interview by Green.
122 Karmel, "Schools in Australia," 56.
123 Karmel, "Schools in Australia," 62.
124 Kim Beazley, "The Labor Party in Opposition and Government," in *The Commonwealth Government and Education 1964–1976*, ed. I. K. F. Birch and D. Smart (Melbourne: Drummond, 1977), 99.
125 "Schools in Australia," 77.
126 JB, "Karmel Revisited," 1982, JB Private papers.
127 Lloyd Logan and Diane Mayer, "The Role of the Teacher," in *Schools in Australia: 1973–1998: The 25 years since the Karmel Report* (Sydney: Australian Council for Educational Research, 1998).
128 Logan and Mayer, "Role."
129 Blackburn, interview by Green.
130 Weller, "Establishment."
131 Blackburn, interview by Green.
132 Karmel, Peter (Chair), "Schools in Australia: Report of the Interim Committee of the Australian Schools Commission." Canberra: AGPS, 1973.
133 Jean Blackburn, interview by Tony Ryan, May 12 & 19, 1994, National Library of Australia.
134 JB to SB, 24 June 1973.
135 JB, "Community Involvement in Education," M733: 13557118, JBPP-NAA.
136 McKinnon, Ken, "The Schools Commission: A Review." In *Schools Commission Seminar*, 1–16. (Melbourne: University of Melbourne, 2010), 3.

137 Malcolm Fraser and Margaret Simons, *Malcolm Fraser* (Melbourne: Miegunyah Press, 2010).
138 Gough Whitlam, *The Whitlam Government: 1972–1975* (Melbourne: Viking, 1985).
139 McKinnon, "The Schools," 3–4.
140 Karmel, interview.
141 McKinnon, "The Schools."
142 Dick Blackburn to SB, 13 November 1973. In possession of SB.
143 Dick Blackburn to SB, 13 November 1973. On Jim Giles of Unley High, see Campbell, *Unley High School*.
144 Blackburn, interview by Ryan.
145 Hugh Blackburn, interview.
146 Hugh Blackburn, interview.
147 Blackburn, interview by Biskup.
148 Blackburn, interview by Ryan.
149 Blackburn, interview by Biskup.
150 Blackburn, interview by Green.
151 Blackburn, interview by Ryan.
152 JB to SB, 21 May 1973.
153 JB to SB, 1 August 1973.
154 JB to SB, 1 August 1973.
155 JB to SB, 20 January 1967.
156 SB to Craig Campbell (email), 10 August 2016.
157 Hugh Blackburn, interview.
158 Helen Palmer, "'Outlook' Ceases Publication," in *Helen Palmer's Outlook*, ed. Doreen Bridges (Sydney: Helen Palmer Memorial Committee, 1982 [1970]).

Chapter 7. Schools Commissioner: Whitlam government years, 1974–1975

1   Jean Blackburn, interview by Peter Biskup, September 27 & November 13, 1990.
2   Blackburn, interview by Biskup.
3   Jean Blackburn, interview by Wendy Lowenstein, July 1, 1994.
4   Hugh Blackburn, interview by Craig Campbell and Debra Hayes, June 8, 2016.
5   Jean Blackburn [JB] to Susan Blackburn [SB], 16 November 1969, in possession of SB.
6   JB, "Handicapped," 1974, M730: 13559820, Jean Blackburn Personal Papers, National Archives of Australia [JBPP-NAA].
7   JB to David Bennett, 6 June c. 1974, M730: 13598820, JBPP-NAA.
8   McKinnon, Ken, "The Schools Commission: A Review." In *Schools Commission Seminar*, 1–16. (Melbourne: University of Melbourne, 2010), 5.
9   Jean Blackburn, interview by Tony Ryan, May 12 & 19, 1994.
10 Blackburn, interview by Ryan.

11   Jean Blackburn, interview by Carl Green, August 21, 1992.
12   Karmel, Peter, (Chair). "Schools in Australia: Report of the Interim Committee of the Australian Schools Commission." Canberra: AGPS, 1973.
13   JB, "Values Directions," M727: 13557773, BPP-NAA.
14   JB, "Values Directions."
15   [JB] to George Reid, 3 September 1974, M731: 13557770, JBPP-NAA.
16   Blackburn, interview by Biskup.
17   JB, "Schools and the Schools Commission." In *The Commonwealth Government and Education 1964–1976*, edited by I. K. F. Birch and D. Smart. Melbourne: Drummond, 1977, 195.
18   "Report to Schools Commissioners on the meeting of Schools Commission and Australian Education Council," 8–9 December, 1978, M727: 13557806, JBPP-NAA.
19   JB, [The Ideology of the Schools Commission]," 1980, JB Private papers, in the possession of SB.
20   Ken McKinnon, interview by Craig Campbell & Debra Hayes, 7 May 2016.
21   Shirley Randell, interview by Craig Campbell and Debra Hayes, 26 May 2016.
22   McKinnon, "The Schools Commission."
23   McKinnon, "The Schools Commission."
24   [JB], "Administration and the Karmel Report," 1973, M728: 13595099, JBPP-NAA. See also Bob Lingard, "Federalism in Schooling since the Karmel Report (1973), *Schools in Australia*," in *Schools in Australia: 1973–1998: The 25 years since the Karmel Report* (Sydney: ACER, 1998).
25   Schools Commission, *Information* (Canberra: Schools Commission, 1974).
26   Christopher Hayen, "The Problems of Distributing School Grants to States," *Canberra Times*, November 4, 1974.
27   McKinnon, "The Schools Commission."
28   McKinnon, K. "The Schools Commission." In *Federal Intervention in Australian Education*, edited by Grant Harman and Don Smart, 135–50. Melbourne: Georgian House, 1982.
29   JB, "The School in the Community," 1974, M733: 13557131, JBPP-NAA.
30   Australian Council for Educational Research. "*Schools in Australia*: 1973–1998." Sydney, 1998.
31   JB, "Providing More Equal Opportunity," 1974, M728: 13595099, JBPP-NAA.
32   Karmel, "Schools in Australia," 109.
33   [JB] to George Reid, 3 September 1974.
34   Central Advisory Council for Education (England). (1967). The Plowden Report. Retrieved July 17, 2016, from http://www.educationengland.org.uk/documents/plowden/plowden1967-1.html.
35   JB, [The Ideology].
36   JB, [The Ideology].
37   JB to SB, 16 August 1975.
38   JB to Peter Tannock, 3 December 1974, M727: 13555997, JBPP-NAA.

39 JB to John Keeves, 11 November 1975. M727: 13557769, JBPP-NAA.
40 JB, "Address to National Task Force Meeting: Melbourne, 29th November 1974," M732: 13598964, JBPP-NAA.
41 Pat Thomson, *Schooling the Rustbelt Kids* (Sydney: Allen & Unwin, 2002), 165.
42 JB. "Memo. Inclusion of non-systemic schools in Disadvantaged Schools Program," 1975, M727: 13555997, JBPP-NAA.
43 JB, "Providing More."
44 JB, "Schools Commission's Disadvantaged Program," 1974, JBPP-NAA.
45 JB, "Address to National Task Force.
46 Blackburn, interview by Biskup.
47 JB to Shirley Randell, 8 May 1978, M732: 13557110, JBPP-NAA.
48 JB to Pam Cahir (Memo), 2 November 1978, M727: 13556003, JBPP-NAA.
49 JB to R. P. McNamara, 17 August 1978, M727: 13555993, JBPP-NAA.
50 Lyndsay Connors, "Time for a Fair Go for Girls," *Canberra Times*, September 2, 1974.
51 Blackburn, interview by Biskup.
52 Peter Beilharz, Trevor Hogan, and Sheila Shaver, *The Martin Presence* (Sydney: UNSW Press, 2015); Jean I. Martin, "Sex Differences in Educational Qualifications," *Melbourne Studies in Education*, 1972 (1972).
53 Daniela Torsh, interview by Debra Hayes and Craig Campbell, August 30, 2016.
54 Blackburn, interview by Green.
55 Dany Torsh to Ken McKinnon, 12 February 1975, M597: 13743432, Ken McKinnon Personal Papers, NAA.
56 McKinnon, interview.
57 JB to SB, 20 July 1975.
58 See Connors, "Time for a Fair Go"; and Dany Humphreys and Ken Newcombe, eds., *Schools Out!* (Melbourne: Penguin Books, 1975).
59 Torsh, interview.
60 Torsh, interview.
61 JB to SB, 16 August 1975.
62 Blackburn, interview by Biskup.
63 McKinnon, interview.
64 McKinnon, interview.
65 Committee on Social Change and the Education of Women. "Girls, School and Society: Report by a Study Group to the Schools Commission." Canberra: Schools Commission, 1975.
66 "Girls, School and Society," 6.
67 JB to Pam Cahir (Memo), 2 November 1978.
68 Blackburn, interview by Ryan.
69 Lyndsay Connors and Jim McMorrow, interview by Craig Campbell and Debra Hayes, December 8, 2015.
70 Gaskell, Jane, and Sandra Taylor, "The Women's Movement in Canadian and Australian Education," *Gender and Education* 15, no. 2 (2003): 151–68; Beilharz, *Martin Presence*, 221.

71 "Girls, School and Society," 1.
72 "Girls, School and Society," 8.
73 "Girls, School and Society," 15.
74 "Girls, School and Society," 147.
75 Lyn Yates, interview by Craig Campbell, 27 November, 2014.
76 Denise Bradley, interview by Craig Campbell and Debra Hayes, October 9, 2015.
77 Beilharz, *The Martin Presence*.
78 "The Schools Commission and the Education of Girls," [1976], M727: 13557797, JBPP-NAA.
79 "Schools Commission and the Education of Girls."
80 "Schools Commission and the Education of Girls."
81 Susan Ryan, *Catching the Waves* (Sydney: Harper Collins, 1999), pp. 152–3.
82 JB to Barry Hill, 27 November 1975, M727: 13555997, JBPP-NAA.
83 JB to Dany Torsh, 6 September 1974, M597: 13743432, Ken McKinnon Personal Papers, NAA.
84 Randell, interview.
85 JB, "Some Ideas and Conclusions Arising out of Reflections in UK. Report," M728: 13595133, JBPP-NAA.

Chapter 8. Schools Commissioner: Fraser government years, 1976–1980

1   Don Novick, "Jean Blackburn: Schools Commission," in *Talking About School*, ed. Don Novick (Adelaide: Education Department of South Australia, 1980).
2   Jean Blackburn [JB] to Susan Blackburn [SB], 30 October 1975, in possession of SB. The co-author of this book was on this trip. Some of the details are recalled from Craig Campbell's travel diary.
3   Deirdre Jordan and Judith Redden, interview by Craig Campbell, December 1, 2015.
4   Jordan and Redden, interview.
5   [JB], "School and Community," 1976, M730: Item 13557016, Personal Papers of Jean Blackburn, National Archives of Australia [JBPP-NAA].
6   Dean Ashenden, interview by Craig Campbell and Debra Hayes, June 7, 2016.
7   JB to SB, 6 February 1976.
8   "Order of Australia: Australia Day Honours List 1976," Government House (Canberra, 1976).
9   JB to SB, 6 February 1976.
10 Dick Blackburn to SB, 1 February 1976, in possession of SB.
11 'Honour returned', *Canberra Times*, July 7, 1976, 8.
12 JB to John Kerr [Governor-General], 18 June 1976, M727: 16557769, JBPP-NAA.
13 JB, Memo, 24 November 1975, M727: 13555997, JBPP-NAA.
14 Ken McKinnon, interview by Craig Campbell and Debra Hayes, May 7, 2016.

Notes

15 P. J. McKeown to Senator Margaret Guilfoyle [Minister of Education], 20 November 1975, M735: 13599180, JBPP-NAA.
16 McKinnon, interview. See also Graeme Starr, *Carrick* (Ballan: Connor Court, 2012), 249.
17 Starr, *Carrick*, 247.
18 JB to SB, 20 February 1976.
19 Australia. Schools Commission, "Report: Rolling Triennium 1977–79," (Canberra, 1976).
20 JB, [Having Argued That the Existing Rationale …], 1977, M740: 13599821, JBPP-NAA.
21 JB to Joan Kirner, 24 September 1976, M727: 13555999, JBPP-NAA.
22 J. L. Carrick, "Guidelines for Education Commissions, 1979–81," 1978, M727: 13557760, JBPP-NAA.
23 JB, "Draft Statement on Guidelines for Chapter 2 of Report," 1977, M740: 13599805, JBPP-NAA.
24 Australian Teachers Federation, Response to 1980 federal government education guidelines, 22 May 1980, 1. In M272: 13557760, JBPP-NAA.
25 J. Jones to JB, 4 May 1978, and other material in M735: 13599178, JBPP-NAA.
26 JB to J. P. Keeves, 24 August 1977, M727: 13556001, JBPP-NAA.
27 JB to SB, c. 1978.
28 K. B. Jackson, "Discussion Paper: The Schools Commission Reports for the Triennium 1979–81: Basic Paper," *Current Issues Brief*, 2/1978.
29 Carrick, "Guidelines."
30 [JB], [The Future and the Schools Commission]," c. 1979, M728: 13557804, JBPP-NAA.
31 Race Matthews, "David Bennett," (Melbourne: Australian Fabian Society, [1985]), 40. See also Shirley Randell, interview by Craig Campbell and Debra Hayes, May 26, 2016. And Jean Blackburn, interview by Peter Biskup, September 27 & November 13, 1990.
32 Joan Kirner, "Personal Comment," *Australian Feminist Studies* 9, no. 19 (1994): 6.
33 Blackburn, interview by Biskup.
34 JB, "Reaction to Phase II Papers: Tanunda Conference on Education in the Eighties," c. 1979, M728: 13589071, JBPP-NAA.
35 JB to Ken McKinnon, 30 October 1979, M727: 13556005, JBPP-NAA. See also S. K. Randell, "The Disadvantaged Country Areas Program," in *Politics in Education* (Brisbane: Australian College of Education, 1980).
36 Randell, interview.
37 Extracts, JB address to NCIS conference on boarding, Canberra 7 May 1977, M731: 13557076, NAA JBPP.
38 JB to SB, 22 October 1969.
39 JB, "Future of Disadvantaged Schools Program," M740: 13599817, JBPP-NAA.
40 JB, "Where Do We Go from Here," 1979, M732: 13599069. See also JB, "[On Disadvantaged Schools Program]," in *National Conference on Disadvantage Program* (1976), M727: 13555999, JBPP-NAA.

41 Nancy Spence to Keiran Batt, [Received] 6 October 1978, M732: 13557104, JBPP-NAA.
42 JB, "Assessing the Needs – in City and Country," *School Bell* (November, 1976): 2ff.
43 [JB], "Educational Disadvantage," 1976, M727: 13555999, JBPP-NAA.
44 JB, "Basic Skills and the Disadvantaged Schools Program," in *Disadvantaged Schools Program*, ed. D. Waters and J. Blackburn (Canberra: Schools Commission, 1978); Don Waters, "Basic Skills and the Disadvantaged Schools Program," in *Disadvantaged Schools Program*. For quotation from Jean, p. 11.
45 JB to S. Randell & Chairman (K. McKinnon)," 1977, M732: 13598971, JBPP-NAA.
46 JB to Mike Douse, 22 March 1977, M727: 13556001, JBPP-NAA. Jean contributed to a committee seeking to establish an 'index of disadvantage' that the Commission might use.
47 JB to Ronald Goldman, 7 September 1977, M727: 13556001, JBPP-NAA.
48 Shirley Randell, "Rough Notes on Visit to Adelaide, 8, 9 April 1979," M732: 13599028, JBPP-NAA.
49 JB, "Visit: Lalor High School, Victoria, 19 July 1979," M737/0: 13599512, JBPP-NAA.
50 JB, "Karmel Revisited," [1982], JB Private papers, in possession of SB.
51 "Policy Planning and Evaluation," 1986, JB Private papers.
52 JB, "Policy Ideas in the Disadvantaged Schools Program," ed. Commonwealth Department of Employment Education and Training, 1989), 20.
53 Lyndsay Connors, "'Schools in Australia': A Hard Act to Follow," *Australian Educational Researcher* 27, no. 1 (2000): 8.
54 R. W Connell, *Schools and Social Justice* (Philadelphia: Temple University Press, 1993), 104.
55 Connell, *Schools*, 106. See also R. W. Connell, V. M. White, and K. M. Johnston, eds., *'Running Twice as Hard': The Disadvantaged Schools Program in Australia* (Melbourne: Deakin University, 1991).
56 JB to Ken McKinnon, 18 May 1976, M727: 13555999, JBPP-NAA.
57 Jim Walker to JB, 31 May 1978, JB Private papers.
58 JB to Kay Schofield, [1978/1979], M732: 13598938, JBPP-NAA.
59 For example, Brian Abbey and Dean Ashenden, "Society and Experience with Particular Reference to Class and Education [rough draft]," 1976, M728: 13556009, JBPP-NAA.
60 JB to Peter Karmel, 2 April 1976, Karmel Papers, C Box 1, National Library of Australia.
61 JB to S.S. Dunn, 9 July 1976, M727: 13555999, JBPP-NAA.
62 R. W. Connell and D. Ashenden, "[Application for Research Grant]," 1976, M737: 13557757, JBPP-NAA. Also, JB to Dean Ashenden, 19 August 1976, M727: 13555999; R. W. Connell et al., *Making the Difference: Schools, Families and Social Division* (Sydney: George Allen & Unwin, 1982).

63 P. J. Fensham to JB, 26 February 1980," [no doc. number], JBPP-NAA.
64 JB to Kay Schofield, 14 December 1979, M727: 13556005, JBPP-NAA.
65 JB, "Notes for Suggested Expanded Outline of National Assessment Report," 1977, M727: 13557755, JBPP-NAA.
66 [JB], "A Positive Statement," 1978, M728: 13557822, JBPP-NAA.
67 K. R. Gilding to JB, 9 February 1977, with Jean's speech attached, M728: 13595089, JBPP-NAA.
68 Blackburn, interview by Biskup.
69 JB to SB, 28 January 1979.
70 JB, "OECD/CERI Project: Funding Provisions for Special Populations," 1979, 1. In M738: 13599612, JBPP-NAA.
71 JB to Alice Day, 14 January 1980, M727: 13556007, JBPP-NAA.
72 JB, "[Notes on US Trip]," 1979, M732: 13599082, JBPP-NAA.
73 JB to Jennifer Presley (Stanford University), 26 March 1979, M727: 13556005, JBPP-NAA.
74 JB, "[Macquarie DSP Speech]," 1979, M732: 13599012, JBPP-NAA.
75 "Jean Blackburn: Tentative Schedule," 1979, M732: 13599082; "Schedule for Ms Jean Blackburn," 1979, M738: 13599614, JBPP-NAA.
76 JB to Jennifer Presley, 22 January 1980, M727: 13556007, JBPP-NAA.
77 JB, "California School Improvement Program," in [Notes on Us Trip]."
78 'US Australia Education Policy Project – Visit 1979,' M732: 13599082, JBPP-NAA; McKinnon, interview.
79 [Macquarie DSP Speech].
80 JB, "Title 1 and the Disadvantaged Schools Program," (Australia-US Education Policy Project, 1979); JB, "Title 1 and the Australian Disadvantaged Schools Program," in *Contemporary Issues in Educational Policy*, ed. G. Hancock, M. W. Kirst, and D. L. Grossman (Canberra: Curriculum Development Centre, 1983).
81 For example, "Commission Meting February 15 and 16," 1978, M740: 13599833, JBPP-NAA.
82 JB to Chairman, Dr Hancock and Mr Bennett, 6 July 1977, M727: 13556001, JBPP-NAA.
83 McKinnon, interview.
84 JB, Visit: St James Christian Brothers College, Queensland', 1980, M737: 13599524, JBPP-NAA.
85 [JB], "The School and Its Principles," c. 1973, M728: 13589551; JB to Tony Delves, 13 November 1979, M727: 13556005, JBPP-NAA.
86 JB, "Unley High School: 19 June 1979," M737: 13599528, JBPP-NAA.
87 "Visit: Henley High School, South Australia, 25 June1979," M737: 13599508, JBPP-NAA.
88 "Visit: Port Adelaide High School, South Australia," 1979, M737: 13599520, JBPP-NAA.
89 "Generalisations from School Visits," 1980, M727: 13556007, JBPP-NAA.
90 Blackburn, interview Biskup.

91 JB to R. P. McNamara, 17 August 1978, M727: 13556003. See also 'Preliminary meeting 8 December 1978 – Students from Non-English Speaking Background'. Draft minutes of meeting, 1978, M729: 13560394, JBPP-NAA.
92 Draft letter, JB to David [Bennett], nd., M730: 13598820, JBPP-NAA.
93 "School and Community."
94 John P. Keeves, "New Perspectives in Teaching and Learning," in *Australian Education*, ed. John P. Keeves (Sydney: Allen & Unwin, 1987), 152.
95 JB, "Committee of Enquiry into Specific Learning Difficulties: Suggested Skeleton Outline of Submission. 3 May 1976," M727: 13555999. See also, JB to Betty Watts, 15 February 1979, M727: 13556005, JBPP-NAA.
96 "Comments on Cameron Paper on Giftedness. 4 November 1974," M730: 13557010, JBPP-NAA. JB to SB, 7 August [1980].
97 Blackburn, interview by Biskup. This narrative contrasts with the probable character of Jean's earlier involvement with Aboriginal groups in the 1960s. See chapter 3.
98 For a comparative history of this, see Jane Gaskell, "The Women's Movement in Canadian and Australian Education," *Gender and Education* 15, no. 2 (2003).
99 JB, "Notes for Monash Lecture," [1976], M727: 13557769, JBPP-NAA.
100 JB to J.G. Scott, 26 July 1977, M727: 13556001, JBPP-NAA.
101 JB, 'Memo to Pam Cahill, Millicent Poole Manuscript', 2 November 1978, M727: 13556003, JBPP-NAA.
102 JB, "Address to AWEC Conference, Adelaide," 1979, M597: 13754468, Ken McKinnon Personal Papers, NAA.
103 Jean Blackburn, interview by Tony Ryan, May 12 & 19, 1994.
104 Daniela Torsh, interview by Debra Hayes and Craig Campbell, August 30, 2016.
105 JB to SB, 1 March 1980. See also W. X. Simmons to K. McKinnon, 27 November 1979, M597: 13754467, Ken McKinnon Personal Papers, NAA; Alice T. Day to K. R. McKinnon, 16 November 1980, M597: 13754467, Ken McKinnon Personal Papers, NAA).
106 JB, [Women's Paid Employment], 1978, M727: 13557753; JB to the editor, 11 January 1978, M727: 13557753, JBPP-NAA.
107 JB to SB, 20 October 1979.
108 JB to SB, 1 March 1980.
109 JB to SB, 28 January 1979.
110 Denise Bradley, interview by Craig Campbell and Debra Hayes, October 9, 2015. See also Denise Bradley, "Education and the Women's Movement in Australia," in *Politics in education* (Brisbane: Australian College of Education, 1980).
111 Blackburn, interview by Biskup.
112 Helen Palmer, "Elitism in Education and the Radical Initiative," in *Helen Palmer's Outlook*, ed. Doreen Bridges (Sydney: Helen Palmer Memorial Committee, 1982 [1978]).
113 Susan Blackburn, interview by Craig Campbell, May 22, 2014.
114 Ashenden, interview.

115 JB to SB, 19 August 1979.
116 JB to SB, 20 October 1979.
117 'Evatt Memorial Foundation', 1980, M728: 13570512, JBPP-NAA.
118 See Minutes, Eighteenth Annual Conference 1977, ACE, M728: 13556043, JBPP-NAA; see also Margaret Bearlin, interview by Craig Campbell and Debra Hayes, July 20, 2015.
119 JB to SB, 17 February 1980.
120 JB, "Work Program 1978," M727: 13557791, JBPP-NAA.
121 "Parents Cannot Ensure Jobs," *Canberra Times*, 17 October 1978. Original speech: [ACSSO Annual Conference Address 1978], M728: 13556015, JBPP-NAA.
122 JB to the Chairman (Schools Commission), 19 November 1979, M727: 13556005, JBPP-NAA.
123 Craig Campbell and Geoffrey Sherington, *The Comprehensive Public High School* (New York: Palgrave Macmillan, 2013 [2006]).
124 Schools Commission [SC], "Schooling for 15 and 16 Year-Olds," (Canberra: Schools Commission, 1980), iii.
125 "15–16 Year Old Project," 1979, M737: 13599427. JBPP-NAA.
126 SC, "Schooling for 15 and 16," 62.
127 SC, "Schooling for 15 and 16," 3.
128 SC, "Schooling for 15 and 16," 12.
129 SC, "Schooling for 15 and 16," 13.
130 SC, "Schooling for 15 and 16," 15.
131 SC, "Schooling for 15 and 16," 16.
132 SC, "Schooling for 15 and 16," 31.
133 Some key ideas in the report occur in JB, "15–16 Year Old Study: Some Random Ravings," c. 1980, M737: 13599437, JBPP-NAA.
134 For example, JB, Memo, 8 November 1979, M732: 13599455, JBPP-NAA.
J135 B, "Upper Secondary School Proposal SA/ACT," 1983, JB Private papers. See also JB to Keren Bissett and Alice Day, 8 July 1980, M727: 13556007, JBPP-NAA.
136 JB to SB, 5 February [1978].
137 JB to SB, 19 August 1979.
138 JB to SB, 8 February 1980.
139 Colin Thorpe to JB, 15 July 1980, JB Private papers.
140 J. R. Giles to JB, 10 June 1980, JB Private papers.
141 Blackburn, interview by Biskup.
142 Blackburn, interview by Biskup.
143 K. R. McKinnon to JB, 28 April 1980, M727: 13557769, JBPP-NAA.
144 McKinnon, interview.
145 Richard Scherer, "Head of Schools Body Not Being Reappointed," *Canberra Times*, 4 December 1980, 8.
146 JB, "Has the Schools Commission a Future?" [1983], JB Private papers.
147 Lyndsay Connors and Jim McMorrow, interview by Craig Campbell and Debra Hayes, December 8, 2015.

Chapter 9. Curriculum theorist and educational activist, 1981–1989

1. Andrew Stephens, "Battle Lines Don't Stop a Crusader," *The Sun*, 9 August 1985.
2. Dean Ashenden, interview by Craig Campbell and Debra Hayes, June 7, 2016.
3. Grant Harman, "The Razor Gang Moves, the 1981 Guidelines and the Uncertain Future," in *Federal Intervention in Australian Education*, ed. Grant Harman and Don Smart (Melbourne: Georgian House, 1982).
4. Jean Blackburn, interview by Peter Biskup, September 27 & November 13, 1990.
5. Jean Blackburn [JB], [Research as Honorary Research Fellow], 1981, Personnel files: Jean Blackburn, University of Adelaide Archives.
6. Margaret Allen, "Remembering Jean Blackburn AO 1919–2001," *Australian Feminist Studies* 17, no. 39 (2002): 256.
7. Alison Mackinnon, interview by Craig Campbell, February 17, 2016.
8. Marilyn Lake, *Getting Equal* (Sydney: Allen & Unwin, 1999), 250–252.
9. Mackinnon, interview.
10. J. H. Bowie and and others, "Submission to the Executive Committee from the Working Party on 'Women at the University of Adelaide'," 1981, Papers of E. H. Medlin, Ser. 631: 198, University of Adelaide Archives. See also "[Papers]," Ser. 1474: 1, Research Centre for Women's Studies Papers, 1981–2010, University of Adelaide Archives.
11. Susan Magarey, *Dangerous Ideas* (Adelaide: University of Adelaide Press, 2014), 196. See also Jean Blackburn, interview by Allison Murchie, March 26, 1994.
12. Denise Bradley, interview by Craig Campbell and Debra Hayes, October 9, 2015.
13. See discussion in Jane Kenway et al., "Making 'Hope Practical' Rather Than 'Despair Convincing': Feminist Post-Structuralism, Gender Reform and Educational Change," *British Journal of Sociology of Education* 15, no. 2 (1994).
14. Susan Magarey, interview by Craig Campbell, November 30, 2015.
15. Susan Magarey to Registrar (University of Adelaide), 23 November 1987. Personnel files: Jean Blackburn, University of Adelaide Archives.
16. Susan Magarey, *Unbridling the Tongues of Women* (Sydney: Hale & Iremonger, 1985). JB, "Launching CHS (Catherine Helen Spence)," 1985, JB Private papers, in possession of Susan Blackburn [SB].
17. Allen, "Remembering Jean Blackburn." See also Mackinnon, interview.
18. Margaret Allen, interview by Craig Campbell, February 16, 2016. The publications: Margaret Allen et al., eds., *All Her Labours*, vol. 1: *Working It Out*, vol. 2: *Embroidering the Framework*. (Sydney: Hale & Iremonger, 1984).
19. Bradley, interview.
20. Deirdre Jordan and Judith Redden, interview by Craig Campbell, December 1, 2015.
21. K. R. Gilding et al., "Teacher Education in South Australia: Proposals for Action," (1980).

22 JB to SB, 24 February 1980, in possession of SB.
23 TEASA Advisory Committee on Post-Secondary Education of Women and Girls, "'Moving Women In': Synopsis of Report from Kay Iseman," 1982, Ser. 1245, Tertiary Education Authority of South Australia Advisory Committee on Post-Secondary Education of Women & Girls, University of Adelaide Archives.
24 Committee of Enquiry into Education in South Australia [Chair: J. P. Keeves], "Education and Change in South Australia: Final Report," (Adelaide: Education Department, 1982).
25 JB, "Background Comment on the Keeves Report: Education and Social Change in South Australia," 1982, JB Private papers.
26 JB, "Curriculum and Public Purposes," in *Who owns the curriculum?*, ed. Craig Campbell (Adelaide: SA Institute of Teachers, 1982), 13.
27 Peggy Mares and Effie Best, interview by Craig Campbell, February 15, 2016.
28 TEASA Advisory Committee on Post-Secondary Education of Women and Girls, "Participation of Women in Senior Administration and Teaching in the Post-Secondary Institutions," 1981, Ser. 1245, Tertiary Education Authority of South Australia [TEASA] Advisory Committee on Post-Secondary Education of Women & Girls, University of Adelaide Archives.
29 JB, "Productive and Excellent Women," *Australian Feminist Studies* 1, no. 3 (1986).
30 K. R. Gilding to JB, 29 October 1982, JB Private papers.
31 R. DeBats et al., *Pathways from School to Society* (Adelaide: Tertiary Education Authority (South Australia), 1981), 233.
32 JB to Roger Wiseman, 11 January 1980, M727: 13556007, JB Personal Papers, National Archives of Australia [JBPP-NAA].
33 "Feminist to Address Women's Conference," *Canberra Times*, September 30, 1981.
34 Stephen Payne, "Schools 'Less Than Helpful'," *Canberra Times*, October 4, 1981.
35 JB, "Address to AWEC Conference, Canberra, October 1981," 1981, JB Private papers.
36 Bradley, interview; Lyndsay Connors and Jim McMorrow, interview by Craig Campbell and Debra Hayes, December 8, 2015.
37 JB to SB, 7 August [1980].
38 JB to SB, 17 January [1982].
39 JB to SB, 24 February [1980].
40 Lezek Kolakowski, *Main Currents of Marxism* (Oxford: Clarendon Press, 1978 [1976]).
41 JB to SB, 17 January 1982.
42 Bradley, interview.
43 JB to SB, 8 February [1980].
44 Hugh Blackburn, interview by Craig Campbell and Debra Hayes, June 8, 2016.
45 Jordan and Redden, interview.

46 JB to SB, 7 August [1980].
47 SB to Craig Campbell (email), 10 August 2016.
48 Muir, Les Thomas and Pryor, Janet, interview by Craig Campbell and Debra Hayes, April 15, 2015.
49 JB to SB, 10 April 1988.
50 JB to SB, 4 May 1988.
51 SB to Craig Campbell (email), 10 August 2016.
52 Mares and Best, interview. Also, Margaret Bearlin, interview by Craig Campbell and Debra Hayes, July 20, 2015.
53 Bradley, interview.
54 Bradley, interview.
55 On the Victorian Labor governments of this period and their educational work, Andrew Spaull, "Schools Policy," in *Trials in Power*, ed. Mark Considine and Brian Costar (Melbourne: Melbourne University Press, 1992).
56 Helen Praetz, interview by Craig Campbell, July 21, 2016.
57 Jean Blackburn, interview by Wendy Lowenstein, July 1, 1994. Also, Praetz, interview.
58 This set of reasons for the enquiry is based on JB, "Seminar, WSRC, April 10th 1987," JB Private papers.
59 For example, [JB], "[Report on School Visits]," c. 1979, M737: 13599427, JBPP-NAA.
60 "[Victorian Certificate of Education]," *Age*, March 7, 1995.
61 Hedley Beare, "Standing the Test of Time," *Age*, January 30, 2002.
62 W. F. Connell, *Reshaping Australian Education 1960–1985* (Melbourne: ACER, 1993); Hedley Beare, "From 'Educational Administration' to 'Efficient Management'," in *American Educational Research Association* (San Francisco: 1989).
63 JB to P. Barcham, 13 November 1979, M727: 13556005, JBPP-NAA.
64 Blackburn, interview by Lowenstein; Jean Blackburn, interview by Tony Ryan, May 12 & 19, 1994.
65 Blackburn, interview by Biskup.
66 Connors and McMorrow, interview.
67 Bradley, interview.
68 Victoria. Education Department, "Ministerial Papers, 1–6: Issued By the Minister of Education for Public Information and Discussion," (Melbourne 1985). (Updated version.)
69 JB, "Seminar, WSRC." Also, Praetz, interview.
70 Blackburn, interview by Murchie, March.
71 Praetz, interview.
72 Blackburn, interview by Biskup.
73 Praetz, interview. See also Ken McKinnon, interview by Craig Campbell and Debra Hayes, May 7, 2016.
74 JB (chair), "Discussion Paper: Ministerial Review of Postcompulsory Schooling," (Melbourne 1984).

75 "Victoria Planning 'Radical' Changes in High Schools," *Canberra Times*, April 17, 1984.
76 Blackburn, "Seminar, WSRC."
77 Praetz, interview.
78 Blackburn, interview by Biskup.
79 Blackburn, interview by Ryan.
80 Praetz, interview.
81 JB, "Occasional Address, La Trobe Graduation," 1988, JB Private papers; "Seminar, WSRC."
82 Praetz, interview.
83 Jan Bassett, *'Matters of Conscience': A History of the Victorian Secondary Teachers Association* (Melbourne: PenFolk, 1995), 164–165.
84 Bill Hannan and Lorna Hannan, interview by Craig Campbell and Debra Hayes, June 9, 2016.
85 JB, "Ministerial Review of Postcompulsory Schooling: Report," (Melbourne: 1985); "Education Minister Releases Blackburn Report," 1985, JB Private papers.
86 Blackburn, interview by Ryan.
87 Susan Blackburn, interview by Craig Campbell, May 22, 2014.
88 See Colleen Farrell, "Responses to Blackburn Report," *Select Reading Lists* (Melbourne: Education Department of Victoria Library Service, 1985).
89 Praetz, interview.
90 Ian Cathie, "Memorandum Re Blackburn Report," 1985, VPRS8536P000315: 6341_74(1), Victorian Public Records.
91 Blackburn, interview by Lowenstein.
92 *VSTA News* 8, no. 9 (May 1, 1985). See also Bassett, *'Matters'*, 164–167.
93 Jack Keating, ed. *Post-Compulsory Schooling in Victoria: A VSTA Position* (Melbourne: Victorian Secondary Teachers Association, 1985).
94 Hannan and Hannan, interview.
95 Peter Karmel, "Summation," in *Education, Change and Society*, ed. Peter Karmel (Melbourne: ACER, 1981); JB, "Changing Educational Emphases for the 1980s," in *Education, Change and Society*, 93–96.
96 *The Tech Teacher* 4, no. 22 (August 21, 1985): 6.
97 Fazal Rizvi, interview by Craig Campbell, December 2, 2014; also, Praetz, interview.
98 Gwyneth Dow, "The Place of History in the Blackburn Report," in *History and the Blackburn Report*, ed. Gwyneth Dow and Stephen Duggan (Melbourne: The History Institute, 1985).
99 Hannan and Hannan, interview.
100 Lyn Yates, interview by Craig Campbell, November 27, 2014.
101 Praetz, interview.
102 Blackburn, interview by Ryan.
103 Yates, interview. See also Luke Slattery, "A Tide That Turned against the VCE," *Age*, October 27, 1992.
104 Spaull, "Schools Policy".

105　Geoff Maslen, "Blackburn Report Proves Prescient," *Age*, May 28, 1991.
106　Blackburn, interview by Biskup.
107　JB, *Changing Approaches to Equality in Education*, John Curtin Memorial Lecture (Canberra: Research School of Social Sciences, Australian National University, 1986).
108　*ACE News* 7, no. 4 (November 1988): 1.
109　Dean Ashenden, "Jean Blackburn," 1988, JB Private papers.
110　JB, "Address by Jean Blackburn, 1988 College Medallist," *ACE News* 7, no. 4 (November 1988): 8.
111　JB to SB, 4 May 1988. On the South Australian job, Bradley, interview.
112　JB, "Girls Earning and Learning in the 1980s," JB Private papers; R. W. Connell et al., *Making the Difference* (Sydney: George Allen & Unwin, 1982).
113　Ashenden, interview.
114　R. W. Connell, *Teachers' Work* (Sydney: George Allen & Unwin, 1985).
115　JB, "Notes for La Trobe Discussion on the Importance of Curricular Content," [1982], JB Private papers.
116　Ashenden, interview; Hannan and Hannan, interview.
117　Dean Ashenden et al., "Manifesto for a Democratic Curriculum," *The Australian Teacher* (February 1984).
118　Brian Crittenden, "Worthwhile with Some Difficulties," 21–22, and Ann Junor, "Lacking a Sense of Urgency," 22–23, *The Australian Teacher*, no. 8 (1984).
119　JB, "Schooling and Public Purposes: Commonality and Difference," c. 1988, JB Private papers.
120　Karen Hobson, "Curriculum Debate 'More Political'," *Canberra Times*, July 9, 1989.
121　Kerry J. Kennedy, "Constructing a National Voice for the School Curriculum," in *Schools in Australia: 1973–1998: The 25 years since the Karmel Report* (Sydney: ACER, 1998). See also the earlier Peter W. Musgrave, "Curricular Research and Development," in *Australian Education*, ed. John P. Keeves (Sydney: Allen & Unwin, 1987).
122　For example, JB, [Proposal Work Technology Society Course], c. 1981, JB Private papers.
123　JB, *The Study of Work in Society: A Curriculum Proposal*, CDC Monograph (Canberra: Curriculum Development Centre, 1987), 3.
124　JB, *Study of Work*, 17.
125　JB, "Has the Schools Commission a Future?" c. 1983, JB Private papers.
126　JB, "From Positive to Negative Discrimination in Education," 1982, JB Private papers.
127　JB, "Policy Response to the Case Studies," in *Alienation from Schooling*, ed. Peter Fensham (London: Routledge & Kegan Paul, 1986), 284–288.
128　JB, "Policy Planning and Evaluation," 1986, JB Private papers.
129　JB, [I Find It Difficult …]," in *Societal Change and Its Impact on Education: Presentations to the WAIER Seminar 1980*, ed. B. Haynes (Perth: Western Australian College of Advanced Education, 1983), 10–20. See also "Arts Graduates as a Major Social Resource," *Lumen* 20, no. 7 (1991).

130 Ashenden, interview.
131 Susan Ryan, *Catching the Waves* (Sydney: Harper Collins, 1999). pp. 222–224.
132 JB, "Curriculum Is Public Business," 1998, JB Private papers. See also Michael Pusey, *Economic Rationalism in Canberra* (Cambridge: Cambridge University Press, 1991).
133 JB, "The Public in Education," in *What Should Government Do?* ed. Peter Coaldrake and J. R. Nethercote (Sydney: Hale & Iremonger, 1989).
134 Brian Hill, "[I'll Come Out …]," in *Societal Change*, ed. Haynes.
135 Joan Kirner, "Personal Comment," *Australian Feminist Studies* 9, no. 19 (1994): 6.
136 Denise Bradley, "Grasping the Opportunities," in *Women and Leadership in Open and Distance Learning and Development*, ed. Asha Kanwar, Frances Ferreira, and Colin Latchern (Vancouver: Commonwealth of Learning, 2013).
137 See reference for Bradley in JB Private papers; Julie Marcus to SB, 12 December 2001, JB Private Papers; Allen, interview; Yates, interview.
138 Praetz, interview.
139 McKinnon, interview.
140 Mares and Best, interview.
141 Dick Blackburn to SB, 16 October 1986. In possession of SB.
142 Ailsa Zainu'ddin to SB, 12 December 2001; Connors and McMorrow, interview.
143 Ashenden, interview.

Chapter 10. Feminist matriarch, 1990–2001

1 Lyndsay Connors in Lyndsay Connors and Jim McMorrow, interview by Craig Campbell and Debra Hayes, December 8, 2015.
2 Denise Bradley, interview by Craig Campbell and Debra Hayes, October 9, 2015.
3 Birthdays, *Canberra Times*, April 7, 1990, 28.
4 Muir, Les Thomas and Pryor, Janet, interview by Craig Campbell and Debra Hayes, April 15, 2015.
5 Margaret Allen, interview by Craig Campbell, February 16, 2016; Celia Frank and Kirsten Marks, *Celebration! The International Women's Day Committee of South Australia* (Adelaide: International Women's Day Committee (SA), 1995).
6 JB, [Notes Towards Planning a Memoir], c. 2000, JB Private papers, in possession of SB [SB]; Judy Gill to JB, 1 May 2001. In possession of SB.
7 [Autobiographical Fragments 2], c. 1995, JB Private papers; Janet McCalman, *Struggletown* (Melbourne: Melbourne University Press, 1984).
8 "[Notes Towards Planning a Memoir]," Judith Gill to Debra Hayes (email), 10 November 2017.
9 Lyndsay Connors to JB, 14 August 2000.
10 JB, "Memoirs: Alternative Approaches," 1999; "Alternatives," nd., JB Private papers; Judith Gill to Debra Hayes (email), 10 November 2017.

11 [Autobiographical Fragments 2].
12 Dean Ashenden, interview by Craig Campbell and Debra Hayes, June 7, 2016.
13 Roger Scott to Craig Campbell (email), 14 December 1990.
14 Jean Blackburn, interview by Peter Biskup, September 27 & November 13, 1990.
15 *Australian*, 25 April 1990, 13.
16 "No Head yet for New Uni," *Canberra Times*, February 16, 1990; Karen Hobson, "Canberra University Gets First Chancellor," *Canberra Times*, March 1; Justine Ferrari, "Canberra's Chancellor Appointed Despite Council Row," *Australian*, March 7, 1990.
17 *Canberra Times*, September 19, 1990.
18 Don Aitkin, interview by Craig Campbell, December 13, 2016.
19 *Canberra Times*, November 15, 1990.
20 JB, "April 19th Speech," 1990, JB Private papers. See also *Canberra Times*, April 20, 3.
21 Connors and McMorrow, interview.
22 University of Canberra. Minutes of the Council. 1990–1991. Accessed 3 January 2017, http://www.canberra.edu.au/about-uc/governance/council/proceedings.
23 Mandle was interviewed by Peter Biskup for the Australian National Library. The interview had not been released in time for this study. The summary of interview includes a statement that there was 'lack of support from Jean Blackburn, the University Chancellor'. See also Jodie Brough, "Canberra Uni '$2m in Debt'," *Canberra Times*, October 3, 1990.
24 *Canberra Times*, October 4, 1990.
25 Graham Eadie, interview by Craig Campbell, December 13, 2016; Alison Mackinnon, interview by Craig Campbell, February 17, 2016; Aitkin, interview; Margaret Bearlin, interview by Craig Campbell and Debra Hayes, July 20, 2015.
26 SB to Craig Campbell (email), 11 January 2017.
27 University of Canberra. Minutes of Council. Meeting no. 16, 13 November 1991.
28 Geoff Maslen, "Education Voice Goes by the Board," *Age*, February 25, 1991, 13.
29 Maslen, "Education".
30 Mary Ryan, *Beyond the Glass Ceiling* (Melbourne: Collins Dove, 1993), 87.
31 Luke Slattery, "Australian Studies Will Be Optional in VCE Next Year," *Age*, December 12, 1991.
32 "A Tide That Turned against the VCE," *Age*, October 27, 1992.
33 Max Tomkins to JB, 12 December 1991.
34 Jayne Taylor, "[Notes]," 1992, Women's Suffrage Centenary South Australia, State Records of South Australia.
35 JB to John Bannon (Premier), 11 April 1992; "[Papers]," GRS 1684/115: 1189, State Records of South Australia.

36 Loine Sweeney to Craig Campbell (email), 20 February 2018. In possession of Craig Campbell.
37 Mary Beasley, interview by Allison Murchie, February 14, 1994.
38 Susan Magarey, interview by Craig Campbell, November 30, 2015.
39 Sweeney to Campbell, 20 February 2018.
40 Sweeney to Campbell, 20 February 2018.
41 Sweeney to Campbell, 20 February 2018.
42 JB, "Minerva Group," 1993, JB Private papers. See also "Celebrating the Suffrage Centenary," 1996, JB Private papers.
43 Deirdre Jordan and Judith Redden, interview by Craig Campbell, December 1, 2015.
44 JB, "Suffrage," 1992–1993, JB Private papers.
45 Sweeney to Campbell, 20 February 2018.
46 Jean Blackburn, interview by Wendy Lowenstein, July 1, 1994.
47 Susan Magarey to Dean Brown, 4 January 1994, GRS 1684/115: 1189, State Records of South Australia.
48 Deborah Tideman, "Discord Mars Suffrage Centenary," *Australian*, January 3, 1994.
49 Press clipping, 1994, JB Private papers. (Newspaper unidentified).
50 Anne Levy, [Sacking of Jean Blackburn], February 22, 1994, in *Parliamentary Debates: Legislative Council* (Adelaide: Parliament of South Australia).
51 Sweeney to Campbell, 20 February 2018.
52 [Papers]; Minutes of Steering Committee no. 18, 3 February 1994, GRS 1684/115, State Records of South Australia.
53 JB and others, "[Transcript of Speeches for Launch of Barbara Hanrahan Memorial Exhibition," in *Oral history collection* (State Library of South Australia, 1994). Also, Jean Blackburn, interview by Kirsten Marks, December 13, 1993; Jean Blackburn, interview by Allison Murchie, March 26, 1994.
54 JB to SB [SB], 31 May 1994; Flinders University, [Program] Tree planting ceremony, 29 May 1994, JB Private papers.
55 Beasley, interview.
56 Hugh Blackburn, interview by Craig Campbell and Debra Hayes, June 8, 2016.
57 Portraits reproduced in Penelope Curtin, ed. *Robert Hannaford: Book and Exhibition by Sally Foster* (Adelaide: Art Gallery of South Australia, 2016).
58 Ashenden, interview.
59 Bill Hannan and Lorna Hannan, interview by Craig Campbell and Debra Hayes, June 9, 2016.
60 Denise Bradley, [Citation for Jean Blackburn], 1993, JB Private papers.
61 JB, "SACAE Graduation Address 9/7/90," 1990. See also "Graduation Address, Victoria University of Technology, May 7th, 1991," JB Private papers.
62 "Deakin Speech, May 11 1990," JB Private papers.
63 "Skills and Content in General Education," *Unicorn* 22, no. 2 (1996).

64 See Susan Ryan, *Catching the Waves* (Sydney: Harper Collins, 1999), 220–237, for an account of 1980s and 1990s in federal education politics.
65 Craig Campbell, Helen Proctor, and Geoffrey Sherington, *School Choice* (Sydney: Allen & Unwin, 2009). Among other authors Jean was reading Giroux and Henig on the rise of school choice policy. JB, "Giroux, Henry A.," c. 1995, JB Private papers.
66 [Major Issue], c. 1997, JB Private papers. See also JB, "Funding Australia's Schools," 1996, JB Private papers.
67 JB and Helen Praetz, "Divided Schooling in a Federal Context," c. 1996, JB Private papers.
68 JB, "A Lesson in School Funding," *The Australian*, July 16, 1996.
69 Ann Morrow, Jean Blackburn, and Judy Gill, "Public Education," in *Going Public: Education Policy and Public Education in Australia*, ed. Alan Reid (Canberra: Australian Curiculum Studies Association, 1998).
70 JB, "Fax to Prof Helen Praetz," 1996, JB Private papers. See also JB, "Public and Private Provision in a Federal Political System," c. 1996, JB Private Papers.
71 "[Possible Reply to Lyndsay Connors]," c. 2000, JB Private papers.
72 Lyndsay Connors to JB, 14 August 2000.
73 Hugh Blackburn, interview.
74 JB to [blank], 15 October 1997. (Form letter.)
75 Mackinnon, interview.
76 JB, "Condensed Biography," c. 2000, in possession of Hugh Blackburn.
77 Alison Mackinnon, *Love and Freedom*, Cambridge University Press, Cambridge, 1997.
78 Anthony Giddens, *The transformation of Intimacy*, Polity Press, Cambridge, 1992.
79 Mackinnon, interview.
80 JB, "Politics of Aged Care," 1990, JB Private papers.
81 "Condensed Biography."
82 JB, "Income Tax Book," 1981–2000, JB Private papers.
83 Hugh Blackburn, interview; Gerard Blackburn, *Pioneering Irrigation in Australia to 1920* (Melbourne: Australian Scholarly Publishing, 1999).
84 JB to SB, 1 September 1995.
85 JB, "Condensed Biography."
86 JB to SB, 13 August 1995.
87 JB, "Income Tax Book."
88 SB, [Personal diary 1963–2001], entry January 9, 1997, in possession of SB.
89 Hugh Blackburn, interview.
90 Dick Blackburn to SB, 19 August 1990.
91 JB, 1999, [Notes for Dick's Funeral], JB Private papers.
92 S. Blackburn, [Personal diary]. See also Judith Gill to Debra Hayes (email), 12 November 2017.
93 JB to Ted Jackson, 30 September 1999. See also SB to Craig Campbell (email), 25 May 2014.
94 SB to Craig Campbell (email), 25 May 2014.

95   JB, [Last Will], 2000, JB Private papers.
96   S. Blackburn, [Personal diary].
97   Bradley, interview.
98   JB, "Condensed Biography."
99   Jordan, and Redden, interview; Judith Gill to Debra Hayes (email), 12 November 2017.
100   Margaret Allen, "Remembering Jean Blackburn AO 1919–2001," *Australian Feminist Studies* 17, no. 39 (2002): 255; Judith Gill to SB, 8 December 2001.
101   Muir and Pryor, interview.
102   SB to Craig Campbell (email), 11 January 2017.
103   Dean Ashenden, "Jean Blackburn (nee Muir)," 2001, in possession of SB.
104   Susan Blackburn, "Notes for Talk at Jean Muir Celebration," 2001, in possession of SB.
105   Denise Bradley, "Jean Blackburn," 2001, in possession of Denise Bradley.
106   Dean Ashenden, "Educationalist Shaped Nation's Minds," *The Australian*, December 12, 2001; Bill Hannan, "Passionate for Schools Equity," *Canberra Times*, December 14, 2001; Hannan, "Jean Edna Blackburn: Shaper of Australia's School System," *Age*, December 14, 2001; Ken McKinnon, "Honestly First Class," *Australian*, December 12, 2001; Miles Kemp, "School System Reformer," *Advertiser*, December 15, 2001; Allen, "Remembering Jean Blackburn."
107   Lyndsay Connors, [Jean Blackburn], 2002, in possession of SB.
108   Peggy Mares to SB (email), 3 January 2002. In possession of SB.
109   "Jean Edna Blackburn 14/7/1919–21/12/2001," 2001, [Funeral program], JB Private papers.
110   Marjorie Pizer to SB, [2001]; Judith Gill to SB, 8 December 2001 & 9 February 2002; John Legge to SB, 5 December 2001; Peter Karmel to SB, 4 December 2001; Elliott Johnston to SB, 7 December 2001; Ted Jackson to SB, December 2001; Julie Marcus to SB, 12 December 2001.

Conclusion: Thinking about the life

1   See Craig Campbell and Helen Proctor, *A History of Australian Schooling* (Sydney: Allen & Unwin, 2014).
2   See Fazal Rizvi on these ideas, interview by Craig Campbell, December 2, 2014.
3   Ken McKinnon, "The Schools Commission," in *Schools Commission Seminar* (Melbourne: University of Melbourne, 2010), 4.
4   Denise Bradley, interview by Craig Campbell and Debra Hayes, October 9, 2015.
5   JB, "From Positive to Negative Discrimination in Education," 1982, JB Private papers. For a comparative analysis of approaches by Karmel and Gonski, see Joel Windle, "The Rise of School Choice in Education Funding Reform," *Educational Policy* 28, no. 2 (2014).

6   Dean Ashenden, "Political Games Hide Hard Facts of Gonski Education Reform," *Echo-Netdaily* (2012), http://www.echo.net.au/2012/08/political-games-hide-hard-facts-of-gonski-education-reform/. Also, Ashenden, "Mr Gonski and the Social Contract," *Inside Story* (22 May 2014).
7   Lyndsay Connors, "'Schools in Australia': A Hard Act to Follow," *Australian Educational Researcher* 27, no. 1 (2000).
8   Bill Hannan, "Passionate for Schools Equity," *Canberra Times*, December 12, 2001.
9   See Geoff Maslen, "A Lifetime of Revolution," *Age*, July 14, 1989.
10 Denise Bradley, "Jean Blackburn," 2001, in possession of Denise Bradley.
11 JB, "Revisiting *Schools in Australia*," nd., JB Private papers.
12 See Tim Rowse, *Nugget Coombs* (Cambridge: Cambridge University Press, 2002), esp. 74–75; Desley Deacon, *Managing Gender* (Melbourne: Oxford University Press, 1989).
13 See Stuart Macintyre, *Australia's Boldest Experiment* (Sydney: New South, 2015), 278.
14 Dean Ashenden, interview by Craig Campbell and Debra Hayes, June 7, 2016, transcript with emails.
15 R. W. Connell, "Long and Winding Road," in *Feminist Sociology*, ed. Barbara Laslett and Barrie Thorne (New Brunswick (NJ): Rutgers University Press, 1997), 157.
16 Ashenden, interview.
17 Susan Blackburn to Craig Campbell (email), 25 May 2014.
18 Bradley, "Jean Blackburn."
19 Margaret Bearlin, interview by Craig Campbell and Debra Hayes, July 20, 2015.
20 Hannah Arendt, "The Crisis of Education," (1954), http://learningspaces.org/files/ArendtCrisisInEdTable.pdf.
21 On Jean and the Australian College of Educators, Margaret Clark, "Jean Blackburn: Courageous Scholar," *Professional Educator* no. 6 (November 2013): 29.

SELECT BIBLIOGRAPHY

Archival and manuscript sources

Blackburn, Gerard. ASIO file. National Archives of Australia.
Blackburn, Jean Edna. ASIO file. National Archives of Australia.
Blackburn, Jean Edna. Personal papers. National Archives of Australia.
Blackburn, Jean Edna. Private papers. Held by Susan Blackburn, Melbourne.
Blackburn, Jean Edna. Student record. University of Adelaide Archives.
Blackburn, Jean Edna. Student record. University of Melbourne Archives.
Blackburn, Jean. Personnel file. University of Adelaide Archives.
Blackburn, Susan. Private papers. [Includes all letters from Jean Blackburn to Susan, and extracts from personal diary.] Held by Susan Blackburn, Melbourne.
Karmel, Peter Henry. Papers. National Library of Australia.
McBriar, Elizabeth Maude. ASIO file. National Archives of Australia.
McKinnon, Ken. Personal papers. National Archives of Australia.
Research Centre for Women's Studies. Papers. University of Adelaide Archives.
Tertiary Education Authority of South Australia Advisory Committee on Post-Secondary Education of Women & Girls. University of Adelaide Archives.
Torsh, Daniela. Papers. National Library of Australia.
Women's Suffrage Centenary South Australia. Files. State Records of South Australia.

Interviews

Aitkin, Don. Interview by Craig Campbell, December 13, 2016, transcript. Held by Debra Hayes.
Allen, Margaret. Interview by Craig Campbell, February 16, 2016, transcript. Held by Debra Hayes.
Ashenden, Dean. Interview by Craig Campbell & Debra Hayes, June 7, 2016, transcript. Held by Debra Hayes.
Bearlin, Margaret. Interview by Craig Campbell & Debra Hayes, July 20, 2015, transcript. Held by Debra Hayes.
Beasley, Mary. Interview by Allison Murchie, February 14, 1994, State Library of South Australia.
Blackburn, Hugh. Interview by Craig Campbell & Debra Hayes, June 8, 2016, transcript. Held by Debra Hayes.
Blackburn, Jean. Interview by Peter Biskup, September 27 & 13 November 1990, transcript, National Library of Australia.
———. Interview by Jack Cross, Adelaide, August 28, 2000, notes. Jean Blackburn Private papers. Held by Susan Blackburn.

———. Interview by Carl Green, August 21, 1992, transcript. In Green, Carl. "Karmel, Labor and Education." BA hons thesis, University of Sydney, 1992. Appendix B.
———. Interview by Wendy Lowenstein, July 1, 1994, transcript, National Library of Australia.
———. Interview by Kirstin Marks, December 13, 1993, State Library of South Australia.
———. Interview by Allison Murchie, March 26, 1994, State Library of South Australia.
———. Interview by Allison Murchie, May 14, 1994, State Library of South Australia.
———. Interview by Peter Read, July 21, 1988, National Library of Australia.
———. Interview by Tony Ryan, May 12 & 19, 1994, transcript, National Library of Australia.
———. Interview by Tony Ryan, January 1, 1995, National Library of Australia.
Blackburn, Susan. Interview by Craig Campbell, May 22, 2014, transcript. Held by Debra Hayes.
Blackmore, Jill. Interview by Debra Hayes& Craig Campbell, June 7, 2016. Held by Debra Hayes.
Bradley, Denise. Interview by Craig Campbell & Debra Hayes, October 9, 2015, transcript. Held by Debra Hayes.
Christensen, Ellen. Interview by Ian Marshall, November 23, 1969, State Library of South Australia.
Connors, Lyndsay, and Jim McMorrow. Interview by Debra Hayes & Craig Campbell, December 8, 2015, transcript. Held by Debra Hayes.
Eadie, Graham. Interview by Craig Campbell, December 13, 2016, transcript. Held by Debra Hayes.
Ferguson, Judy. Interview by Craig Campbell, February 16, 2016, transcript. Held by Debra Hayes.
Hamilton, Louisa. Interview by Susan & Hugh Blackburn, November 20, 2013, with notes added August 6, 2014. Held by Susan Blackburn.
Hannan, Bill, and Lorna Hannan. Interview by Craig Campbell & Debra Hayes, June 9, 2016, transcript. Held by Debra Hayes.
Harcourt, Geoffrey, and Joan Harcourt. Interview by Craig Campbell, March 21, 2016, transcript. Held by Debra Hayes.
Jordan, Deirdre, and Judith Redden. Interview by Craig Campbell, December 1, 2015, transcript. Held by Debra Hayes.
Karmel, Peter. Interview by Carl Green, June 12, 1992. In Green, Carl. "Karmel, Labor and Education." BA hons thesis, University of Sydney, 1992. Appendix C.
Kirner, Joan. Notes of interview, 2011. Accessed 4 June 2016 from http://www.ourcommunity.com.au/leadership/leadership_article.jsp?articleId=4911.
Mackinnon, Alison. Interview by Craig Campbell, February 17, 2016, transcript. Held by Debra Hayes.
Magarey, Susan. Interview by Craig Campbell, November 30, 2015, transcript. Held by Debra Hayes.

Mares, Peggy, and Effie Best. Interview by Craig Campbell, February 15, 2016, transcript. Held by Debra Hayes.
Martin, Frank. Interview by Carl Green, August 18, 1992. In Green, Carl. "Karmel, Labor and Education." BA hons thesis, University of Sydney, 1992. Appendix D.
McBriar, Elizabeth Maud. Interview by Bernard O'Neill, September 30, 1992, State Library of South Australia.
McKinnon, Ken. Interview by Debra Hayes & Craig Campbell, May 27, 2016, transcript. Held by Debra Hayes.
Muir, Les. Interview by Susan Blackburn, May 16, 23, 25, 31 and June 8, 1981. Held by Susan Blackburn.
Muir, Leslie Thomas, and Janet Pryor. Interview by Craig Campbell & Debra Hayes, April 15, 2015, transcript. Held by Debra Hayes.
Praetz, Helen. Interview by Craig Campbell, July 21, 2016, transcript. Held by Debra Hayes.
Randell, Shirley. Interview by Craig Campbell & Debra Hayes, May 26, 2016. Held by Debra Hayes.
Rizvi, Fazal. Interview by Craig Campbell, December 2, 2014, transcript. Held by Debra Hayes.
Torsh, Daniela. Interview by Debra Hayes & Craig Campbell, August 30, 2016, transcript. Held by Debra Hayes.
Tucker, Ernie. Interview by Jean Ely, July 2007. In *Contempt of Court: Unofficial Voices from the DOGS Australian High Court Case 1981*, edited by Jean Ely, 107–22. Melbourne: Dissenters Press, 2010.
Wilson, J. J. Notes of interview by Carl Green, August 11, 1992. In Green, Carl. "Karmel, Labor and Education." BA hons thesis, University of Sydney, 1992. Appendix E.
Yates, Lyn. Interview by Craig Campbell, November 27, 2014, transcript. Held by Debra Hayes.

Government reports for which Jean Blackburn was involved in the preparation and writing

Australia. Schools Commission. "Report for the Triennium 1976 to 1978." Canberra, 1975.
———. "Report for Triennium 1979–1981." Canberra, 1978.
———. "Report: Rolling Triennium 1977–79." Canberra, 1976.
———. "Report: Rolling Triennium 1978–80." Canberra, 1977.
Committee of Enquiry into Education in South Australia (1969–1970). "Education in South Australia: Report." Adelaide, 1971.
Committee on Social Change and the Education of Women. "Girls, School and Society: Report by a Study Group to the Schools Commission." Canberra: Schools Commission, 1975.
Commonwealth Schools Commission. "Schooling for 15 and 16 Year-Olds." Canberra: Schools Commission, 1980.

DeBats, R., J. Blackburn, A. Martin, and C. Starrs. *Pathways from School to Society: A Review of the 1980 School to Work Transition Program in South Australia.* Adelaide: Tertiary Education Authority (South Australia), 1981.
Interim Committee for the Australian Schools Commission. "Schools in Australia: Report of the Interim Committee for the Australian Schools Commission, May 1973." Canberra, 1973.
Victoria. Ministerial Review of Postcompulsory Schooling. "Discussion Paper." Melbourne, 1984.
Victoria. Ministerial Review of Postcompulsory Schooling. "Report." Melbourne: 1985.

Published work by Jean Blackburn

[By year of publication]

"'Shine, O Shine Them Pots!'" *Outlook: An independent socialist review* 3, no. 4 (1959): 12.
"Changes Brewing." *Outlook* 5, no. 4 (1961): 9.
Blackburn, Jean, and Ted Jackson. *Australian Wives Today.* Melbourne: Victorian Fabian Society, 1963.
[Book Review: Selleck, *The New Education*]. *The Australian Rationalist* 1, no. 4 (1970): 28–29.
"Assessing the Needs: In City and Country." *School Bell*, 1976, 3pp.
"School and Community." In *Parents and Professionals: A new partnership in special education,* edited by Paul Whiting, 65–72. Brisbane: Australian Association of Special Education, 1976.
[On Disadvantaged Schools Program]. In *National Conference on Disadvantage Program*, 4pp., 1976.
"Boarding Schools as Seen by the Schools Commission." In *New Perspectives in Boarding Schools*, 98–106: National Council of Independent Schools, 1977.
"Schools and the Schools Commission." In *The Commonwealth Government and Education 1964–1976: Political Initiatives and Development*, edited by I. K. F. Birch and D. Smart. Melbourne: Drummond, 1977.
[Keynote Address]. Paper presented at the Schools can make a difference: National Conference on educational disadvantage, Melbourne, 1977.
"Basic Skills and the Disadvantaged Schools Program." In *Disadvantaged Schools Program: Basic Skills: Two Views*, edited by D. Waters and J. Blackburn, 5–11. Canberra: Schools Commission, 1978.
"Quality Is Not What It Was." In *Quality of Australian Education*, 13–15. Canberra: Australian College of Education, 1978.
"Basic Skills and the Disadvantaged Schools Program." *Western Australian Parent and Citizen* 24, no. 3 (1979): 29–33.
Title I and the Disadvantaged Schools Program. 22pp.: Australia-US Education Policy Project, 1979.

"Rationales: Financing, Organisation and Governance of Education for Special Populations." In *Principles and Issues*, 19pp: Centre for Educational Research and Innovation: OECD, 1980.
[Book Review: Dow, *Learning to Teach*]. *Education News* 17, no. 1 (1980): 43–44.
"Changing Educational Emphases for the 1980s." In *Education, Change and Society*, edited by Peter Karmel, 81–99. Melbourne: ACER, 1981.
"The Disadvantaged Schools Program: Retrospect and Prospect." In *New Directions in School and Community Studies: Volume 2*, 7–21. Canberra: Canberra College of Advanced Education, 1981.
"Becoming Equally Human: Girls and the Secondary Curriculum." *VISE News*, July/August 1982.
"Curriculum and Public Purposes." In *Who Owns the Curriculum?*, edited by Craig Campbell, 12–13. Adelaide: SA Institute of Teachers, 1982.
"Some Dilemmas in Non-Sexist Education." *Secondary Teacher* 33, no. 1 (1982): 10–11.
[Book Review: Connell et al. *Making the Difference*]. *Australian Journal of Education* 26, no. 3 (1982): 330–32.
[Book Review: Connell et al. *Making the Difference*]. *Parent and Citizen Journal* 33, no. 6 (1982): 26–27.
"Title 1 and the Australian Disadvantaged Schools Program." In *Contemporary Issues in Educational Policy: Perspectives from Australia and USA*, edited by G. Hancock, M. W. Kirst and D. L. Grossman, 227–40. Canberra: Curriculum Development Centre, 1983.
"Unequal Resource Distribution." In *The Education of Minority Groups: An Enquiry into Problems and Practices of Fifteen Countries*, edited by Centre for Educational Research and Innovation (OECD). Aldershot (UK): Gower, 1983.
Blackburn, Jean, and D Morley. "Curricular Issues in Educational Provision for the 15–18 Age Group." In *The Schooling of 15–18 Year Olds in South Australia*, edited by B King, C Manhood and G Willmott, 18–24. Adelaide: South Australian Group of Chief Executives of Tertiary Institutions, 1983.
"Schooling and Injustice for Girls." In *Unfinished Business: Social Justice for Women in Australia*, edited by Dorothy H. Broome. Sydney: Allen & Unwin, 1984.
"The Participation and Equity Program in Historical Context." In *National Conference on the Participation and Equity Program*, 25–28. Canberra: Australia. Commonwealth Participation and Equity Program Coordinating Committee, 1984.
"National Promotion of Quality in Schooling: A Review of the Quality in Education Report." *Youth Studies Bulletin* 4, no. 4 (1985): 122–27.
"Policy Response to the Case Studies." In *Alienation from Schooling*, edited by Peter Fensham, 284–88. London: Routledge & Kegan Paul, 1986.
"Productive and Excellent Women: Equity, Productivity, Excellence and Women in Tertiary Education." *Australian Feminist Studies* 1, no. 3 (1986): 15–26.
"Reading 5." In *Gender and Education: Sociology of the School*, edited by Paige Porter. Melbourne: Deakin University Press, 1986.

Changing Approaches to Equality in Education. John Curtin Memorial Lecture. Canberra: Research School of Social Sciences, Australian National University, 1986.

"Schooling Women." *Australian Feminist Studies* 2, no. 4 (1987).

The Study of Work in Society: A Curriculum Proposal. CDC Monograph. Canberra: Curriculum Development Centre, 1987.

"Address by Jean Blackburn, 1988 College Medallist." *ACE News*, 1988, 8.

"Gender." In *Imagining the Australian Curriculum*, edited by David McRae, 17–19. Canberra: Curriculum Development Centre, 1989.

"The Public in Education." In *What Should Government Do?*, edited by Peter Coaldrake and J. R. Nethercote, 220–31. Sydney: Hale & Iremonger, 1989.

Public Schooling: The Democratic Commitment. Melbourne: Victoria: State Board of Education, 1990.

"Arts Graduates as a Major Social Resource." *Lumen* 20, no. 7 (24 May 1991): 2pp.

"A Lesson in School Funding." *The Australian*, 16 July 1996.

"Skills and Content in General Education." *Unicorn* 22, no. 2 (1996): 6–10.

Morrow, Ann, Jean Blackburn, and Judy Gill. "Public Education: From Public Domain to Private Enterprise?" In *Going Public: Education Policy and Public Education in Australia*, edited by Alan Reid, 9–17. Canberra: Australian Curriculum Studies Association, 1998.

Other sources

Allen, Margaret. "Remembering Jean Blackburn AO 1919–2001." *Australian Feminist Studies* 17 no. 39 (2002): 255–258.

Allen, Margaret, Jean Blackburn, Margaret King, and Alison Mackinnon, eds. *All Her Labours*. Vol. 1, Working It Out. Sydney: Hale & Iremonger, 1984.

Ashenden, Dean. "Educationalist Shaped Nation's Minds." *The Australian*, 12 December 2001.

———. "Mr Gonski and the Social Contract." *Inside Story* (22 May 2014).

Ashenden, Dean, Jean Blackburn, Bill Hannan, and Doug White. "Manifesto for a Democratic Curriculum." *The Australian Teacher*, February 1984, 13–20.

Australian Council for Educational Research. "Schools in Australia: 1973–1998: The 25 Years since the Karmel Report." Sydney, 1998.

Australian Women's Archives Project. "New Housewives' Association (1946–1950)." *The Australian Women's Register*. http://www.womenaustralia.info/biogs/AWE1114b.htm.

Barcan, Alan, *Sociological Theory and Educational Reality: Education and Society in Australia since 1949*. Sydney: New South Wales University Press, 1993.

Bassett, Jan. *'Matters of Conscience': A History of the Victorian Secondary Teachers Association*. Melbourne: PenFolk, 1995.

Bayne, Mollie, ed. *Australian Women at War*. Melbourne: Left Book Club of Victoria, 1943.

Beazley, Kim. "The Labor Party in Opposition and Government." In *The Commonwealth Government and Education 1964–1976: Political Initiatives*

and Development, edited by I. K. F. Birch and D. Smart, 94–119. Melbourne: Drummond, 1977.
Beilharz, Peter, Trevor Hogan, and Sheila Shaver. *The Martin Presence: Jean Martin and the Making of the Social Sciences in Australia*. Sydney: UNSW Press, 2015.
Bessant, B., and A. D. Spaull. *Politics of Schooling*. Melbourne: Pitman, 1976.
Blackburn, Susan. "Children of the Revolution." 5pp, 2011.
———. "Food." In *Growing up in Adelaide in the 1950s*, edited by Susan Blackburn, 199–219. Sydney: Hale and Iremonger, 2012.
———. "A Golden Age for Children's Reading in Adelaide: A Memoir." *Journal of the Historical Society of South Australia* 38 (2010): 108–17.
———. *Maurice Blackburn and the Australian Labor Party, 1934–1943, a Study of Principle in Politics*. Melbourne: Australian Society for the Study of Labour History, 1969.
Bridges, Doreen, ed. *Helen Palmer's Outlook*. Sydney: Helen Palmer Memorial Committee, 1982.
Bulbeck, Chilla. *Living Feminism: The Impact of the Women's Movement on Three Generations of Australian Women*. Cambridge: Cambridge University Press, 1997.
Caine, Barbara. "Mothering Feminism/Mothering Feminists: Ray Strachey and the Cause." *Women's History Review* 8, no. 2 (1999): 295–310.
Campbell, Craig, and Helen Proctor. *A History of Australian Schooling*. Sydney: Allen & Unwin, 2014.
Clark, C. M. H. "Faith." In *Australian Civilization*, edited by Peter Coleman, 85–87. Melbourne: Cheshire, 1962.
Clark, Manning. *The Quest for Grace*. Melbourne: Viking, 1990.
Clark, Margaret. "Jean Blackburn: Courageous Scholar." *Professional Educator*, November 2013, 29.
Coltheart, Lenore, ed. *Jessie Street: A Revised Autobiography*. Sydney: Federation Press, 2004.
Connell, R. W. *Schools and Social Justice*. Philadelphia: Temple University Press, 1993.
Connell, R. W., D. J. Ashenden, S. Kessler, and G. W. Dowsett. *Making the Difference: Schools, Families and Social Division*. Sydney: George Allen & Unwin, 1982.
Connell, R. W., V. M. White, and K. M. Johnston. *Poverty, Education and the Disadvantaged Schools Program (DSP)*. Sydney: Macquarie University, 1990.
———, eds. *'Running Twice as Hard': The Disadvantaged Schools Program in Australia*. Melbourne: Deakin University, 1991.
Connell, W. F. *Reshaping Australian Education 1960–1985*. Melbourne: ACER, 1993.
Connors, Lyndsay. "'Schools in Australia': A Hard Act to Follow." *Australian Educational Researcher* 27, no. 1 (2000): 1–29.
Crittenden, Brian. "Arguments and Assumptions of the Karmel Report: A Critique." In *The Renewal of Australian Schools: A Changing Perspective in Educational Planning*, edited by J. V. D'Cruz and P. J. Sheehan, 17–31. Melbourne: Australian Council for Educational Research, 1978.

Curthoys, Ann, and John Merritt, eds. *Australia's First Cold War 1945–1953: Society, Communism and Culture.* Vol. 1, Australia's First Cold War. Sydney: George Allen & Unwin, 1984.

Damousi, Joy. *Women Come Rally: Socialism, Communism and Gender in Australia, 1890–1955.* Melbourne: Oxford University Press, 1994.

Davidson, Alastair. *The Communist Party of Australia: A Short History.* Stanford: Hoover Institution Press, 1969.

D'Cruz, J. V., and P. J. Sheehan. "Culture and the Schools Commission in Educational Renewal." In *The Renewal of Australian Schools: A Changing Perspective in Educational Planning*, edited by J. V. D'Cruz and P. J. Sheehan, 3–11. Melbourne: Australian Council for Educational Research, 1978.

Debelle, Penelope. *Red Silk: The Life of Elliott Johnston Qc.* Adelaide: Wakefield Press, 2011.

Dow, Gwyneth, and Stephen Duggan. *History and the Blackburn Report: Implications for Schools and Universities.* Melbourne: The History Institute, 1985.

Dow, Hume, ed. *Memories of Melbourne University: Undergraduate Life in the Years since 1917* Melbourne: Hutchinson of Australia, 1983.

———, ed. More Memories of Melbourne University: Undergraduate Life in the Years since 1919. Melbourne: Hutchinson, 1985.

Dudley, J., and I. Vidovich. *The Politics of Education: Commonwealth Schools Policy 1973–95.* Melbourne: ACER, 1995.

Dunstan, Don. *Felicia: The Political Memoirs of Don Dunstan.* Melbourne: Macmillan, 1981.

Finch, Lyn. "Could 'Winnie the War Winner' Organise Women? Problems of CPA Women During World War II." *Hecate* 10, (1984): 7–27.

Fitzpatrick, Kathleen. "Introduction." In *Australian Women at War*, 5–6. Melbourne: Left Book Club of Victoria, 1943.

Frank, Celia, and Kirsten Marks. *Celebration! The International Women's Day Committee of South Australia.* Adelaide: International Women's Day Committee (SA), 1995.

Franzway, Suzanne. *Staking a Claim: Feminism, Bureaucracy and the State.* Sydney: Allen & Unwin, 1989.

Fraser, Malcolm, and Margaret Simons. *Malcolm Fraser: The Political Memoirs.* Melbourne: Miegunyah Press, 2010.

Gaskell, Jane. "The Women's Movement in Canadian and Australian Education: From Liberation and Sexism to Boys and Social Justice." *Gender and Education* 15, no. 2 (2003): 151–68.

Gilding, Michael. *The Making and Breaking of the Australian Family.* Sydney: Allen & Unwin, 1991.

Grimshaw, Patricia, and L. Strahan, eds. *The Half-Open Door.* Sydney: Hale and Iremonger, 1982.

Hannan, Bill. "Jean Edna Blackburn: Shaper of Australia's School System." *Age*, 14 December 2001.

Harman, Grant, and Don Smart, eds. *Federal Intervention in Australian Education: Past, Present and Future.* Melbourne: Georgian House, 1982.

Hasluck, Paul. *The Government and the People 1939–1941*. Canberra: Australian War Memorial, 1952.
———. *The Government and the People 1942–1945*. Canberra: Australian War Memorial, 1970.
Hocking, Jenny. *Gough Whitlam: His Time: The Biography*. Vol. 2, Melbourne: Miegunyah Press, 2014.
Horner, D. M. *The Spy Catchers: The Official History of ASIO, 1949–1963*. Sydney: Allen & Unwin, 2014.
Hoy, Alice. *A City Built to Music: The History of University High School, Melbourne, 1910 to 1960*. Melbourne: University High School, 1961.
Humphreys, Dany, and Ken Newcombe, eds. *Schools Out! Verdicts by Australian Children*. Melbourne: Penguin Books, 1975.
Hyams, Bernard. "Education." In *The Dunstan Decade: Social Democracy at the State Level*, edited by Andrew Parkin and Allan Patience, 70–90. Melbourne: Longman Cheshire, 1981.
Inglis, Amirah. *The Hammer and Sickle and the Washing Up: Memories of an Australian Woman Communist*. Melbourne: Hyland House, 1995.
Johnston, K. "A Discourse for All Seasons? An Ideological Analysis of the Schools Commission Reports, 1973 to 1981." *Australian Journal of Education* 27, no. 1 (1982): 17–32.
Jones, A. W. "Peter Karmel: The Greatest Educational Statesman of the Century: The Unification of South Australian Secondary Education." In *A Broader Vision: Voices of Vocational Education in Twentieth-Century South Australia*, edited by Erica Jolly. Adelaide: the editor, 2001.
Kaplan, Gisela. *The Meagre Harvest: The Australian Women's Movement 1950s–1990s*. Sydney: Allen & Unwin, 1996.
Keating, Jack, and Kira Clarke. "The Schools Commission and School Funding." *Professional Educator* 9, no. 4 (2010): 40–43.
Keating, Jack, ed. *Post-Compulsory Schooling in Victoria: A VSTA Position*. Melbourne: Victorian Secondary Teachers Association, 1985.
Keeves, John P. "Educational Privilege and Disadvantage." In *Australian Education: Review of Recent Research*, edited by John P. Keeves, 346–77. Sydney: Allen & Unwin, 1987.
Kenway, Jane, Sue Willis, Jill Blackmore, and Leonie Rennie. "Making 'Hope Practical' Rather Than 'Despair Convincing': Feminist Post-Structuralism, Gender Reform and Educational Change." *British Journal of Sociology of Education* 15, no. 2 (1994): 187–210.
Kerin, Rani. *Doctor Do-Good: Charles Duguid and Aboriginal Advancement, 1930s–1970s*. Melbourne: Australian Scholarly Publishing, 2011.
———. "'Mixed up in a Bit of Do-Goodery': Judy Inglis, Activist Anthropology and Aboriginal History." *History and Anthropology* 18, no. 4 (2007): 427–42.
Kirner, Joan E. "Societal Change and Education in Retrospect: Reactant's Paper." In *Education, Change and Society*, edited by Peter Karmel, 119–26. Melbourne: ACER, 1981.
Kirner, Joan. "Personal Comment." *Australian Feminist Studies* 9, no. 19 (1994): 1–7.

Lake, Marilyn. *Getting Equal: The History of Australian Feminism*. Sydney: Allen & Unwin, 1999.
Macintyre, Stuart, and R. J. W. Selleck. *A Short History of the University of Melbourne, 1850–1939*. Melbourne: University of Melbourne Press, 2003.
Macintyre, Stuart. *Australia's Boldest Experiment: War and Reconstruction in the 1940s*. Sydney: New South, 2015.
——. *The Reds*. Sydney: Allen and Unwin, 1998.
MacKenzie, Norman. *Women in Australia*. Melbourne: Cheshire, 1962.
Mackinnon, Alison. *Love and Freedom: Professional Women and the Reshaping of Personal Life*. Cambridge: Cambridge University Press, 1997.
——. "A Woman of Conviction: A Tribute to Sister Deirdre Jordan, 22 October 1999." *Australian Feminist Studies* 15, no. 31 (1999): 15–18.
Magarey, Susan. "Setting up the First Research Centre for Women's Studies in Australia, 1983–1986." *Australian Feminist Studies* 13, no. 27 (1998): 81–90.
Marginson, Simon. *Educating Australia: Government, Economy and Citizen since 1960*. Cambridge: Cambridge University Press, 1997.
——. "The Whitlam Government and Education." In *It's Time Again: Whitlam and Modern Labor*, edited by Jenny Hocking and Colleen Lewis, 244–72. Melbourne: Circa Books, 2003.
Marshall, Vern. "Schools." In *The Bannon Decade: The Politics of Restraint in South Australia*, edited by Andrew Parkin and Allan Patience, 209–21. Sydney: Allen & Unwin, 1992.
Martin, Jean I. "Sex Differences in Educational Qualifications." *Melbourne Studies in Education*, no. 1972 (1972): 96–123.
Mathews, Rivkah. "Rivkah Mathews." In *More Memories of Melbourne University: Undergraduate Life in the Years since 1919*, edited by Hume Dow, 55–72. Melbourne: Huchinson, 1985.
McCalman, Janet. *Journeyings: The Biography of a Middle-Class Generation 1920–1990*. Melbourne: Melbourne University Press, 1993.
McKinnon, K. R. "The Schools Commission: Policies and Politics in a Statutory Body." In *Federal Intervention in Australian Education: Past, Present and Future*, edited by Grant Harman and Don Smart, 135–50. Melbourne: Georgian House, 1982.
McKinnon, Ken. "Honestly First Class." *The Australian*, 12 December 2001.
McLaren, John. *Free Radicals of the Left in Postwar Melbourne*. Melbourne: Australian Scholarly Publishing, 2003.
Miller, Pavla. *Long Division: State Schooling in South Australian Society*. Adelaide: Wakefield Press, 1986.
Mitchell, Winifred. "A Pilgrim's Progress." In *Against the Odds: Fifteen Professional Women Reflect on Their Lives and Careers*, edited by Madge Dawson and Heather Radi, 201–17. Sydney: Hale & Iremonger, 1984.
Moss, Jim. *Representatives of Discontent: History of Communist Party in South Australia 1921–1981*. Melbourne: Communist and Labour Movement History Group, 1983.

Novick, Don. "Jean Blackburn: Schools Commission." In *Talking About School: Parents and Evaluation: A Discussion Paper,* edited by Don Novick, 34–37. Adelaide: Education Department of South Australia, 1980.
O'Lincoln, Tom. "Against the Stream: Women and the Left, 1945–1968." (1980): 8pp. https://www.anu.edu.au/polsci/marx/interventions/rebelwomen/against.htm.
O'Neal, Bernard, Judith Raftery, and Kerrie Round, eds. *Playford's South Australia: Essays on the History of South Australia, 1933–1968.* Adelaide: Association of Professional Historians, 1996.
Papadelos, Pam, Dee Michell, and Penelope Eate. "'Bending and Morphing': The Department of Women's Studies at the University of Adelaide Continues Past Its Twenty Year Anniversary." *Outskirts* 31 (2014).
Poynter, John, and Carolyn Rasmussen. *A Place Apart: The University of Melbourne: Decades of Challenge.* Melbourne: Melbourne University Press, 1996.
Praetz, Helen. *Building a School System: A Sociological Study of Catholic Education.* Melbourne: Melbourne University Press, 1980.
Priestley, Raymond. *The Diary of a Vice-Chancellor: University of Melbourne 1935–1938.* Melbourne: Melbourne University Press, 2002.
Pusey, Michael. *The Dynamics of Bureaucracy: A Case Analysis in Education.* Sydney: John Wiley & Sons, 1976.
———. *Economic Rationalism in Canberra: A Nation-Building State Changes Its Mind.* Cambridge: Cambridge University Press, 1991.
Rasmussen, Carolyn. *The Blackburns: Private Lives, Public Ambition.* Melbourne: Melbourne University Press, 2019.
———. *The Lesser Evil? Opposition to War and Fascism in Australia, 1920–1941.* Melbourne: History Department University of Melbourne, 1992.
———. *'A Whole New World': 100 Years of Education at University High School.* Melbourne: Australian Scholarly Publishing, 2010.
Read, Peter. *Charles Perkins: A Biography.* Melbourne: Penguin, 1990.
Rowse, Tim. *Nugget Coombs: A Reforming Life.* Cambridge: Cambridge University Press, 2002.
Ryan, Mary. *Beyond the Glass Ceiling: Women Leaders in Education.* Melbourne: Collins Dove, 1993.
Ryan, Robin. "Rethinking the Economics of Education: Evolving Thoughts of Professor Peter Karmel and the Australian College of Educators." *Archival Brief,* 2013.
Ryan, Susan. *Catching the Waves: Life in and out of Politics.* Sydney: Harper Collins, 1999.
Schedvin, C. B. *Shaping Science and Industry: A History of Australia's Council for Scientific and Industrial Research, 1926–49.* Sydney: Allen & Unwin, 1987.
Selleck, R. J. W. *The Shop: The University of Melbourne 1850–1939.* Melbourne: Melbourne University Press, 2003.
Sendy, John. *Comrades Come Rally! Recollections of an Australian Communist.* Melbourne: Nelson, 1978.

Smart, Don. "The Accelerating Commonwealth Participation 1964–1976." In *The Commonwealth Government and Education 1964–1976: Political Initiatives and Development*, edited by I. K. F. Birch and D. Smart, 24–47. Melbourne: Drummond, 1977.

Smart, Judith. "Homefires and Housewives: Women, War and the Politics of Consumption." *Victorian Historical Journal* 75, no. 1 (2004): 96–109.

———. "The Housewives' Associations 1915–1950: Australia's First Consumer Organisations." In *Consumer Australia: Historical Perspectives*, edited by Robert Crawford, Judith Smart and Kim Humphrey, 75–95. Newcastle upon Tyne: Cambridge Scholars, 2010.

Smith, Charlene. *40: A Short History of the University of Canberra*. Canberra: University of Canberra, 2009.

Smith, Graham F. *Speak up, Reach Out: A Life to Reckon With*. Adelaide: Wakefield Press, 2015.

Spaull, A. D. *Australian Education in the Second World War*. Brisbane: University of Queensland Press, 1982.

———. *John Dedman: A Most Unexpected Labor Man*. Melbourne: Hyland House, 1998.

Spaull, Andrew. "Schools Policy." In *Trials in Power: Cain, Kirner and Victoria 1982–1992*, edited by Mark Considine and Brian Costar. Melbourne: Melbourne University Press, 1992.

Starr, Graeme. *Carrick: Principles, Politics and Policy*. Ballan (Vic): Connor Court, 2012.

Stevens, Joyce. *A History of International Women's Day*. Sydney: IWD Press, 1985.

———. *Taking the Revolution Home: Work among Women in the Communist Party of Australia 1920–1945*. Melbourne: Sybylla Cooperative Press, 1987.

Street, Jessie. *Jessie Street: A Revised Autobiography*. Sydney: Federation Press, 2004.

Tanner, Lyndsay. "The Policy Formulation Process of an Australian Political Party in Opposition: A Case Study of the Australian Labor Party's Schools Commission Policy." *Melbourne Studies in Education*, no. 1983 (1983 1983): 44–75.

Teese, Richard. *For the Common Weal: The Public High School in Victoria 1910–2010*. Melbourne: Australian Scholarly Publishing, 2014.

Turner, Ian. *Room for Manoevre: Writings on History, Politics, Ideas and Play*. Melbourne: Drummond, 1982.

Weller, Patrick. "The Establishment of the Schools Commission: A Case-Study in the Politics of Education." In *The Commonwealth Government and Education 1964–1976: Political Initiatives and Development*, edited by I. K. F. Birch and D. Smart, 48–70. Melbourne: Drummond, 1977.

Wells, Andrew. "The Old Left Intelligentsia 1930 to 1960." In *Intellectual Movements and Australian Society*, edited by Brian Head and James Walter, 214–34. Melbourne: Oxford University Press, 1988.

White, Doug. "Create Your Own Compliance: The Karmel Prospect." In *The Renewal of Australian Schools*, edited by J. V. D'Cruz and P. J. Sheehan, 46–58. Melbourne: Australian Council for Educational Research, 1978.

Whitlam, Gough. *The Whitlam Government: 1972–1975*. Melbourne: Viking, 1985.
Whitlock, Gillian, and Chilla Bulbeck. "'A Small and Often Still Voice'? Women Intellectuals in Australia." In *Intellectual Movements and Australian Society*, edited by Brian Head and James Walter, 145–69. Melbourne: Oxford University Press, 1988.
Williams, Ross, ed. *Balanced Growth: A History of the Department of Economics, University of Melbourne*. Melbourne: Australian Scholarly Publishing, 2009.
Windle, Joel. "The Rise of School Choice in Education Funding Reform: An Analysis of Two Policy Moments." *Educational Policy* 28, no. 2 (2014): 306–24.
Yates, Lyn, Cherry Collins, and Kate O'Connor. "Australian Curriculum Making." In *Australia's Curriculum Dilemmas: State Cultures and the Big Issues*, edited by Lyn Yates, Cherry Collins and Kate O'Connor, 3–22. Melbourne: Melbourne University Press, 2011.
Yates, Lyn. "Australian Research on Gender and Education 1975–85." In *Australian Education: Review of Recent Research*, edited by John P. Keeves, 241–68. Sydney: Allen & Unwin, 1987.
——. "Theorising Inequality Today." *British Journal of Sociology of Education* 7, no. 2 (1986): 119–34.

INDEX

Abbey, Brian 238
Abeyasekere, Dayal 179–180, 279, 281
Abeyasekere, Susan *see* Blackburn, Susan
Aboriginal Advancement League 97, 124–125
    Aboriginal and Torres Strait Islanders xviii, 2, 48, 97, 123–126, 282–283, 321, 328, 331
    politics and organisations 90, 112, 114, 123–126
    Schools Commission 182, 210, 211, 224, 248, 359
Adelaide Festival of Arts 112, 122, 180, 253, 332
Adelaide Left Club 112–113
Advertiser (newspaper) 81, 103, 250, 356
Age (newspaper) 214, 285, 301, 326, 355
Aitkin, Don 319, 322–323, 340
Allen, Margaret 270–271, 311, 356
Alpers, Liz 346, 353
Arendt, Hannah 370
Argus (newspaper) 47
Ashenden, Dean 109, 154, 161, 204, 220, 238, 252, 278, 283, 303, 304, 305, 310, 314, 316, 340, 355, 356, 363, 367, 368
ASIO (Australian Security Intelligence Organisation) xxiii, 78, 88, 90–91, 97, 101–102, 103, 104, 105, 117, 118, 124–125, 156, 160, 218
Australian College of Education/Educators xxiii, xxiv, xxv, 249, 255, 303, 315, 339, 356, 370
Australian Council for Educational Research (ACER) 151, 198, 226, 238, 240, 272–273

Australian Education Council 139
Australian Education Union 348
Australian National University 68, 302, 317, 318, 319, 323, 324
Australian Teachers Federation 174, 195, 226, 305
Australian Wives Today (1963) 97, 111, 118, 126–130
Australian Women's Education Coalition (AWEC) 249–250, 274–276
Australia-Soviet Union Friendship League/Society 50, 56, 120
bank nationalisation campaign (1947) 63, 82
Bannon, John 327, 334
Barraclough, Helen 278, 279, 281, 345, 349, 352
Bayne, Molly 72
Beare, Hedley 285
Bearlin, Margaret 137, 221, 321, 370
Beasley, Mary 327, 328, 329, 334, 335–337, 338, 339
Beazley, Kym (Snr) 159, 165, 171, 174, 186, 187, 348
Bedford Park Teachers College xv, 141, 142, 152, 154–155
    see also Sturt College of Advanced Education
Benko, Andrew 97
Bennett, David 174, 183, 188, 216, 227–228, 247
Best, Effie 282, 283, 346, 354
Blackburn Review and Report (1983–1985) 152, 266, 284–301, 325, 326, 328
Blackburn, Bill (William) 76, 77, 78, 79, 80, 90, 99, 115, 119, 120, 133, 180, 181, 206, 246, 252, 279, 281, 345–346, 348

Blackburn, Dick (Gerard) xvi, xxiii, 46, 47, 53, 55–56, 71, 73–80, 91, 94, 96, 97, 98, 100, 101, 104, 107, 108–109, 114–115, 116, 118, 120, 121, 122, 123, 128, 130, 131, 132, 159, 175, 179, 181, 221, 252, 253, 261, 278, 279, 281, 288, 311, 312, 340, 345–346, 348–352, 357
Blackburn, Doris 55, 56, 57, 76, 122, 123, 124, 178, 179
Blackburn, Hugh 114–115, 130, 135, 147, 156, 175–176, 179, 182, 207, 246, 252, 261, 278–279, 281, 288, 327, 339, 345, 349, 350, 352, 354, 356
Blackburn, Jean
  adolescence 28–33
  autobiography xxii, 10, 13, 21, 24, 314, 315–316, 353
  birth 1, 21
  career xvi, xvii, 2, 54, 95, 135, 141, 303, 341, 361, 366
  childhood 7–22, 92, 314, 353
  death, funeral and memorial gatherings 352–357
  educational thought xvii–xviii, 34, 59, 110, 121, 129, 132, 138, 150–152, 176–177, 194–198, 218–219, 237–238, 255, 273–275, 302, 319–320, 356, 358–361, 366–369
  health xix, 80, 92, 123, 133–134, 178, 221, 278, 281, 296, 312, 313, 316, 323, 336, 340, 348, 353, 359
  honours and honorary degrees 150, 255, 261, 301–302, 303, 341–342, 354
  leaves parental home 54–55
  married life and motherhood 76–78, 97–98, 108–109, 114–115, 119–122, 175–176, 252–253, 348–351, 369
  night school 35, 37–38
  old age 278, 281, 313–355
  reading 13, 23, 25, 37, 81, 86, 93–94, 132, 138, 155, 276, 348, 369
  religion 21–22, 32
  retirement 255, 267, 343, 347, 348–349, 352
  romances and marriage 55, 61, 74, 76–77
  sex and sexuality 31, 86, 208, 250–251, 278, 304, 349, 351
  teacher 32, 35–37, 39, 105–107, 130–132, 145
  teachers college and CAE lecturer 135–138, 152–154, 172
  travel abroad 122, 214–215, 217–220, 241–244, 252, 279, 295–296
  union member 69–71
  university chancellor 317–324, 340
  visiting or adjunct scholar 267–269, 315
  work habits and manner 37–38, 214, 245, 269, 283, 287–288, 313, 353
  see also War Organisation of Industry; New Housewives; Schools Commission; University of Melbourne; Communist Party of Australia; Labour Club
Blackburn, Louisa 42, 51, 53, 54, 55, 59, 74, 253, 254, 351
Blackburn, Margaret (Meg) 252, 279, 281, 345
Blackburn, Maurice xxiii, 47, 53, 55, 56, 76
Blackburn, Maurice, Jr. 76
Blackburn, Naomi 279, 281, 345, 345
Blackburn, Robyn 279, 281, 345, 345
Blackburn, Susan xxiii, 13, 30, 79, 81, 90, 99, 100, 109, 115, 117, 119, 120, 121, 122, 133, 155, 179–180, 181, 205, 218, 220, 246, 253, 279, 281, 295, 327, 345, 349, 350, 351, 352, 353, 354, 355, 356, 357

Index

Blake, Jack 51
Blessing, Rae 135
Bloch, Cathy 203
Bowles and Gintis, conference 237
boys' education 16, 207–208, 209–211, 245, 249, 274, 276, 359
Bradley, Denise 114, 132, 211, 251, 269, 272, 276, 278, 283, 286, 311, 341–342, 353, 355, 364, 368
Brennan, Marie 287
Bretherinton, Rod 53
Bridge, Ken 154
Brilliant, Rivkah 30, 50, 53, 282, 346
Brine, Judith 319, 322
Brown, Dean 334–335, 336
Butler, Eric 82
Cahir, Pam 213, 253
Cain Labor government (Vic) 284–285, 362
Calwell, Arthur 64
Campaign for Peace in Vietnam 137, 155–156, 367
Carrick, John 223, 225, 228
Cashmore, Jennifer 327, 329, 334, 337
Cathie, Ian 296
Catholic Action 45, 50, 71, 101, 159
Catholic schools 157, 158, 163–164, 174, 185, 186, 187, 222, 226, 229, 252, 292, 364
Caust, David 116–117, 123, 178
Caust, Tess 85, 87, 116–117, 119, 154, 253, 276, 280
centenary of women's suffrage (SA) x, xvii, 327–339
Chifley Labor government 65, 69, 87
China and Chinese education 102, 111, 217–220, 277
    Jean and, xxii, 103, 111, 217–220
Christensen, Ellen 107, 348
Clark, Manning 45, 58, 255
Clerks Union, Federated 69–71, 73
Cohen, Sam 53
Cold War xix, 78, 87, 88, 90, 97, 101–104, 131, 133, 160, 358, 362, 365

Committee of Enquiry into Education in South Australia *see* Kamel Enquiry (SA)
communism, Marxism and socialism xiii, xviii, 10, 21, 28, 33, 37, 39, 43, 46, 47, 49, 50, 52–54, 56, 58, 62, 63, 70, 78, 81–82, 83, 89–90, 92, 94, 97, 102, 103–104, 108, 111, 112, 117–120, 154, 155, 180, 203, 219, 238, 252, 270, 350, 358, 271, 277–278, 299, 367, 368
Communist Party dissolution referendum 96, 101
Communist Party of Australia (CPA/ACP) 47, 48, 55–56, 71, 83, 87–88, 94, 100, 101–103, 108, 110–111, 180, 252, 312, 350
    Jean joins ACP xviii, 92, 39, 43
    Jean leaves ACP xviii, 96, 108–110, 114, 116, 132
    Jean's experience xvii, 46, 49, 62, 69, 83–84, 88–89, 92, 98, 100, 116, 117, 133
    patriarchal character 58, 88–89, 94, 111
    World War II 49–50, 57
    see also Cold War; New Housewives; peace movement
Connell, R. W. (Raewyn) 194–195, 199, 236, 238, 304
Connell, W. F. 139, 143
Connors, Lyndsay xxiv, 202–203, 206, 209–210, 236, 265, 276, 279, 286, 311–312, 316, 319, 321–322, 342, 345, 353, 356, 363, 368, 370
Coombs, H. C. (Nugget) 68–69, 117–118, 221, 302, 366
Cooper, Malcolm 125
Copland, Douglas 44
Council for Scientific and Industrial Research (Organisation) 63, 79, 118, 121, 279
Council for Women in War Work 72, 83
Critchley, Tom 69

Crittendon, Brian 305, 326
Curriculum Development Centre 244, 307
curriculum, school 34, 137, 139, 143, 170, 176–177, 209, 211, 234, 239, 245, 273, 305
    core and common curriculum 201, 261, 306, 309, 363
    Jean's thinking xix, 16, 176–177, 201–202, 239–240, 258–260, 268, 285–287, 290–291, 297, 299, 300, 304, 306, 307–308, 325–326
    national curriculum 306, 307, 343
    secondary school 26–28, 121, 152, 175, 257, 295, 326
    see also Disadvantaged Schools Program; *Manifesto for a Democratic Curriculum*; work and society curriculum
Curtin, John and Labor government 50, 62–63, 65, 69, 73, 76, 302
Dalgety company 6–7
Dawkins, John 310, 317, 318–319
Day, Alice 241–242
de Beauvoir, Simone xxv, 133, 368, 369
Dedman, John 50, 63, 64–66, 69, 70, 72, 78, 302, 366
Defend Our Government Schools (DOGS) 162, 226
Depression, Great, 2, 8, 13, 18, 21, 26, 33, 46, 86, 314
Deveson, Ivan 324
Disadvantaged Schools Program xii, xviii, 165, 168, 182, 190, 194–202, 214, 222, 223, 230–237, 239, 242, 243, 244, 245, 249, 256, 262, 364
Dow, Gwyn 299
Dow, Hume 75
Duguid, Charles 90, 124–126
Duguid, Phyllis 90
Dunstan, Don 112, 124, 143, 278, 348, 353, 361
Dutt, Palme 33

Edgar, Don 198, 229
Edmonds, Flo 85
Education and Research Development Committee (ERDC) 238
Education Department (SA) 105, 131, 137, 141, 143, 155, 229, 234, 251, 262, 272, 273, 280
Education Department (Vic) 34, 39, 281–282, 288
Education Department, Commonwealth xvi, 162, 189, 235
education policy
    Catholic schools 157–159, 160, 163, 169, 174, 185, 186–187, 222, 225–226, 229, 261, 299, 343, 364
    communities, parents and schools 121, 132, 149, 151, 162, 165, 166, 168, 169, 172, 174, 175, 176, 185, 187, 188–189, 193, 195–197, 199–200, 211, 217, 219–220, 224–225, 228, 229–230, 232, 244, 247, 256, 260, 300, 304, 326, 343
    equality of opportunity xii, xviii, 137, 144–145, 148–149, 150–151, 158, 161, 165–168, 188, 181, 194–196, 198, 206, 209, 212, 222, 224, 227, 230–231, 233, 238, 241, 248–249, 258, 259–260, 263, 267, 291, 305–306, 344, 355, 357, 359, 360–361, 368
    evaluation of programs 197–198
    federal and state issues 166, 170, 172, 184–185, 189–191, 223, 224, 226, 227, 274, 334, 344
    funding and resourcing schools 149, 157–159, 162–163, 165–166, 183–190, 194, 216, 224–225, 233–234, 344, 359, 364
    gifted and talented 248
    intelligence testing 149, 151, 167
    migrant and ethnicity issues xviii, 182, 194, 203, 210, 211, 224, 239, 240, 247, 259, 261, 303, 359
    multiculturalism 247, 343

neoliberalism (economic rationalism) xvi, 69, 143, 227, 306, 310–311, 312, 326, 362
  rural and remote 150, 157, 173, 182, 210, 229–230, 292
  scholarships 48, 255
  school choice 165, 185, 189, 222, 344
  teachers 168, 170, 176, 188, 196–197, 202, 220, 228, 229, 232, 233, 237, 239, 240, 277, 304
  universities 309, 317, 319–321, 359–360
  youth: education, training and employment 255–260, 274, 290–291, 307
  see also Disadvantaged Schools Program; Special Education; post-compulsory education; girls' education
Ennor, Hugh xvi
Esselbach, Rod 135
Evatt Memorial Foundation 255
Evatt, H. V. 73, 255
Farrago (student newspaper) 47, 50, 51
fascism, rise of 2, 33, 45, 46, 56, 70
feminism, Jean and xviii, 358, 365–368
  before 1970: 1–2, 10, 21, 26–27, 57–58, 72–73, 77, 85–87, 92–94, 111, 126–130
  from 1970: 155, 203–212, 248–250, 269–271, 311, 327–336, 346
  see also New Housewives; girls' education
Fensham, Peter 239, 294
Ferguson, Judy *see* Goss, Judy
Fife, Wal 264
Fitzpatrick, Brian 47, 69, 76
Fitzpatrick, Kathleen 72
Flinders University 114, 141, 333, 339, 341
Fordham, Robert 284, 285, 286, 289, 296
Forster, Catherine 23, 28
Foxcraft, Edmund 68

Franzway, Suzanne 354
Fraser Coalition government 189, 198, 222–224, 264–265, 310
Friends of the Soviet Union *see* Australia-Soviet Union Friendship League
funding education *see* education policy: funding schools
Gale, Fay 268, 333
Gartens, Gloria 85
gender and education *see* boys' education; Feminism; girls' education; *Girls, School and Society*
Gibson, Ralph 48, 51, 76
Gilding, Kevin 136, 154, 240, 271–272, 273, 274, 296, 346
Giles, J. P. (Jim) 234, 263
Gill, Judith x, 268, 315, 344, 353, 354, 356–357
girls education xiii–xiv, 154, 202–205, 211–212, 248–250, 272–275, 307
  see also Girls, School and Society
Girls, School and Society 181, 202–214, 248, 249–250
Gonski, David, and reports, xxv, 360
Goss, Joe 98–100
Goss, Judy 98–100, 280, 351
Gott, Ken 110
Habermas, Jurgen 237–238, 277
Hall, Bob 156
Hamilton, Louisa *see* Blackburn, Louisa
Hancock, Greg 161, 174, 215, 241
Hannaford, Robert x, 340
Hannan, Bill 287, 294, 296, 297, 305, 306, 324, 326, 355, 356, 363
Hannan, Lorna 294, 340
Harcourt, Geoffrey 113, 141, 155–156
Harcourt, Joan 113, 115
Hawke Labor Government xiv, 189, 284, 310, 342
Hawthorn State School 35–37
Hayden, Bill 216, 319
Healy, Jim 50
Hill, Brian 310

Holburn, Muir 69–70, 71
Howard Coalition government 343
Hoy, Alice 26, 27
Hudson, Hugh 143, 151, 218
Humphreys, Dany *see* Torsh, Daniela (Dany)
Huntingdale Technical School (Vic) 246
Illich, Ivan 177
Inglis, Amirah *see* Turner, Amirah
Inglis, Judy 114, 116, 123–124, 126
Inglis, Ken 114
Innovations Program (Schools Commission) 169, 188, 194
Interim Committee for the Australian Schools Commission xv, 159–174, 176, 177, 187, 194, 195, 197, 203
International Women's Day 90–91, 250, 315, 338
Iseman, Kay *see* Schaffer, Kay
Jackson, Glenda 332, 334
Jackson, Mary 118
Jackson, Ted 118, 126–127, 129, 351, 357
Johnston, Elizabeth 73, 80, 90, 101, 107, 281, 282, 346
Johnston, Elliott 80, 101, 102, 117, 132, 281, 282, 328, 346, 351, 357
Jones, A. W. 143, 174
Jordan, Deirdre xvii, 218, 271, 277, 279, 318, 333, 339, 342
Junor, Ann 305
Karmel Enquiry (SA) 138, 139–153, 154, 159, 162, 176, 272, 361
Karmel Report (Interim Schools Commission) *see Schools Australia*
Karmel, Peter xv, xvi, 54, 114, 141–143, 145, 148, 149, 150, 159–163, 164–165, 174, 215, 221, 238, 244, 261, 310, 318, 323–324, 348, 357, 369
Keeves Report (SA) 272–273
Keeves, John 198, 226, 272–273
Kemmis, Stephen 277, 287
Kennett Liberal government 296, 324, 326, 345

Keynesian economics 43, 63, 68, 143
Khrushchev, Nikita 108, 109, 110, 111
Kindergarten Union 144
Kirner, Joan 162, 174, 176, 192, 216, 224–225, 228, 229, 255, 264, 286, 293, 303, 311, 324, 333, 348, 368
Klein, Viola 81, 127, 129
Knowles, Ada 26–27, 28, 29, 32, 46, 55, 57
Korean War 102, 103, 104
Kwong Lee Dow 302
Labor Party (ALP) xv, 53, 56, 63, 71, 76, 84, 87, 101, 111, 126, 140, 156, 157, 158–159, 188
Labour Club (University of Melbourne) 39, 42, 43, 45, 46–53, 54, 55, 69, 71, 278, 282
Laidlaw, Dianne 334, 335, 336, 337, 338
Lalor High School (Vic) 234
Latham, J.G. 47
Left Book Club 47, 50, 72, 76
Legge, Jack 45, 47
Legge, John 357
Levy, Anne 327, 329, 330, 331, 336–337
Linden Park Primary School 97, 120–121
Lloyd Street Higher Elementary School 14–18
    Jean as a student 14–18, 19, 24
Logan, Mal 318, 319
Macintyre, Stuart 348
Mackinnon, Alison 268, 270, 315, 346–347, 353, 356
Magarey, Susan xvii, 269–270, 327–329, 333, 335
Mandle, Bill 322
Manifesto for a Democratic Curriculum 305–306
Mares, Peggy 129, 137, 272, 273–274, 282, 356
Marjoribanks, Kevin 267–268, 333
Marshall, Dorothea 26
Marshall, Graham 294, 297

Index

Martin, Frank 174, 192, 364
Martin, Jean 203, 208, 211, 213
Maslen, Geoff 301, 364
Matthews, Rivkah *see* Brilliant, Rivkah
McBriar, Alan 51, 53
McBriar, Maud 53, 90, 91, 118, 156, 278, 282–283, 351, 357
McKinnon, Ken xiii, 172, 173–175, 186, 190–193, 204–205, 208, 215, 224, 225, 237, 244, 245, 248, 255–256, 263–264, 267, 279, 284, 286, 288, 293, 311, 324, 345, 355, 362, 369
McLeod, Jessie 122, 253
McLeod, Jock 122
McMenamin, Anne 155
McQueen, Humphrey 154
Medley, John 52
Menzies governments 50, 62, 68, 69, 78, 101
Menzies, Robert 41, 63, 78
Miles, J.B. 94, 98
Miller, Mary 116, 117, 118
miners' union and strike (1949) 84, 87–88, 92
Mitchell, Roma xvii, 318, 328, 329, 335
Mitchell, Winifred 83, 85, 88–89, 92
Monash University 248, 253, 278, 281, 317, 318, 345, 357
Morrow, Ann 325, 344
Moss, Jim 105
Muir, Allan 8–9, 11, 12, 17, 20, 279, 314, 355
Muir, Caroline 5
Muir, Claire (Clarice Edna) 3–5, 6, 8, 10–11, 13–14, 18–19, 21, 31, 37, 40–41, 54, 74–75, 122, 178, 179
Muir, Jean *see* Blackburn, Jean
Muir, Leslie 3, 4, 5–8, 10–13, 16, 17, 18, 19–20, 21, 24, 26, 31–33, 34, 35, 37, 39, 40–41, 54, 59, 60, 74, 75, 97, 122, 254, 281, 313–314, 359
Muir, Leslie Thomas 8, 11, 14, 17, 19, 31, 279–280, 314, 322, 354, 355

Muir, Thomas 3–4
Murray Smith, Stephen 110
Myrdal, Alva 81, 127, 129
Nation (magazine) 126
National Women's Conference (1943) 73
Neill, Anne 96, 101–102, 104, 120, 125, 132–133
New Housewives Association 83–90, 315
New Left 154, 155, 180, 217
New Theatre 70, 103–104, 116, 119
Newnham, Peter 277
Non-aggression pact, German-Soviet Union 48–49, 51
O'Donohue, Lowitja (Lois) 125, 340
Organisation for Economic Co-operation and Development (OECD) 139, 241–242
Ormond College 40
Outlook (magazine) 97, 110–112, 113, 127, 130, 180
pacificism, Jean and 18, 33, 37, 46, 47
    see also peace movement
Palmer, Helen 47, 53, 62, 97, 110–112, 180, 252
Palmer, Nettie 45, 53, 57, 77
parents of school children *see* education policy: communities, parents and schools
peace movement 42, 47, 48, 56, 58, 71, 91, 101–104, 108, 111, 113, 118, 120, 156, 367
    see also Women's International League for Peace and Freedom
Perkins, Charles 124
Peters, R.S. 138
Pfitzner, Eric 135–136, 156
Pizer, Marjorie 53, 69–70, 71, 357
Playford Liberal Country League government 82–83, 137, 361
Point McLeay reserve 123
Point Pearce reserve 123, 124
Polglaze, Jean 44
Porter, Don 51, 100, 119

Porter, Rosemary 51, 100, 118, 119
post-compulsory education 267, 284–301
postmodernism, Jean and xviii, 269, 270, 312
post-war reconstruction xiii, 65, 78, 94, 358, 367
Powell, Lindy 328
Powell, Ruby 106
Praetz, Helen 285, 288, 291–292, 296, 299–300, 311, 339, 344, 356
Presbyterian Girls School (PGC) 27, 106–107, 114, 126, 130, 131, 133, 155, 346
Priestly, Raymond 46
Pritchard, Katherine Susannah 58, 73
progressive and alternative schools, Jean on 201–202, 286–287, 363–364
Pullen, Barry 324, 325
Pusey, Michael xvi
Pyle, Haury 105
Radford, William 150–151
radical education 137, 153, 154, 157, 177–178, 197, 205, 229, 262, 289, 363–364
Randell, Shirley 214, 231, 234, 245, 303, 339
Rechabites 5, 8
Redden, Judith 219, 231, 277, 279, 342, 354, 364
Reid, Elizabeth 203
Review of Post-compulsory Schooling *see* Blackburn Review and Report
Richardson, James 141–142
Rizvi, Fazal 299
Ross, Hyrell 74–75, 180
Russell, Eric 53, 108–109, 113–114, 141, 142, 180, 252
Russell, Judith 142. 156, 180
Russell, Marion 288, 289, 296, 339
Ryan, Susan xii–xiv, 203, 213, 221, 265, 284, 310, 334, 342, 368
Santamaria, B. A. 45, 50
Schaffer, Kay 272

Schooling 15–16 year-olds, project and report 245–246, 255–261
Schools Australia 163–171, 176, 188–189, 203, 348
Schools Commission, Australian/Commonwealth
  1973–75 (under Labor government) 173–175, 181–216, 361
  1975–1983 (under Coalition governments) 189, 222–237, 239–250, 255–265, 309
  1983–1988 (under Labor government) 189, 265, 284, 310
  origins 157–172
  special projects xii, 171, 187–188, 212, 227–228
  termination 310, 321
Scott, John 294
Scott, Roger 317–318
  see also Blackburn Review and Report; Schooling 15–16 year-olds
Sharkey, Lance 56, 98
Shell Oil 7, 20, 54, 97
Slade, Gwen 116, 119
Slater, Dympsie 85
Slattery, Luke 326
Smith, Graham 102, 116, 119, 155
Soviet Union (USSR) 21, 47, 48–50, 52, 56, 57, 70, 81, 87, 89, 100, 102, 103, 108–110, 111, 120, 129, 180, 252, 312
Spanish Civil War 21, 36, 45–46, 69, 365
Special Education and Schools Commission 183–184, 193, 195, 219, 247–248
Spegele, Roger 345, 352
Spence, Catherine Helen 93, 270, 327
Stalin, Josef 45, 50, 108, 358
Stanford University 243, 244, 319
State Board of Education (Vic) xvii, 267, 284, 286, 287–288, 289, 324–325
Steele, Joyce 140
Steinle, John 234

Strachey, Ray 77, 93
Street, Jessie 73, 85, 87, 348
Stretton, Hugh 112, 113, 114, 115, 153, 340, 355
Student Christian Movement 42, 47, 137
Sturt College of Advanced Education 152, 172, 175, 271–272
Summers, Anne 155, 204, 334
Sunday Mail (newspaper) 102, 120, 133
Swan, Trevor 66, 67–68, 69, 75
Sweeney, Loine x, 328, 330, 334, 337, 338, 339
Tannock, Peter 174, 197, 198, 216, 223, 244, 267
Taylor, Gwen 57
Taylor, Jayne 327
teacher education 35, 135, 141, 170, 194, 271–272, 277, 317
teacher unions 137, 164, 174, 229, 235, 273, 284–285, 286, 287, 289, 293, 294, 296–298, 324, 348
   see also Australian Teachers Federation; Victorian Secondary Teachers Association; Technical Teachers Union of Victoria
teachers 36, 155, 168, 170, 176, 188, 196–197, 202, 220, 228, 229, 232, 233, 237, 239, 240, 277, 304
teaching 15, 26–28, 196, 312
Technical and Further Education (TAFE) 284, 288, 290, 295
technical schools (secondary) 131, 151–152, 158, 284, 286, 292, 295, 299, 301
Technical Teachers Union of Victoria 287, 289, 293, 299
Teesdale-Smith, Cecil 107, 252
tertiary education
   colleges of advanced education 172, 271–272, 317
   universities 271–272, 285, 317–321
Tertiary Education Authority South Australia 229, 268, 271–274, 309

Thomson, Pat 199, 276
Tickell, Gerry 287, 289
Torsh, Daniela (Dany) 204–206, 213–214, 249–250
Turner, Amirah 112
Turner, Ian 44–45, 46, 102, 110, 112
Union of Australian Women 88, 89, 105
United Associations of Women 73, 85, 87
United Kingdom 332
   education policies 145, 168
   Jean travels to 215
United States of America 21, 37, 57, 309
   education policies 140, 145, 168, 241
   Jean travels to xxiii, 241–244
universities *see* tertiary education: universities
University High School 24, 34, 228
   Jean as a student 1, 19, 20, 23–35, 36, 57, 59, 202
University of Adelaide 80, 113, 118, 124, 261, 333
   economics 108, 113, 114, 141, 143
   education 97, 130, 135, 218, 267–268
   history 112, 113, 114, 346
   women's studies and research centre 250, 268–269, 327
University of Canberra xvii, 317–324, 340, 342
University of Melbourne xiii, xxv, 16, 25, 32, 40–55, 59–60, 113, 114, 228, 301
   economics and commerce 42–44, 63, 95, 141
   see also Labour Club
University of South Australia 311, 315, 341, 353, 354
University Women's College 27, 55, 57
Unley High School (SA) 97, 115, 121, 147, 155, 175, 246
Vickers, Margaret 199, 253

Victorian Certificate of Education (VCE) 295, 300, 325, 326
Victorian Secondary Teachers Association (VSTA) 287, 294, 296, 301
   opposition to Blackburn Report 297–298
Vietnam War, opposition to xv, 137, 155–156, 367
Wagstaff, Ernest 7
Walker, Jim 154, 198, 237–238, 319
War Organisation of Industry, Department of xx, 62–70, 79, 91, 144, 148
Ward, Margaret 116, 119, 280
Warneke, Con 36–37, 55, 122
Waten, Judah 74, 109, 180, 280
Waters, Don 232–233
Western Teachers College 135–138, 154, 356
White, Doug 199, 287, 305
Whitlam Labor government xii, xv, 127, 158, 216, 221, 222, 361
Whitlam, Gough xv, 158, 159, 160, 163, 165
Widdup, David 204, 205, 208, 226
Williams, Bruce 44, 80
Williams, George 136
Witt, Edward 3–4
Woiker, The (newsletter) 70–71
Women and Labour Conference (1982) 270–271
Women's Charter 73, 85, 87, 92
Women's Christian Temperance Union (WCTU) 84, 85, 90, 328, 331, 338
Women's Electoral Lobby (WEL) 213, 328
Women's International League for Peace and Freedom (WILPF) 56, 103, 137, 156
women's movement *see* feminism
women's studies xviii, 250, 272, 328
   see also University of Adelaide: Women's Studies

women's suffrage centenary *see* centenary of women's suffrage
Woods, Claire 131, 356
work and/in society curriculum (Australian Studies) 295, 299–300, 305, 307–308, 325
World War I (Great War) 2, 7, 17, 21, 28, 44, 84
World War II xvii, xx, 48–49, 57, 61–75, 76, 78, 83, 139, 184, 309, 365
Yates, Lyn 211, 299, 300, 311
Yeatman, Anna 155, 251
youth unemployment *see* education policy: youth: education, training and employment; Blackburn Review and Report

ABOUT THE AUTHORS

Craig Campbell is an historian of education based at the University of Sydney. His books include *A History of Australian Schooling* (2014) and *School Choice* (2009). He is a recent editor of the *History of Education Review* and the online *Dictionary of Educational History in Australia and New Zealand*.

Debra Hayes is Professor of Education and Equity in the Sydney School of Education and Social Work at the University of Sydney. Her research investigates the inequitable effects of schooling in contexts where there are high levels of poverty and difference. Her early work was strongly influenced by Jean Blackburn's writing.